TRANSFORMING EUROPE

A volume in the series

Cornell Studies in Political Economy
Edited by Peter J. Katzenstein

A full list of titles in the series appears at the end of the book.

TRANSFORMING EUROPE

EUROPEANIZATION AND DOMESTIC CHANGE

EDITED BY

Maria Green Cowles, James Caporaso,
and Thomas Risse

Cornell University Press

Ithaca and London

First published 2001 by Cornell University Press
First printing, Cornell Paperbacks, 2001

Printed in the United States of America

Library of Congress Cataloging-in-Publication Data
Transforming Europe : Europeanization and domestic change / Maria Green Cowles, James Caporaso, and Thomas Risse, editors.
    p. cm. — (Cornell studies in political economy)
    Includes bibliographical references and index.
    ISBN 0-8014-3793-8 (cloth)—ISBN 0-8014-8671-8 (pbk.)
    1. Europe—Economic integration.   2. Policy sciences—European Union countries.   3. Nationalism—European Union countries.   I. Green Cowles, Maria.   II. Caporaso, James A., 1941– .   III. Risse-Kappen, Thomas.   IV. Series.
    HC241 .T43 2001
    337.1′4—dc21   00-011003

Cornell University Press strives to use environmentally responsible suppliers and materials to the fullest extent possible in the publishing of its books. Such materials include vegetable-based, low-VOC inks and acid-free papers that are recycled, totally chlorine-free, or partly composed of nonwood fibers. Books that bear the logo of the FSC (Forest Stewardship Council) use paper taken from forests that have been inspected and certified as meeting the highest standards for environmental and social responsibility. For further information, visit our website at www.cornellpress.cornell.edu.

Cloth printing   10 9 8 7 6 5 4 3 2 1

Paperback printing   10 9 8 7 6 5 4 3 2 1

To our students

CONTENTS

PREFACE

This project results from a transatlantic collaboration in origins, development, and composition. It has had a long gestation. In 1995, Jim and Maria began discussing a joint research project that would examine the "next phase" of European integration studies: the impact of the European Union on the member states. Meanwhile, Thomas was developing similar ideas. In March 1996, at the Conference of Europeanists in Chicago, Thomas invited Jim, Maria, and others to discuss a joint research project focusing on Europeanization and domestic change. When the three of us sat down together to discuss our respective research agendas, our transatlantic project was created.

With the support of the European University Institute's Robert Schuman Centre, we convened our first workshop at the EUI's Villa Schifanoia in February 1997 to explore the transformation of Europe and to identify key issues and concepts. We met again in November 1997 at the Center for West European Studies, University of Pittsburgh, where individual authors presented their first drafts. We are particularly grateful to Alberta Sbragia and for the Center's Department of Education, Title VI, funding of the event. In Pittsburgh, we developed and agreed on a three-step approach to study the impact of Europeanization on domestic structures, which then formed the conceptual framework of this book. The authors met a final time in June 1998 at the Villa Schifanoia to discuss their work in light of the conceptual framework developed in Pittsburgh. Again, we are grateful for the hospitality and financial support provided by the EUI's Robert Schuman Centre whose director, Yves Mény, supported our endeavor all along the way. Following the Fiesole workshop, contributors presented their chapters at various workshops and conferences including the Europeanists' Conference of the Council of European Studies, Baltimore, March 1998, and the annual convention of the

American Political Science Association in Washington, D.C., in September 1998.

This book benefited enormously from the critical comments of many scholars both in the United States and in Europe. Fritz Scharpf's contribution, as a critical discussant at every single meeting, was tremendous and cannot be overestimated. From the Pittsburgh meeting on, Vivien Schmidt joined him in this task. Our conceptual framework also owes quite a bit to Tanja Börzel's research. Moreover, for comments and contributions, we are very grateful to Stefano Bartolini, Simon Bulmer, Laura Cram, Michelle Egan, Albrecht Funk, Jonathan Golub, Liesbet Hooghe, Walter Mattli, Gary Marks, Yves Mény, Andrew Moravcsik, Mark Pollack, Martin Rhodes, Philippe Schmitter, Mitchell Smith, Yasemin Soysal, Martin Staniland, Sabrina Tesoka, Bastiaan Van Apeldoorn, Amy Verdun, and Antje Wiener. Finally, we benefitted from the anonymous reviews commissioned by Cornell University Press and also from the detailed and excellent comments by Peter Katzenstein.

For assistance in the final preparation of the manuscript, we thank Klaus Roscher, Alison Weston, and, in particular, Emily Schuster and Federica Bicchi. We are grateful to Michelle Everson for compiling the index. We thank Nancy Winemiller for her support throughout the editing process. Roger Haydon's unsurpassed professionalism guided the book from the very beginning. Our deep gratitude goes to the contributors, whose insights, patience, and diligence made this truly a collaborative process. We also thank the friends, colleagues, and family members without whose support this project would not have been possible.

Working on a transatlantic project for more than four years has brought new meaning to the phrases "e-mail exchange" and "computer viruses." It has taught us the pleasure (and the agony) of working with three different personalities. It has also enabled us to celebrate together the birth of Maria's daughter, and the marriages of Jim and Thomas. And we've discovered that, after four years of intensive co-editing, we are still friends.

MARIA GREEN COWLES
JAMES CAPORASO
THOMAS RISSE

Washington, D.C.
Seattle, Washington
Florence, Italy

TRANSFORMING EUROPE

CHAPTER ONE

Europeanization and Domestic Change: Introduction

Thomas Risse, Maria Green Cowles,
and James Caporaso

This volume explores the impact of Europeanization—which we define as the emergence and the development at the European level of distinct structures of governance—on the domestic structures of the member states. We are particularly interested in understanding whether and how the ongoing process of European integration has changed nation-states, their domestic institutions, and their political cultures. The book highlights the impact of Europeanization on formal structures such as national legal systems and national as well as regional administrations. At the same time, it explores the ability of the European Union (EU) to shape informal structures such as business-government relations, public discourses, nation-state identities, and collective understandings of citizenship norms.

Our volume offers three central contributions. First, Europeanization matters. In nearly every case, Europeanization has led to distinct and identifiable changes in the domestic institutional structures of member states. Every single member state in our project has had to adapt to the Europeanization process. Yet, for reasons discussed below, we find neither wholesale convergence nor continuing divergence of national policy structures, institutions, and other patterned relationships. Rather, our book points to "domestic adaptation with national colors" in which national features continue to play a role in shaping outcomes.

We are very grateful to all those who commented on this introductory chapter, especially the participants of the project workshops in Florence, February 1997, at the University of Pittsburgh in November 1997, and again in Florence in June 1998. In particular, we thank Stefano Bartolini, Tanja Börzel, Michelle Egan, Peter Katzenstein, Christoph Knill, Andrew Moravcsik, Mark Pollack, Fritz Scharpf, Vivien Schmidt, and Philippe Schmitter for their helpful suggestions. We are also grateful to Joseph Jupille for the initial development and design of Figure 1.1.

Second, our book moves beyond traditional debates about whether or not Europeanization strengthens or weakens the state. We did not find this focus helpful in capturing the dynamics of our empirical findings. Our findings do not support the claim that, in general, Europeanization tends to strengthen state autonomy vis-à-vis society. Nor do they give credence to the argument that, on balance, Europeanization has little if any impact on the EU's most powerful states. Even the "big three"—the United Kingdom, France, and Germany—have had to adapt to Europe across a variety of issue-areas.

But Europeanization as a process involving the gradual erosion of national sovereignty does not weaken the state, either, through the transfer of competence and control to the supranational level. The weight of evidence strongly points in the direction of continuous interaction and linkages between national and European levels. Indeed, it is hard to even speak of levels in a system in which European and domestic influences are so thoroughly melded (Rometsch and Wessels 1996).

Third, Europeanization changes nation-states by exerting adaptational pressures. Europeanization by itself is a necessary but not sufficient condition for domestic change. When there are changes at the European level, the first question one must ask is how closely these changes fit with what already exists at the domestic level. Poor fit implies strong adaptational pressure; good fit implies weak pressure. A country whose domestic institutions are perfectly compatible with Europeanization experiences no adaptational pressure. In such a case, we expect no domestic institutional change.

Where adaptational pressures exist, we do not necessarily foresee significant domestic change. National and subnational governments may simply avoid doing anything to respond, in which case there will be an implementation deficit. Whether or not a country adjusts its institutional structure to Europe will depend on the presence or absence of mediating factors. Our book identifies five such intervening factors: multiple veto points in the domestic structure, facilitating formal institutions, a country's organizational and policymaking cultures, the differential empowerment of domestic actors, and learning.

This three-step approach—Europeanization, adaptational pressures, mediating factors—represents the conceptual framework of this book. Our central message is clear. Strong movements in Europeanization as well as strong adaptational pressure do not necessarily translate into domestic structural change. These forces must pass through and interact with facilitating and/or obstructive factors specific to each country.

Our chapters are broadly informed by a historical institutionalist approach. Historical institutionalism implies an interest in explaining ("endogenizing") preferences and identities. It also implies that institutions evolve, sometimes slowly and piecemeal, sometimes rapidly and comprehensively, and that institutional change at the European level is likely to intersect with pre-existing domestic institutions. Institutional adaptation can be difficult, not only because of the costs of bringing domestic institutions in line with Europeanization but also because domestic institutions represent long-standing habits of doing things. In this sense, the possibilities for institutional change are path dependent.

Europeanization and Domestic Structures: Clarifying Key Concepts

Europeanization

We define Europeanization as *the emergence and development at the European level of distinct structures of governance*, that is, of political, legal, and social institutions associated with political problem solving that formalize interactions among the actors, and of policy networks specializing in the creation of authoritative European rules. Europeanization involves the evolution of new layers of politics that interact with older ones. The exact patterns of interaction are not specified as part of the definition but are instead kept as "free parameters," to be examined empirically. Political institutionalization involves the development of formal and informal rules, procedures, norms, and practices governing politics at the European, national, and subnational levels.

By recognizing the interactions among several levels of governance (supranational, national, and subnational), our definition of Europeanization differs from traditional uses of the term. Initially, scholars generally referred to Europeanization as institution-building at the European level. For example, research has focused on the development of EU interest groups largely divorced from their national counterparts, and on the growth of exclusive policy competences at the European level. Slowly, scholars began to focus on the effects of Europeanization at the national level. Olsen (1995a,b), Andersen and Eliassen (1993), and Rometsch and Wessels (1996), for example, examined how Brussels activities impacted the national political institutions and policymaking styles of member states (see also Mény, Muller, and Quermonne 1996). Kohler-Koch (1997) and others (e.g., Kohler-Koch and Eising 1999) have documented this process at the subnational level by examining the influence of the European Union on regional governments, policies, and outcomes. Haverland (1999) and Duina (1999) looked at the domestic implementation of specific European rules and regulations. Others reviewed the impact of Europeanization processes within a particular country (Bulmer and Paterson 1987; Katzenstein 1997a; V. Schmidt 1996a) or focused on Europeanization indirectly as the movement from a classical state system to an institutionalized polity (Stone Sweet and Sandholtz 1998a). To date, however, there has been very little systematic study of why, how, and under what conditions Europeanization shapes a variety of domestic structures in a number of countries.

In defining Europeanization, we also differentiate this process from that of internationalization or globalization more broadly defined. Several works have examined the linkage between globalization and domestic institutions and/or policymaking. Keohane and Milner (1996) provide a substantive overview of how globalization impacts government and society across a number of policy areas. Europeanization itself might respond to "globalization" processes by reinforcing their trends or by shielding EU member states against their undesired effects. Although tracing these links is not the focus of the book, we distinguish between Europeanization and globalization trends to the extent possible in order to identify their independent effects. In the telecommunications sector, for example, the liberalization of the American market exerted strong pressures on Europe to follow suit. EU policies further increased these pressures by forcing the member states to liberalize and to deregulate the sector. Such measures were already underway in some countries (particularly the United Kingdom, but also partly Germany and France; cf. chapter 4) and, thus, could not have been caused by Europeanization pressures. But the Europeanization of telecommunications had an impact in other cases, particularly Italy, where liberalization and deregulation met firm domestic resistance initially. Careful process-tracing and attention to the time sequences between EU policies and domestic changes allow us to distinguish between globalization effects, on the one hand, and the impact of Europeanization, on the other. The same procedure holds true for other alternative accounts. We check, for example, whether purely domestic factors might explain structural changes in some cases, with little or no independent effects from Europeanization.

In this book, we choose to focus on the impact of Europeanization domestically—that is, at the national and subnational levels. Much of the book is preoccupied with what goes on at the domestic level, even though we recognize that ultimately the causal processes go both ways—activities at the domestic level affect the European level and vice versa.

Changes in Domestic Structures

The broad proposition that Europeanization affects domestic politics is noncontroversial. Politics within European countries are influenced daily and in countless ways by the actions and legislation of the European Union. In addition, more and more policy areas are being affected by policymaking in Brussels. We need to specify a dependent variable that is separate from specific policy decisions, policies, or domestic politics in general. "Domestic structure"—while apparently broad—gives us more focus.

"Structure" implies more than changes in policies or preferences. In the most general sense, structures are patterned relationships which are stable over time. "Domestic structures," then, comprise those components of a polity or society consisting of regularized and comparatively stable interactions. Probably the most significant component of domestic structures are institutions. As defined by the sociological literature (e.g., March and Olsen 1989; Powell and DiMaggio 1991), institutions are systems of rules, both formal and informal. Formalized institutions are organizations with written norms and procedures prescribing behavior. But organizations also encompass informal understandings, for example, organizational routines and cultures. Formal institutions, including political and social systems, usually consist of informal structures, too, such as policy networks, epistemic communities, and so on. Our notion of domestic structures entails both formal and informal institutions. Most authors in this book adopt such a broad understanding of institutions when they talk about "policy styles," "integrated leadership," "institutional culture," or informal networks among executives and interest groups (see chapters 3, 7, 8, and 9).

If the focus of this book were solely on such domestic political and societal structures, we could have used the term "institutions." But we also examine Europeanization effects on collective understandings of actors, be it norms of citizenship (chapter 10) or collective identities pertaining to the nation-state (chapter 11). Thus, the broader term "domestic structure" seems appropriate.

Domestic structure approaches are by now well established both in comparative politics and in international relations. Originally developed in the field of comparative foreign economic policies (Gourevitch 1986; Katzenstein 1978), these approaches have found widespread applications in a variety of issue-areas (cf. Evangelista 1997). The concept has been extended to capture elements of political culture including the understandings and meanings attached to political and societal institutions as well as collective identities (e.g., Katzenstein and Okawara 1993; Katzenstein 1984, 1997a). Our project fits well into what international relations scholars called "the second image reversed" (Gourevitch 1978), that is, the international sources of domestic change.

In this volume, we focus on two categories of domestic structure. The first is *policy structures*. Policy structures imply more than changes in policy subject matter at the domestic level. We are interested in the political, legal, and administrative structures that interpret and carry out policies. Policy structures are issue-area specific and might vary quite substantially across policy sectors in a given domestic polity. The chapters on gender equality policies (chapter 2), transport (chapter 3), telecommunications (chapter 4), and public finances (chapter 5) focus on such policy structures, both formal and informal.

The second category is somewhat broader and concerns *system-wide domestic structures* pertaining to the nation-state, its society and economy as a whole. Often, these structures are embedded historical and cultural practices. Conant investigates the impact of Europeanization on national legal systems (chapter 6), and Knill and Lenschow (chapter 7) focus on national administrative traditions, whereas Börzel (chapter 8) concentrates on territorial structures. For Cowles (chapter 9), the dependent variable consists of the structure of business associations and of business-government relations. Finally, Checkel (chapter 10) investigates changes in citizenship norms, whereas Risse (chapter 11) focuses on collective understandings about the nation-state.

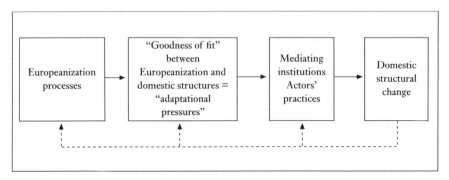

Figure 1.1   Europeanization and domestic structural change

A "Three-Step" Approach to Europeanization and Domestic Structural Change

In this book we have tried to establish a research agenda for relating Europeanization to domestic politics. To tackle the potentially complex effects of Europeanization, we propose a framework of domestic adaptational change that each empirical chapter applies to its respective policy area (see Figure 1.1).[1] This framework works in three steps.

Steps 1 and 2: Europeanization and "Goodness of Fit"

First, we identify the relevant Europeanization processes—formal and informal norms, rules, regulations, procedures, and practices—at the European level. Which processes are relevant depends on the question the author poses. If the area of interest is citizenship rights, Europeanization implies a particular set of processes; if the interest is road haulage and telecommunications, it implies another. We cast our net widely so as to include legal practices, rulings of the European Court of Justice (ECJ), EU directives and policy mandates, state-society relations, and even informal understandings and meanings of EU norms. These Europeanization processes constitute the starting point of our framework. They necessitate some adjustments on the domestic level of the member states so that states can be in compliance with EU norms, rules, and procedures. Whether these policy adjustments (e.g., transposing EU rules into domestic law) lead to domestic structural change is our central research question.

The second step in the framework identifies the "goodness of fit" between the Europeanization processes, on the one hand, and national institutional settings, rules, and practices, on the other. (For a similar approach, see Duina 1999.) This

---

[1]   Part of this framework follows suggestions by Fritz Scharpf and Tanja Börzel.

degree of "fit" constitutes what we identify as "adaptational pressures." In principle, the degree of adaptational pressures determines the extent to which domestic institutions would have to change in order to comply with European rules and policies.

But what does "adaptational pressure" actually imply? The effect of Europeanization on domestic structures involves a process by which one set of institutions—the European rules, regulations, and collective understandings—interact with another set of institutions—the given domestic structures in the member states (Olsen 1995b). The degree of adaptational pressure generated by Europeanization depends on the "fit" or "misfit" between European institutions and the domestic structures. The lower the compatibility (fit) between European institutions, on the one hand, and national institutions, on the other, the higher the adaptational pressures.

We distinguish between two causal pathways by which Europeanization exerts adaptational pressures on domestic structures. First, European policies might lead to a "policy misfit" between EU rules and regulations, on the one hand, and domestic policies, on the other. These policy misfits then exert adaptational pressures on underlying institutions, particularly political and administrative structures (see chapters 2–5). Second, Europeanization might also exert direct adaptational pressures on embedded domestic institutional structures. As Börzel argues in chapter 8, Europeanization took away core competencies of the German and Spanish regions, leading to a severe "unequal distribution of say and pay" (see also chapters 6 and 9). But Knill and Lenschow demonstrate in chapter 7 that Europeanization can also challenge ingrained national administrative styles. Europeanization might even threaten deeply rooted collective understandings of national identity (see chapter 10, and chapter 11).

This conceptualization of the "goodness of fit" has important implications. Since political, economic, legal, and societal institutions differ among member states, the degree of adaptational pressures varies as well. In some cases, EU rules and regulations might be easily incorporated and complied with in the respective national settings, because they match the domestic system of rules and regulations. Sometimes, member states changed their domestic practices and institutions prior to new European policies. In the transport sector, the United Kingdom liberalized and deregulated its domestic market before the EU became active in this area, and the proposed EU legislation largely matched the British rules. The Netherlands undertook major reforms prior to the European intiatives in the late 1980s (see chapter 3). There was little adaptational pressure for these two countries.

In other cases, European norms and practices ran completely counter to national rules, practices, and administrative traditions (e.g., in Italy and Germany, in the case of transport). The regulatory mode of some EU policies in the environmental area was alien to Germany's administrative structure, problem-solving philosophy, organizational routines, and state-society relations (Héritier, Knill, and Mingers 1996; see chapter 7). These latter cases of adaptational pressures are of special interest for us, since it is only here where we can show the impact of Europeanization on domestic structural change.

Finally, the very meaning of Europeanization might vary from country to country. As Risse argues in chapter 11, European integration resonated quite differently with given elite identities pertaining to the nation-state in the United Kingdom, France, and Germany. Only the German elites could easily incorporate "Europe" into their understandings of Germanness in the post–World War II era, while the notion of Europeanness has remained alien to most British elites.

Thus, EU rules and procedures tend to create quite different degrees of adaptational pressures, depending on the goodness of fit between EU regulations and domestic institutional procedures as well as collective understandings. The examples also indicate that the degree of institutional fit may vary from policy sector to policy sector (and sometimes even within one issue-area; cf. chapter 7). With regard to policy structures, we do not expect to find that some countries generally face significantly less adaptational pressures than others. We are skeptical that the congruence between the EU and Germany in terms of constitutional order as well as underlying norms and conventions (Bulmer 1997, 61–72; Katzenstein 1997b, 33–45) translates into generally low adaptational pressure for the Federal Republic.

In sum, at least two possibilities of such fit or misfit need to be distinguished. First, the adaptational pressure might be low, and not much structural adaptation is required. Actors easily incorporate EU institutions and regulations in their domestic ways of doing things. An institution is unlikely to resist changes in its environment if these are consistent with its own constitutive principles. Such cases are not very interesting in the framework of our book, since they do not require domestic institutional change. Yet as we show in the concluding chapter 12, not a single country in our sample represents such a case across issue-areas and institutional structures.

Second, the interesting cases are those where the adaptational pressures are significant. If adaptational pressures are very high, European institutions seriously challenge the identity, constitutive principles, core structures, and practices of national institutions. In such cases, the institutional, material, and cultural adaptations are exceedingly costly and national institutions will be defended at great cost. Some countries might even vote for "opt-outs" (e.g., the United Kingdom resisted the single currency for Europe) or try to change EU policies and institutions. We expect some sort of stalemate between EU institutions and domestic institutions resulting in severe implementation deficits or gaps between the prescribed institutions and actual behavior. In France, the EU's Equal Pay and Equal Treatment Directives have led to minimal responses, whereas there has been a flurry of legal activity in the UK, often spurred by feminist groups (see chapter 2). In Italy, there was almost no response to the EU transportation policy (cf. chapter 3). Another case in point is the refusal among the majority of the British political elites to identify with Europe (see chapter 11). Yet, large gaps between existing institutional structures and adaptational requirements can lead, over time, to a serious performance crisis of the institution and finally result in radical and rapid transformations (Olsen 1995b).

In other cases, however, member states adjusted their domestic institutional arrangements to Europe, even though they faced high adaptational pressures. Although Italy refused to adapt institutionally in the transport sector, it undertook structural reforms in public finances to qualify for the euro (see chapter 5). What accounts for the variation in structural change—the dependent variable of this book? This question points to the third step in our conceptual framework.

Step 3: Mediating Factors—Institutions and Actor Strategies

In cases of high adaptational pressures, the presence or absence of mediating factors is crucial for the degree to which domestic change adjusting to Europeanization should be expected. Our book looks at structure and agency in such cases. Concerning structure, we explore the institutional and cultural conditions that facilitate or prohibit flexible responses to adaptational pressures. We distinguish among three structural factors that might enable or block adaptational change: multiple veto points in the domestic structure, facilitating institutions, and cooperative cultures.

Multiple Veto Points.   The existence of multiple veto points in a given policy-making structure has been identified as a major factor impeding structural adaptation (Tsebelis 1995). The more power is dispersed across the political system and the more actors have a say in political decision making, the more difficult it is to foster the domestic consensus or "winning coalition" necessary to introduce institutional changes in response to Europeanization pressures. Scharpf and others, for example, have argued that the particular features of interlocking politics in Germany, a federal state with multiple veto players, lead to a "joint decision trap." It inhibits innovative solutions and problem solving and only allows for incremental adjustments (Scharpf 1985; Scharpf, Reissert, and Schnabel 1976). As Héritier argues in chapter 3, multiple veto points in the Italian political system blocked the country's structural adaptation to Europeanization pressures in transport policies.

Thus, the existence of multiple veto points in a given policy-making structure is likely to inhibit or at least to considerably slow down adaptation to Europeanization pressures, if no other mediating factors are present. But there are also institutional factors that might help to overcome such veto points.

Mediating Formal Institutions.   Facilitating formal institutions provide actors with material and ideational resources to induce structural change. As Caporaso and Jupille point out in chapter 2, the British Equal Opportunities Commission (EOC) was crucial in providing women's organizations with the means to use EU Equal Pay and Equal Treatment Directives in furthering gender equality. The absence of such an institution in France explains to a large degree the variation in adaptational change between the two countries. As Conant shows in chapter 6, the British common law tradition provides a mechanism that is functionally equivalent to referring cases to the European Court of Justice (ECJ). Thus, the presence of facilitating institutions empowering actors explains why structural adaptation sometimes occurs.

Multiple veto points, on the one hand, and facilitating formal institutions, on the other, exert their effects on the capacity of actors to induce structural change in opposite directions. But both factors have in common that they are compatible with a "logic of consequentialism" assuming utility-maximizing actors with fixed interests and preferences. These institutional factors do not influence actors' views of the world, interests, or identities. Rather, they provide resources or means to further these given interests and identities. The British EOC did not create women's organizations with the desire to achieve equal pay and equal treatment; it merely provided them with an additional opportunity and resource to further their goals. Our third institutional factor leaves the logic of consequentialism behind.

Political and Organizational Cultures.   Political and organizational cultures— and the prevailing collective understandings of appropriate behavior embedded in them—also affect whether domestic actors can use adaptational pressures emanating from Europeanization to induce structural change. These cultural understandings define the realm in which actors can legitimately pursue their interests following a "logic of appropriateness," which sees action as rule-based: "Action involves evoking an identity or role and matching the obligations of that identity or role to a specific situation" (March and Olsen 1998, 951). Actors ask, "What kind of situation is this?," "What should I do now?," or "What rule applies here?"[2]

One (informal) institutional mechanism to overcome multiple veto points is the existence of a consensus-oriented or cooperative decision-making culture (see Börzel 2001, and Katzenstein 1984). Benz and others have argued, for example, that German cooperative federalism embedded in a consensus-oriented negotiating culture explains why the "joint decision trap" is less relevant than Scharpf and others originally assumed (Benz 1994). As Börzel argues in her contribution (chapter 8), the German Länder used the mechanisms of cooperative federalism to regain the competences they had previously lost to the European level. Structural adjustment was achieved because the German regions relied on a consensus-oriented decision-making culture. In contrast, the Spanish regions initially failed to adjust to Europe because of the confrontational policymaking culture in the relationship between the central state and the regions. Conant (chapter 6) explains the variation in referral rates to the ECJ by local courts with differences in national legal cultures and traditions. It is less appropriate in the French statist political culture, with a strong centralization of political power, to use the Article 177 procedure than in Germany, with its dispersal of power.

---

2. We owe this point to Jeffrey Checkel.

Finally, Risse (chapter 11) deals with the impact of Europeanization on even more deeply embedded factors: collective identities pertaining to the nation–state. He argues that changes in the prevailing nation–state identities of political elites are more likely to occur the more ideas about Europe and visions of European order resonate with given identities pertaining to the nation–state.

So far, we have identified mediating institutional factors that facilitate or prohibit structural change in response to significant pressures for adaptation to Europeanization. But institutions do not change institutions; actors do. Institutions might provide opportunities to actors or even affect their interests and identities. These actors ultimately have to exploit these opportunities in order to produce structural changes. We identify two mediating factors relating to agency.

Differential Empowerment of Actors.   Structural changes lead to a redistribution of power capacities among the relevant actors in a political, social, or economic system. Milner (1988) and Rogowski (1989) argued more than ten years ago that exposure to international trade and increased economic interdependence leads to a shift in societal interest coalitions in favor of export-oriented sectors. Moravcsik (1994) focused on this issue by arguing that national executives have powerful resources (initiative, institutions, information, and ideas) that enable them to alter the domestic balance of power in favor of executives. By transferring policies from the domestic to the European arena, executives acquire some home-turf advantages. Although autonomy is diminished with regard to their foreign counterparts, it widens the autonomy of executives in relation to other domestic actors.

Not everyone agrees with this assessment. Marks (1993), Sandholtz (1996), V. Schmidt (1997), and others have claimed that domestic societal and other subnational actors gain new resources through the process of Europeanization, since the EU enables them to circumvent the national executives. Instead of strengthening their prerogatives, national executives find their governmental authority "under siege."

The current debate has mainly focused on national executives, but we expect that Europeanization leads to a redistribution of power among a variety of domestic actors, from legislatures, courts, regional governments, to interest groups and companies. As Cowles points out in chapter 9, the Europeanization of business-government relations in common commercial policy resulted in the empowerment of the French industry association vis-à-vis the state. Thus, we expect that domestic actors use Europeanization as an opportunity to further their goals. In the case of Italy and Economic and Monetary Union (EMU), for example, Europeanization served as a mechanism to bolster a specific group of pro-EMU elites while silencing the otherwise considerable societal opposition against the reform of public finances (see chapter 5). In a similar way, Italian business was capable of overcoming the considerable domestic opposition to the liberalization of telecommunications, once the EU had started regulating this area (chapter 4). How far domestic actors are able to exploit new opportunities depends on their previous resources and identities provided by domestic institutions (access to the public sphere and decision-making bodies, financial means, information, legitimacy; see Kitschelt 1986).

Learning.   The mechanisms of differential empowerment and redistribution of power resources do not assume that actors change their interests or identities. Rather, differential empowerment enables actors to further these given interests and to induce structural change. But Europeanization might lead to more fundamental changes in actors' interests and identities. Learning constitutes an agency-centered mechanism to induce such transformations.

There is a vast literature on policy learning, of course (Sabatier and Jenkins-Smith 1993; Levy 1994). We need to distinguish between instances in which actors merely adjust means and strategies to achieve their given goals and preferences ("single-loop learning," according to Argyris and Schön 1978) and situations that lead actors to change these goals and preferences themselves ("double-loop learning" or "complex learning"). We use the term only for these latter occasions, since learning otherwise becomes analytically indistinguishable from strategic adjustment. Learning that results in changes in actors' interests and identities occurs rather rarely. But, as Checkel argues in chapter 10, elite learning played a significant role in changing the interests of German political elites regarding citizenship norms. Such learning usually takes place after critical policy failures or in perceived crises when actors reassess their set of preferences (see chapters 8 and 9) or even collective identities (see also chapter 11).

Europeanization, goodness of fit, and mediating factors: these are the three steps in our conceptual framework to explain domestic change. We expect structural change in response to Europeanization to occur if and when (a) it generates significant adaptational pressures in the domestic environment; and (b) facilitating factors are present, enabling actors to induce or push through institutional change.

Contribution to Current Theoretical and Empirical Debates

Competing Theories of Institutional Change: Functionalism,
Liberal Intergovernmentalism, and Historical Institutionalism

As Figure 1.1 shows, a full specification of our model of Europeanization rests on a circular flow, a system of causal relationships closed by feedback loops. Although the causality between Europeanization and domestic structure runs in both directions, we have chosen to emphasize the downward causation from Europeanization to domestic structure. Our approach contrasts with much of the literature on European integration, which treats the process of integration as the end point of a causal process beginning with domestic and transnational societal interests and ending with European outcomes (policies, ECJ proceedings, activities of other key institutions).

While functionalism and liberal intergovernmentalism have important differences, both posit a causal sequence running from individuals and groups to national and intergovernmental decision making. Functionalism stresses the autonomous power and energy of transnational society, especially when coupled to entrepreneurial international institutions and agents. For both Jean Monnet and Ernst Haas, the raw material of politics lay in the society and economy (unions, corporations, professional and craft organizations) and in practical problems faced by individuals in trying to solve them cooperatively (Haas 1958). Functionalism is based on a rather straightforward social pluralism in which political institutions matter little in shaping and channeling interests to central governments. Intergovernmentalism stresses the importance of states as the ultimate locus of decision making. It also emphasizes the ability of governments to structure agendas, as well as their capacity to control international organizational actors. The "liberal" part of liberal intergovernmentalism starts with social and economic interests and describes how these interests work their way through the domestic political system and affect the preferences of central decision makers. National politics is much more important for liberal intergovernmentalism than for functionalism. But the causal chain runs from the bottom up, and until we get to the negotiation phase, the process can again be described as straightforward social pluralism.

The most elaborate version of a bottom-up theory is Andrew Moravcsik's liberal intergovernmentalism. In the article "Preferences and Power" (1993), he proposes a two-step theory of regional integration. The chiefs of government who represent states are rational self-interested actors, capable of taking in information about the orientations of interest groups and calculating what their positions imply for European integration. The first step in the integration process has to do with the identification, mobilization, and aggregation of preferences to arrive at something called a national interest.

The second component of liberal intergovernmentalism concerns bargaining and negotiation in international arenas. National governments take their preferences (and there may be a gap between societal and governmental preferences) into international negotiations and bargain with their counterparts in other countries about preferred outcomes. This part owes much to standard bargaining models, just as the first part owes much to pluralism and interest group theory. The formation of preferences can be told as a relatively straightforward story of social pluralism, heavily informed by Olsonian interest group theory and the logic of collective action (Olson 1965).

The third part of Moravcsik's theoretical synthesis comes in his book *The Choice for Europe* (1998). Here, he adds institutions to the mix of preference formation and bargaining. The presence of institutions does not signify a dramatic turn to institutionalism, in the sense that institutions are now responsible for shaping the preferences of actors or affecting identities. Instead, institutions enforce agreements, make bargains credible, and provide a rule-based structure as a bulwark against defection: "To secure the substantive bargains they had made, finally, governments delegated and pooled sovereignty in international institutions for the express purpose of committing one another to cooperate" (Moravcsik 1998, 3–4).

While our project can be seen as a top–down effort to understand the dependence of domestic institutions and actors on European integration, Moravcsik systematically insulates domestic preferences from feedback effects of Europeanization. Preferences are seen as results of "the economic incentives generated by patterns of international economic interdependence" (Moravcsik 1998, 6). They "vary in response to exogenous changes in the economic, ideological, and geopolitical environment within which European integration takes place" (23) but not in response to Europeanization itself. Addressing himself to the issue of monetary policy, Moravcsik emphasizes global economic pressures of which Europe (but not Europeanization) is a part. Monetary cooperation in Europe came about because of forces in the global political economy, not because of the policy and institutional impact of the EU.

Moravcsik's account differs substantially from our own and from Sandholtz's argument in "Membership Matters" (1996) that the EU as an institution, and the norms and practices that members learned, made a difference in the monetary bargains struck. Allowing only upward flows, Moravcsik ignores the potential endogeneity of domestic structures and preferences—the ways in which domestic institutions and preferences of domestic actors are dependent on Europeanization, and not just on the broader international political economy changes generated by integration.

Our approach contrasts with both functionalism and liberal intergovernmentalism. Functionalism has virtually no theory of the political process and central governmental bargaining, nor do practitioners of this approach carefully assess the feedback effects of institutional integration on domestic structures. We agree with liberal intergovernmentalism that interstate bargains are important, but they constitute the start of an interesting story for us. Institutions are not primarily passive devices to reduce transaction costs, manage interdependence, and lock-in agreements. Institutions are also vehicles for implementing policies and spreading norms and expectations, sometimes against the wishes of key domestic constituencies. Institutions are explicitly political because different domestic constituencies have conflicting stakes in whether the new institutions take root. We need only think of the reaction of employers to equal pay legislation in the UK (see chapter 2) or of the German industry's opposition to the creation of new business-government relationships in Brussels (see chapter 9).

While broadly consistent with Pierson's historical institutionalist account of European integration (1996), we move beyond his relatively narrow principal-agent focus in a way that both advances historical institutionalism and gives its critique of intergovernmentalism added bite. Pierson takes liberal intergovernmentalism as his point of departure, proceeding to attack it by explaining first, how "gaps" in member-state control can arise, and second, why these gaps can be difficult for member states to redress. Four factors produce gaps in member-state control: the partial autonomy of EU institutions, politicians' restricted time horizons, the ubiquity of unintended consequences, and shifts in domestic preferences. Our approach takes all of these factors seriously but speaks most directly to the last two. In particular, Pierson gives short shrift to the fourth factor, changed domestic preferences, which are more thoroughly theorized in our account. Pierson cites only two sources of such shifts: "altered circumstances or new information," and electorally induced changes in government (1996, 139–40). We add an additional source of changes in domestic preferences, as these arise from changes in domestic structures. This focus identifies endogenous changes in preferences, that is, changes resulting from the process of Europeanization itself. We propose a more serious challenge to intergovernmentalism.

In sum, the political content of institutions is not exhausted by principal-agent analysis. Institutions are politically significant in ways not likely to be captured by an approach that sees institutions as actors with delegated authority, always carefully monitored and controlled by principals (the member states). Rather, institutions and policy change at the European level (Europeanization) have a much more political effect, namely to create tensions and inconsistencies between European and domestic structures. Such tension is the source of adaptational pressure. The nature and degree of this pressure will be, in part, a function of the fit between European and domestic institutions. The lack of fit, and the changed domestic structures and preferences that it can produce, lead to a more lively conception of politics than that inspired by functionalism, liberal intergovernmentalism, or existing historical institutionalist work. Far from representing the successful completion of a task (functionalism), locking in commitments (liberal intergovernmentalism), or the simple slippage that results when principals with fixed preferences delegate authority to agents (historical institutionalism), Europeanization takes on a more active political role in spurring domestic change. We move historical institutionalism further toward a "thicker" or sociological understanding of institutions and institutional change (March and Olsen 1989, 1998).

Convergence or Divergence?

Suppose that adaptational pressures exist and that they indeed cause change at the domestic institutional level. How can we describe this change? What qualities will it have and in what direction will it tend to go? It is often assumed that European and global integration create pressures for uniform outcomes, both at the level of policy and institutions. In this view, there is a single and homogenous institutional response to adaptational pressures that each country moves toward, either for reasons of efficiency, "best practice," or overall compatibility. Some globalization arguments emphasize that structural convergence is dictated as much by the need to fit into the existing structure as by concerns about efficiency.

Is this view correct with regard to Europeanization and the member states? Prior to answering this question, we should reiterate that we need to strictly distinguish between policy outcomes, policies to achieve these outcomes, sector-specific institutional structures, and "system-wide" political, economic, and social structures.

As to EU directives, for example, Article 189 of the EC treaty requires similar policy outcomes ("results") but leaves to the member states "the choice of form and method" (i.e., policies), let alone political and administrative structures. Similarly, the famous EMU convergence criteria required that the participants achieve similar results in terms of low inflation, limits on budget deficits, and the like. It was left to the discretion of member states whether they went after pension funds, cut subsidies to industry, or raised taxes—as long as they reduced their budget deficit to the 3 percent GDP level. But EMU also required some structural convergence among the member states' institutions, namely, the independence of their central banks from national governments.

This book is only interested in convergence of this latter kind, which can be labeled "structural isomorphism." Structural isomorphism requires a growing convergence in the formal and informal institutional structures as defined above, for example, in the organization of courts and bureaucracies; the nature of parliaments; the rules governing the relationship between the executives, financial ministries, regional authorities, and interest groups; and, finally, the meanings, understandings, and collective identities surrounding these institutions. This is a stronger hypothesis, since structural changes are more difficult to achieve than policy changes. Structural convergence may be observed in specific policy areas or in particular segments of society, but it ultimately leads to what Unger and van Waarden call "system convergence," or the increasing similarity among entire political, economic, and social systems (1995, 4–6). We are interested in both the policy and systemic convergence processes.

One can distinguish between economic and sociological approaches to structural convergence. Economic approaches to convergence rely mainly on market competition in one of two forms, either imitation of "best practice" or simply survival of the fittest. In either case, efficiency is the governing logic; the only real difference is whether it is consciously pursued by the agents or a residual effect of competition. Whether one is talking about corporate governance, systems of industrial relations, or regulatory environments, considerations of efficiency are constantly relevant (Woolcock 1996, 179). In the globalization literature (Notermans 1993; Strange 1996), convergence provides a device to integrate international and domestic levels of analysis. Globalization theorists argue that global economic forces reduce the differences in national economic policies, make left-wing and social democratic policies difficult to maintain, and dictate a neoliberal approach to monetary and fiscal policies (see the discussion by Garrett 1998b). Globalization undermines distinctive national policy styles. Structural convergence is achieved in terms of the "retreat of the state," with national policy autonomy as the main casualty.

If we apply this line of reasoning to Europeanization and the EU member states, structural convergence would occur particularly in areas exposed to the pressures of global market forces. The more Europeanization is about market integration and the removal of trade and investment barriers ("negative integration"; see Scharpf 1996), the more adaptational pressures lead to structural isomorphism. Policy emulation as well as the domestic empowerment of pro-liberalization forces provide the two mechanisms by which structural convergence is achieved. As we discuss in the conclusion (chapter 12) in more detail, only Schneider's discussion of telecommunications (chapter 4) fits this particular argument.

Many sociological institutionalists also expect structural convergence, but for reasons other than efficiency. According to them, the world is replete with institutions and any given institution is embedded in an environment of other institutions. Institutional convergence occurs because institutions frequently interact or are located in similar environments. They are likely to look alike over time, that is, to develop similar formal organizational rules and structures, informal practices, and collective understandings (March and Olsen 1998). DiMaggio and Powell suggest several mechanisms to explain institutional isomorphism (1991, 74–77), among them coercive, mimetic, and normative processes. Coercive mechanisms operate when institutions are highly dependent on other institutions, either in terms of resources or because of strong cultural expectations in the larger society in which both operate. Mimetic processes operate when means–ends relationships are unclear and institutions imitate "successful" examples. This mechanism resembles the "best practice" mentioned above; the underlying logic is not to increase efficiency, however, but to reduce uncertainty and complexity. Normative mechanisms work when credentials, professional status, and ethical concerns are at issue.

Europeanization provides fertile ground for each of these mechanisms. The EU is an environment characterized by a high level of interactions, dense issue networks, and dependence of institutions on inputs from their environment. Borrowing, imitating, and bending to Europeanization seems quite plausible. We find evidence of some convergence in almost every chapter of this book.

The literature on Europeanization seems to confirm this tendency. Rometsch and Wessels (1996, 351–52) suggest that convergence among national and European political and administrative institutions is driven by the increasing "fusion" and dense interaction among bureaucrats on all levels of decision making. Similarly, it follows from the arguments by DiMaggio and Powell (1991) that convergence can be expected the more a policy sector or issue-area is Europeanized, that is, the more national institutions and their actors regularly interact with European institutions and the more the former are dependent on the latter. Kohler-Koch (1996) posits a mimetic process when suggesting that convergence takes place when domestic actors are supplied with key governing concepts such as regulations or court directives.

Although there are good reasons to expect some degree of structural convergence, there are equally good reasons to assume continuing structural and institutional differences among the member states. First, there is a permissive condition. As mentioned, the legislative and regulatory vehicles of the EU, particularly the directives and the doctrine of mutual recognition, allow great discretion and flexibility in implementing legislation, let alone institutional adaptation. Directives (as opposed to regulations) leave each state to devise its own way of implementing their goals. The doctrine of mutual recognition can be seen as an overall regulatory standard that requires member states to accept the standards of other members for purposes of regional commerce. It signifies a move away from harmonization and uniform policies toward compatible but different systems of national regulation.

Second, we can deduce from liberal intergovernmentalism that national institutional differences are likely to prevail among the EU member states, at least as far as the more powerful members are concerned. If Europeanization results from interstate bargaining based on the domestic power and preferences of societal actors, the institutional solutions negotiated at the European level are unlikely to require major adaptation by the powerful members. The existing structural differences among the EU member states should remain untouched. Our empirical findings disconfirm this particular argument, even though we do find continuing structural differences.

Third, the sociological argument for convergence neglects the role of history. Many domestic institutions facing adaptational pressures from Europeanization have been around much longer than the EU. The German territorial structure of semi-autonomous regional units (now called "federalism") goes back to the Middle Ages. The French centralized l'état-nation (nation-state) has been around for centuries. The EU is unlikely to wash these differences away. The same aspect of Europeanization, say, the Equal Treatment Directive, implies different things depending on whether national legislation is already in line with European policy, whether such legislation departs radically from the European norm, or whether none exists at all. Europeanization not only generates different adaptational pressures, but its very meaning might differ from country to country. The European Central Bank (ECB) means one thing to Germany and another to France and Italy. Since countries are far from uniform in terms of existing policies and institutions, Europeanization is likely to generate different responses across the fifteen member states. This is also the finding of the study edited by Rometsch and Wessels (1996), which corresponds to our approach.

A final reason for expecting partial convergence has to do with the set of mediating variables in every political system. No matter what level of adaptational pressure is felt, every country will have a different set of institutions and actors to mediate between these pressures and the institutional outcomes. Sometimes these pressures will facilitate, sometimes they will obstruct, and at other times they may encourage piecemeal adaptation. These mediating institutions refract the policies made in Brussels so that a distinctive national stamp is placed on these policies as well as the domestic institutions. Full convergence is unlikely at both the policy and institutional levels. This does not imply that Europeanization has no structural effects. Far from it. It just implies differentiated responses.

Overview

The empirical chapters of the book are ordered according to the type of domestic structures dealt with. The first part of the book investigates the effects of Europeanization on *policy structures*. Caporaso and Jupille (chapter 2) investigate the impact of Europeanized gender equality policies (EU directives and ECJ rulings) on the domestic structures in France and Great Britain. They argue that the adaptational pressure was higher in the British than in the French case but that mediating institutions such as the Equal Opportunities Commission facilitated domestic structural change in the United Kingdom.

Héritier (chapter 3) analyzes the impact of EU transport liberalization policies in Britain, the Netherlands, Germany, and Italy. While Britain and the Netherlands faced only limited adaptational pressures, Germany and Italy were required to transform existing administrative structures to a large degree. Germany managed to change its administrative structure owing to institutional capacities to overcome multiple veto points and a consensual decision-making culture. Both mediating factors were missing in Italy, which resisted the change.

Schneider (chapter 4) examines the impact of Europeanization on the liberalization of telecommunications in Germany, France, and Italy. Although the ultimate outcome was convergence with regard to liberalized and deregulated telecommunications markets, the changes in France and Italy cannot be explained without reference to EU policies that strengthened and accelerated global trends.

Sbragia (chapter 5) examines the reform of public finances in Italy, which enabled the country to meet the Maastricht convergence criteria for Economic and Monetary Union (EMU). She argues that Europeanization empowered a small group of core executives who overcame the considerable domestic opposition against reform by exploiting the considerable support for European integration among the political elites and the Italian public.

The second part of the book investigates the impact of Europeanization on *"system-wide" domestic structures*, as defined above. Conant (chapter 6) examines the degree to which legal systems in France, Germany, and the United Kingdom have been transformed in response to the development of distinct European legal procedures. In particular, she looks at the variation in referral rates to the ECJ, following the Article 177 procedure. She argues that the transformation of national judicial structures remains incomplete and that the variation can be explained by the differences in national institutional systems.

Knill and Lenschow (chapter 7) investigate administrative responses in Britain and Germany to EU environmental policies. Both countries faced adaptational pressures in some cases, while EU environmental directives fit existing administrative styles in other cases. The authors argue that change was the more likely, the less the required adjustments contradicted core features of national administrative styles and cultures.

Börzel (chapter 8) examines the responses of the German Länder and of the Spanish autonomous regions to the loss of competences to Brussels. Although both countries faced similar adaptational pressures, the German states regained their competences rather easily in a system of cooperative federalism. In contrast, the Spanish regions had first to overcome their confrontational attitude toward the central government in order to recover some lost competences.

Cowles (chapter 9) investigates the impact of the Transatlantic Business Dialogue on relations between firms, business associations, and governments in the United Kingdom, France, and Germany. The adaptational pressures were particularly strong in the French and German cases. In France, firms and business associations used their new, direct access to the European level to gain more independence from the French state. It was much harder for German business organizations, who resented the German firms' leading role, to accept the new business-government relationship.

Checkel (chapter 10) examines changes in the understandings of German citizenship norms responding to both the Council of Europe's citizenship rules and recent developments in the EU. He claims that elite learning and societal pressures resulted in a gradual change of German citizenship identity away from the old jus sanguinis toward dual citizenship.

Risse (chapter 11) investigates the degree to which Europeanization changed collective understandings relating to the nation-state in the United Kingdom, France, and Germany. Although he does not find much change in the British case, German nation-state identity incorporated Europe and Europeanness already in the late 1950s. France is probably the case with the most profound effect of Europeanization, since Europe was incorporated in the former Gaullist understanding of the l'état-nation since the 1980s.

The concluding chapter summarizes the findings of the empirical chapters in view of the theoretical and conceptual framework of the book.

CHAPTER TWO

The Europeanization of Gender Equality Policy and Domestic Structural Change

James Caporaso and Joseph Jupille

Social policy began life as something of a poor cousin to the more fundamental economic aims of the European Community. Despite substantial growth at the European level, social policy remains a central component of domestic politics, and conceptions and systems of social protection vary meaningfully across European Union (EU) member states. We outline the Europeanization of one of the central pillars of EU social policy, gender equality, and assess its impact on domestic structures in France and the United Kingdom. The chapter proceeds in five parts. The first section describes the Europeanization of gender equality policy and operationalizes the abstract concepts laid out in the introduction. The second section sets forth the logic of our case selection and offers a comparative assessment of the French and British cases. The third and fourth sections consist of case studies assessing the degree and nature of domestic structural change in France and the United Kingdom as a result of the Europeanization of gender equality policy. The final section summarizes the argument and findings.

Gender Equality: Europeanization and Domestic Structures

Europeanization

Our focus in this chapter is equal pay and the equal treatment of men and women. While these areas have been the subject of considerable EU-level leg-

We thank participants in the project workshops, and especially Thomas Risse and Maria Green Cowles, for detailed comments on several earlier drafts. We also thank Karen Alter, Renaud Dehousse, Peter Katzenstein, Sally Kenney, Amy Mazur, Martin Rhodes, Jo Shaw, and two anonymous reviewers for comments, helpful research advice, and/or access to documents.

islative and judicial activity (CEC 1995a), we place three elements at the center of our analysis: Article 119 of the Treaty of Rome (post-Amsterdam Article 141), the 1975 Equal Pay Directive (EPD), and the 1976 Equal Treatment Directive (ETD).[1]

Article 119.   Article 119 of the Treaty of Rome stated that each member state shall ensure and maintain "the application of the principle that men and women should receive equal pay for equal work," going on to define pay as "the ordinary basic or minimum wage or salary and any other consideration, whether in cash or in kind, which the worker receives, directly or indirectly, in respect of his employment from his employer." The article was based on, but was narrower than, earlier International Labor Organization (ILO) standards calling for equal pay for work of "equal value." Its narrowness and the relatively tenuous foundations of EU law in the late 1950s made it difficult to imagine how this provision would have practical effect. Indeed, in the decade following the entry into force of the Treaty, member states made very little effort to implement the equal pay principle (Hoskyns 1996, 60–68).

Unlike much of the treaty, Article 119 "was written in clear and specific terms and appeared to impose a precise obligation on the member states" (Burrows and Mair 1996, 16). Despite this, the question as to whether Article 119 conferred directly effective and justiciable rights upon individuals remained unresolved until the European Court of Justice (ECJ) took it up in *Defrenne II*.[2] In its judgment, the Court found that "direct and overt discrimination may be identified solely with the aid of the criteria based on equal work and equal pay referred to by [Article 119]." Because it identified "precise" and "unconditional" criteria for assessing direct discrimination, Article 119 had direct effect: it conferred rights upon individuals that they could invoke against their states (Pescatore 1983, 161). The Court subsequently developed this line of reasoning in a number of cases.

Directives.   Article 1 of the Equal Pay Directive (EPD) states that "the principle of equal pay for men and women outlined in Article 119 of the Treaty ... means for the same work or for work to which equal value is attributed, the elimination of all discrimination on grounds of sex with regard to all aspects and conditions of remuneration." This Directive affirms the intent of Article 119 and expands its meaning to include equal pay for work of equal value.

1. Council Directive 75/117/EEC of 10 February 1975 on the approximation of the laws of the member states relating to the application of the principle of equal pay for men and women (*Official Journal of the European Communities* [O.J.] L 045, February 19, 1975, 19); Council Directive 76/207/EEC of 9 February 1976, on the implementation of the principle of equal treatment for men and women as regards access to employment, vocational training and promotion, and working conditions (O.J.L 039, February 14, 1976, 40).

2. Case 43/75, *Gabrielle Defrenne v. Société anonyme belge de navigation aérienne Sabena*, 1976 European Court Reports (E.C.R.) 455.

The 1976 Equal Treatment Directive (ETD) took up concerns raised by women's groups and policymakers about gender discrimination beyond the area of pay. Article 1 exhorted member states "to put into effect the principle of equal treatment for men and women as regards access to employment, including promotion, and to vocational training and as regards working conditions." The ETD went further than the EPD in scrutinizing and attempting to remedy deeply ingrained, low-visibility, and indirect forms of discrimination. In its 1986 *Marshall I* judgment, the ECJ found that Article 5 of the ETD was "sufficiently precise to be relied on by an individual and to be applied by the national courts."[3] In other words, the right to equal treatment, much like the right to equal pay, had direct effect and could be invoked by individuals against EU member states.

Other Aspects of Europeanization.   The ECJ, national courts, the European Commission, and domestic and transnational actors engage in the clarification, interpretation, monitoring, and enforcement of these provisions. Without the landmark decisions of the ECJ regarding the direct effect and superiority of EU law, EU gender equality policy might not yield results. The ECJ and domestic courts cooperate to clarify and interpret European law through the preliminary ruling procedure (formerly Article 177, now Article 234), and the Commission monitors and enforces implementation through the infringements procedure (formerly Article 169, now Article 226). Women's groups and other societal actors engage the European Commission, the Council of Ministers, the European Parliament, and national governments at the policy formulation and implementation stages. Thus, the measures we examine here have to be interpreted within the broader framework of EU, national, and transnational institutions, policies, and behavior, all of which form part and parcel of Europeanization.

Goodness of Fit

Starting with Europeanization, in this chapter we assess the goodness of fit between Europe and domestic provisions. In the area of pay, we use pay disparities as a first-cut indicator of goodness of fit. Here fit is "good" to the extent that substantive equality (e.g., pay equality between men and women) in the member states satisfies the expectations or requirements of European policy and law. Other indicators concern how European and national levels define terms such as "equal," "pay," "treatment," "work," and "value." To the extent that they are defined similarly in the two spheres, fit is good and adaptational pressure will be relatively low. Procedurally, both Directives require member states to provide avenues for legal recourse to perceived victims of discrimination. Other requirements include job-evaluation schemes facilitating the comparison of the value of different jobs and provisions for ensuring the inclusion of equality principles into collectively

---

3. Case 152/84, *M. H. Marshall v. Southampton and South-West Hampshire Area Health Authority*, 1986 E.C.R. 723.

bargained agreements. To the extent that such domestic procedures satisfy the requirements of European law, fit will be good and Europeanization will generate relatively little adaptational pressure.

Mediating Institutions

Adaptational pressure does not translate frictionlessly into domestic structural change. Instead, preexisting institutions and practices mediate these pressures and influence structural outcomes. The number of mediating factors is potentially quite large and requires us to make choices about what to include and exclude from our analysis. We choose to retain a strictly institutional focus on public agencies and legal arenas and state-society relations. We do not systematically consider broader political and less institutionalized factors, such as the orientation of the ruling majority or coalition, or even more institutionalized factors, such as differences in industrial relations regimes. These choices do not imply that we think all excluded variables are unimportant.

Agencies and Legal Arenas.   The presence of public bodies competent in equality matters may condition the translation of adaptational pressure into structural change. We assess such bodies along several dimensions. Their degree of autonomy vis-à-vis political (especially majority) parties and other public bodies conditions the translation of Europeanization into domestic structural change. Low autonomy suggests that agencies will have little influence in either direction on domestic structures. Highly autonomous agencies can either amplify or attenuate pressures for change, depending on their own preferences. Correlated with autonomy but analytically separate is the degree to which agencies specialize in the area of gender equality. As the degree of specialization increases, we expect agencies to amplify adaptational pressure and to correlate with greater domestic structural change. By contrast, where multifunctional agencies with broader mandates (e.g., labor inspectorates) have simply added gender equality to their competencies, we expect that, at a minimum, they will exert little influence on the degree of structural change. Finally, we consider the functions fulfilled by public agencies. To the extent that agencies are mandated to transform pressures for change (emanating from Europe or elsewhere) into actual change, we expect them to amplify the effects of Europeanization. Agencies called upon to advocate on behalf of victims of discrimination, rather than simply investigating their claims, would seem to fulfill this transformation function. In addition, authoritative agencies, capable of imposing sanctions, should promote greater change than do purely advisory or consultative bodies.

State-Society Relations.   By state-society relations, we understand such issues as the relative autonomy of state and society from each other, their relative strength or the strength of their component parts, and organizational capacity and access to the political and legal system. Here the stylized distinction between pluralist and corporatist systems suggests itself, since most systems exhibit elements of both, and these are best viewed as points along a continuum rather than as polar types (Keeler 1985). In pluralist systems, societal actors (interest groups) and the state are distinct and interact voluntarily and through multiple channels. Groups emerge and dissolve of their own volition, tend to compete among themselves, and neither control nor are controlled by the state. The state, in this conception, serves as the passive arena within which group conflict and interaction occur. Corporatist systems, by contrast, blur the boundaries between society and the state. Societal actors formally participate in state or quasi-public institutions, may depend upon the state for recognition, legitimation, or resources, and may in turn defer to it in any number of ways (Schmitter 1974; Wilson 1982, 176–79). These differences correlate with other, possibly important, mediating institutions such as norms about the relative effectiveness of the market in addressing social concerns.

Overall, state-society relations will influence domestic structural change as a function of the organization, relative power, preferences of, and linkages between state and societal actors. Where the state is relatively strong, as in corporatist systems, it can facilitate or hinder change, depending on its preferences. The degree to which pluralist systems facilitate or hinder adaptation is a function of the preferences and power of the relevant societal groups. Where women's groups are relatively strong and mobilized within a pluralist system, we expect adaptation to be facilitated. Where they are weak relative to other groups with different views (for example, employers' associations), adaptation may be hindered.

Domestic Structural Change

Finally, we arrive at our dependent variable, domestic structural change. How can we think about this abstract concept in a more operational way? We focus on three dimensions of domestic structures: legislation, individual rights, and the domestic institutional balance.

Domestic Legislation.   The products of domestic legislation are the laws of the land, the highest expression of the binding authority of the state. Laws are systems of rules that are interrelated, making it difficult to alter one part without making changes in other places. Legislation is structural in the sense that it provides a framework for making choices that is not ad hoc and personal but is instead based on rules, and is commensurately difficult to change. However, relative to individual rights and the domestic institutional balance, legislation is comparatively easy to change, and should be more sensitive to pressures emanating from Europeanization.

Individual Rights.   The acquisition of new individual rights, if it originates in European legal sources and is sustained and dependable, is a change in domestic structure. To focus on the rights of individuals before an international court such as the ECJ raises questions about legal standing and the constitutional character of the European Community. In a traditional, treaty-based international organization, the ECJ would limit itself to resolving interstate conflict. This interstate architectural principle provides few, if any, direct links between individuals and either the institutional machinery or textual content of international treaties. The original Treaty of Rome lacked a serious statement of individual rights and provided little by way of enforcement of those scattered rights that might (through interpretation) have been said to exist.

Thus, from the standpoint of developing individual rights under Community law, the architecture of the EU seems weak. Before substantial progress could be made, the Treaty had to be transformed from a decentralized compact among states into a constitution, with direct effect in and supremacy over national law (see Mancini 1991; Stone 1994). This transformation has proceeded in several stages and is ongoing (O'Keeffe 1996, 902–3). While reception remains uneven and depends on political and institutional factors in the member states, it is important nevertheless.

Domestic Institutional Balance.   Europeanization may also affect the balance of power among domestic institutions. Moravcsik (1994) emphasizes changes in the executive-legislative balance to the benefit of the former. Alter and Vargas (2000) emphasize shifts in the balance of power among domestic groups. Legal integration theorists suggest that judicial cooperation between national courts and the ECJ through the preliminary reference procedure can alter the relative importance of lower and higher domestic courts and can strengthen the judiciary as a whole vis-à-vis domestic executives and legislatures (Alter 1996b).

Although we take Article 177 proceedings as prima facie evidence of domestic structural change insofar as they produce a complex fusion of domestic and supranational legal orders, we focus primarily on the extension of judicial review. Judicial review involves the assessment (review) of the laws of one level of government in light of laws (including the constitution) of another level. Some hierarchy is implied in the very idea of judicial review. When the ECJ set forth the doctrines of direct effect and supremacy, it implied that it would have the ability to review and overturn domestic laws. Despite strong resistance, today judicial review is accepted in all EU member states, with varying degrees of conviction. Because this legal innovation relied on domestic courts to serve as agents of change, it appears more as a triumph for the rule of law rather than a triumph of external (European) over domestic institutions (Alter 1998a, 121).

Europeanization of Gender Equality: France and the UK Compared

We apply these arguments to France and the United Kingdom. Pairing these countries provides theoretically meaningful variation on a number of the factors that should condition the translation of pressure from Europeanization into domestic structural change.

Goodness of Fit and Adaptational Pressure

Pay Disparity.   The United Kingdom traditionally manifests one of the largest male–female pay differentials in the Community, France one of the lowest (Table 2.1). Broader measures of gender inequality point in the same direction (Perrons 1994). On the hypothesis that higher disparities indicate poor fit between the aspirations of EU equality policies and domestic conditions, we expect greater pressure on the United Kingdom than on France.

Article 119.   In general, we expect Treaty articles to exhibit greater fit with original member states (that participated in their design) than with later entrants. More important, in the case of Article 119, France already had domestic equal pay legislation on the books and, fearing competitive disadvantage, forcefully insisted on the inclusion of the equal pay principle in the Treaty of Rome. Other member states agreed to the provision to satisfy the French. Given this high goodness of fit, we expect very little adaptational pressure on France as a result of Article 119. The United Kingdom, by contrast, played no part in shaping Article 119, and we expect the Article to exert greater adaptational pressure on it.

Equal Pay Directive.   Adoption of the EPD in 1975 only marginally increased the adaptational pressure on France. The Directive extended the "equal pay for *equal work*" principle to the principle of "equal pay for *work of equal value*." While innovative in the EU, this extension was consistent with existing French provisions. Britain, by contrast, had resisted the equal value provision prior to enactment of the EPD (McCrudden 1983, 197). Instead, it set up an equal pay for "like

Table 2.1   Gross hourly earnings, all industry (% difference, men–women)

Country	1972[a]	1977[a]	1983[b]	1990[c]	1995[d]
Belgium	31.9	29.3	26.0	24.1	16.8
France	22.9	24.2	19.9	19.2	23.4[f]
Germany	29.4	27.5	27.5	26.8	23.1
Italy	23.6	19.9[e]	12.8	17.3	23.5
Luxembourg	41.7	37.5	35.0	34.9	16.1
Netherlands	34.2	25.2	26.0	24.7	29.4
United Kingdom	41.2	29.0	30.5	31.8	26.3

[a] CEC 1979, 98.
[b] Mazey 1988, 65.
[c] Manual employment only (CEC 1994, 5).
[d] Eurostat, *News Release* no. 48/88, June 8, 1999.
[e] Data for April 1976.
[f] Data for 1994.

work" standard and left the creation of a job evaluation scheme for assessing "like work" to employers' discretion. Because employers faced a disincentive to establish job-evaluation schemes (insofar as they opened the door to equal pay claims), women's rights were not ensured, and the British act did not fully implement the Directive. In sum, we expect the EPD to generate substantially greater pressure for change on the United Kingdom than on France. A glance at Table 2.2, which reveals eleven Article 177 proceedings in the area of equal pay involving the United Kingdom and zero involving France, provides initial confirmation of this expectation.

Equal Treatment Directive.   The fit between European and French provisions is poorer in equal treatment than in equal pay. We exploit this within-country, cross-issue variation in our research design. The within-country comparison controls for extraneous variables and permits us more effectively to isolate the causal effects of Europeanization on domestic structural change. According to the European Commission, French law implementing the ETD insufficiently defined "equal treatment" and "indirect discrimination" and failed to clarify acceptable derogations from the equal treatment principle (for example, regarding "positive" discrimination in women's favor). Most important, the Commission felt that provisions for access to public employment that discriminated on the basis of gender brought French law out of conformity with European law (CEC 1981, 44–49). Looking again at Table 2.2, we observe that whereas equal pay produced no direct judicial pressure on France, the ETD produced six ECJ judgments, three each under the preliminary ruling (Article 177) and infringement (Article 169) procedures. These data suggest that adaptational pressure on France resulting from the ETD was considerable.

The United Kingdom's Sex Discrimination Act of 1975 preceded the ETD and so did not directly transpose terms and definitions from the Directive into national law. The Commission's review of United Kingdom implementation of the Equal Treatment Directive found several areas of nonconformity. Most important, British law failed to nullify collective agreements containing clauses contrary to the principle of equal treatment, excluded household and small employers, and maintained certain unjustifiable sex-based job restrictions. In mid-1980 the Commission formally notified the United Kingdom that it was in breach of the Directive in these three areas, as compared with a single formal notification for France (CEC 1981, 212–13). In sum, then, we expect pressure on both France and the United Kingdom in this area, with slightly more in the British case.

Mediating Institutions

Equality Agencies and Tribunals.   Public agencies responsible for promoting gender equality exist in every EU member state (European Parliament 1995). In France, Mazur argues, these bodies reflect the symbolic nature of equality politics

Table 2.2 Legal proceedings in the area of gender equality, through 1997

	Belgium	Denmark	Germany	Ireland	Netherlands	United Kingdom	France	Italy	Luxembourg	Total
					Article 177 Rulings on Equal Pay					
1971	1									1
1975	1									1
1978	1									1
1980						1				1
1981						2				2
1982						2				2
1984					4					4
1986			2							2
1988				1						1
1989		1	1			1				3
1990			1							1
1991			1							1
1992			1							1
1993			1		1	2				4
1994			7		4	2				13
1995		1	1							2
1996			2		1	1				4
Total	3	2	17	1	10	11	0	0	0	44
					Article 169 Actions on Equal Pay					
1983			1			1				2
1985		1							1	2
1993	1									1
Total	1	1	1	0	0	1	0	0	1	5

Table 2.2 (cont.)

	Belgium	Denmark	Germany	Ireland	Netherlands	United Kingdom	France	Italy	Luxembourg	Total
Article 169 Actions on Council Directive 76/207										
1983						1		1		2
1985			1							1
1988							2			2
1996							1			1
Total	0	0	1	0	0	1	3	1	0	6
Article 177 Rulings on Council Directive 76/207										
1984			3							3
1986					1	3				4
1990		1			1	1				3
1991							1			1
1992						1				1
1993			1			1	1			3
1994	1		1			1				3
1995			1			1				2
1996						1				1
1997		1	3				1			5
Total	1	2	9	0	2	9	3	0	0	26
Grand Total	5	6	28	1	11	22	6	1	1	81

Sources: CEC 1997, 109; CEC 1998a, 102.
Note: The Commission reports figures for the Equal Pay Directive and Article 119 together.

(Mazur 1995a). The impressive flurry of institutionalization that attended to the Socialists' 1981 electoral victory created agencies highly dependent upon (i.e., lacking autonomy from) the party (Forbes 1989, 27–28; Lovenduski 1997, 104–5). In addition, French equality agencies tend to be limited to consultative rather than policymaking or even advocacy roles. They enjoy no mandate to facilitate or engage in equality litigation, which comparative studies identify as a crucial element in promoting change (Kilpatrick 1997, 29). Bodies with real power, such as the Labor Inspectorates and the unions, do not specialize in gender equality issues and consequently lack expertise. As a result, litigation strategies on behalf of gender equality fail to take root (Fitzpatrick 1993, 46, 90; Blom et al. 1995, 36). Simply put, there is little reason to believe that French equality agencies and tribunals can or will capitalize—or permit interested groups and individuals to capitalize—upon Europeanization.

In the United Kingdom, by contrast, the Equal Opportunities Commissions (EOCs) in Britain and Northern Ireland enjoy a broad mandate proactively to assert and defend the rights of working women. The two commissions actively pursue a litigation strategy with a strong European component. Their relative autonomy, popularity, linkages with women's groups, and flexibility insulate them from the vagaries of electoral politics (Forbes 1989, 32) and increase their impact on United Kingdom gender equality policies and structures. In addition, the United Kingdom already had in place, when the two EC Directives were passed, a basic structure to hear and try cases on equal pay and equal treatment. During the first two years following entry into force of the Equal Pay Act, individuals brought almost 2,500 equal pay claims, resulting in 1,072 cases before the industrial tribunals, and the Employment Appeals Tribunal (EAT) decided more than fifty equal pay cases (CEC 1979, 50–51). We can think of the combination of the equality commissions and the industrial tribunals as a relatively specialized and partly preexisting facilitative structure for the European transformation of gender equality.

State-Society Relations.   Gender equality replicates many features of French sectoral corporatism (Muller 1992). Interest groups require official recognition of their representativeness, which tends to limit their autonomy (Keeler 1985). Hall singles out French women's groups for their lack of organization and dependence upon alliances with major politicians and political parties (Hall 1990, 87, 89; Forbes 1989, 27–28). The organic involvement of the French feminist movement with public actors and political parties puts women's groups in a dependent position and weakens the foundations of the feminist movement itself (Lovenduski 1990, 145, 158; Mazur 1995b, 86, 91).

The United Kingdom, by contrast, exhibits a strong, active, and highly mobilized interest-group system organized along pluralist lines (highly specialized, yet grouped into peak associations, and imbued with a bargaining culture). Bretherton and Sperling (1996) describe a wide-ranging, dynamic, and highly interactive network of United Kingdom women's groups that does not depend upon state sponsorship. We expect groups in labor, feminist organizations, and those generally concerned with equality of opportunity to take an active role in pressing claims for greater gender equality.

France and the United Kingdom also contrast in the relative importance of the market for establishing the price of labor. Here, France tends to rely more on *étatiste* solutions. Mazey suggests that "French governments of both Left and Right—in keeping with French policy style—have been strongly interventionist in this policy sector" (Mazey 1998, 147). The United Kingdom, by contrast, especially during the Thatcher and Major periods, demonstrates a relative preference for the market as a mechanism for solving pricing issues. Its "statism" is more liberal than France's (Schmidt 1995, 90–94). Because equal pay and treatment legislation "assert clearly an intention to disrupt normal market forces" (Fenwick and Hervey 1995, 447; Perrons 1994), we expect this dimension of French domestic structure to facilitate adaptation to European gender equality requirements, and British structures to attenuate it.

We summarize these basic points in Table 2.3. The top half of the table summarizes adaptational pressures on the two countries generated by each issue (reading across the rows) and within each country across issues (reading down the columns). We label each substantive element of the analysis and score the degree of pressure it generates. Similarly, the bottom half summarizes mediating institutions, drawing out their expected impact in terms of the translation of Europeanization into domestic structural change. The scores are largely subjective, but we believe that they faithfully reflect the evidence adduced above.

Overall, we expect greater change in the UK, since it is here that we find a combination of large mismatch between the EU and the national level and, at the same time, a favorable balance to alter domestic institutions and practices. To strengthen the analysis, we extract additional variation and provide greater leverage on our claims by reading down the columns of the table. Here, we can hold mediating institutions constant and examine variations in structural change within each country resulting more precisely from variations in goodness of fit across issues.[4] Attention to within-country variation permits a more finely grained analysis of the hypothesized relationships between Europeanization and domestic change. We proceed now to our case studies to explore these expectations.

Europeanization of Gender Equality and French Domestic Structures

Domestic Laws

Most of the changes in French domestic structures resulting from Europeanization have taken this weakest (because least structural) form. Equal pay generated the least pressure because of the strong consistency of French procedures and

---

4. We thank Thomas Risse for encouraging us to pursue this option.

Table 2.3 Adaptational pressure and mediating institutions compared

| | Adaptational Pressure | | | |
| | UK | | France | |
Factor	Description	Pressure	Description	Pressure
Pay disparity	Relatively high	High	Relatively low	Moderate-Low
Article 119	Did not influence Article 119	High	Decisively shaped Article 119	Low
EPD	No equal value provisions; voluntary job evaluation schemes breach procedural requirement	High	Longstanding equal value provisions; slight procedural incongruity	Low
ETD	Failure to nullify inconsistent collective agreements and unjustified restrictions of equal treatment principle	High	Gender restrictions in public-sector employment, collective agreements, and nightwork for women	Moderate-High

| | Mediating Institutions | | | |
| | UK | | France | |
Factor	Description	Impact	Description	Impact
Public bodies	Specialized, relatively autonomous, advocacy bodies	Facilitate	Multifunctional, politically dependent, advisory bodies	None or attenuate
State-society relations				
Interest intermediation	Pluralist	Facilitate	Sectoral corporatist	Attenuate
Reliance on market	Relatively high	Attenuate	Relatively low	Facilitate

EPD = Equal Pay Directive.
ETD = Equal Treatment Directive.

practices with EU requirements. The European Commission's 1979 review did find that French legislation failed properly to implement the EPD insofar as it tied certain public-sector benefits in cash or in kind to head of household status, understood at that time as a man (CEC 1979, 133). Compared to most other member states, however, French transgressions were slight. The Commission began infringement proceedings but dropped them after France adjusted the offending provisions (Kilpatrick 1997, 30). Thus, Europeanization resulted only in very slight changes to French equal pay legislation.

Turning to the ETD, the Commission noted several deficiencies in French implementing legislation (CEC 1981). As a result of these lacunae and the infringement actions that they generated, the ECJ, in three separate rulings, found French equal treatment legislation to be unsatisfactory. The first of these cases concerned access to public-sector employment.[5] A 1982 French law generally established the principle of gender equality but, by way of exception from the general principle, established gender-distinct lists for several categories of employment that required physical strength or skill allegedly possessed only by men (e.g., police work). After the Commission began infringement proceedings in 1983, France partially amended its legislation to drop certain of the job categories concerned. In a 1988 judgment, the ECJ found that the French provisions contravened tenets of Community law.

Among other interesting features of the case, we find the fact that it never gave rise to a preliminary ruling to be meaningful. One of the largest public-sector unions had already contested the gender distinction before the French Conseil d'État. The Conseil did not see fit to refer the question of the compatibility of the French provision with the Equal Treatment Directive to the ECJ. In its judgment of April 16, 1982, the Conseil d'État held that the French law, in the interest of the proper functioning of certain public services, justifiably established for men and women differential access to certain jobs (Pettiti 1989, 162). Given a chance to weigh in through the Commission's infringement action, the European Court of Justice disagreed and found that the French provisions should be amended to conform to Community law.

The second case concerned French law 83–635 of July 13, 1983, which sought to bring French labor and criminal codes into conformity with the ETD.[6] Article 19 of the French law permitted the temporally unlimited maintenance of a number of special rights for women, including several having to do with older women workers and mothers, in collective agreements enacted prior to the entry into force of the Directive. The Commission contended that such provisions were excessively general, permitting any and all clauses of collective agreements that granted special rights to women, and concluded that the French law contravened the ETD.

The French government responded that the provisions were necessary to maintain prevailing parenting and marriage norms, and that as the products of difficult negotiations among the social partners, the measures would be exceedingly difficult to modify. The ECJ dismissed these arguments in short order and found that the measures were inconsistent with Community law (Lanquetin and Masse-Dessen 1989). France subsequently passed a law on 10 July 1989 requiring the social partners to bring their collectively bargained agreements into conformity with EC law, as required by the ECJ judgment (Savatier 1990, 468). In subsequent jurisprudence, France's Cour de Cassation upheld the conclusions drawn by the ECJ (Hennion-Moreau 1992, 740). However, Europeanization compelled relatively minor changes, affecting fewer than two hundred clauses of the thousands of French collective agreements in effect at the time (*EIRR* 1989).

5. Case 318/86, *Commission of the European Communities v. French Republic*, 1988 E.C.R. 3559.
6. Case 312/86, *Commission of the European Communities v. French Republic*, 1988 E.C.R. 6315.

Structure of Rights

Three cases, one from a domestic French court and two from the European Court of Justice, demonstrate that there has been some change in the structure of individual rights as a result of the Europeanization of gender equality. However, they also attest to the limits of change in France.

In the domestic case, decided in La Rochelle, a labor inspector discovered nine women working in a photo-processing laboratory at 4:30 in the morning and charged their employer, Mr. Beyly, with violating Article L-213-1 of the French labor code. The code prohibited, with certain exceptions, nighttime work for women. In an audacious ruling, the La Rochelle police court found that the French code did not conform to the ETD, which permitted gender distinctions only with respect to pregnancy or maternity leave, and thus could not be used to prosecute the defendant. The case stands out in two respects. First, the domestic court suggested the existence of an individual right on the basis of European law. Second, the court, judging Community law to be adequately clear and precise, did not see fit to put the question to the European Court of Justice (Hennion-Moreau 1992, 741). In the event, the relationship between French and European laws, and the rights to which the latter might give rise, required further clarification.

Two ECJ cases clarified the matter. In *Stoeckel*,[7] the French public prosecutor charged Mr. Stoeckel with infringing the same Article L-213-1 of the French labor code. The defendant argued before the Illkirch criminal court that the provision contravened the ETD. The court asked the ECJ whether Article 5 of the ETD was "sufficiently precise to impose on a Member State an obligation not to lay down in its legislation the principle that nightwork by women is prohibited," as laid down in the French code. Reiterating its *Marshall* jurisprudence, the ECJ held that Article 5 of the ETD was "sufficiently precise to impose on member states the obligation not to lay down by legislation the principle that night work for women is prohibited, even if that obligation is subject to exceptions, where night work for men is not prohibited." In so doing, the Court affirmed Mr. Stoeckel's right to invoke Article 5 of the Directive as against the French provisions.

The case of *Levy*[8] replayed many of the features of *Stoeckel* but added consideration of the respective place of European and international law in the French hierarchy of norms (Vanhamme 1994–95). *Stoeckel* had concluded that French night-work provisions were inconsistent with the ETD. However, the Metz police court involved in the *Levy* case noted that France had enacted the offending provision in order to implement its 1953 commitment (under ILO Convention No. 89) to ban night work for women. The court thus asked the ECJ about the relationship between EU law and national legislation intended to implement a treaty obligation incurred prior to the signature of the Treaty of Rome. Where they conflicted, the Metz court asked, which took precedence?

7. Case C-345/89, *Criminal proceedings against Alfred Stoeckel*, 1991 E.C.R. I-4047.
8. Case C-158/91, *Criminal proceedings against Jean-Claude Levy*, 1993 E.C.R. I-4287.

The ECJ held that domestic courts were required to ensure the application of Article 5 of the ETD, even against conflicting national legislation, "unless the application of such a provision is necessary in order to ensure the performance by the Member State concerned of obligations arising under an agreement concluded with non-member countries prior to the entry into force of the EEC Treaty." Because the French code implemented a prior international commitment, therefore, and because the Court was concerned about protecting the rights of third countries with which France had entered into Treaty obligations, it in effect denied Mr. Levy's invocation of EU law as against the conflicting French provision.

In the area of individual rights, in sum, we observe limited change. First, within the domestic arena, there exist very little expertise and tradition of invoking individual rights as against the state. This creates a vicious circle in which cases that are brought are time-consuming and frequently lost in the face of lawyers and judges inexperienced in the area of gender equality; hence, fewer cases are brought, experience does not develop, and so forth (Fitzpatrick 1993, 223). Second, and related, in contrast to the overall willingness of French courts to use the preliminary ruling procedure (Golub 1996b), they have used it very little in the area of gender equality. No public agency exists that is both motivated and empowered to exploit the possibilities offered by European law, and private groups do not seem prepared to step into the public void. Third, the rights that have been created have been circumscribed, especially to the extent that they repose on European law that relates ambiguously to international law in the French hierarchy of legal norms (Pettiti 1988; Savatier 1990; Wuiame 1994).

Institutional Balance

We find very little evidence of changes in the French domestic institutional balance as a result of the Europeanization of gender equality. The domestic equal treatment case, coming out of the La Rochelle criminal court, indicates some institutional change. The leading French labor law journal, *Droit Social*, published a scathing critique of the judgment accusing the court of arrogating lawmaking functions from national legislators (Savatier 1990). To the extent that this charge is true, it would represent domestic structural change of an important kind. The Europeanization of gender equality has not noticeably advanced trends in judicial review. With respect to state-society relations, the tantalizing idea that Europeanization might "pluralize" France's more structured corporatist-type system finds no support in our analysis. If changes in the institutional balance have occurred in the area of gender equality, they are subtle and difficult to establish.

Summary

As expected, we find very little evidence of domestic structural change in France resulting from Europeanization. However, we find greater change in response to the Equal Treatment Directive than the Equal Pay Directive, conforming to the predicted pattern that greater adaptational pressure produces greater domestic change. Europeanization has propelled some changes in domestic legislation. Individual rights have been created, although their invocation remains rare and their effects remain in doubt. Changes in the domestic institutional balance are not apparent. More speculatively, we must at least consider the possibility that Europeanization affects deeply and historically rooted notions of work and family roles. Many reacted negatively to the ECJ's night-work judgments, suggesting that the Court had attacked measures viewed by most French as important protective measures and symbols of progress (Pourtaud 1997; Sciarra 1996). Were Europeanization to cause a rethinking (or, in the extreme, abandonment) of traditional notions of work and family, we would be in the presence of domestic structural change of the most profound sort.

Europeanization of Gender Equality and British Domestic Structures

Domestic Legislation

To what extent has Europeanization, in particular Article 119 and the two Directives, influenced British gender equality legislation? In terms of the relationship between European and domestic legislation, no causal connection appears possible. The EC directives were passed in 1975 and 1976, whereas the Equal Pay Act was passed in 1970 and the Sex Discrimination Act in 1975. However, the British Equal Pay Act "was developed, partly at least, in anticipation of future United Kingdom membership" in the EC (McCrudden 1983, 197). To be sure, pressure groups had been lobbying for equality legislation independently of Europe (Davies 1987, 23–25). However, as even an unsympathetic observer notes, it was also clear that equal pay legislation would be necessary to comply with Article 119 as well as subsequent EC legislation. In fact, conformity with EC laws was used as an argument in favor of national legislation as early as 1969, and before that, various government ministries had been asked to review the consequences of membership in 1967 (Davies 1987, 25). At a minimum, then, United Kingdom law reflects an anticipated connection between European and domestic levels.

Whatever the connection to the original drafting of these laws, the Equal Pay Act and the Sex Discrimination Act were both amended to bring them more into line with European requirements. Both were subjected to continuous pressure by the comparison of these national acts with EU legislation. Under pressure of Europeanization, the Sex Discrimination Act was redrafted so as to narrow exceptions in the areas of pregnancy, retirement, and protective legislation. Here, we focus on amendments to the Equal Pay Act (EPA).

The basic narrative is as follows. The EPA was passed in 1970 and provided for equality in pay for "like work." However, a number of serious shortcomings existed in the law, especially where the plaintiff did not have a comparator, that is, someone in a similar job in the same establishment. In cases where the employer did not agree to set up a job–evaluation scheme, the employee had no legal recourse. Since most of the inequality was between job categories rather than within them, this was a serious matter. Thus, the issue of comparison was crucial and remains so. Women could be prevented from claiming discrimination simply because there were no men doing the same job.

Potential victims of discrimination faced a difficult situation. If women performed the same job as men and were paid less, discrimination would be easy to demonstrate. But in the more common case, where women and men worked at different jobs and women were paid less, they would have no comparators (no one doing exactly the same work with whom to be compared). Clearly, unless equal value standards were admitted, no progress could be made. Women's groups and others within Britain pushed for amendment to the 1970 act so as to admit the phrase "work of equal value." However, little happened until the EC passed the Equal Pay Directive in 1975. This Directive explicitly included the "equal value" language and imposed a deadline for its enforcement of February 1978. After this date, and upon its 1979 review of domestic measures implementing the Directive, the European Commission felt that the United Kingdom had not properly implemented the Directive (primarily because of the shortcomings enumerated above) and instituted infringement proceedings.

The ECJ's judgment came in 1982, and it found the United Kingdom in violation of the Directive.[9] In response, the Department of Employment came up with proposals for amending the act. Women's groups, the EOC, and the House of Lords met the proposals with stiff resistance, objecting in particular to the one-year delay they would have created before giving effect to the ECJ judgment (Clarke 1984). Notably, the government abolished the delay (moving implementation forward to January 1, 1984) after the EOC suggested that additional delay "would amount to an infringement of the UK's obligations under Community law" (Clarke 1983, 1130). In 1984 the Equal Pay (Amendment) Regulations were passed. This is certainly not the end of the story, as the EOC and women's groups have continued throughout the 1980s and 1990s to invoke European law in compelling the United Kingdom government to amend domestic legislation (Ellis 1996).

We conclude that Europeanization has generated substantial changes in British legislation. The British women's movement and the EOC deftly exploited leverage offered by EU law, obtaining legislative success even in the face of a hostile political majority (Bashevkin 1996; Meehan and Collins 1996). The gap between the content of the Equal Pay Act (1970) and EU equal pay provisions, coupled with other aspects of Europeanization and facilitative domestic structures, combined to propel domestic legislative change. While many charge that the United Kingdom has not responded in good faith (Ellis 1996), the finding of formal legislative change is clear, with substantive change a crucial but somewhat separate issue.

9. Case 61/81, *Commission of the European Communities v. United Kingdom of Great Britain and Northern Ireland*, 1982 E.C.R. 2601.

Individual Rights

EU gender equality law has affected individual rights in the United Kingdom in numerous areas. Among them are pregnancy and maternity, equal pay, more generous standards for the use of comparators, indirect discrimination, and the shoring up of social rights in the face of market factors. Because we cannot examine all of these areas, we focus instead on legal activity in just a few areas, to give a flavor of the jurisprudence in the areas of equal pay and equal treatment.

The courts, both domestic and European, have made progress in the area of equal pay, and they have relied on the standard of European law in doing so. Several cases provide suggestive insights regarding the development of individual rights before Community law.[10] *Worringham v. Lloyds Bank Ltd.*[11] addressed a situation in which male employees were required to contribute to an employer's pension plan, but females were only required to do so after the age of twenty-five. The employer adjusted upward by 5 percent the salaries of males so that, while their gross pay exceeded that of women, their take-home pay was equal. The Equal Pay Act permitted this discrimination. However, it contravened Article 119, and when presented with a preliminary ruling request, the ECJ decided that pension contributions constituted pay under Article 119 and deemed the practice discriminatory (Morris and Nott 1991, 114).

A second equal pay case centers on the troubling issue of a male comparator. In *Pickstone v. Freeman*, Mrs. Pickstone, employed as a warehouse operative, claimed equal pay with a checker working in the same establishment. The Industrial Tribunal, Employment Appeals Tribunal, and Court of Appeal all held that she could use the checker as a comparator because there were males doing the work she did (at the same pay). Thus, the presence of a single male working the same job for the same pay would prevent equal pay actions using a comparator from a different job. The House of Lords, in an important judgment, found in favor of Mrs. Pickstone, and did so via a radical route—the purposive interpretation of the relevant act of Parliament. Arguing special circumstances, it referred to the *Hansard* debates on the equal pay amendment, thus compromising a long-standing British legal norm of strict construction of legislative acts. Here, reference to higher European standards altered both the procedure and the substance of equal pay (Morris and Nott 1991, 123–24).

The ECJ has also fostered rights against indirect pay discrimination, which is particularly prominent in part-time work. In *Jenkins v. Kingsgate Ltd.*,[12] the ECJ ruled that "paying part time workers at a lower hourly rate might be indirectly discriminatory toward women if employers could not show that a material factor other than sex justified the differential" (Kenney 1995, 374). The Court thus asked the

10. Kenney (1992, 81) provides a detailed listing.
11. Case 69/80, *Susan Jane Worringham and Margaret Humphreys v. Lloyds Bank Limited*, 1981 E.C.R. 767.
12. Case 96/80, *J. P. Jenkins v. Kingsgate (Clothing Productions) Ltd.*, 1981 E.C.R. 911.

firm in the *Jenkins* case to provide justification for the lower pay, thus shifting the burden of proof to the employer.

Equal treatment has given rise to numerous judgments affecting individual rights in the United Kingdom, including the famous *Marshall* case establishing the direct effect of Article 5(1) of the ETD. In other cases, the ECJ has advanced procedural rights for claimants by prohibiting the UK from sealing off the equal treatment of men and women from the jurisdiction of European law. In *Johnson v. Royal Ulster Constabulary*,[13] the head of the Northern Ireland police decided to introduce firearms into the police force and in the process fired all the women on the force. The women on the force challenged this decision and claimed unequal treatment. The United Kingdom argued exceptions from the Equal Treatment Directive and tried to insulate the matter from judicial review. The Court sided with the women in deciding that the policy unjustifiably derogated from the ETD, establishing in the process the existence of directly effective rights under Articles 3(1) and 4(1) of the Directive. Despite their procedural victory, the women suffered a substantive defeat, as the ECJ did not clearly weigh-in on remedies and left it to the Northern Ireland tribunal to decide whether special circumstances justified the firing of women officers (Kenney 1995, 374). In the event, by *Marshall II*[14] the Court had established the direct effectiveness of Article 6 of the ETD, granting rights to contest the effectiveness of remedies offered by member states (Moore 1996, 142).

The creation and enforcement of European rights has suggested several things. European measures have been interpreted as providing a higher and more encompassing standard of gender equality by providing rights and remedies not available under (interpretations of) domestic legislation. In many, if not most cases, the discrimination claims made "would have failed without the benefit of EC law" (Steiner 1983, 399; Crisham 1981, 609). Weiner contends more generally that the putatively "fundamental right" to gender equality would lack effect in the United Kingdom but for EU law (1990, 599). There are many areas where little progress has been made, where the burden of proof is on those who challenge domestic legislation and practices, financial aid is rarely forthcoming, and legal representation is spotty. Despite these limitations and the obvious failure to achieve substantive equality, we cautiously conclude that Europeanization of gender equality policy has had an effect on the structure of individual rights in the United Kingdom. This represents structural change of the first order, a change in legal standing for individuals and a change in the relationship between domestic and European law.

Institutional Balance

Finally, and perhaps most significantly, the Europeanization of gender equality has contributed to the changing relationship between Parliament and the judiciary in

13. Case 222/84, *Marguerite Johnston v. Chief Constable of the Royal Ulster Constabulary*, 1986 E.C.R. 1651.
14. Case C-271/91, *M. Helen Marshall v. Southampton and South-West Hampshire Area Health Authority*, 1993 E.C.R. I-4367.

the United Kingdom. Historically, the laws of Parliament have been supreme, the final statement of the will of the people, and not subject to review by another body. While the story is complicated, this relationship has changed, so that Parliament now accepts the jurisdiction of the ECJ, along with the supremacy of European law.

This innovation compromises the time-honored principle of the sovereignty of the UK Parliament. The web of national and European legal and political relationships proved to be tangled. British and Community legal orders do not move in separate orbits, identify separate issues, and mark off separate jurisdictions. For all practical purposes, they deal with the same subject matter. This commingling of laws requires adjudication as to which level is appropriate and controlling. With EU accession, "British courts soon found themselves required to engage in judicial review to ensure the compatibility of domestic with Community law" (Levitsky 1994, 348). The doctrine of supremacy, it seems in hindsight, implied judicial review.

Judicial review refers to the evaluation of legislation by a judiciary for consistency with broader principles of law. Parliament now accepts as a practical matter something like judicial review, even though it fudges the question of sovereignty by arguing that it has decided, through legislation, to accept the practice. Acts of Parliament are subject to the judicial scrutiny of the ECJ. Sometimes these acts are interpreted more broadly than they were previously by domestic courts. But the pressure to bring them into line with European law has meant that the direction of interpretation has been, on average, more expansive. The case that illustrates this most clearly is *Macarthy's Limited v. Smith*,[15] an equal pay case. This case went through four levels of courts in the United Kingdom. At issue was whether the Equal Pay Act of the United Kingsdom (1970) implemented Article 119. Upon receiving a request for a preliminary ruling, the ECJ ruled that it did not adequately do so. After receiving the judgment of the ECJ, the U.K. Court of Appeal decided in favor of the employee (Levitsky 1994, 361). The case is significant not just because of the pressure to bring U.K. legislation in line with European law but also because the legislation in question was passed after the United Kingdom accession to the EC. It therefore forced the U.K. courts to choose between enforcing a British statute that was passed after 1972 (when the United Kingdom acceded to the EC) and a directly effective European law (Levitsky 1994, 354). More recently, in *R. v. Secretary of State for Employment ex parte Equal Opportunities Commission*, the House of Lords reviewed and overturned a later domestic statute in light of earlier-enacted EU equality law, giving the United Kingdom the "taste of a constitutional court" (Szyszczak 1995, 19) in the process. This, again, is structural change of the highest order. Longstanding notions of the respective powers of courts and the legislature are being revised as a result of pressure emanating from the Europeanization of gender equality policy.

15. Case 129/79, *Macarthys Ltd v. Wendy Smith*, 1980 E.C.R. 1275.

Gender Equality and Domestic Transformation in Comparative Perspective

To summarize our results, the United Kingdom had a more positive profile for change, both from the standpoint of "misfit" (or incongruity) of its basic laws and procedures with those of Europe, and from the standpoint of the array of domestic factors facilitating change. France faced neither the same adaptational pressure nor the same array of public agencies and interest groups that would facilitate its translation into domestic structural change. Our examination of the evidence supports the conclusion that, as a result of the configuration of pressure and receptiveness, Europeanization has resulted in greater change—in legislation, in individual rights, and in the domestic institutional balance—in the United Kingdom than in France. The role of an independent and specialized equality agency, as part of a facilitative domestic environment, has proven especially important in translating pressures from Europeanization into domestic change, most notably through an active litigation strategy with a strong European component (Kilpatrick 1997; Alter and Vargas 2000). While the trajectory has been steeper in the United Kingdom (i.e., more rapid and profound), and while variations across these two countries will likely persist, they do demonstrate partial convergence toward greater incorporation of European norms.

What does our comparative case study imply for the larger theoretical issues addressed in this volume? First, we confirm the importance of top-down influences, all while underlining the causal weight of domestic mediating variables. Given the differences among countries regarding these mediating factors, convergence is likely to be limited.

Second, we find evidence to support a livelier and more conflictual role for institutions in the process of Europeanization than is implied by transaction cost and national choice approaches. The impact of European change on domestic structures is not due primarily to agency problems, to incomplete contracting, to limited time horizons, or to unintended consequences. Instead, European policies and institutions run up against domestic structures, often creating confusion and conflict. The resulting process of adaptation is highly political, an outcome broadly supportive of historical institutionalism.

Is the effect of Europeanization large, or significant? Our implicit argument in this chapter is that the question requires a standard. In comparison to need, to the everyday problems faced by women subject to discrimination on factory floors and in office cubicles, the response is, surely, "too little." If we use the overall successes of some nation-states (within a domestic context) as the yardstick, the effects of Europeanization will again seem small. Our comparison here is more modest. We compare two EU member states and ask about the impacts of institutional and policy developments at the European level on their domestic structures. While the mean around which this expected variation is thus lowered, we believe the impact to be significant. It may be true, to echo a phrase from

James Rosenau's 1966 review of Ernst Haas's *Beyond the Nation-State*, that we are trying to measure "small changes along a vast periphery." While measurement is accordingly difficult, the changes are less small today, more significant than those analyzed by Haas in the ILO, and still proceeding. The story is far from over.

CHAPTER THREE

Differential Europe: National Administrative Responses to Community Policy

Adrienne Héritier

Community legislation is unquestionably a factor to be reckoned with in member-state policymaking. But the extent and mode of its impact on domestic policies and administrative structures will depend on the existing policy practices and the political and institutional structures of the country in question. In cases where there is a mismatch between an established policy of a member state and a clearly specified European policy mandate, there will be an expectation to adjust, which in turn constitutes a precondition for change.

Assuming the existence of a need for change, the ability to adapt will depend on the policy preferences of key actors, and the capacity of institutions to implement reform, realize policy change, and administratively adjust to European requirements. The policy preferences of key actors are influenced by the distributional consequences of the policies to be adopted (Milner 1996); the capacity to change depends on the degree of integrated political leadership, caused by a lack of formal veto points (Tsebelis 1995), or a decisional tradition capable of surmounting formal and factual veto points by way of consensual tripartite decision making. Where there is a divergence or mismatch between European and national policies, and the policy preferences of political leaders are defined by a willingness to adapt, the absence of formal veto points and a cooperative decisional tradition will enhance the capacity to change and to adjust administrative structures in compliance with European policy mandates. The most far-reaching consequence—tantamount to innovation—is the replacement of old administrative structures with a comprehensive set of new ones. A less far-reaching form of adjustment occurs by "tinkering at the edges of old structures" (Lanzara 1998, 40), whereby new administrative units are patched onto existing organizational structures in order to accommodate the Europe-imposed policies. Another important measure of change is whether public actors, public and private actors, or only private actors are engaged in administering the sector and whether administrative functions pass from one form to another.

By contrast, the existence of a high number of formal or de facto veto points, which are not compensated by consensual decision-making patterns, makes adjustment to European policy demands more difficult and administrative change less probable because bids for change are blocked by veto players. This poses no problem as long as there is a basic congruence between the national policy, its administrative implementation structures, and European policy demands, one that allows the latter to be smoothly absorbed into current procedures and structures. If, however, there is a clear mismatch between national policies and European policy demands, political structures ridden with formal and factual veto points and the absence of cooperative decisional traditions will lead to non-implementation and in consequence to no, or only marginal, change in administrative structures.

The impact of European policies on domestic administrative structures, which are channeled through their responses to European policy demands, are discussed here for market-making policy in the specific case of liberalization of road haulage and rail transport for Britain, the Netherlands, Germany, and Italy. The general argument, that it is largely the institutional structures and decision-making styles of member states which account for their capacity to transform existing administrative structures where existing policies differ from European legislation, is empirically explored by comparing these four countries. More specifically, I examine the extent to which established national policies diverge from European policy demands and, where there is a clear mismatch, to what extent the four coun-tries are able to muster the necessary institutional reform capacity in order to generate the required change in administrative structures so as to comply with European policy exigencies.

I show that Britain, because of its conformity with the market-liberal policy demands of Europe, did not have to undertake any changes in road transport regulation; the liberalization of rail transport had already been carried out of its own accord. It used its capacity of concentrated political leadership, derived from the existence of few formal veto points, to realize an extensive reform, thoroughly changing the administrative structures in rail transport before Europe had proceeded to a policy of liberalization.

In the Netherlands, with few formal veto points, the key actors basically agreed with the European goals of liberalization. Policy change and, concomitantly, a reform of administrative structures was facilitated by building on its institutionally well-developed capacity for corporatist consensual decision making—a form of concentrated political leadership that allowed for the compensation of the potential losers of reform. The reforms generated substantial changes in administrative structures in both the road and rail sectors, that is, innovation.

In contrast to Britain and the Netherlands, there is a sharp mismatch between Germany's established policy practices and administrative structures and European reforms, particularly in the road haulage sector. The policy preferences of key actors were thus split between a pro- and anti-liberalizing camp. Given the multiple veto points in the German federalist system, the pressure from Europe accelerated an extensive reform of road transport and helped the pro-liberalization faction win, thereby ushering in a change of policies and administrative structures. The abolition of quantitative regulation of market access and pricing made existing administrative structures obsolete. The liberalization of rail transport was driven by domestic reform rather than by the more modest European policy demands. In spite of in-built veto points, it was achieved by a large-scale multipartite bargaining process that mobilized and bundled all relevant political forces, building a reform consensus and pushing through the reform by paying off opponents. This led to a significant administrative reform, amounting to system innovation.

Italy, in contrast, possesses strong institutional and sectoral fragmentation and a multitude of veto points. Until very recently, the potential losers under a reform policy, the small hauliers and the railway unions—in spite of a clear mismatch with European policy expectations and European pressure—impeded policy and administrative change. A tradition of consensual tripartite policymaking that would help overcome decisional barriers does not exist.

In what follows, I first offer brief empirical accounts of national administrative responses to European reform policy in transport and subsequently interpret the results in light of a explanatory approach that links a rational, goal-oriented actor stance with an institutionalist perspective.[1]

The Liberalization of Transport Policy in Europe and Its Impact on Domestic Administrative Structures

Road Transport

A common transport policy, which was mandated by the Treaty of Rome, did not take off until the late 1980s and early 1990s. The main reason was that member-state governments had different preferences for road transport liberalization. Germany and Italy, with their highly regulated markets, were reluctant to liberalize and demanded a harmonization of all regulation prior to deregulation in order to create a level playing field. Britain and the Netherlands, who in principle favored liberalization, called for an immediate deregulation of the European road haulage market. Once the deadlock in the Council of Ministers over these conflicting positions was overcome, the Court order to start liberalizing the service sector and the political impetus of the Single Market Program led to mandatory tariffs for international road transport being abolished in 1988. With respect to fiscal measures,

1. The empirical data for the analysis of transport policy are based on the joint research project "Changing Policy Patterns through Europeanization," by Adrienne Héritier, Dieter Kerwer, Christoph Knill, Dirk Lehmkuhl, Michael Teutsch, and Anne-Cécile Douillet, financed by the Deutsche Forschungsgemeinschaft under the Leibniz Fund Program.

the European Community (EC) issued a directive in 1992 setting minimum levels for fuel taxes and, in 1993, for vehicle taxes. Furthermore, member states were allowed to introduce annual user charges for road infrastructure. (These charges, known as the regional vignette, are the fees paid for running trucks on the motorways of a foreign country.) As far as capacity regulation (market access) is concerned, the European Commission proceeded to a stepwise conversion of bilateral quotas for international transport into a multilateral Community system. By far the most difficult issue was the introduction of cabotage, the operation of nonresident hauliers in foreign domestic markets. In 1990 and 1993, regulations were introduced that extended the number of cabotage licenses until 1998, after which time all restrictions were to be abolished.

With the exception of Britain and the Netherlands, the European policy requirements substantially challenged the existing national policies and administrative structures, particularly in the case of Germany and Italy. The Netherlands had already started to deregulate their road haulage sector in the mid-1980s, and Britain had liberalized its market as early as 1967. The instrument that remains is the control of the individual qualification as a precondition for market access. In brief, there is no mismatch between European policy demands and British and Dutch policy and, hence, no need to adjust administrative structures. Rather, the latter run parallel and reinforce each other. For Germany and Italy, by contrast, European legislation entailed a high need for adjustment, the consequences of which may be observed in terms of transformation of national policies and administrative structures.

When EU legislation introduced the liberalization of road transport in 1993, this was already an established practice in Britain, where the first important steps of market liberalization had been taken at the end of the 1960s. As a consequence, the British policy was confirmed by European reforms. At the heart of British road haulage policy has been a concept of minimal state intervention implying only one instrument of economic regulation—that of market access linked to certain individual qualifications. The decision on whether an applicant meets the qualitative criteria of market access lies with the regional licensing authority, the Traffic Commissioner. Market prices are influenced through vehicle and fuel taxes, for which Britain has the highest rates throughout the EU. Because the coordinative functions in road transport have been handed over to the market, there is no administration of licenses or prices. Given the European-British parallelism of policy objectives, the need to adapt to Community policies after 1993 was marginal with respect to the policy instruments applied and the underlying administrative structures (Knill in press[a]).

In the Netherlands, road haulage reform ran parallel to the European reforms. The old system of market regulation, which had concentrated on controlling the transport capacity of individual units requiring administrative authorization procedures, was succeeded in 1985 by a regime solely controlling professional qualifications, financial soundness, and reliability as preconditions for market access. It was changed by drawing up a covenant between the ministry, branch associations, and enterprises agreeing to eliminate, step by step, the quantitative restrictions of market access to introduce a liberalized regime.[2] In order to strengthen the market position of the small hauliers, they were offered tax credits and subsidies. Thus, increases in diesel taxes were compensated by a reduction in vehicle taxes (Lehmkuhl in press). Research and development schemes were launched for the development of advanced transportation and "green" technologies; the restructuring of firms and sectoral organizations is subsidized by the state.

Since one central instrument of market regulation—the quantitative limitation of market access—was abolished, some administrative institutions became obsolete. Thus, the functions of the Transport Licence Commission and the State Traffic Inspectorate, which had controlled the overall transport capacity by road by examining applications for entry into the market or for extension of a firm's capacity on the basis of a proof of "transport necessity," were not needed any longer. As a consequence it was incorporated into the Stichting Nationale en Internationale Wegvervoer Organisatie (NIWO), a private foundation dominated by industry, formerly responsible for international licensing and now responsible for individual licensing and hence control of market access. While individual licensing has been privatized, inspection has remained a public task performed by the State Traffic Inspectorate. Its role has gained in importance in that it is now more involved in policy formulation and implementation with the intention to intensify cooperation between the regulator and regulatees in order to promote voluntary compliance. Moreover, in the course of deregulation a new public-private institution was established to strengthen the market position of the Dutch haulier industry. The Holland International Distribution Council, which is a nonprofit organization of employers, road transport associations, the Port of Rotterdam, and Schiphol Airport, is the result of an agreement between government and industry to promote "ondernemen Nederland" as a European distribution center and the "Gateway to Europe" (Lehmkuhl in press).

Germany was significantly affected by the outcome of European road haulage liberalization. Under the old regulatory regime, state intervention in transport was taken for granted by all relevant political actors, and market functions were viewed with scepticism. The instruments used were a mix of quantitative and qualitative restrictions to market access, and vehicle and fuel taxes. Licensing procedures and rate controls had been introduced in the 1930s for long-distance transport, for which only a limited number of licenses were available until the 1990s. More recently, however, owing to European influence, there has been a move away from quantitative restrictions toward the strengthening of individual qualitative access criteria. As regards price controls, in the 1960s bracket tariffs were introduced, and tariff commissions, consisting of experts from transport associations, were authorized to set rates. These fixed tariffs were abolished in 1994.

2. Mandatory tariffs had been abolished in the 1970s.

Hence, in Germany, too, deregulation rendered unnecessary some administrative units formerly responsible for the setting of fares and their control.[3] The commission responsible for setting tariffs between 1961 and 1994 was disbanded. The federal agency formerly responsible for the control and implementation of the regulations,[4] in which the hauliers' associations had played an important role, lost its core functions and instead was given new—rather marginal—tasks, such as market observation.[5] Furthermore, the haulier co-operatives (*Straßenverkehrsgenossenschaften*), which, in close cooperation with the hauliers' associations, had previously controlled the application of rates and waybills, partly lost their functions and were reduced to such responsibilities as providing insurance for their members and technical control functions. A new administrative task was established with the regional vignette in the fiscal sector. This new toll for road usage is administered by a federal agency, the *Bundesamt für Verkehr* (Teutsch in press).

In contrast to the Netherlands and Germany, Italy, instead of adjusting its policies to the European reform demands, maintained the quantitative restriction of market access and a regulation of market prices. A 1974 regulatory reform increased intervention by introducing compulsory bracket tariffs to control prices for transport services. But no less than nine years elapsed before its implementation in 1983. During this transition period, substitute bracket tariffs were developed for certain products, such as cement and petroleum. The latter are set by collective economic agreements determined by industry and hauliers in bipartite negotiations. Their outcome is, furthermore, relevant for determining general compulsory tariffs because the representatives of the haulier associations, who sign the collective economic agreements, also negotiate the mandatory tariffs. Thus, the setting of transport prices develops in a multitude of different negotiating systems that offer a bonanza for transport interest groups and contribute to the politicization of the sector. The frequent disregard for negotiated prices triggered a new avalanche of detailed regulation (Kerwer in press). With respect to fiscal measures, the Italian system of taxation and charges was already in line with the European objectives, because all road users are treated equally. For example, a system of motorway tolls had been in place for a long time. The impact of taxation, however, is modified by another fiscal instrument—the generous tax credits granted to registered road hauliers since 1990. For many years, the government has compensated road hauliers for fuel taxes. This tax credit scheme was challenged by the European Commission because it was considered to be illegal state aid, with discriminatory consequences for non-Italian hauliers. Fiscal instruments have also been

---

3. As regards the quantitative restriction of licenses, the formal abolition of their restriction was postponed. However, the licensing system had been simplified in 1991, which together with the increase of licenses caused by the inclusion of the former East German Länder, led to a significant increase in capacity (Teutsch in press).

4. The former Bundesanstalt für Güterfernverkehr, since 1994 the Bundesamt für Güterverkehr. It now is directly subordinated to the Ministry of Transport and entirely financed by public funds, whereas it was previously funded by fees and (and occasional fines) paid by road hauliers (Teutsch in press).

5. What remains is monitoring compliance with technical and social regulation.

employed to improve the economic structure of the transport sector, offering specific loans and social tax credits such as the support of mergers, which was again
contested by the Commission but not subsequently abolished. Taken together,
these instruments—market access, price regulation, and tax credits—amount to a
clear attempt to protect the market from international competition in the interest
of Italian hauliers (Kerwer in press).

Rail Transport

As regards rail transport, for decades, the structure of the railway industry as a
single enterprise owning the infrastructure and providing the services had not been
questioned. Railways were considered natural monopolies because of their technical and economic characteristics: high fixed or sunk costs, and recurrent—
and extensive—phases of excess capacity (Baumol, Panzar, and Willig 1982). They
were also supposed to achieve general goals, such as regional integration within
a nation-state, and to secure mobility for all (public service obligation). Public
ownership and nationally integrated railway systems were legitimated on these
grounds. As public service enterprises, railways were subject to state intervention
and political steering and had little management autonomy.

In spite of the overwhelming symptoms of crisis, particularly a loss of market
shares in intermodal competition, a European policy of rail liberalization was not
undertaken until the mid-1980s (Erdmenger 1981, 88), when the notion of "contestable markets" (Baumol, Panzar, and Willig 1982; Denkhaus 1997, 3) was
introduced. As a consequence, the idea of railways as a natural monopoly was
increasingly questioned. In order to introduce market elements, rail transport is
divided into two sectors: infrastructure, which is not easily accessible for competitors owing to the high sunk costs (e.g., investment in railway track, stations); and
service operation, in which market competition can take place (vertical division).
Accordingly, Community policies (91/440/EEC) introduced a mandatory division
of accounts between the costs of construction, maintenance, and operation of
infrastructure on the one hand, and the provision of transport services on the
other. This arrangement allows the state railway enterprises to increase financial
transparency and to assess economic performance. The next step is the mandatory
organizational separation of infrastructure and services by the end of 1997
(Commission 1996, 36), which creates separate business units and financial responsibility for the different transport sectors (e.g., freight, passenger service), rolling
stock, and the management of the infrastructure network. Furthermore, a regulation (91/440/EEC) allows new operators to gain access to the rail network in order
to provide passenger and freight transport services. The deregulation, however, has
been limited to international transport and to enterprises with specific characteristics (e.g., international combined freight transport) but will be extended to all
freight operations in the future (Commission 1995b, 19). The European Commission also encourages the dividing of railways into subsystems by forming various
regionally integrated companies (horizontal division).

In all countries, the railway systems were faced with similar problems of market losses in intermodal competition, of financial crisis, and of inflexibility under the auspices of political leadership. However, countries responded differently to the long-standing crisis of the railways and European policy initiatives, depending on whether similar reforms had already been envisaged at the national level and depending on state capacity to bring about change. The British Railways Act (1993), which was realized on the grounds of purely domestic initiatives and was not spurred on by European policy developments, marks a watershed in the history of British Railways. It not only implies the transformation of a public-sector monopoly into private ownership but also the introduction of different forms of competition and the establishment of formal contractual regimes between the different actors involved. The new system set in place a far-reaching vertical and horizontal fragmentation of a formerly integrated structure. With respect to the vertical dimension, the institutional separation of train and infrastructure operations was established. The whole infrastructure of British Railways was transferred to Railtrack, which is responsible for infrastructure provision and maintenance, the supply of access to tracks and stations and the management of time-tabling, train planning, and signaling. Referring to horizontal separation, British Railways' train operating businesses were split up into different units. The three passenger businesses were broken up into twenty-five train operating companies, and the freight and parcels businesses into seven companies. Passenger rolling stock was separated from the train operating companies and divided up into three rolling-stock leasing companies, which took over all domestic passenger trains of British Railways. The organizational break-up was followed by the privatization of these services. The twenty-five passenger services were franchised to private companies, and Railtrack was subject to stock market flotation.

Interorganizational coordination is achieved by means of a contractual matrix of horizontally and vertically separated companies. Train operators, for instance, contract with Railtrack to obtain access to track. Privatization has been accompanied by the establishment of a regulatory framework to control and oversee the operations of private actors. The Rail Regulator deals with aspects of competition and monopoly control. The Office of Passenger Rail Franchising awards passenger rail franchises on the basis of competitive tendering and allocates subsidies (Knill in press[a]). Thus, independent from and preceding European measures, Britain took important steps toward a fundamental reform of the system.

The second country in which considerable policy change occurred, primarily fuelled by domestic reform goals, is the Netherlands. The Dutch are keen to defend their competitive position in an integrated transport market. In particular, the port of Rotterdam authority pointed to the growing problems of road congestion in its hinterland and demanded the strengthening of rail transport and inland navigation in order to defend the Netherlands's position as a gateway to Europe. Hence, the Netherlands favored the removal of trade restrictions and supported the EU policy for an integrated European transport market. It incorporated ideas from the European reform discussion into their own comprehensive domestic reform for the realization of an environmentally friendly transport policy. The reform, in line with EC 91/440, provided a vertical division between infrastructure and the operation of services. The railway system now consists of several independent legal entities divided into a government-commissioned sector, which performs infrastructure-related tasks, and a market-oriented sector, which conducts operational services such as cargo transport, station maintenance, and passenger transport. Cargo transport received the legal status of a shareholder company, enabling it to make contracts with and to sell shares to third parties. The assignment of all infrastructure development to government-commissioned agencies, by contrast, ensures that government controls this development (Lehmkuhl in press).

In the same way as its Dutch counterpart, the German railway system underwent a significant process of change, predominantly spurred by domestic reform goals. The basic idea of the reform was to strengthen commercial thinking by initiating step-by-step regulatory change and a new regime opening the domestic rail transport market to outside competition. The reform process was accelerated by a feeling of imminent crisis after the publication of information on startling future deficits, a problem exacerbated by German unification and the need to incorporate the East German railways. The former state monopoly was transformed into a joint-stock company, with the federal government as its sole stockholder. This legal statute gives the Deutsche Bahn AG some independence from ministerial guidance. In line with EC Directive 91/440, the new legislation provides an internal organizational division into different branches and accounting units, such as for infrastructure, operation of services in long-distance and short-distance transport, as well as freight transport. Ten different divisions were created within the Deutsche Bahn AG that act independently of one another and are responsible for the mutually offered services. With the regulatory reform introducing intramodal competition, any rail operator can buy slots from the national railways infrastructure branch and run trains on its network. A new regulatory body was created, the Federal Railway Agency, which is responsible for licensing railway undertaking and technical control. Investment in infrastructure is financed predominantly through interest-free loans granted by the German government on the condition that these investments remain within the scope of government-defined goals (Teutsch in press).

Italy has made its own—only partly successful—attempts of reform while at the same time resisting European reform expectations. The general tendency was to enhance the railways' autonomy in relation to the administration, giving Ferrovie dello stato (FS) more autonomous management competences. In the 1990s, the state railways were legally privatized. Although the public administration is still the sole owner, the railways now have the status of a joint-stock company. Hierarchical coordination has been abolished and replaced by contractual coordination. The "program contract" defines the investments into the rail infrastructure and into rolling stock; the "service contract" defines the services that have to be provided by the railways. These contracts remove the former system of cross-subsidies between infrastructure financing and the operation of services. In addition, measures were adopted to promote the freight transport unit, supplemented by initiatives in the area of intermodal transport. Hence, with respect to organizational reforms, Italian reform policy has been congruent with European policy goals but did not introduce market elements in rail transport, making the Italian response to the European invitation to reform rail policies only very limited.

The Empirical Evidence in Light of the Theory

The empirical accounts show that European policies have a differential impact on member-state policies and administrative structures, depending on the given policy mismatch and member-state willingness and capacity to adjust. Assuming that there is a mismatch, I argue that a European policy mandate affects the preferences of actor groups in member states: those who expect to be winners of the Europe-induced change will support corresponding political and administrative adaptations, while those who expect to lose, will oppose them. However, the new preferences and the cleavages they generate do not automatically translate into policy responses and administrative changes. Instead, they are shaped by the policy preferences of the key political actors involved and the existing political and administrative institutions. Coalitions are formed and bargains struck in response to the new European policy demands (Keohane and Milner 1996). European pressure to act may create a political space for reform, a window of opportunity (Kingdon 1984) that may be exploited by the strategic action of political elites in the specific institutional context of a domestic political system. The outcomes—the change or the resistance to change—are a result of conflict, bargaining, and compromise among individuals or groups representing diverse interests.

It is expected that given a need for adaptation because of a mismatch between the European policy mandate and the existing national policy practice, and given domestic key actors' preference for policy reform—institutional conditions, the existence of few veto points, and strengthened integrated political leadership—policy change and a concomitant transformation in administrative structure are more likely (Milner 1996; Keohane and Milner 1996; Tsebelis 1995). The derived properties of integrated political leadership are such that key political actors have a medium- to longer-term time perspective toward government service. Closely related to this is the credibility that governments have for maintaining commitments to losers of reform measures (Frieden and Rogowski 1996, 43). If these conditions of integrated political leadership and key actors' preferences for a policy change are given, it is then to be expected that there will be a clear change in existing policies and, hence, administrative structures. A functional equivalent to the concentration of institutions is the tradition of formal, consensual decision making, which offers a basis for resolving the redistributional conflicts that would otherwise prevent change.

Conversely, it is proposed that given a need for adjustment and preferences for change, there is little response to European policy expectations if political leadership is fragmented; there are a high number of formal and factual veto points in the political decision-making process, if key decision makers have short-term office perspectives; and government has little credibility for maintaining commitments to the losers of the reform. For instance, a federalist system in which substates have a say in policymaking and strong unions are not incorporated into a tradition of neocorporatist decision making will face powerful veto actors able to impede change (Keohane and Milner 1996, 21). As a consequence, either no or only minor administrative change will take place. On the side of the administrative change, I distinguish between various modes and degrees of transformation. The most far-reaching change is a substitution of old structures with new ones—that is, innovation.

An incremental change consists of a patching-up of old structures in the sense of adding new elements with new underlying principles to old structures ruled by old principles. The policy elements suggested by Europe diverge in terms of principles and instruments. The result of "patching up" existing structures as a response to required changes are hybrid administrative structures consisting of various and diverse administrative principles and policy instruments (Héritier, Knill, and Mingers 1996).

Enlargement, another form of incremental change, is defined as adding additional elements ruled by the same principles to the existing structures. The administrative activities and instruments applied increase but do not conflict with established principles.

Absorption, the next mode and degree of change, implies that new policy requirements are accommodated without administrative structures being changed. It presupposes that new policies do not conflict with existing administrative principles. In particular, if they are formulated in an ambiguous way, only loosely linking problems to solutions, the implementing organizations have more room to specify the instrumental aspects of the tasks to be achieved and can do so in a mode that does not compromise existing procedures and structures. It may then more easily incorporate new policy demands without jeopardizing routine procedures and established structures (March 1981; Cyert and March 1992). Finally, there is the possibility of no change taking place (i.e., non-implementation) because new policy elements are taken on board.

Each of these different degrees and modes of change is scrutinized from a public-private perspective. Are administrative functions "handed over to" or "taken over by" private actors, or vice versa? Or are there new forms of public-private cooperation in performing administrative tasks?

Thus, the extent of change is assessed along two empirical dimensions: first, the instruments applied to obtain specific policy targets, such as command and control or the use of market incentives or information and persuasion; and second, the formal and factual horizontal and vertical division of tasks among public actors and public and private actors in policymaking and implementation. How are the empirical stories of the four countries to be interpreted against the background of these general considerations? In the case of road haulage in Britain, we have the strong preferences of key actors for a reform that, on the basis of the marked capacity of integrated executive leadership, was put into practice even before a corresponding European policy mandate was imposed. Since all this had already been accomplished in the late 1960s, the precondition of policy mismatch vis-à-vis the European policy mandate, which creates a need of adjustment, was not given.

Basically, the same holds for the reform of rail transport. Britain opted for a radical reform without needing European policy support. A political space for reform was created and was facilitated by the awareness of the extent of the financial problems affecting British Railways. Once again, integrated executive leadership and the lack of formal veto points facilitated a far-reaching policy and administrative change. The Railways Act of 1993 constitutes a watershed in British rail history and involved fundamental changes to the state-owned British Railways. The reform bill was only slightly modified in the House of Commons, despite the presence of important opposing actors (including the Labour Party, the railway unions, and interest associations, such as Transport 2000) that could rely on broad public support. However, the institutional structure of the political system (concentration of power in government, and a first-past-the-post electoral system) allows for a considerable assertiveness on the part of government policymakers, even in the face of sizable opposition. Factual veto points, such as the railway unions, were relatively weak because they held different views on and had different interests in privatization. As a consequence, they did not coordinate their policies, thus being unable to offer a political counterweight to the government's policy. Moreover, from its experience with other public-sector reforms, government had gained experience in privatizing. They had learned that liberalization should be introduced before, or parallel with, privatization and ownership of infrastructure, and that networks should be separated. Dividing up a public-sector enterprise into different business units prior to privatization reduces the power of the former public enterprises in flotation and weakens the unions (Knill in press[a]), thereby reducing the political clout of potential factual veto actors. Thus, although not Europe-induced as such, there has been a fundamental change of administrative structure and instruments in the British rail sector that amounts to an innovative system change along both empirical dimensions, instrumental and organizational.

In the case of the Netherlands, a different capacity for integrated political leadership materialized and brought significant administrative changes about in road and rail transport. Political forces were effectively bundled through a consultative and consensual decision-making process involving all relevant actors. Therefore, it was possible to overcome de facto veto powers. The Dutch government, with its relative stability and corresponding medium- to long-term time horizons of key decision makers, had sufficient credibility in the eyes of the potential losers to induce them to support the reform in return for offered subsidies.

Thus, in the road sector, the reform was brought about in a process of joint decision making by state and associative actors. The previous system of market regulation was changed by drawing up a covenant between the ministry, branch associations, and enterprises agreeing to a clear change of instruments and to eliminate step by step the quantitative restrictions of market access to introduce a liberalized and deregulated regime. To strengthen the market position of the losers, specifically the small hauliers, compensation in the form of tax credits and subsidies was offered (Lehmkuhl in press).

Rail reform was largely shaped in a negotiation process of "fighting coopera-tion" between Nederlandse Spoorwegen (NS) and the Ministry of Transport. State actors used the pressure exerted by European legislation to achieve their goals. The NS, in turn, managed to weaken the radical market reform proposals of the Ministry of Transport. As potential veto players, the railway unions sup-ported the railway reform in the hopes of revitalizing rail transport and because they were offered compensation (social provision for early retirement) to cushion redundancies linked with the splitting up of the railways. This type of integrated political leadership, in the form of sectoral neocorporatist bargaining and agree-ment, is able to incorporate political veto players and to commit them to a reform.

The reform led to a substantial change in policy and, hence, administrative structures in the road and rail sectors along both dimensions—instruments and the formal division of tasks between public and private actors. In road haulage, with the abolition of all quantitative restrictions of market access, former market-regulating bodies lost their functions and were incorporated into a private institu-tion (Lehmkuhl in press). The division of competences has changed in favor of industry, while the state maintains a role of overall guidance. This is underlined by the creation of a new public-private body which was created along established lines of public-private cooperation, constituting an enlargement of existing structures along already established principles.

A far-reaching administrative reform, albeit not as extensive as the British one, was also realized in the rail sector. It created independent organizational units in what is considered to be a contestable market, that is, the operation of services. However, in the infrastructure, which is still regarded as a natural monopoly, state guidance is maintained. Hence, the Dutch reform may be qualified as half a system innovation, combining new market instruments and multiple organizations struc-tures linked by incentives in one area (operation) and leaving hierarchy (state inter-vention) in infrastructure. This is more than "patching-up," because it does not consist of merely grafting "alien" instruments and administrative units upon an established administrative structure ruled by different principles but goes halfway in a far-reaching reform.

The preconditions for building an integrated political leadership for reform were less favorable in Germany. For one thing, the political institutional structure is more decentralized. For another, the hauliers' associations, which considered themselves the losers in the reform, had a strong hold in the self-regulation and administration of the sector. In the political contest between pro- and anti-liberalizers, European reform policies played a decisive role. They helped to over-come the de facto veto points, that is, the opposition of the road hauliers with their vested interests in maintaining market regulation, tipping the scales in favor of the pro-liberalization party and leading to the abolition of license restrictions and price regulations. The political opposition of the hauliers' associations was overcome. The outcome of administrative changes in the German transport sector as a consequence of this far-reaching reform has been a deliberate and clear-cut application of instruments and change in the sector's administration. Some bodies lost their functions, either entirely or partly, and were either abolished or given new, soft tasks. Hence, the changes involved the elimination of administrative units owing to the introduction of market instruments and a search for new tasks for obsolete structures.

The reform measures in the rail sector, from the beginning, took into account that the German political system is ridden with formal and factual veto points. The reformers deployed a strategy based on a broad political consensus. Opposition demands—by the Social Democratic Party, regarding public responsibility for infrastructure development; by the Länder over fiscal questions and the safeguarding of their competences in future rail decisions; and by trade unions in respect of responsibility for infrastructure, pay levels, and social provisions—were all incorporated. Thus, as part of the deal, the potential losers under the reform were offered compensation payments. The process was very much promoted by the expert function of a governmental advisory commission of high repute with a well-balanced membership, working at arms' length from political influence. Its report became an authoritative source for rail reform legislation. European legislation was used by the German rail reformers to advance rather than initiate their own policy purposes (Teutsch in press).

In rail reform, in much the same way as the Dutch case, the German reform consists of comprehensive measures of instrumental change and a new division of functions between public actors, and public and private actors, which go halfway in system innovation.

Italy, by contrast, has all the classical institutional ingredients necessary to impede reform. The main reason for the freezing of the old (interventionist) policies lies in a lack of integrated political leadership characteristic of Italy's series of short-lived and conflict-ridden multiparty governments unable to overcome associational veto points. The latter are constituted by the small hauliers, who play an important role in the regulation and administration of the sector. The "padroncini," as they are referred to, often resort to contortionist practices and call for strikes, in order to press the Ministry of Transport for new tax subsidies and to prevent deregulation, and their attempts are usually successful. Since this pattern repeats itself, over and over again, the short-lived governments—in the past decade, transport ministers remained in office for about one year—cannot honor all the tax promises made over time. The obvious consequence is a loss of credibility in the eyes of the small hauliers unwilling to support a policy of deregulation in exchange for promises of compensation (Kerwer in press). In terms of administrative change, this means there was no transformation of road transport regulation in the sense of the Europe-promoted deregulation; instead, the change that occurred served to deepen the old anti-liberalization administrative approach.

The Italian rail reform, taken either as domestic measures or driven by European policy initiatives, never gathered momentum because it was soon caught up in the multiple veto points of the political decision-making process. The government proved unable to bundle together enough political forces to push through its major political reform initiative, the "direttiva Prodi," which was stopped by the de facto veto power of the railway unions. The latter fear that the new organizational division of functions ("spezzatino ferroviario," the railway ragout) would weaken their negotiating capacity and that the financial independence of the railway management may lead to redundancies in the overstaffed Ferrovie dello Stato (FS). This reform proposal draws heavily on the European directives, but even though it contains fundamental changes, it was never subject to any type of consultation process of potential veto actors. Apparently, not even the Department of Transport took part in the drafting by the finance ministry (Kerwer in press). Other possible sources to promote change, such as the mobilization of independent economic expertise to furnish arguments for reform, as used by the German government in the reform process, were not exploited. Parliament, committed to special interests, did not support a comprehensive reform but has attempted to satisfy particular regional demands for investment and the operation of lines; the railway management itself has been ambivalent with respect to the reform.[6] Thus, several factors tended to weaken the prospects of integrated political leadership. As a result, the outcome of the Italian attempts at rail reform have remained modest indeed. There has been some change at the organizational and instrumental level, with hierarchy (at least formally) being replaced by contractualization in the relationship between FS and the administration. In practice, however, decision-making routines have not changed much but have instead been accommodated by the new structure, and market competitive elements in the operation of services have not been introduced at all (Kerwer in press).

The empirical evidence confirms the proposition that, given a mismatch between European policy expectations and given preferences for change of key political leaders, the capacity of integrated political leadership accounts for the degree of administrative change. However, what the empirical cases also show is that integrated political leadership need not consist of pronounced executive power with few formal veto points. Instead, integrated political leadership may also derive from a well-functioning consensual leadership style such as in the Dutch case for road haulage and rail reform, and in the German case in the reform of the rail sector. Thus, given a willingness to change, these two forms of integrated political leadership produce change.

The changes in administrative structure resulting from the partly Europe-induced changes range from extensive in road haulage and rail transport

---

6. Despite its debts, the FS has increased investment in rail transport in recent years—partly due to political pressure from the Italian Parliament, which made approval of a contract dependent on a long list of amendments. This clientelistic intervention by the parliament ran counter to the objective of contractualization between the administration and the railways (Kerwer in press).

in Germany and the Netherlands, to marginal in Italy. For Britain, owing to its policy congruence with European legislation, there was no need to adjust. As to the nature of change in these countries where adjustment occurred, there was a clear change in regulatory instruments from hierarchical intervention (e.g., fare-setting, quantitative regulation of market access) to market mechanisms. While this decision implied that administrative units in road haulage became obsolete, in most cases the administrative units that lost their functions were not abolished but were instead incorporated into other institutions or given new, "soft" tasks. The changes brought about in the rail sector both at the instrumental and organizational level are substantial. Tasks are divided up in a new way among various levels of public actors (central, regional), and between public and private actors (privatization).

CHAPTER FOUR

Institutional Reform in Telecommunications: The European Union in Transnational Policy Diffusion

Volker Schneider

In continental Europe, the state has traditionally played a central role in the provision of communication infrastructures and the control of communication contents. Since the rise of the modern state, postal and telecommunications systems have been highly relevant for military purposes, as well as for internal security. For a long time the provision of long-distance communication facilities was not only considered to be an indispensable infrastructure, but, even more important, it was also thought to be a major component in the "logistics of power" of the state (Mann 1986). Thus, the provision and operation of communication systems were considered to be state monopolies, and the respective administrations and public enterprises were, in a qualitative as well as a quantitative sense, important elements of the public sector. This institutional division of labor between state and society, which had been immutable for centuries, began to change dramatically within only one decade.

During the 1980s and the 1990s in many countries, former public monopolies have been broken up and transformed into competitive markets, and the various government-administered bodies and state enterprises have been restructured into private corporations. In most cases, these companies have even been sold through the stock market.

While there are a number of causes for this transformation, for example, technical and other structural changes to modern society, a major driving force in Europe was the missionary impetus for liberalization and privatization on the part of the European Commission. Since the late 1980s, the Council of Ministers and the Commission have issued a long series of directives and other decisions calling

I benefited from comments on this chapter by Maria Green Cowles, Peter Katzenstein, Fritz Scharpf, and Vivien Schmidt.

for changes in public procurement behavior, market regulation, and standardization in this sector. These were ultimately directed toward a near-total liberalization of all kinds of telecommunications networks and services within the European Union (EU) in the year 1998.

In this chapter I consider the question of how the EU-led transformation of formerly public-sector telecommunications industries evolved within the three largest continental EU countries (Germany, France, and Italy). I examine how the domestic processes of these countries were conditioned or amplified not only by the regional context of European integration but, above all, by the international environment. In all three countries, there was a "misfit" between the proposed EU directives and the existing telecommunications monopolies. However, both France and Germany began to liberalize their telecommunications markets in response to global deregulation pressures. Thus, their liberalization efforts were made parallel to—and at times, in advance of—the emerging European policies. Hence, Europeanization produced less adaptational pressures in these countries. In Italy, however, while global movements toward liberalization and deregulation of telecommunications were important, they were not sufficient to allow the Italian government to overcome domestic opposition to telecommunications reforms. The Europeanization policies, however, placed significant pressures on the Italian government to change its strategy and "impose" some regulations on the parliament. Indeed, the government largely adopted EU directives when creating its own regulations. Thus, the Europeanization of telecommunications policy can better account for the timing and nature of Italian telecommunications policy in the 1980s. That being said, it is made clear in this chapter that all three cases of "misfit" between national structures and European policy and regulation cannot be explained without reference to the global level.

I begin by outlining how the European Community entered the telecommunications policy domain and what the major outcomes at this supranational level have been. Subsequently, I sketch the similarities and dissimilarities in the reform outcomes of the three national policies, explaining these in the final section of the chapter against the background of competing theories and approaches of public sector reform in this area. I conclude that a "dynamic transformation" model might best account for changes in telecommunications policies that occurred not only in the European Union but worldwide. Europeanization did not provide the underlying push for telecommunications reform, but it did serve as a kind of catalytic transmission of these pressures.

The Europeanization of Telecommunications

The emergence of structural reform in the telecommunications sector as an issue of European policymaking is a process that started in the late 1970s and early 1980s. Essentially, three stages can be distinguished in its development. In every stage, however, the driving force of policy integration has been the European Commission acting as a "corporate actor" in its own right, endowed with specific resources and pursuing distinctive goals.[1]

Interestingly, until 1977 there were no EC activities in telecommunications at all. The member states shared the opinion that the Treaty of Rome did not give any authority to the Commission in this field. When the Commission made attempts to take action, for instance, the October 1968 attempt to promote the harmonization of public procurement of posts and telecommunication administrations, it met harsh opposition by the Council of Ministers. The actual forum for European coordination was the Conférence Européenne des Administrations des Postes et Télécommunications (CEPT), set up in 1959, which issued nonmandatory recommendations for the harmonization of national technical systems.

It was only at the end of the 1970s that the Commission became more active by promoting information policy and trade policy programs. Taking advantage of the debate on the prospective information age, the Commission issued a report in 1979 that addressed the role of networks in economic competition and the necessity of cooperation for developing new networks and services.

This indirect strategy allowed the Commission to appear as a legitimate actor in the telecommunications sector while not directly attacking the power of the Post, Telegraph, and Telephone (PTT) administrations. As a result, the Commission created a task force for information technology and telecommunications in 1983. This was later absorbed by Directorate General (DG) XIII, which became the DG for Telecommunications, Information Industries and Innovation in 1986. Subsequently, various programs were launched by the Commission, such as ESPRIT and RACE, aimed at the development of a pan-European telecommunications infrastructure. Through these programs, the actor network involved in European telecommunications policy expanded. The Commission's allies and supporters stemmed primarily from large European industrial firms (such as Philips, Siemens, Alcatel, Olivetti), thus consolidating and slowly improving the Commission's power position.

A new stage began in the mid-1980s, when the Commission prepared its Green Paper on telecommunications, basically the blueprint of the subsequent reform program. The process took place when the good old Bell system in the United States had broken up and also when the United Kingdom as well as Japan undertook to liberalize and privatize their telecommunications sectors. At this historic juncture the Commission took the initiative and, using the United States and Japan as role models, promoted its own aspirations for similar sectoral transformations and for the future development of an integrated European information and communication sector. The Commission's strategy was to create a common market in the European information and communication sector, which primarily meant harmonizing technical norms and legal regulations and supporting R&D in this area.

---

1. For the history of EC telecommunications policy, see Schneider and Werle (1990); Cohen (1992); Chamoux (1993); Schneider, Nguyen, and Werle (1994); Simon (1994); and Schneider and Vedel (1999).

The major objective of the Commission thus was the introduction of competition within national markets. To implement this aim, it made use of Article 90, paragraph 3 of the Treaty of Rome. This portion of the Treaty confers on the Commission a kind of autonomous regulatory power in order to ensure the application of the Treaty provisions.

Such an unconventional move by the Commission, initiated in 1988 with a Directive liberalizing the terminal markets, was a frontal attack against national PTT administrations that were monopolizing this sector. In addition, this was a strategy to gain autonomy vis-à-vis the intergovernmental EC decision maker, the Council of Ministers, provoking strong criticism from most European governments, including the United Kingdom. The French government, which was not only against this procedural form but also against most of the policy goals, aimed to stop EC liberalization plans on this occasion by bringing a suit in the European Court of Justice (ECJ) against the Commission for overstepping its powers. Several months later, Italy, Belgium, Greece, and Germany also supported the suit. Other, more liberal member states such as the United Kingdom, despite their anger at the Commission's style, refrained from this action because they generally approved the aims of the Commission Directive. Germany opposed this legal action for procedural reasons. In 1991, the Commission's actions were upheld by the ECJ.

In 1988, during the time of the French suit against the Commission, EU telecommunications policy seemed to be blocked by two opposing power alliances that held rather diverging interests with respect to the Commission's policy goals. On the one hand, a group of member states, essentially led by France, largely opposed an extensive liberalization of telecommunications policy. On the other hand, countries such as the United Kingdom and the Netherlands, with additional support from Germany, deemed a more liberal telecommunications policy desirable. The situation changed slightly when the two camps reached a compromise in December 1989.

This settlement did not last very long, however. The forces unleashed by the liberalization and privatization processes in some key industrial countries (the United States, the United Kingdom, and Japan) and the growing globalization of telecommunications were feeding back on telecommunications sectors at the European and the domestic levels. A key event took place when the governments decided to introduce full competition in traditional telephony. In the summer of 1993, the Council of Ministers agreed that national telephone operators were obliged to allow competition in conventional telephony from 1998 onward, with the exception of four less-developed member states.

There is no doubt that this move was very much influenced by the big European telecommunication operators, who aspired to form international alliances—such as the Franco-German cooperation or the British alliance with a big American telecommunication company—and thus become global players. Regulators in the United States as well as in Europe were linking the authorization of these alliances to an acceleration of domestic liberalization (Schneider and Vedel 1999). For instance, when the Franco-German alliance under the code name Atlas (later

Phoenix and Global One) was announced in 1993, the *Financial Times* commented: "There is widespread concern that a Franco-German link-up before 1998, bringing together the world's second- and third-largest operators, will 'sew up' much of the European market in advance of 1998."

As this short history has shown, in only one decade, telecommunications policy at the EU level had developed from a non-issue to a central area of EC competition and industrial policy. As highlighted in Table 4.1, from the first Council Directive on mutual recognition of terminal equipment to the 1995 and 1996 directives liberalizing even networks and infrastructures, the EU decisions were not just nice intentions in intergovernmental cooperation but resulted in deep structural changes in the member countries. A recent implementation report determined that the harmonization of the countries' telecommunications reforms with the EU policies was "very good" and that only minor variations existed in the transposition and final implementation of the various liberalization and harmonization directives (CEC 1998b).

How significant these changes at the national level of Germany, France, and Italy were, and how they came about, are examined below. Here, it should be emphasized that national transformations were not simply reactive policy implementations of EU reform programs in the form of a simple "institutional download" from the supranational to the domestic level. In fact, EU policymaking was a rather complex process in which governmental and nongovernmental actors of the different member states were involved at all stages. In addition, the strong commitment of such supranational European institutions as the European Commission and the European Court of Justice in this process indicates that the overall result should not be explained by intergovernmental bargaining alone. It clearly

Table 4.1 Important telecommunications policy events at the EC/EU level

1983	Commission outlines strategies for a common telecommunications policy. Establishment of expert group SOGT.
1984	Council recommendation on harmonization in the field of telecommunications.
1986	Council directive on mutual recognition of terminal equipment.
1987	Green Paper on the Common Market for telecommunications services and equipment.
1988	Commission Directive on competition in the markets in telecommunications terminal equipment.
1989	Council decision to gradually liberalize telecommunication with the exception of telephony and public infrastructures.
1990	Commission Directive on telecommunications services liberalizing all services with the exception of telephony, mobiles and satellite communications. Council Directive on Open Network Provision requiring the separation of operating and regulating functions.
1993	Council decision to open all telecommunications services to competition as of 1.1.1998.
1994	Council resolution on universal service principles. Commission Directive extending competition to satellite communication. Council decision to liberalize telecommunications infrastructures as of 1.1.1998.
1995	Commission Directive liberalizing the use of alternative infrastructures as of 1.7.96.
1996	Commission Directive extending competition to mobiles. Commission Directive to implement full liberalization of the telecommunications market.

was overdetermined by the self-interest of the European Union as a relatively autonomous actor in this policy process. (For a similar perspective stressing supranational factors, see Stone and Sandholtz 1998b.)

The Transformation of Telecommunications in Germany

As mentioned above, it would be too simple to reduce the German reform process solely to the implementation of EC directives. However, domestic telecommunications policymaking and the major institutional reform measures in this sector during the past ten years cannot be understood without taking the EU level into account. As I will show, the transformation of German telecommunications is a nice example of a reform policy driven simultaneously by domestic, European, and even global factors.

The first time the German telecommunications sector became a matter of foreign policy—not counting international technical coordination—was in the late 1970s, as the first waves of liberalization and deregulation originating in the United States reached Europe.[2] At that time, as the technological revolution in microelectronics increasingly impinged upon telecommunications, relevant public and private policy actors in Germany were confronted with increasing pressure. Major "pushers" were foreign governments, such as the United States and Great Britain, as well as international and domestic computer firms that demanded the remaining protected markets be opened for terminals and new telematic services. This triggered a series of domestic institutional reform activities.

Inspired by American deregulation, in 1980 Germany's Monopoly Commission began to scrutinize the procurement behavior of the German public telecommunications operator, Deutsche Bundespost, and the telecommunications equipment market in general. In its report the Monopoly Commission criticized existing cartels, asked for a number of liberalization measures in the terminal market, and proposed that some degree of service competition be introduced into the public telecommunications network. At this time, however, neither domestic political actors nor the business community sufficiently supported this reform initiative.

A few years later, the domestic landscape changed significantly and support for telecommunications liberation became apparent. In 1982, a new coalition government of Christian Democrats and Liberals under Chancellor Helmut Kohl came into office and took over some of the reform proposals. Within the new cabinet a prominent critic of the PTT monopoly, Christian Schwarz-Schilling, became PTT minister. Even so, three years passed before reform plans materialized. In 1985 the federal government established a special advisory commission charged with the

2. For diverse historical descriptions and interpretations of the German telecommunications reform process, see Webber (1986); Grande (1989); Schneider and Werle (1991); Humphreys (1992); Schmidt, S. K. (1991, 1996); and Werle (1999).

development of a coherent reform program to restructure the telecommunications sector.

There are a number of indications that this telecommunications reform initiative was very much linked to the start of liberalization talks at the EC and Organization for Economic Cooperation and Development (OECD) level. With proposals that were issued almost parallel to the formulation of the Green Paper on telecommunications by the EC Commission, and with policy experts who served on both the European and German telecommunications reform groups, the German advisory commission formulated a list of reform proposals highly converging with the EC policy guidelines. Most of the commission's suggestions were subsequently included into a structural reform law that the German legislature passed in 1989. Major institutional changes included the transformation of the postal, banking, and telecommunications divisions of the former Bundespost into separate public corporations. Further reforms were the liberalization of the terminal market and several market openings in the area of telematic services. Telephone service, however, was still considered a public monopoly, to be kept within the realm of the Bundespost.

These initial openings, however, also called for changes in related areas. Liberalization and deregulation created "auto-dynamics" comparable to chain reactions. The opening of markets without improving the efficiency and flexibility of the government administrative bodies led to an unstable situation. Thus, a logical next step was the transformation of the three public entities into corporations with a private legal framework, to be sold in parts on the stock exchange.

In Germany, this process was propelled by reunification, charging the Bundespost with the burden of giant reconstruction investments in the former GDR. This created enormous financial problems for the new public company. Formal privatization and the partial selling of these separate corporations on the stock market promised to solve most of these difficulties. To that end, a privatization bill was introduced in the Bundestag in February 1994, which was adopted in July and came into force at the end of that year. From 1995 onward, the three Bundespost companies—Telekom, Post, and Postbank—became private corporations. The first issue of Deutsche Telekom shares sold quite successfully in November 1996.

In 1996, a further reform step led to a Telecommunications Act aimed at the complete elimination of monopoly barriers still present in the traditional telephone sector. This corresponded to the major EU telecommunications policy goal of achieving complete liberalization in telecommunications in 1998. A related step was the delegation of regulatory tasks (such as licensing and tariff controls) to a newly created independent regulatory agency, taking over the functions of the old PTT ministry, which had been dissolved at the end of 1997. In the new institutional structure, the telecommunications operator Deutsche Telekom still has some universal service obligations, including the nationwide provision of telephone service at affordable rates. The costs of these services are collected through payments of the new competitors to a special fund. In all other areas of telecommunications, from telephone to computer networks, there is now fierce competition between a large number of firms. (For a recent review of the process, see Werle 1999.)

The Transformation of Telecommunications in France

In France, the liberalization of telecommunications has been on the political agenda since the mid-1980s.[3] Interestingly, the first steps in agenda setting had been undertaken by the head of the French telecommunications administration, Jacques Dondoux. In February 1985, at a *Financial Times* colloquium, Dondoux argued that state monopolies and the universal services model were outdated and had completed their historical role. New liberalization constraints originating in structural changes in the United States, the United Kingdom, and Japan would require that France itself modify its traditional telecommunications structures (Cohen 1992, 257).

One year later, the conditions for such transformations significantly improved by the electoral victory of "right-wing" political forces and the appointment of Prime Minister Jacques Chirac. That same year, the cable TV market was opened to private operators. In 1987, a private mobile telephony operator was licensed and the terminal market was liberalized. In the summer of the same year, however, a proposed law aimed at opening the provision of telecommunications services failed because of rising opposition.

When the Socialists returned to power in 1988, a broad public debate on the future of postal services and telecommunications was launched. Between 1988 and 1994, the French government tried to support the single telecommunications market while carefully avoiding political conflicts. Thus, while the government officially criticized the Commission's liberalization plans, it also proposed and implemented a number of laws leading to significant institutional changes. First, the telecommunications division of the former French PTT, France Télécom (FT), was transformed into a public corporation, becoming fully separated from the postal branch. Second, two segments of the telecommunications market, mobile services and value-added services, gradually were liberalized. Within the network infrastructure, FT retained a monopoly, although private networks were allowed to coexist as long as they were not opened to third parties.

Since 1994, however, France has openly accelerated its liberalization measures. This shift followed a report prepared by the head of the regulatory directorate at the PTT ministry, stating that FT's monopoly could not ultimately withstand the liberalization of mobile and satellite communications. The report urged the government to follow through on its plans to open the French telecommunications

3. For the French reform process in telecommunications, see Vedel (1988, 1991); Humphreys (1990); Cohen (1992); Chamoux (1993); and Schneider and Vedel (1999).

industry to competition and thus, to prepare France Télécom for a tougher international and national economic environment.

In January 1996, a bill was introduced implementing the EU liberalization goals with respect to traditional telephony. Adopted by the French Parliament in June 1996 and implemented at the end of the following year, the law opened all telecommunications services, including traditional telephony, to competition. Finally, an independent regulatory agency was established to monitor operators' activities, to administer the universal service fund, and to solve conflicts among operators. Licenses, however, were still distributed by the Ministry of Economic Affairs, Finance and Industry.

Finally, the privatization of France Télécom was also addressed. In summer of 1994, a report on the future of France Télécom, submitted to the French government, called for the sale of a minority share of the public operator while maintaining the employees' civil servant status. However, this measure was opposed by Prime Minister Balladur in an effort to avoid any unpopular measures on the eve of presidential elections. After Chirac's electoral victory in May 1995, however, France Télécom's privatization was no longer taboo. Through special legislation passed in the summer of 1996, France Télécom was transformed into a national corporation. In 1997 a minority share of its assets was sold on the stock market. The change to a Socialist government in 1998 somewhat slowed down the reform process but did not change the direction of this long-term institutional restructuring. Thus, France has transformed its telecommunications system from a state monopoly to a largely privatized and competitive market.

The Transformation of Telecommunications in Italy

In Italy, the reform process differed to some extent from the two other countries, because reform motives were not only motivated by liberalization and deregulation but also by the need to centralize what had been a fragmented organizational landscape. In contrast to the spirit of the time, the goal of centralization became a dominant concern because of excessive institutional fragmentation in the Italian telecommunications system. Unlike the French and German systems, the Italian one consisted of several different telecommunications operators. Azienda die stato per i servizi telefonici (ASST), Società Italiana per l'Esercizio Telefonico (SIP), and Italcable were the largest ones. SIP and Italcable have been controlled by the state-dominated Società Finanziaria Telefonica (STET) holding company. In Italy, demands for institutional telecommunications reform had been on the political agenda since the reconstruction in the 1950s. The recent wave of institutional reforms in the telecommunications sector, however, has its origins in the late 1970s and early 1980s. The combination of a moderate tariff policy in telecommunications and high inflationary pressures during the seventies pulled Italy into a period of severe economic crisis. At the same time, global industrial changes challenged Italy's industrial policymakers to adapt to the new situation. Thus, in 1981, the minister of state-owned industry formulated a development plan for the electronic sector that also included telecommunications. Prime Minister Spadolini established an expert commission directed by Franco Morganti to study the situation in the telecommunication sector and to develop recommendations for action. The Morganti Commission submitted a report in July 1982. A few months later, however, the Spadolini cabinet resigned. When the report was finally reissued in 1984 following a series of political upheaval in Italian politics, it noted the need to address new international changes in telecommunications. Thus, the report's main recommendations focused not only on the highly fragmented Italian system but also on the global liberalization and deregulation of telecommunciations markets. By explicitly pointing to the increasing Europeanization and internationalization of the telecommunications sector, the Morganti Commission recommended the complete liberalization of the terminal market and the new telematic services. At the same time the commission defended the conservation of the public monopoly at the network level (Morganti et al. 1988). To put an end to the fragmented organizational shape, the commission proposed to integrate the different operators— ASST, SIP, and Italcable—into a "monopolio intelligente."

Again, due to changes in the Italian government, the Morganti Commission's reform proposals were not taken up until March 1987, when the new PTT minister in the Fanfani cabinet, Antonio Gava, issued a law proposing both centralization and liberalization measures. However, despite increasing domestic and European pressure toward institutional reform, the bill became victim to bureaucratic infighting and never arrived at the Council of Ministers. An unfortunate alliance between bureaucrats and trade unions—opposing the fusion of SIP and ASST—in addition to internal conflicts within the governmental coalition, obstructed the reform initiative.

It took another two years and two further governments to relaunch the reform program. In early 1989, the new PTT minister, Oscar Mammì, submitted another bill to the Council of Ministers, which passed it on to the Senate. In the summer of 1989, the bill was dealt with in the Camera. Its main proposals included the integration of the traditionally fragmented system into a kind of "super-STET" or super-SIP, a solution that was advocated particularly by Romano Prodi, who was at that time the head of the huge state industrial complex IRI, the Istituto di Reconstruzione Industriale. The plans, according to EU policy guidelines, were to liberalize a number of market segments and to separate service and network provision from regulative tasks, making the traditional PTT ministry responsible for the latter. While the Mammì proposal finally succeeded in being placed on the parliamentary agenda, major conflicts of interest still remained. A final breakthrough only succeeded when the Italian government, in December 1991, used the institutional weapon of government imposed regulation. This put parliament under pressure to come to a decision, and in January 1992 the Mammì bill was finally adopted. Through the new law, the former public operators ASST, SIP, Italcable, and Telespazio were merged into a new public enterprise, which some time later was named "Telecom Italia." (In 1997, a large majority of shares of this new entity was sold on the stock exchange.) In addition, a number of EU liberalization directives were adopted and transposed into national law, and new guidelines for tariff policy were established.

This domestic reform process could not be understood without reference to Europeanization. A number of liberalization measures, for example, had been introduced by government regulations adopting EC directives. Most significant were the Liberalization of Services Directive and the Open Network Provision Directive, which put the Italians under heavy pressure to compete with their European counterparts. Government officials understood this quite well. When the new PTT minister, Maurizio Pagani, announced his centralization plan in December 1992, a journalist asked: "Mr. Minister, this is not the first time that somebody is blocking the reform. What will you do this time?" The minister answered: "We have to. We have no alternative. How could we otherwise meet European competition?" (*Come potremmo, altrimenti, fronteggiare la concorrenza europea?*)[4] Thus, Italy had no choice but to respond, sometimes reluctantly, to the increasing economic pressure toward liberalization, for which the European Union played the intermediating force. Franco Morganti thus wrote: "The recent history of Italian liberalization originated entirely in Brussels" (1994, 3).

Public Sector Reform by Global Policy Diffusion: The Role of the European Union

In this section, I examine the interaction of three national reform processes with European policy development and the role of the EU in explaining the development pattern. In doing so, the first step is to ascertain which factors explain similarities and differences among the three reform processes. The second step to determine the actual role that EU decisions, actions, and policies have played in this transformation process.

It is striking how similar the outcomes of the three public sector reforms have been:

1. All three countries have largely liberalized their telecommunications sector, with the last step to full liberalization taking place in 1998.
2. All three countries have privatized their former public operators and have sold them (partly) on the stock market.
3. All three countries have introduced independent regulatory agencies that monitor, license, and regulate.

The degree and significance of these institutional changes from the old "organizational paradigm" to a new institutional model is depicted in more detail in Table 4.2.

4. *Mondo Economico*, December 1992, 29.

Table 4.2 Institutional changes in German, French, and Italian telecommunications

Institutional change	Telecommunications type	Old institutional model pre-1980			New institutional model post-1998		
		Germany	France	Italy	Germany	France	Italy
Liberalization							
	Terminals	●	●	●	○	○	○
	Networks	●	●	●	○	○	○
	Data communications (X.25)	●	●	●	○	○	○
	Leased lines	●	●	●	○	○	○
	Mobile communications	●	●	●	○	○	○
Privatization							
	Legal structures	■	■	■□	□	□	□
	Capital	■	■	■□	■□	■□	□
De-/Regulation							
	Independent regulatory agency	◆	◆	◆	☑	☑	☑

Legend. ● Monopoly ○ Competition ■ Public □ Private ◆ no independent regulatory function ☑ independent regulatory authority.

In sharp contrast to expectations expressed in political science literature at the end of the 1980s and early 1990s (Morgan and Webber 1986; Webber 1986; Rubsamen 1989; Grande and Schneider 1991), the outcomes of institutional reform in the different countries look quite similar at the end of the 1990s. To a large degree, therefore, structural convergence has taken place. (Recent studies emphasizing greater divergence than convergence, however, seem to be still impressed by empirical data of the early 1990s; see, e.g., Vogel 1996.)

Yet, structural convergence does not mean that there is no variation in detail. Since EU directives only set the basic framework for the transposition of EU directives into national law, the different member states have some degree of freedom in their domestic adaptations. To be certain, the European Commission is investing considerable energy in monitoring and in constantly evaluating this adaptation process in order to assure a high degree of harmonization. In its status reports, the Commission identifies some countries that have partly deviated from or delayed the implementation of the various directives. From a broader analytical view, however, these divergences are of minor importance. Compared to the enormous institutional shift from public monopoly to private competition, the concrete differences in licensing procedures, new regulatory procedures, or percentages of the capital to be sold at the stock market are trivial. If the shift from the old to the new model in telecommunications were to be measured in feet, the variation in outcomes is a matter of inches.

Meaningful differences between the three countries only appear if we look at the overall processes pattern. Here it can be seen that French and German reform policies started during the late 1980s and developed highly synchronously since then, in close connection to policy development at the EU level. Italy, in contrast, displayed a peculiar development rhythm. It started later and moved slower in the European liberalization and privatization process. In the end, it only reluctantly switched to structural reforms.

How can the similarities in outcomes and the differences in the process be explained? A well-known explanation in contemporary literature emphasizes similarities and convergence based on technological factors and economic competition. In this explanation scheme, the similar results in the different institutional reform processes are essentially related to economic and technological globalization, in particular to the recent revolution in communication and information technology penetrating and transforming traditional market structures just by technological necessity and economic efficiency.

But during the 1980s, other literature—although acknowledging the important role of technology—related sectoral reforms more to changing power relations between dominant social groups. In this respect, the shift was identified with strategic changes in economic policy by neoconservative governments of the time, such as in Thatcher's Britain, Reagan's America, and Kohl's Germany (Morgan and Webber 1986; Webber 1986; Lehmbruch at al. 1988). Political and ideological variables, indeed, have been supportive for a general cutback of the state in these countries—which is not, however, the major factor explaining this significant transformation. Deregulation in the United States was not just a neoconservative idea; rather, it had much broader support, already gaining prominence during the Carter era (Derthick and Quirk 1985). Moreover, the alternation between "left" and "right" governments in France showed that there were only slight but not essential differences between socialist and conservative governments in this sectoral policy. That the German Social Democrats supported the anti-reform alliance during all three reform steps was mainly due to general partisan opposition behavior in the German party system. If they had shared governmental responsibility, they would have supported the various reform measures.

I argue below that a number of forces and structural constraints at the transnational and European level—largely independent of political ideologies and political systems—were pushing all countries toward converging institutional transformations. One of these forces would be "European integration" in the telecommunications industrial sector. The European Commission's decisions to promote the goal of an internal market and to develop various EU R&D programs were clearly significant (Sandholtz and Zysman 1989; Schneider and Werle 1990). However, while the missionary impetus of the European Commission played an important role in the diffusion of liberalization and deregulation policies among EU member countries, it would be too simplistic to conceive EU policy as an exclusive force or "single independent variable" of the enormous domestic changes in the telecommunications sector. While there were specific forces emanating from the EU level to adjust domestic institutions to EU requirements, the EU itself did not create these pressures but played an important intervening or intermediary role in transmitting, channeling and amplifying adaptation constraints at the global level into its regional context.

A more convincing explanation thus has to reconstruct the changes within a global context, where institutional transformation was ultimately triggered by global economic and technical changes being transmitted and reinforced by international organizations and other channels of policy diffusion. A core thesis I develop here is that the reform policies in Germany, France, Italy, and in many other countries ultimately were the effects of a global chain reaction that actually was started by major institutional changes in U.S. telecommunications during the 1970s and early 1980s. This institutional break-up then spread, in several "shock waves," to other countries. International organizations and trade regimes such as the OECD and the General Agreement on Tariffs and Trade (GATT), and, above all, the European Community, then played the role of transmitters and amplifiers in this diffusion process.

Compared to other explanations of increasing international privatization and liberalization by diffusionist approaches (Ikenberry 1990; Vogel 1996), the following "dynamic transformation" model has some important differences. The two major deficiencies in the above-mentioned approaches are that (1) the inter- and supranational level of politics is largely absent, and (2) diffusion is conceived as a rather continuous process. It is more plausible to reconstruct the overall transformation as a *dynamic* and *multilevel* process, in which pressures toward structural adaptation not only worked between and through nation states but also via inter- and supranational organizations. The second aspect is that the pressures to adaptation were not constant during the whole process but increased over time, in a self-stimulating manner. In the end they became so strong that even countries with mighty institutional rigidities and low governmental capacity for action had been constrained to adapt to the new model of liberalized markets and privatized enterprises.

In this perspective, the overall transformation was started by an institutional "big bang" in the United States. That this happened when and where it did seems to be explained by the fact that (1) during the 1970s, the United States had been technologically much more advanced than other countries, and (2) the foregoing institutional structures could more easily erode or break up in this specific form of political system. An important explanation is that sectoral structures in the United States were less deeply entrenched than elsewhere. In Europe and Japan, where telecommunication systems had been run as conventional publicly administered bodies, institutional characteristics generally had been laid down in statutory laws or even within constitutions. In the United States, in contrast, the dominant operator was a private firm only indirectly controlled by the state. The Communication Law of 1934 delegated much of the legal framework to an independent regulatory agency, the Federal Communications Commission (FCC). In Germany, in contrast, the major aspects of the institutional structure have been determined at the constitutional level, based on a legal tradition dating back to the mid-nineteenth century.

The varying depth of the institutional entrenchment of sectoral governance structures (by constitution, by statutory law, or by regulation) thus implies different degrees of adaptability. Constitutional entrenchment clearly offered the best protection against change to institutions, although this, of course, also depends on the respective procedural rules for the modification of constitutional provisions. The legal systems in which change can occur most easily are those in which mere conventional statutory legislation is required for a given institutional change. Clearly, the American system fits this category, because large parts of institutional arrangements in U.S. telecommunications may be changed unilaterally by a regulatory agency or by a court reviewing a given regulatory rule. In this case the respective policy subsystem essentially has only one "veto player" (Tsebelis 1995). Just as the Bell system had the legal form of a private corporation and its monopolistic position was only protected by regulations, the institutional status could be changed more easily than in the other three cases studied here. A further facilitating factor was that the various changes in U.S. telecommunications were strongly supported by a powerful alliance between the computer industry and a great number of multinational corporations from other economic sectors.

The complete set of variables explaining different capacities for institutional transformation are therefore

—the interest structure (essentially the interest positions of the major political actors for or against institutional changes, weighted with their power resources);
—the degree of institutional entrenchment (measured by the "transformation energy" as described above), and
—the collective action capacity of the policy network deciding upon these changes (roughly measured by the number of "veto players" in this policy subsystem).

Among the six countries I have mentioned so far (the United States, Great Britain, Japan, Germany, France, and Italy), the United States appeared to combine the most favorable conditions for institutional change (see Table 4.3). It displayed a strongly reform-prone interest structure, the lowest degree of collective institutional entrenchment, and the highest degree of action capacity in this sector. It is thus not a coincidence that the earliest transformations occurred in the United States—initially, by the way of "institutional erosion" and, finally, culminating in the famous AT&T divestiture (Coll 1986). In an increasingly interdependent and competitive world economy, however, the first step to liberalization had serious ramifications. The first move toward institutional reform in one country increased the pressure on other countries to follow this path. Seen from a trade perspective, liberalization in one country without similar efforts in all others will lead to critical competitive disadvantages. The "first mover" in deregulation is strongly motivated to support liberalization policies in other countries—by traditional economic diplomacy or by transnational alliances with domestic groups in other states. A similar logic works in an industrial policy perspective, where regulations are seen as a competitive burden for the domestic industry if they are not "exported" and "internationalized." Both forms of interdependence create chain reactions based on self-stimulating feedback toward global deregulation and liberalization.

The "first move" in the United States amplified the technological pressures toward institutional change in European countries. AT&T's divestiture not only

Table 4.3   Differential probability toward institutional change

Probability	Interest structure	Institutional entrenchment	Collective action capacity	Cases/Countries
High	Reform prone	Weak	High	USA: regulative arena
	Reform prone	Medium	High	Great Britain & Japan
	Reform prone	Medium	Medium	USA: legislative arena
	Strongly status quo prone	Medium	High	France
	Moderately status quo prone	High	Medium	Germany
Low	Strongly status quo prone	Medium	Weak	Italy

opened the U.S. telecommunication system for new competitors but also liberated AT&T from old restrictions, enabling it to move outside its established areas—into the computer business and to foreign countries. This triggered the formation of complex policy alliances. On the one hand, the U.S. trade administration established negotiations (through bilateral talks as well as through multilateral bargaining within the OECD and the GATT) with the highly regulated European countries in order to create fair trade conditions. On the other hand, some foreign subsidiaries of U.S. multinationals asked for liberalization, especially in the United Kingdom, Germany, and France, thus generally supporting liberalizers and deregulators in Europe.

From this active international agenda setting (the push path), we can distinguish a passive form of international policy diffusion. This is based on a "pull mechanism" triggered by major changes in how the situation is perceived and defined. In this respect, a major perceptional shift can be identified during the early 1990s. After a certain threshold in the global spread of liberalization and privatization was reached, public monopolies and government-administered bodies no longer were regarded as protective shields but were increasingly considered obstacles in the way of meeting the challenges of an increasingly competitive environment. The pull mechanism, too, works as a self-stimulating process. The stronger the pressure for privatization, the larger the privatized area of telecommunications operators becomes. It is a type of self-stimulating feedback (a popular topic in recent economic analysis).

This interpretation means that the reason the winds of change in the three countries blew the old order in telecommunications away was a combination of domestic interests in political reform and external pressures to reform, as well as incentives toward adaptation that increased over time. The more countries that joined the liberalization path, the greater the adaptation pressure for the others.

In addition to this global diffusion picture, an important regional factor has to be included in the model: the effect of supranational or regional integration in the process of policy diffusion. Key factors are the European Union industrial and competition policy on the one hand, and the role of European law on the other.

As we have seen, institutional transformations in Germany, France, and Italy originally were influenced by the U.S. strategy to gain reciprocity in trade and to open international markets in this sector. International institutions and organizations, such as the OECD and the GATT, had been used as bargaining arenas for this purpose since the early 1980s. In the first phase, these efforts were largely unsuccessful, improving only when the European Commission and the European Court of Justice joined the policy arena.

As discussed in this chapter, the European Commission entered telecommunications policy in the mid-1980s by dramatizing the changes in the United States and Japan. Through the mobilization of specific policy resources, the European Community became an important corporate actor in this policy domain. From this perspective, EC telecommunications policy did not only follow the preferences of the majority of its member states but also the self-interest of its supranational institutions, such as the European Commission and the Court of Justice. Both institutions dispose of specific resources to produce compliance even by dissenting member states. Only recently has the autonomous role of these actors in the process of European integration gained more attention in the literature (S. K. Schmidt 1997).

From this perspective the changes in the United States and the subsequent transformations in Japan had the effect of mobilizing the European Commission to anticipate the adaptation pressures in the coming years. The European Commission's main arguments were that European industry would lose industrial ground if their member governments delayed institutional readjustment for too long. From the mid-1980s onward, the Commission advanced the view that Europe would become an industrial colony of United States and Japan if it did not join the liberalization forces.

By this strategy the European Commission even entered into a kind of paradoxical political alliance with the United States, supporting American requests for deregulation and liberalization with the long-term goal of improving the competitiveness of European industry. Essentially, the European Commission promoted institutional adaptation through a strategy combining elements of neoliberalism with neomercantilism, i.e., state-led adaptation of industrial sectors through the introduction of competition (Schneider and Werle 1990). Turning this strategy into practice meant, on the one hand, to support the European computer and telecommunications industry by massive R&D programs (e.g., ESPRIT and RACE) and, on the other hand, to promote a number of liberalization measures. The blueprint of this combined approach was published as the telecommunications Green Paper in 1987 (Ungerer 1988).

Both strategies were highly successful. The promotion of liberalization was supported by a number of European Court of Justice decisions that essentially extended the principle of competition into the realm of former public monopolies and publicly administered bodies. During the early years of liberalization, the state monopolist telecommunication administrations tried to defend their status quo. But over time, they gradually changed their preferences. More and more challenged by open competition, they increasingly considered their public status as a competitive disadvantage and became interested in restructuring as a private law company. Since the early 1990s, most of the former PTTs thus changed to private corporations that, in the end, were sold on the stock exchange.

The different "horizontal" pull-and-push forces of policy diffusion, therefore, clearly have been amplified by supranational, "vertical" relations, forcing institutional changes in countries that generally did not support such changes or did not have the capacity to enforce such reform efforts. As we have seen, this was the case in Italy, where institutional change without pressure from Brussels would have been unthinkable. Italy only reluctantly complied with EU requirements and, in the end, essentially forced various structural reforms through parliament. In the Italian political system, the veto points—the dominance of status quo-oriented interests and the fragmented political decision structure—created too many obstacles for swift structural adaptation. Much of this inertia could only be overcome through pressures from Brussels. In effect, Europeanization prompted the government to realize that it had no choice but to change its policy strategies.

Supranational pressures from the European Union also supported and amplified the process of structural reform in Germany and France. In both countries, the European Commission actually entered into transnational alliances with domestic reformers; and in both countries, decisions of the European Court of Justice significantly improved the position of liberalizers, despite the straddling goals of their governments in the Council of Ministers (Schneider, Dang-Nguyen, and Werle, 1994).

In the end, institutional changes in the three countries led to a far-ranging convergence in telecommunications industry structures. It should be emphasized that this breakup was not restricted to some core countries of the European Union but gained momentum on a Europe-wide scale. This is astonishing. That this kind of convergence originates not only with the three cases selected but also represents a general trend in the industrialized world is shown by other comparative studies (Grande 1994; Høj, Kato, and Pilat 1995). But convergence does not mean homogenization. The introduction of competition, the elimination of market barriers, and the privatization of former government-administrated bodies does not mean that in all countries identical market structures will emerge. The structural outcome not only depends on the opportunity space that is created by the different reform processes at the European and national levels but also on the way in which these new opportunities will be exploited by different national economic actors.

In most of the advanced industrial countries, the telecommunications sectors have changed dramatically during the past two decades. The focus of this chapter was structural changes in Germany, France, and Italy and the relationship between these domestic changes and telecommunications policymaking at the EU level. It was shown that all three countries, despite some apparent differences in structural and institutional conditions at the national level, converged to highly similar institutional arrangements in the past decade. The national changes were part of a global transformation process that started in the United States and subsequently diffused to other important industrial countries. The adaptation toward this global sectoral change was strongly supported by the European Community, which prompted reluctant states to restructure their telecommunications sectors. All three countries finally privatized and liberalized their telecommunications systems, producing rather similar results. Significant differences only appeared in the process or time dimension—in how and when these three countries adapted to the new organizational paradigm.

Finally, it is important to consider how the findings in this chapter compare to those in the rest of the book. My core message is not that globalization generally will lead to structural convergence, or that globalization beats Europeanization. Rather, under a specific set of conditions, global pressures to adaptations are becoming so strong and intense that only a small spectrum of structural pattern can survive in this competitive environment. Political and economic analysis could borrow here from evolution theory, in particular from ecological and macroevolutionary concepts. In this respect, the pressure to adapt is not simply a function of the degree of "misfit," that is, differences between the structure of an evolutionary unit (organism, technical artifact, social institution) struggling to survive in a given context and the relevant structures of its environment. As ecological approaches are showing, pressures to adaptation can vary greatly according to the intensity of selection. In a certain environment, a persisting misfit may be punished by extinction. In other environments, greater variation in structure might be possible. Global competition in the telecommunication sector was interpreted as pressure toward structural adaptation, which during the 1990s attained such an intensity that virtually all countries have become forced to transform their sectors toward privatization and liberalization. Europeanization in this context did not create these pressures, but it certainly provided a kind of catalytic transmission of this constraint in order to produce favorable conditions for European industry to survive in the context of increasing global competition.

CHAPTER FIVE

Italy Pays for Europe: Political Leadership, Political Choice, and Institutional Adaptation

Alberta Sbragia

T he Treaty of European Union, popularly known as the Maastricht Treaty, allowed European institutions to exert very strong pressure on the member states to reshape the contours of domestic public finance. By setting a clear limit to the ability of member-state governments to spend more than they taxed, the Treaty represented a defeat of the Keynesian ideas that had, whether implicitly or explicitly, shaped much fiscal policy in many member states. The decision to move to Economic and Monetary Union (EMU) carried with it very strong pressures on many member states to adapt to the new paradigm of public finance embedded in the Treaty. Maastricht, by addressing public finance, Europeanized a critical policy area previously off the agenda of European integration.

It did so, however, in a deceptively nonintrusive fashion. EMU involved neither programmatic intervention, regulatory reform, nor the reshaping of rights. While it did set parameters of appropriate fiscal behavior, it did not restrict the ability of member states to raise or lower taxes or to raise or lower public expenditure. At its core, it simply forced member-state governments to fund expenditure through taxation (or other forms of revenue generation, such as privatization). In that sense, it seemed to many nonspecialists to provide less intense pressure on member states than many far more detailed directives adopted by institutions in Brussels.

The truth could not have been more different. The policy agenda embodied in the Maastricht Treaty was extraordinarily powerful because public finance is so central, so absolutely fundamental, to the modern state. Detailed directives about a policy sector are typically far less intrusive in practice and less significant in impact than even the most seemingly innocent restrictions related to taxing and

For extensive comments on the draft manuscript, I am particularly grateful to Maria Green Cowles.

spending. As Joseph Schumpeter argued in 1918, "The public finances are one of the best starting points for an investigation of society, especially though not exclusively of its political life" (Schumpeter 1954, 7). In many ways, public finance constitutes the heart of the state.

In fact, the structure of public finance in the member states in the postwar period had shaped the nature of their welfare state, the degree of redistribution of both income and wealth, and activities of their publicly owned enterprises. As Theda Skocpol has argued, "A state's means of raising and deploying financial resources tells us more than could any other single factor about its . . . capacities to create and strengthen state organizations, to employ personnel, to coopt political support, to subsidize economic enterprises, and to fund social programs" (Skocpol 1985, 16). Although the European Union is distinctive and, as I have argued elsewhere, powerful, partly because it does not have much money to spend (Sbragia 2000), Maastricht allowed the European Union to structure, at least to some extent, how the member states raised and spent *their* money. Europeanization set the standard by which "misfits" would be defined, identified, and excluded.

While the constraints imposed by Maastricht were difficult for nearly all member states, they were the most daunting for Italy. The misfit between Italian public finances and the Maastricht requirements was widely considered the most significant in the European Union. Italy's public finances had for decades been shaped more by the needs of coalition governments, which had ignored the types of institutional mechanisms—such as "fiscal contracts"—used by other multiparty governments to control public spending (Hallerberg 1999). At the time of the signing of the Maastricht Treaty, the feasibility of adaptation on Italy's part was so slim that a general consensus developed which argued that Italy would be unable to join EMU in the first wave of countries. In fact, many suspected that the constraints had been selected by the Bundesbank precisely to keep Italy out of the future Euro-zone.

Italy, nonetheless, did join the Euro-zone in the first wave of countries, and it thus maintained its status as a founding member of all the institutions created by the process of European integration. In this chapter I set out the pressures imposed by Maastricht and then examine the shape of Italian public finance during the period 1991–97, arguing that the adaptational pressures faced by Italy were extraordinary. I then go on to give a brief summary of the financial adaptation undertaken by Italian governments as well as the institutional changes that underpinned such adaptation. Finally, I examine three mediating factors that help account for those policy responses. The first is the empowerment by Maastricht of those elites in Italy concerned with public finance reform. The second is the nearly universal general support for European integration among all elites and a willingness to consider arguments for austerity couched in terms of "Europe." Third, the "permissive consensus" on Europe, which existed among the Italian electorate, provided crucial support for such elites and enabled the silencing of opposing forces at critical times in the process of belt tightening.

The Politics of Austerity

Maastricht led to the retrenchment of public expenditure and/or increases in taxation in most member states. Although the scholarly literature on retrenchment is not extensive, it does emphasize either strategies of concealment or the importance of key institutions relatively insulated from electoral and societal pressures. Paul Pierson, in his study of welfare-state retrenchment in Britain and the United States, argues that among the strategies available to advocates of retrenchment, "obfuscation which involves efforts to manipulate information concerning policy changes is the most important" (Pierson 1994, 19).

Boisseau and Pisani-Ferry, in explaining why French policymakers maintained a commitment to the *franc fort* in spite of the costs to employment and economic growth of such a policy, identify the power and the long, seven-year term of the French president, for whom foreign policy concerns are paramount, as one key institutional element. As long as being a co-leader of Europe remained the number one French foreign policy goal, the *franc fort* policy trumped alternative policies that would have stressed economic growth (Boissieu and Pisani-Ferry 1998).

While obfuscation does not seem to have played an important role in Italy, as the sacrifices needed to reduce the budget deficit were spelled out rather clearly, the electoral insulation characteristic of the French presidency is relevant to the Italian case. Italy, it is argued here, reshaped its public finances enough to enter EMU at least partly because Maastricht empowered an elite, a "core executive" concerned about public finance, which had been relatively ineffectual in its prior efforts to rein in deficit spending. Helped by the power of the (indirectly elected) Italian president, who became unusually strong in a period of political uncertainty, this relatively small elite both captured the executive and proceeded to strengthen that executive vis-à-vis the legislature and the once-hegemonic political parties. Key unelected leaders laid the groundwork—by reshaping industrial relations to bring down the inflation rate, addressing pension reform in order to make structural cuts, cutting expenditure or stabilizing the public debt—for the elected Prodi's government final Herculean initiative in 1996 and 1997 to cut the deficit. Even in that government, an unelected minister played a critical role. Although, as we argue, a "permissive consensus" supportive of integration existed in Italy at both the elite and mass level, many of the attempts at budget cutting or at least stabilization were carried out by ministers who were not members of parliament.

The European Constraint: The Maastricht
Convergence Criteria

The Treaty of European Union explicitly set out the conditions member states would need to meet in order to join EMU. Although almost none of the member-state governments signing the treaty could meet those conditions, political elites clearly saw the Maastricht criteria as "targets" to work toward rather than as criteria that had to be met upon signing. In fact, the Treaty gave the governments until 1999 to meet the criteria.

In essence, the Treaty laid out a blueprint for public finance of a type and nature which is very unusual and, in fact, probably unique in the annals of taxing and spending. The criteria addressed inflation, the stability of the exchange rate, the interest rate, the ratio of government (including all subnational and local government) debt to gross domestic product (GDP) at market prices, and the ratio of the government deficit to GDP at market prices. A member state's suitability for membership in EMU was to be decided on explicit criteria laid out either in the body of the Treaty of European Union or in protocols attached to the Treaty.

Briefly, a member state's inflation rate, observed over a period of one year before the examination, could not exceed by more than 1½ percentage points that of, at most, the three best-performing member states in terms of price stability. Inflation-prone countries were forced to try to minimize their inflation so as to approach the EU's low-inflation economies.

Second, the exchange rate had to be such that the member state would have been a member of the exchange rate mechanism (ERM) of the European Monetary System (EMS) for at least the two years before the examination. Countries whose currency was too weak for the ERM were to be excluded.

Third, interest rates were to converge. The Treaty required that membership only be granted if, over the year previous to the examination by the European Commission, a member state has had an average nominal long-term interest rate that does not exceed by more than two percentage points that of, at most, the three best-performing member states in terms of price stability.

Fourth, the ratio of public sector debt to GDP was to be at 60 percent, and fifth, the budgetary deficit was to be 3 percent. In both the case of the public debt and the deficit, the Treaty stipulated that if the debt was above 60 percent, it should be "sufficiently diminishing and approaching the reference value at a satisfactory pace"; the budget deficit, if over 3 percent, should have "declined substantially and continuously and reached a level that comes close to the reference value."

The Maastricht convergence criteria, as they are known, were designed to ensure price stability and thus to ensure the credibility and soundness of the new currency and the European Central Bank. The size of the budgetary deficit played a critical role in the thinking behind the criteria. If deficits were brought under control, central banks would be less subject to pressure to underwrite the deficits through monetary policy, and if monetary policy could be tight, inflation would likely fall. In turn, lower deficits would help reduce at least the rate of public-sector debt growth. Convergence across the member-state economies would be maximized.

In fact, the deficit came to symbolize the changes demanded by Maastricht. It gradually became clear that it would be the most difficult criterion for many member states (including France and Germany) to meet. First of all, the deficit—commonly stated as a percentage of GDP—is a clearly recognizable and quantifiable figure. It easily summarizes the gap between the government's revenue and its expenditure in a single year. Whereas tax structures and the structure of national debt (the ratio between long term and short term, for example) vary in complex ways across countries, the figure of the deficit expressed as a percentage of GDP is a relatively easily comparable piece of data. Finally, it is a key piece of information of interest to financial markets. It is important to note that this figure does not stipulate whether a small deficit is a result of cutting expenditure or raising taxes—either method of raising revenue is acceptable to financial markets and was acceptable to the drafters of the Maastricht Treaty.

Moreover, the pressures emanating from EMU differed in several important ways from those emanating from other European Union (EU) policies. First, lack of compliance with traditional EU legislation is not often sanctioned; when applied, sanctions are in the form of European Court of Justice (ECJ) judgments rather than financial penalties or exclusion from EU decision making, and the costs of noncompliance are not easily understood in either operational or symbolic terms. By sharp contrast, lack of compliance with the criteria established for entry into EMU was to be clearly sanctioned by the refusal of membership into the Euro-zone. Such exclusion carried very well understood costs: exclusion from what was to be the "inner core" of the European Union and the imposition by the financial markets of comparatively high interest costs on public-sector borrowing. Second, the criteria for compliance were quantified and easily understood. The 3 percent budget deficit limit was particularly comprehensible. Third, noncompliance would have a clearly visible physical manifestation—the retention of the national currency when many others would have been allowed to adopt the Euro.

Italy's Public Finances: A Symbol of "Lack of Fit" with the Maastricht Convergence Criteria

In 1991, the "lack of fit" between Italian public finances and the convergence criteria was striking. Tables 5.1 and 5.2 give a sense of the magnitude of the deficits and public debt that had accumulated in the 1970s and 1980s. In the 1970s, budget deficits in Italy outpaced those in other EC countries, even when adjusted for business cycles and inflation (Fratianni and Spinelli 1997, 215). Italy's annual public deficit had been above 10 percent of GDP nearly every year since 1981. Budget deficits in the 1980s were so large that by 1993, the interest on the public debt totaled 28 percent of all public expenditure and represented by far the largest category of public expenditure. In January 1991, the public debt amounted to more than Italy's GNP.

The targets set by Maastricht were clearly so restrictive from Italy's standpoint that it is not surprising most observers thought that Italy was almost certainly

Table 5.1 Budget deficits in Italy and other EC countries, 1971–80

Country	Deficit/Income	Cycle-adjusted	Cycle and inflation-adjusted
Italy	−8.3	−8.3	−6.3
Belgium	−5.0	−5.5	−3.6
Denmark	0.9	1.2	1.3
Germany	−2.1	−2.3	−1.6
France	−0.3	−0.7	−0.4
Netherlands	−1.5	−2.0	−2.3
UK	−3.1	−3.2	−2.3
EC average	−3.1	−3.3	−2.4

Source: European Economy, November 1984, 125 in Fratianni and Spinelli, 1997, 215.

Table 5.2 Public debt and deficit (as % of GDP)

Year	Public Deficit	Public Debt	Primary Balance[a]
1970	3.7	38.0	2.1
1975	11.6	57.6	8.1
1980	8.5	57.7	3.2
1981	11.4	59.9	5.2
1982	11.3	64.9	4.2
1983	10.6	70.0	3.1
1984	11.6	75.2	3.6
1985	12.6	82.3	4.6
1986	11.6	86.3	3.1
1987	11.0	90.5	3.1
1988	10.7	92.6	2.6
1989	9.9	95.6	1.0
1990	10.9	97.8	1.3
1991	10.2	101.4	0.0
1992	9.5	108.0	−1.9
1993	9.6	117.3	−2.6
1994	9.0	121.4	−1.7
1995	7.5	122.9	−3.5
1996[b]	5.9	122.7	−4.3
1997[b]	4.4	121.1	−5.4
1998[b]	2.6	117.9	−6.4

Source: Data collected from annual reports to parliament by the Treasury and Budget ministries; and from data presented by the Governor of the Bank of Italy, Antonio Fazio to the Interministerial Committee on Economic Planning in Banca d'Italia, *Bolletino Economico*, No. 25 (October 1995): 152–5, Vincent Della Sala 1997, 23.

Note: The figures include central, regional, provincial and local governments, along with all state public agencies and enterprises.

[a] Primary balance removes interest payments from calculation of expenditure and revenue.

[b] Bank of Italy estimates.

doomed to exclusion. In fact, Italy came to symbolize an extreme misfit—a member state whose public finances were so incompatible with the European standard that its chances of adapting in time to join the first wave of EMU entrants were thought to be nil.

The state of public finance in Italy was linked to institutional factors that allowed deficit-financed spending to go nearly unchecked. An electoral system of proportional representation had encouraged the formation of multiparty coalition governments that were financially irresponsible. (Multiparty governments were still in place after the reform of 1994, which did not have the impact many had expected.) Generally, five parties were included in the coalition. Second, Italy's geopolitical situation and deep divisions in society—between a "red" or Communist Party-dominated culture, and a "white" or Christian Democratic Party-dominated culture—meant that the Christian Democratic Party had to be included in every coalition. Thus, as Hallerberg (1999) points out, the Christian Democrats could not be punished by exclusion in the next coalition (and the Christian Democrats themselves would have found it difficult to exclude their partners from future coalitions as their own maneuverability was limited) if they reneged from an agreement. This meant that the typical mechanisms used by multiparty coalitions in other West European governments to keep spending in check were absent in Italy, even if the parties in the multiparty coalition had agreed collectively to set spending levels.

Finally, the prime minister could not act to enforce fiscal discipline. Prime ministers were institutionally weak—so weak, in fact, that some have characterized Italy as an "acephalous democracy" (Fabbrini 1995, 72). Given the extraordinary power of political parties (summarized by the Italian term *partitocrazia*—rule by party), prime ministers as well as finance ministers were subject to the dictates of party secretaries rather than being able to act autonomously. In many ways, they were mere figureheads (Spotts and Wieser 1986, 4–8; Pasquino 1989). And the political parties had little interest in limiting deficits: the Christian Democrats wanted to avoid taxing their supporters while the parties of the left wanted public expenditure to fund various programs related to social welfare.

Thus, spending ministers had a great deal of autonomy: they were constrained neither by a strong prime minister, nor a strong finance minister, nor multiparty negotiations resulting in fiscal contracts designed to keep spending within agreed-upon parameters. Further, the legislature was unusually strong vis-à-vis the executive (most of the key leaders of the Christian Democratic Party were in the legislature rather than the government), so that spending requests from the parties in parliament reinforced the pro-spending dynamic found within the cabinet. The kinds of institutional arrangements required to achieve the European standard of financial soundness were absent. Italy suffered not only from deficits and public debt, but, perhaps most significantly, it also suffered from a lack of those institutional arrangements that had been adopted by its European neighbors to ensure sound public finance.

The Effect of Europeanization on Public
Finance and Institutions

Although some analysts have argued that the economic and (national) political benefits for Italy of joining EMU were precarious at best (Garrett 1998a), successive
Italian governments, beginning in 1992, did begin either to rein in spending,
stabilize the debt, address the key problem of pension reform, or raise taxes in an
effort to address the Maastricht criteria. The effort lasted from 1992 through 1997,
the key reference year for admission to the Euro-zone. The belt tightening has been
so serious that in 1998 and 1999, it was seen as one of the key reasons for Italy's
sluggish economic growth.

Italy was helped in meeting the 3 percent criterion by the impact of falling
interest rates. This "cushion" is still of concern to institutions such as the
European Central Bank. Was Italy able to defer key structural reforms by the
windfall provided by lower interest rates? Some economists have concluded that
if interest rates on the public debt had remained stable since 1994, the budget
deficit in 1997 would have been 4.8 percent of GDP rather than 3 percent (Blitz
and Barber 1999, 2; Chiorazzo and Spaventa 1999). On the other hand, falling
interest rates could be seen as a reward for the budgetary sacrifices Italy had
accepted.

Even if the most skeptical analysts are correct, it is important to remember that
the budget deficit in 1991 stood at 10.2 percent of GDP. The magnitude of expenditure cuts and tax increases have been startling: between 1989 and 1998, taxes
were raised 4.6 percent of GDP compared to 0.7 percent in the rest of Western
Europe (Blitz 1999, 11).

The public finance reforms undertaken by Italy in order to adapt to Maastricht
required institutional changes—one that allowed reform in many expensive policy
areas intrinsic to the welfare state. Such institutional changes can be thought of as
beginning to put in place a structure of government that can act with the kind
of fiscal responsibility typical of many Western European democracies. Italian
"exceptionalism" makes this task rather daunting, but the pressures exerted by
Maastricht have been so strongly felt that significant changes have indeed occurred.
Much more needs to be done, but again Maastricht catalyzed a process that is still
ongoing.

The basic challenge is one of institutionalizing mechanisms known to facilitate
fiscal responsibility in a system that has previously avoided nearly all such mechanisms. Historically, the Italian multiparty system differed from its European counterparts in that the parties dominated governments and the public administration,
the legislature dominated the executive, and the executive was internally run as a
set of fiefdoms with no strong centralizer. Ministers were appointed according to
the strength of their factions within their respective political parties and answered
to those factions rather than to the president of the Council of Ministers (Spotts
and Wieser 1986). Power, in other words, was institutionally dispersed while simultaneously being concentrated in political parties.

The Maastricht criteria were agreed upon just as the Italian political system, which had been in place since 1948, began to collapse. Parties began to weaken vis-à-vis governments, and a window of opportunity for institutional change appeared. Institutional changes favoring more fiscal responsibility were, in fact, adopted. Some of them are likely to last, while others are more precarious. Still, those institutional changes directly linked to fiscal rectitude are widely considered the most permanent and significant of all the insitutional changes attempted.

Three key processes stand out. One is the gradual increase, since the Amato government of 1992–93, in power within the cabinet of the premier (Giuliani 1999). Although the Italian premier still is far from wielding the authority of a British prime minister or a German chancellor, there has been an increase in his standing within the cabinet.

Second, and perhaps most important for the long-term health of Italian public finance, the Treasury has been strengthened considerably as part of the process of strengthening the executive vis-à-vis the legislature and of centralizing authority over public money within the government itself. In 1997, legislation formally folded the ministry for the budget and economic programming into a new Treasury Ministry. A "super ministry" was thereby created that enjoyed more formidable powers over budgetary policymaking than had the old Treasury Ministry (Fabbrini 1998a; Felsen 1999; Vassallo 2000). Furthermore, those units within the old Treasury Ministry concerned with European Union issues have become even more central in the new ministry (Felsen 1999; Vassallo 2000). In a similar vein, the procedure for adopting a budget within the legislature was changed so that the process was less likely to increase spending not desired by the government (Hallerberg 1999, 27).

Third, the power of the government vis-à-vis Parliament has been strengthened. In September 1997 the Chamber of Deputies adopted an important reform of its internal operating procedures, strengthening the general power of the government in parliament (Fabbrini 1998a). Of particular significance is the government's increased use of "delegated powers." These allow the government to obtain from parliament the authority to act (largely) independently of parliament in the areas authorized by the parliamentary act authorizing the delegation.

While the initial objective of this instrument had been for the more efficient transposition of EC directives into Italian legislation, it has now been used to carry out far-reaching reforms in areas such as pensions (pensions have been reformed three times in the 1990s), health, and labor policy (Giuliani 1999, 12). The use of these powers for restructuring key elements of the welfare state has been critical. Giuliani concludes that the effort to join the Euro led to "a complex restructuring of strategic policy areas which is still continuing. For this reason the European influence spilled over different sectors such as pension policy, health policy, labor and industrial policy, cohesion policy, and, generally speaking, every high-spending policy sector" (Giuliani 1999, 23). The use of delegated powers was a key institutional mechanism allowing the government to increase its influence over a legislature that would have found it nearly impossible to carry out such sensitive reforms following traditional procedures.

Mediating Factors

In the Italian case, the gap between what was required for entry to the Euro and the state of public finance was so great that adaptational pressures were enormous. Yet the magnitude of the lack of fit and the fact that money rather than legislation of a regulatory nature was involved in closing the gap presented huge obstacles to successful adaptation. If Italy could have escaped its status as a "misfit" by passing regulation, the probability of success would have been much higher than it actually was. After all, it is common for legislation not to be implemented, a fact that makes such legislation easier to adopt. Legislation authorizing expenditure, however, is always implemented, for those entitled to receive money from the welfare state ensure that such implementation occurs. Similarly, public money cannot be spent unless legislation authorizes it. Expenditure cuts cannot therefore be ignored, either. The very nature of public finance made it impossible for Italy to pass legislation and then simply ignore it.

Given the intrinsic difficulties of adapting to European standards in a "hard" arena like public finance, how do we account for the fact that Italy joined the Eurozone with a deficit for 1997 of 2.7 percent of GDP? Which domestic actors were mobilized? What resources did they use? How did a political system known for its inability to make tough choices manage to contract its deficits enough to gain admission to a club whose rules for admission were designed by an institution (the Bundesbank) known for its commitment to sound public finance? We point to the impact of the core executive concerned with public finance, the nearly universal support for European integration found in the Italian political class, and a strong permissive consensus on Europe among the mass electorate.

The Core Executive

Adaptation does not occur spontaneously, and in Italy the process of adaptation was long and difficult. The actors and institutions that played a key role were members of the core executive concerned with EMU and with public finance more generally. Analysis drawing on the concept of core executive, as developed by Rhodes and Dunleavy (1995), focuses on the network of agencies, institutions, and actors that make up the "government machine" and handle conflict as well as provide coordination within that same machine. Many members of the core executive are technocrats, officials who play key roles in fashioning government policy but are not elected. In the Italian case, the core executive involved with EMU necessarily became involved in issues related to public finance. That involvement continued when they left Maastricht and returned to Rome.

The members of the core executive who negotiated the EMU portion of the Maastricht Treaty never numbered more than sixteen. Dyson and Featherstone argue that the core executive—"the small technocratic steering group established to co-ordinate policy on EMU"—operated with very little detailed ministerial input when the group negotiated in the Intergovernmental Conference (IGC).

Carli, the main minister concerned with negotiating EMU, was from a technocratic background himself, having previously served as governor of the Bank of Italy (Dyson and Featherstone 1996, 275). His advanced age and illness during the Intergovernmental Conference, however, led to his providing only general negotiating guidelines. Thus, "a small group of senior civil servants in the core executive [were able] to 'drive' the process of domestic policy formation and EC-level negotiation on EMU, with only limited ministerial intervention" (Dyson and Featherstone 1996, 277). That group would be heard from again.

The institutions represented by the sixteen key negotiators represent in large measure the institutions that became important in advancing the ideas of retrenchment in order to meet the Maastricht criteria. These included Economic Affairs in the Foreign Ministry, the Bank of Italy, and the Treasury. In the period examined in this chapter, this core executive continued to exert very significant influence. Furthermore, it was joined by others who also came from a technocratic/finance background. Finally, it would probably be fair to include President Scalfaro in the core executive concerned with public finance, for his choice of prime ministers was critical to the process by which reformers obtained key decision-making offices and shaped the government's agenda. Members of the expanded core executive were often influential in the cabinet, which previously had been under the control of the parties. Some eventually became elected officials, while others obtained key decision-making ministerial posts without being elected. Whatever position(s) they held in the period 1992–97, however, members of the "public finance core executive" were united in their firmly held belief, born of historical experience, that a *vincolo esterno*—an external constraint—was essential for Italy's economic well-being (Dyson and Featherstone 1996; Fratianni and Spinelli 1997, 257). The Maastricht convergence criteria represented that *vincolo* and thus were seen as the best way for Italy to improve its public finances, viewed by this group as "the Achilles' heel of the country" (Fratianni and Spinelli 1997, 254).

The Emergence of an Influential Public-Finance Core Executive

Those key civil servants who negotiated EMU had been worrying about both monetary policy and public finance since Carlo Azeglio Ciampi had been appointed governor of the Bank of Italy in late 1980. After the bank's monetization of deficits in the 1970s, it had become clear that "the quality of monetary policy cannot be divorced from the course of public finance. Price-level stability is likely to depend more on the stabilisation of the debt-to-GDP ratio than on central bank independence" (Fratianni and Spinelli 1997, 234). During the 1980s, however, deficits kept ballooning, and those concerned about such deficits were effectively sidelined by the power of the political parties. *Partitocrazia* and sound public finance were largely incompatible, and those advocating the latter were no match for the power of the former.

The terms of engagement began to change, however, with the fall of the Berlin Wall in November 1989. The old fear of Communism, which had underpinned the

Christian Democratic Party's vote for so many decades, dissolved rather quickly among the electorate. The Italian Communist Party (PCI), for its part, transformed itself into the Democratic Party of the Left (PDS) at its party congress in February 1991. Trade unions and the General Confederation of Italian Industries (Confindustria) both detached themselves from their traditional partisan allies. A new regional party, Lega Nord, made a mark in the regional and local elections of 1990 and 1991 by questioning the distribution of public resources to the South (long a stronghold of Christian Democratic patronage). In the April 1992 national elections, Lega Nord became the second largest party in northern Italy, after the Christian Democrats. In June 1991 and April 1993, referenda calling for electoral reform met with overwhelming electoral success. Finally, in what came to be known as the "clean hands" operation, magistrates began to accuse key members of the political class of corruption.

The scandals surrounding the Socialist Party were so great that its leader was forced to allow the new president of the republic, Oscar Luigi Scalfaro, to choose the new prime minister from a list of three candidates. In June 1992, Scalfaro chose Giuliano Amato, who had been minister of the Treasury in the late 1980s and was very familiar with the workings of the European Monetary System (EMS). As the magistrates' attack escalated, the parties had to worry about their organizational survival so that Amato was able to act far more independently than had been the norm for Italian premiers.

Amato entered office with Italian finances in a state of crisis. Shortly before his entry into office, the lira began to fall dramatically on the foreign currency markets and kept falling. In response, Amato gave key economic posts in his government to nonpolitical technocrats, approved an emergency tax increase, and constructed a tripartite agreement with the unions and employers designed to bring down inflation, cut public expenditure, and reduce Italy's trade deficit. Although a significant portion of the membership of the trade union that had traditionally been closely linked to the Communist Party contested the agreement, the union's secretary general signed it.

Finally, the Amato government introduced the first far-reaching tax reform since the end of World War II, and in return the unions agreed to curb wages without demanding that the government provide public funds as a trade-off (Locke 1995, 190). When the lira was forced to leave the EMS in September, the Senate and the Chamber of Deputies agreed to delegate to the government the power to change benefits in the areas of health, pensions, public-sector employment, and local finance (Hellman and Pasquino 1993, xxiv–xxvii). "The European bell had rung" (Fabbrini 1998b) when the lira was ousted from the EMS; approaching the Maastricht deficit criteria became the new catechism for the governments that succeeded Amato. His (relative) independence from the parties, his inclusion of technocratic ministers, and his strengthening of the executive vis-à-vis the legislature were all signals that those worried about public finance would get a hearing.

The Amato government was followed by Scalfaro's choice of Ciampi, the governor of the Bank of Italy, as the new prime minister. Ciampi became the first nonelected prime minister in postwar Italy, and after refusing to consult with party leaders before choosing his ministers, his government too included nonelected "technicians." Having represented Italy during the EMU negotiations, he was a key member of the public finance core executive. Now he found himself in a politician's role without having been elected. He asserted the independence of the executive from the parties and proved extremely able in reshaping industrial relations in Italy so as to dampen inflationary pressures.

The national parliamentary elections of March 1994 produced a government headed by Berlusconi, a political newcomer, whose (nonelected) minister of the Treasury (Lamberto Dini) was from the Bank of Italy. The government was short-lived. At the beginning of 1995, Scalfaro refused to call new elections as Berlusconi demanded, and they finally agreed on Dini as the new and nonelected prime minister. Dini took the portfolio for the Treasury as well. It was a completely "technical" government, for not one member of the Dini government was a parliamentarian, and it was completely unelected (Pasquino 1989, 150). Dini overhauled the pension system and, helped by another crisis of the lira, cut expenditure so much that when he left office the projected deficit for 1997 was 4.4 percent of GDP.

In April 1996, the "technocratization" of Italian government seemed to come to a halt with the installation of a political (i.e., elected) government. A center-left coalition—including the ex-Communist PDS and various center parties drawn from the left wing of the now-defunct Christian Democratic Party—symbolized by the Olive Tree, came to power. Romano Prodi (a former economics professor), who was to become president of the European Commission in 1999, led the Olive Tree coalition. While Dini, Prodi's foreign minister, was now a parliamentarian, Ciampi was still not an elected official. He was seen as so central to the Olive Tree's efforts to enter EMU, however, that he was able, as a condition of his accepting the portfolio of Treasury minister, to force a merger between the Treasury minister and the Ministry of Budget and Economic Programming. Such a merger had been discussed for many years to no avail; Ciampi, however, was determined to strengthen the power of the Treasury minister within the cabinet and used his leverage to accomplish that. His leverage was based on the exceptional credibility he was thought to have with Kohl and with other European leaders skeptical of Italy's efforts at retrenchment. His success in forging a "superministry" symbolized the ascendancy that the public finance reformers had achieved since the collapse of the *partitocrazia*.

The Prodi government, on taking office in 1996, found that the relatively rosy projections of the previous Dini government were not materializing. Estimates of economic growth were not met, and interest stayed higher than expected. Rulings by the Constitutional Court regarding pension benefits made the financial situation even bleaker.

The budget submitted by the Prodi government would not bring down the deficit to 3 percent in 1997. Italy would be able to do so only in 1998, one year after the reference year laid out in the Treaty. Explanations differ: some argue that Prodi had not yet managed to convince the PDS that further huge cuts were needed (since 1992, the Italian budget had been cut by 16 percent of GDP), while others think that the Prodi government believed that the Bundesbank would succeed in postponing EMU and thus provide Italy with an extra year in which to make adjustments. Whatever the reason, Prodi's position changed after his meeting (in September 1996) with the new Spanish prime minister, Aznar, who told Prodi that Spain was going to try to enter EMU in the "first wave." Prodi promptly asked for twice the cuts approved by Parliament in July. Significantly, the parliamentary debate focused on whether the deficit should be narrowed by expenditure cuts or increased taxes—not on whether the deficit should be addressed. Ciampi, by threatening to resign if the entire package was unacceptable, strengthened the position of those committed to serious reform. In November 1996, Dini and Ciampi oversaw the reentry of the lira into the exchange rate mechanism (ERM) of the EMS, and Italy was on track for admission to the Euro-zone.

In summary, the collapse of the old system of *partitocrazia* allowed those committed to public finance reform to define the new policy space that emerged with the serious weakening and even disappearance of the traditional parties. In essence, Italy faced the chance to choose a new policy agenda, and Maastricht provided one possible agenda. This agenda was indeed the one chosen because an essentially technocratic elite, committed to public finance reform, captured that policy space.

The Treasury and the Bank of Italy in particular were able to define the key policy issues that had to be addressed. They were able to link the attractive goal of "joining Europe" with the need for restructuring public expenditure in very painful ways. Europeanization defined what could have been an ideological vacuum in such a way that public finance reform was privileged over other types of reforms that were also desperately needed (the reform of the public administration, for instance). The Maastricht convergence criteria served as a catechism for those elites most concerned with Italy's integration into the world economy, its macroeconomic welfare, and its credit rating in the financial markets. The requirements set down by Maastricht provided members of the core executive concerned about deficits with a common program around which to mobilize and a common platform upon which to act.

One of the key reasons the criteria were so compelling is that the penalty for not meeting them was exclusion. Although a reform agenda for Italy in 1992 might well have included many other arenas that needed serious attention, the strictures of Maastricht left no room for competing priorities within a reform agenda. Nothing could trump the reform of public finance without paying the severe cost of being excluded from EMU. U.S. President Ronald Reagan had deliberately used the "politics of deficits" as a strategy in his attempt to cut taxes and force the retrenchment of the American welfare state (Pierson 1994, 154). In the Italian case, the Maastricht deficit limit allowed the reformers to use the politics of deficits as the key referent in the political discourse. Maastricht gave the reformers credibility.

Maastricht, backed by the threat of exclusion, empowered the core executive committed to sound public finance. Organizationally, such empowerment increased the power of the Bank of Italy and the Treasury vis-à-vis politicians and political parties. Ideationally, it privileged a discourse emphasizing low deficits, low inflation, and declining debt. Italy participated in "an EC-wide process of displacement of power to finance ministries and central banks consequent on the EMU process" (Dyson and Featherstone 1996, 296). Such a displacement was far more evident in Italy than in most other member states because the parties had been so powerful, the Treasury had been comparatively weak, and deficits had not been stigmatized. Although the odds against the reformers were high, they were able to draw on the nearly universal support among both elites and the mass electorate for European integration. Those two additional mediating factors are important in understanding how the core executive could be as successful as it was.

Elite Support for European Integration

Italian elites have traditionally been very supportive of European integration. Once the Communist Party changed its position and supported Italian participation in the European Community, it became difficult to find anyone who questioned the appropriateness of Italian participation in the process of integration. All the parties' platforms support integration, and the approval of EU legislation in the Parliament during the process of transposition draws only a handful of negative votes. Italy's foreign policy imperative is simply that Italy must remain in the center of the process of integration; it must not allow itself to become marginalized or be driven to the periphery. That elite support has been a valuable political resource, for arguments for austerity couched in terms of "Europe" had much greater resonance than arguments packaged in the wrappings of the virtue of sound public finance.

Austerity justified by "Europe" was legitimate partly because the threat of exclusion was a particularly potent one for Italian elites. In fact, the possibility of being marginalized from "Europe" represented the worst fear of all for the Italian political class. Throughout the postwar period, the single overriding goal of Italian foreign policy had been not to be marginalized within Europe. In a system in which domestic politics were byzantine and always took up the lion's share of the political elite's attention and time, the desire to be included rather than any specific strategic or substantive goal drove Italian foreign policy. Italy, unlike France, did not wish to lead, but it very much wanted to be included.

The decision by Spain to seek entry in the first wave without asking for any softening of the Maastricht criteria, and the realization that the Bundesbank would be extremely important in Germany's view of who was an acceptable member of EMU, made the threat of exclusion painfully credible. Whether Prodi used the Spanish decision to convince the PDS to support further cuts or whether Prodi himself became convinced that the 3 percent figure had to be met at whatever cost is unclear. What is clear and most important is that the Spanish decision exposed Italy to the very real possibility of being the only major Mediterranean country that would not be a founding member.

Italian policymakers had not counted on being left alone; isolation was un-acceptable. Better to make further huge cuts in the welfare state than to be iso-lated in Europe. As Amato had said in 1992, Italy would become Europe's Disneyland without membership in the Euro. Prodi, Dini, Ciampi, and D'Alema (the leader of the PDS) all became convinced that EMU would represent the key grouping within the European Union and that Italy simply could not afford to be excluded. Italy rejoined the exchange rate mechanism as soon as it could, even though Italian exports had boomed during the four years in which the lira was outside the ERM.

"Europe" in Italian political discourse means, quite simply, the European Union. The term represents an institutional rather than a geographic or cultural entity. In brief, it is symbolized by Brussels. Belonging to the project of European integra-tion is so fundmental to the way the Italian political class (including the trade union elite) views itself and the world it inhabits that a fundamental challenge to "Europe" as such is nearly impossible to mount. That view gave those concerned with public finance reform a key political and cultural resource.

Mass Support for European Integration

The Italian mass electorate is generally viewed as among the most supportive of integration of any electorate in the European Union. This support crystalized in 1997 in a very important way. After successfully cutting the budget in 1996, dis-turbing budget projections forced the Prodi government to seek further cuts in 1997. Proposed reforms focused on pensions. However, this round of cuts was too much for one of the Olive Tree's far-left allies. Rifondazione communista (RC), the party that had been formed by those who disagreed with the transfor-mation of the Communist Party into the PDS, was critical to the Olive Tree's majority in the Chamber of Deputies but announced that it would not support Prodi's budget cuts. It withdrew its support from the government, and the Prodi government resigned. It is very likely that the entanglement of European issues with an interparty dispute was inadvertent, but nonetheless the road to the Euro was threatened.

The reaction to the RC was almost universally hostile. Crowds booed Bertinotti, the RC's leader and the man held responsible for the party's decision to withdraw from the government, at public functions. Telegrams and letters flooded into RC headquarters from party members. Newspapers on the left mercilessly criticized Bertinotti. Party officials distanced themselves from him. After a compromise, the government resumed operating, but the extraordinary reaction from the public had indicated how deep was the desire to do what was necessary to enter the Euro-zone. Some argue that Italians favor the Euro because the process of qualifying has lowered interest rates and had other specific economic benefits. The quality of support, however, would rather indicate that belonging to Europe matters to Italians more as a form of identity than as a form of economic association. Being "European" certainly includes an economic dimension, but above all it seems to

resonate as a club to which Italians want to belong, are proud of, and see as responsible for the prosperity and stability that Italians have enjoyed during the past fifty
years.

The argument made here is that three key mediating factors accounted for the
ability of Italy to accomplish what most had thought impossible. The first was
the ability of elites found in institutions supportive of public finance reform—the
Bank of Italy and the Treasury prominent among them—to define the political
space opened up by the collapse of the established groups in such a way as to link
the attractive goal of "joining Europe" with the need for restructuring public
finances in very painful ways.

The second factor has to do with the fundamental feeling among Italians that
they belong to "Europe." The Italian identity is fundamentally a European one, as
opposed to, for example, the British. That factor helped create a permissive consensus for the very significant budgetary cuts and belt tightening that accompanied the effort to join the Euro-zone. If Maastricht provided the catechism, the
dynamics of Italian identity vis-à-vis Europe accounted for the Italian electorate's
willingness to accept it as a catechism. The expenditure cuts and tax increases that
allowed Italy to enter EMU were the consequences of both the effectiveness of a
core executive concerned with reshaping policy and the permissive consensus
among both elites and mass publics when issues of European integration are
involved.

In 1991, Italy was a misfit, according to the criteria developed at Maastricht.
Although its economy was fundamentally strong, its exports globally known, and
its standard of living the envy of most people in the world, its public finances were
so weak that it was widely viewed as unlikely to be admitted to a very selective
club. In the pre-Maastricht world, Italy had simply been a country with a basically
strong economy accompanied by big deficits and an ever-growing public debt.
After Maastricht, Italy was a misfit. The weakness of its public finances clearly
overshadowed its economic strengths. The Maastricht convergence criteria defined
Italy as a problem in spite of its generally strong economic fundamentals.

The lack of fit between the convergence criteria and Italian indicators was so
large that, once applied, the term "misfit" seemed appropriate. Yet that very des-
ignation empowered those officials most concerned with public finance sufficiently
so that they adapted institutions and budgets so as to join the emerging European
order. It was an effort not predestined to success; in fact, many assumed Italy would
simply be unable to mobilize the political capital necessary for such a major restructuring. Given the previous track record of Italian governments, it was a remark-
ably sustained effort supported by successive governments and the president of the
republic. Technocrats, key members of the core executive in public finance, played
a role previously unknown in the country of *partitocrazia*. In fact, entering EMU
could be seen as the revenge of long-suffering officials against the party officials
who, in their view, had allowed the Italian budget to deteriorate so badly that one
of the strongest economies in Europe could be labeled a misfit.

The Europeanization of public finance, therefore, was of tremendous significance for the transformation of the Italian state. It began a process of "normalizing" Italian budgetary procedures and institutions so that Italy began to converge with its European neighbors. It still has a long way to go, but the direction seems set. Many have argued that Italians view the notion of Europe as an external force that can correct the ills of the Italian system of governance. The impact of EMU would seem to lend credence to that hope.

CHAPTER SIX

Europeanization and the Courts: Variable Patterns of Adaptation among National Judiciaries

Lisa Conant

T he European Court of Justice (ECJ) has been hailed as the motor of legal integration, responsible for designing a European legal order that transforms domestic structures by successfully enlisting the cooperation and authority of national courts. The direct link between national courts and the ECJ through the Article 177 preliminary ruling mechanism is lauded as the critical force behind national adaptation to Europeanization. The Article 177 reference procedure and judicial doctrines on the direct effect and supremacy of European law summon the participation of national judiciaries in the European legal system. Such participation constitutes a change in the basic structure of national judicial institutions: interactions with the ECJ involve appeals to an institutional authority beyond the state and the incorporation of an external source of law.

Most literature on the impact of Europeanization on national legal structures has concentrated on the acceptance of the supremacy of European law. Contending legalist, neorealist, neofunctionalist, and bureaucratic politics explanations of this process of transformation share a convergence thesis: compelling legal and functional logic (Mancini 1991; Weiler 1994), the strategic accommodation of national interests (Garrett 1992; Garrett, Kelemen, and Schulz 1998), the self-interest of legal actors (Burley and Mattli 1993; Mattli and Slaughter 1998), and intercourt competition (Alter 1996b) all ultimately inspire acceptance of European legal supremacy in each member state.

Yet, despite the formal acceptance of European legal doctrines, recent research identifies substantial cross-national and subnational divergence in the extent to

I thank Karen Alter, Karen Anderson, David Cameron, Jeff Checkel, Maria Green Cowles, Michelle Egan, Clea Finkle, Albrecht Funk, Thomas Risse, Fritz Scharpf, Vivien Schmidt, and Sabrina Tesoka for their comments on earlier drafts.

which national courts participate in the European legal system (Golub 1996a; Stone Sweet and Brunell 1998; Weiler and Dehousse 1992). Article 177 referrals vary widely across member states and within different segments of national judiciaries. Sending a reference to the ECJ for a preliminary ruling is far from a routine procedure for most domestic courts.

Existing accounts of this variable judicial dialogue cannot explain different patterns of participation across and within national judiciaries. Previous scholarship has established that single factors such as population size (Golub 1996a; Weiler and Dehousse 1992), distinctions between monist and dualist legal traditions, or the existence of constitutional courts do not correspond with Article 177 referral rates across member states (Alter 1998b; Slaughter, Stone Sweet, and Weiler 1998; Stone Sweet and Brunell 1998). Legalist, neorealist, neofunctionalist, and bureaucratic politics explanations, designed to explain the convergence of support for supremacy of European law, predict relatively uniform patterns of adaptation to the European legal system, although the bureaucratic politics argument expects distinctions in the participation of lower and upper courts.

Transactionalist arguments depart from this literature by addressing variable judicial participation in the European legal system. Proponents of this approach attribute aggregate national reference rates to societal demand for European law enforcement. Intra-European Union (EU) trade and/or the size of the non-national EU population serve as proxies for societal demand, where transnational interactions generate disputes that require resolution at the European level (Golub 1996a; Stone Sweet and Brunell 1998). This argument makes an important contribution in identifying variations in demand for European justice. However, by disregarding factors that influence individual access to courts, transactionalism overlooks processes of structural adaptation and fails to account for variation in references. Patterns of Article 177 referrals indicate that the impact of Europeanization is neither uniform nor automatic.

In this chapter, I demonstrate that the transformation of domestic judicial structures remains incomplete. I argue that national institutional variation, and its consequences for state-society relations, create variable pressures for national judges to participate in the European legal system. Variation in (1) aggregate political structure, (2) institutionalized access to legal arenas, and (3) substantive domestic law affect the extent to which national courts respond to Europeanization by interacting with the ECJ.

First, following the work of James Q. Wilson on political organizations, I argue that the dispersion of political power within government influences patterns of societal interest organization. Political structures that disperse power inspire active interest organization, while political structures that concentrate power suppress interest organization (Wilson 1973). Following the work of Marc Galanter, I argue that interest organization facilitates the pursuit of legal rights by providing the information and financing necessary to sustain litigation before courts (Galanter 1974). Europeanization disperses power and, therefore, should promote greater interest organization across the EU. However, a convergence toward active interest organization is likely to develop only in the long term. Broad patterns of state-society relations change gradually. Terry Moe's observation of societal responses to changing political opportunities is illustrative:

> It is counterproductive to pretend that [Mancur] Olson's (1965) logic of collective action cranks up to generate brand new interest groups. The reality is that these new groups would arrive on the scene too late to play the game. For most issues most of the time, a set of organized interest groups already occupies and structures the upper reaches of political decision making, and these are the players. (Moe 1990, 129–30)

As a result, member states whose domestic political structures approximate the dispersed European system, providing closer institutional fits, will be host to the patterns of active societal interest organization that facilitate European legal challenges. This aggregate institutional factor accounts for cross-national variation in domestic responsiveness to Europeanization of the law.

Second, the presence of institutions that expand access to legal arenas, through legal aid or independent enforcement action, enables the pursuit of European rights by segments of society that ordinarily cannot mobilize effective collective action. Supported by the state or private initiatives, these institutions provide the organizational resources necessary for effective litigation. Because these institutions typically target particular populations or issue areas, this factor will generally account for variation in the impact of Europeanization across court systems and fields of law.

Third, the presence of conflicts between national and European law generates grievances that motivate legal challenges. Conversely, the absence of European provisions in some fields eliminates the ECJ as a source of recourse against unfavorable national law, and parallel rules obviate the need for dispute resolution in court. To the extent that conflicts between national and European provisions vary across issue areas, this factor will also account for variation in the impact of Europeanization across specialized court systems and fields of law.

Factors that account for subnational variation among courts and issue areas, access to legal arenas and discrepancies between national and European law, ordinarily influence adaptation independently of political structures that mediate aggregate national transformation. Only in extreme instances, where national law virtually never conflicts with European law, or where endemic conflict coexists with a wealth of institutions that expand access to legal arenas, would forces behind subnational variation exert a substantial impact on aggregate national trends.

The empirical analysis concentrates on the transformation of judicial structures in France, Germany, and the United Kingdom (U.K.). Variations across these member states in political structure, access to legal arenas, and substantive domestic law provide an opportunity to assess the influence of institutional factors on patterns of judicial response to Europeanization. In the first section of this chapter I assess the pressures for domestic adaptation that emanate from the European legal system. I compare the goodness of fit between European and national institutions in each country to establish specific expectations about judicial behavior in each case. In the next section, I evaluate interactions between national courts and the ECJ to assess whether institutional factors account for variation in the rate and extent to which national courts in these three member states instrumentalize the European legal system. I operationalize domestic transformation by comparing patterns of Article 177 referrals in French, German, and U.K. courts.[1] Finally, I assess the empirical findings and the alternative transactionalist explanation.

Adaptational Pressures: European Law and Domestic Institutions

Europeanization of the law places identical demands on national judges. However, the goodness of fit between domestic institutions and European requirements determines the extent to which Europeanization generates pressures for adaptation in national legal structures. Political structures that constitute closer institutional fits to the European system promote aggregate national transformation, while those that conflict with the European system impede aggregate national transformation. Institutions that expand access to legal arenas also promote transformation in the issue areas and court systems they target. Finally, poor fit between national and European institutions is a promoter of transformation in the case of substantive law, where conflicts are a precondition for any judicial action. Below, I discuss European rules and institutions that elicit national judicial participation in the European legal system. Then, I discuss variations in the political structures of France, Germany, and the United Kingdom and their implications for judicial dialogue at the European level.

Courts and Europeanization: Preliminary Rulings and Judicial Doctrine

Judicial mechanisms that constitute forces of Europeanization include the Article 177 reference procedure and a set of doctrines developed in ECJ case law. Article 177 of the Treaty of Rome (1957) provides the Court of Justice with the jurisdiction to provide preliminary rulings on questions raised by national courts concerning the interpretation and validity of Community law. Designed to facilitate national administration of Community policy and promote a uniform interpretation of European law, the Article 177 procedure provides a means to introduce novel European legal rules into domestic legal orders once governed almost exclusively on the basis of national law (Alter 1998a, 126–35).

The Court of Justice then engaged national judiciaries in Europeanization by obliging them to enforce European law. The ECJ's doctrines of direct effect and

---

1. National judicial transformation occurs outside the parameters of Article 177 references as well, for example, when national courts operate as European courts by interpreting European directives that have been transposed into national law and by interpreting European law independently or on the basis of prior preliminary rulings.

supremacy exert the initial pressures to introduce European rules into domestic legal systems. The doctrine of direct effect holds that certain provisions of Community law confer rights and impose obligations on individuals and public authorities (Article 189, Treaty of Rome; Bermann et al. 1993, 180).[2] National courts directly apply these rights and obligations as they derive from European provisions, without the need for national implementing legislation. Individual lit-, igants invoke directly effective Community measures in national courts to settle disputes that formerly would have been resolved on the basis of purely national rules. The doctrine of supremacy holds that European law is supreme to national law and that national courts are obligated to give primacy to Community law over conflicting national law (Hartley 1994; Mancini 1991; Stein 1981; Weiler 1994).[3] Combined, these doctrines empower national courts to exercise judicial review of domestic legislation and enable individuals to replace unwelcome national measures with European provisions.

The ECJ increased pressures for domestic adaptation to Europeanization by declaring that governments can be liable for damages caused to individuals by a failure to apply Community law. National courts order financial compensation for individuals who suffer losses from the nonimplementation or inadequate implementation of European law.[4] State liability for infractions of Community law simultaneously increases individual incentives to pursue their European rights and member-state incentives to apply Community law.

This judicially constructed system attracts attention as a powerful mechanism to transform national legal structures. However, highly variable patterns of interaction between national courts and the ECJ suggest that national judges have not responded uniformly to this invitation to participate in the European legal system. Preexisting domestic institutions condition this variable response to Europeanization.

Domestic Institutional Variation and Responsiveness to Europeanization

Variations in political structure across France, Germany, and the United Kingdom have consequences for the prevailing pattern of state-society relations, which in turn determines the responsiveness of domestic actors to the Europeanization of

2. Casc 26/62, *NV Algemene Transport—en Expeditie Onderneming van Gend & Loos v. Nederlandse Belastingenadministratie*, 1963 European Court Reports (E.C.R.) 1; Case 41/74, *van Duyn v. Home Office*, 1974 E.C.R. 1337; Case 43/75, *Defrenne v. Société Anonyme Belge de Navigation Aerienne Sabena*, 1976 E.C.R. 455; Case 152/84, *Marshall v. Southampton and South-West Hampshire Area Health Authority*, 1986 E.C.R. 723.

3. Case 24/64, *Costa v. ENEL*, 1964 E.C.R. 585; Case 106/77, *Amministrazione delle Finanze dello Stato v. Simmenthal S.p.A.*, 1978 (E.C.R.) 629.

4. Case 6 & 9/90, *Francovich and another v. Italy*, 1991 E.C.R.-I 5357; Case 392/93, *Regina v. HM Treasury, ex parte British Telecommunications plc*, 1996 E.C.R.-I 1631; Case 178–79, 188, 190/94, *Dillenkofer and others v. Germany*, 1996 E.C.R.-I 4845; Case 46 & 48/93, *Brasserie Du Pecheur Sa v. Germany, Regina v. Secretary of State for Transport, ex parte Factortame Ltd and others*, 1996 E.C.R.-I 1029; Case 5/94, *Regina v. Ministry of Agriculture, Fisheries and Food ex parte Hedley Lomas (Ireland) Ltd.*, 1996 E.C.R.-I 2553.

law in each country. In the tradition of Wilson, I argue that political structure influences the propensity for interest group formation and activity: the separation of power among branches of government, the dispersion of power across levels of government, and/or the sharing of power among multiple governing parties can generate multiple opportunities for interest groups to intervene in the decision-making process. Conversely, the concentration and centralization of power create few opportunities for interest groups to gain access to decision-making channels: if petitions to the chief executive fail, few viable alternatives exist. Therefore, the greater the decentralization and dispersion of political authority, the greater the incentive for the formation and agitation of interest groups (Wilson 1973). Groups are not necessarily most effective in decentralized systems, but they have more points of access to attempt to influence policy, and as a result, they have a greater incentive to organize.

Wilson concentrated on the role of political associations in legislative arenas, but the presence and activism of interest groups is also immediately relevant to legal arenas. In his research on the role of law in reform efforts, Galanter defines a position of structural advantage in litigation that is shared by "repeat players," who strategically structure litigation by capitalizing on expertise gained through multiple interactions in court or easy access to specialized legal professionals. Their knowledge allows repeat players to forum-shop for friendly judges, select the best test cases, press to settle whenever the risk of an adverse judgment is high, and target officials who can transform legal victories into tangible gains (Galanter 1974).

Repeat players usually include government agencies, relatively large and wealthy business enterprises, and organized interest groups. Privately organized groups and state-supported public interest agencies can both help individuals draw on legal expertise, increase their litigative persistence and bargaining position, aggregate claims that are too small relative to the cost of judicial remedies, and monitor implementation, giving those who would normally pursue just "one shot" in court the structural advantages of repeat players (Galanter 1974). Multiple empirical studies confirm that organized groups tend to prevail over individuals before courts (Epstein and Rowland 1986; McCann 1994; Olson 1990).

I extend the insights of these two scholars to argue that societal interests will be most likely to be organized for strategic litigation where political structures disperse power. Strategic litigation will also be more likely in fields that affect business interests and in fields where institutions expand access to legal arenas for individuals. By uncovering good test cases and more accommodating judges and by supporting appeals, strategic litigation then contributes to a higher level of Article 177 referrals.

European political structures disperse power widely: action must typically be initiated by the European Commission, adopted by overwhelming to unanimous agreement in the Council of Ministers, approved by the European Parliament in some instances, and ultimately implemented by member states. The European system also confers substantial power to the judiciary, including judicial review of secondary legislation and review of governmental action for compatibility with a "higher law" (treaties). European judicial review is ultimately accessible to European institutions, national governments, and citizens alike. EU scholars have observed that this decentralized structure offers many access points (Grande 1996) and has begun to attract interest groups (Hayward 1995). However, because effective interest organization develops gradually, societal responsiveness to European opportunities will not emerge rapidly across the EU. Where domestic structures also disperse power, societal interests will be better organized to engage in the strategic litigation that promotes judicial participation in the European legal system. Therefore, the goodness of fit between European political structures and domestic political structures determines the scope of adaptational pressure that Europeanization exerts across member states.

The extent to which domestic political structures parallel the European pattern varies substantially across the French, German, and United Kingdom cases. France and the United Kingdom both concentrate political power in the institutions of the central state, while Germany disperses political power in a system of cooperative federalism. The French Constitutional Council exercises an extremely limited form of constitutional review, and United Kingdom courts do not function as coequal branches of government, but the German Constitutional Court does serve as a formidable check on governmental action. The following specification of domestic political structures illustrates that Germany represents the closest institutional fit with the European system.

In France, political power is largely concentrated in the executive branch, where the government passes laws related to its own domain (*pouvoir reglementaire*) that constitute 90 percent of French legislation (Provine 1996). The implementation of French law is also highly centralized within the national administration. France has undergone reforms to decentralize power and give more autonomy to local districts (Schmidt 1990), but this decentralization is not comparable with federal governance. France has a civil law jurisdiction with a narrow range of opportunities for constitutional review, a political culture that has historically rejected and limited judicial lawmaking (*le gouvernement des juges*), and a long tradition of public law that stresses administrative efficiency (Provine 1996; Schwarze 1993, 1996; Stone 1992; Szyszczak and Delicostopoulos 1997). Constitutional review, and the power of the French Constitutional Council, may have expanded since the 1980s (Stone 1992; Mullen 1998), but judicial review of legislation and judicial power are still substantially more circumscribed in France than in Germany. Most important, constitutional challenges to French law are possible only before legislation is promulgated, and can be initiated only by the president, prime minister, chief of either the National Assembly or the Senate, or a group of sixty members of either chamber of parliament (Provine 1996; Stone 1992). That is, only governing elites, but not French citizens, can request constitutional review.

By contrast, in Germany political power is shared by federal and Länder institutions, where the federal government is largely responsible for writing most legislation and Länder governments are responsible for implementation. Länder governments' direct representation at the federal level in the Bundesrat also gives them the power to approve or reject all federal legislation that affects Länder, which amounts to two thirds of all federal legislation (Goetz 1995; Sbragia 1992). German governments also rule in two-party coalitions, which further diffuses governmental authority and requires a consensual form of decision making. Postwar (West) Germany has a civil law jurisdiction with extensive forms of constitutional review, a political culture that accepts judicial censure and authority, and a well-established tradition of public law that stresses individual protection from arbitrary administration (Blankenburg 1996; Ladeur 1995; Schwarze 1996). German legislation can be challenged on constitutional grounds at any point after promulgation. Moreover, while the federal government, Länder governments, and one third of the Bundestag members monopolize the right to request abstract constitutional review, individual citizens can request concrete constitutional review of suspect law (Stone 1992, 232).

In the United Kingdom, political power is concentrated in the governing cabinet of the party that controls parliament. Single-district, first-past-the-post electoral rules generate legislative majorities for a single party, and party discipline generally ensures that Parliament will approve the prime minister's proposed legislation. The United Kingdom has a common-law jurisdiction[5] with no constitutional review, a political culture that values minimal judicial interference in politics, and the absence of a long-standing public law tradition to control administrative action. Parliament is sovereign, that is, domestic legislation is not subject to constitutional review. Judges practice a form of judicial review that holds government and the administration accountable to existing legislation, but judges do not review the legislation itself. British institutions narrowly construe statutory interpretations by judges and subject all judicial interpretation to parliamentary overrule (Kritzer 1996; Schwarze 1996; Sterett 1997). Therefore, the government can legislate the legality of any action if it seeks to exempt itself from a constraint imposed by prior judicial censure of its actions.

Given these political structures, where German groups can hope to influence politics through both land and federal institutions and through individual applications for administrative and constitutional review, German groups should be better organized for political action and legal challenge than their British and French counterparts. Indeed, German patterns of interest intermediation are highly organized: functionally organized groups enjoy consultation at the Länder level, and peak interest organizations participate in the review of draft legislation at the federal level (Hayward 1995). And victories before German courts cannot be easily overturned through administrative fiat or legislative overrule. The German system contrasts with France, where less organized societal interests, generally excluded from decision making and less confident that

5. England and Wales share a common-law system, and the system in Northern Ireland is similar to that in England and Wales. Scotland has its own legal system, which combines elements of common and civil-law traditions. Data for interactions with the European legal system treat the United Kingdom as a single entity (Kritzer 1996, 81).

judicial action will provide recourse (Provine 1996), are more likely to express demands in periodic waves of confrontation with the government. The German system also contrasts with the United Kingdom, where the governing party can overrule any court decision by statute and successfully exclude even highly organized groups from decision-makers, a situation illustrated most dramatically by Margaret Thatcher's exclusion of trade unions during the 1980s (Goetz 1995; Sbragia 1992).

Therefore, because German political structures inspire higher aggregate levels of interest organization than British and French political structures, and because interest organization facilitates legal challenges, Germany should be more responsive to Europeanization of the law. German citizens and interest groups see a familiar institutional landscape in the EU (Goetz 1995; Sbragia 1992): they need only add a layer to their existing system to seize opportunities at the European level. As a result, German courts will face the greatest bottom-up societal pressures to participate in the European legal system. Conversely, British and French political structures should both be more resistant to Europeanization, which demands a politicized form of legal activism that is not well established in either country. To conclude, on the basis of domestic political structure, German courts should participate the most frequently in the European legal system, while French and British courts should participate less often.

Finally, I also expect that domestic variation in institutionalized access to legal arenas and the substantive content of law will influence adaptational patterns in particular court systems and fields of law. Pressures for adaptation will increase wherever institutions facilitate individual legal challenges, given substantive conflict between national and European law. And in the case of more powerful commercial interests who independently engage in strategic litigation, pressures for adaptation will increase in the presence of conflicts between national and European law. Therefore, references should cluster within issue areas subject to strategic litigators and legal conflicts.

An Incomplete Judicial Architecture: Europeanization and the Transformation of National Legal Structures

Cross-National Patterns of Transformation in French, German, and U.K. Courts

The impact of Europeanization on national judicial transformation varies across France, Germany, and the United Kingdom in a pattern that is consistent with variation in domestic political structures. National judicial participation in the European legal system varies substantially across these three member states. Courts in Germany have referred almost twice as many questions to the ECJ under Article 177 as courts in France, and both French and German references dramatically outpace U.K. references (see Table 6.1). The United Kingdom joined the European Community fifteen years later than France and Germany, but the timing

Table 6.1   Total Article 177 references to December 31, 1994

Germany	901
France	501
United Kingdom	186

Source: Court of Justice of the European Communities 1995, 261.

Table 6.2   Average annual Article 177 referral rates

Average Annual Number of References	United Kingdom	France	Germany
During the fourteen years following the	1974–87	1965–78	1965–78
first reference	5.4	5	20.1
From the fifteenth year after the first	1988–94	1979–94	1979–94
reference to 1994	15.7	24.4	39.4

Source: Court of Justice of the European Communities 1995, 162.

of entry contributes little to an explanation of the variable referral rates among these three member states.

Despite their status as original members, Germany and France have never experienced similar referral rates. On average, German courts referred questions at a rate four times greater than French courts from 1965 to 1978, and German courts continued to refer at a substantially higher rate than French courts from 1979 to 1994 (see Table 6.2). The average referral rate of U.K. courts approximately matched the average French referral rate during each member states' initial fourteen years of participation in the Article 177 procedure. However, while average French referral rates climbed approximately fivefold after this initial period, average U.K. referral rates only trebled (see Table 6.2).

The United Kingdom remains the source of disproportionately few references. After approximately two decades of membership, U.K. courts refer many fewer questions to the ECJ than member states with broadly similar economic and demographic profiles such as Germany, Italy, and France. U.K. courts do not even keep pace with the courts from member states with smaller economies and populations, such as Belgium and the Netherlands (see Table 6.3). British courts have exceptionally low rates of participation in the Article 177 procedure based on either their population base (Golub 1996a; Weiler and Dehousse 1992) or on their intra-EU trade activity (Table 6.3; Golub 1996a; Stone Sweet and Brunell 1998).

However, U.K. courts' citations of ECJ rulings indicate that they engage the European legal system to a much greater extent than their referral rates suggest. A Lexis search for U.K. citations to European jurisprudence counted 478 citations (Kritzer 1996, 170), in comparison with only 186 referrals for preliminary rulings. The practice of invoking existing case law is consistent with the common-law system, which formally respects the binding force of legal precedents. Indeed, within a year of accession to membership, a British high court judge, Lord Denning, issued highly restrictive guidelines to justify Article 177 references. One

Table 6.3   Total Article 177 references, 1990–95

Germany	300
Italy	211
France	166
The Netherlands	119
Belgium	107
United Kingdom	87

Sources: Commission of the European Communities, "Thirteenth Annual Report on Monitoring the Application of Community Law, 1995," COM (96) 600 final, 415; Commission, "Twelfth Annual Report on Monitoring the Application of Community Law, 1994," *Official Journal of the European Communities* C-254 1995, 164; "Tenth Annual Report to the European Parliament on Commission Monitoring of the Application of Community Law, 1992," *Official Journal of the European Communities* C-233 1993, 212; Commission, "Eighth Annual Report to the European Parliament on Commission Monitoring of the Application of Community Law, 1990," *Official Journal of the European Communities* C-338 1991, 77.

of Lord Denning's explicit instructions to U.K. judges is to follow a previous ECJ ruling rather than refer a similar question, unless the judge specifically seeks to challenge past jurisprudence. Over twenty years of membership, and a relaxation of doctrinal guidelines on references in the 1980s (Craig 1998, 205–6), have not been followed by a convergence of British referral rates with those of other member states (Golub 1996b; Court of Justice 1995, 262). Yet if U.K. referrals and citations are considered together (664 invocations of European law), U.K. judicial participation begins to approximate French patterns of referral.

It would be highly unlikely that a parallel Lexis search for French citations, were it available, would yield similar results because the citation of precedents is alien to French legal institutions. Indeed, the civil-law origin of the European legal system is responsible for the fact that preliminary rulings of the ECJ formally apply to the parties of a case and have no general effect (Toth 1990, 202, 321, 465; Cohen 1996, 435–37). Even the ECJ refrained from making any explicit references to its own rulings for a long period, reinforced existing case law by repeating past provisions verbatim in new rulings, and only began to cite previous judgments directly as of 1973, after common-law states joined the European Community (Hartley 1994, 84; Schermers and Waelbroeck 1987, 86).

If the United Kingdom common-law tradition helps account for an unusually low rate of Article 177 references from U.K. courts, the substantial divergence between German referral patterns and French and British invocations of European law is consistent with variation in political structures among these three states. The decentralization and dispersion of political power in Germany, including individual access to constitutional review, should promote more interest organization, which in turn facilitates strategic litigation for political ends. A comparison of domestic civil litigation indicates that German society is more litigious than British or French society (see Table 6.4). If Germans use courts more

Table 6.4 Domestic civil litigation rates, 1989 and 1982 (per 100,000 inhabitants)

Country/Year	Civil procedures	First instance adversarial	Appeal de novo
West Germany (1989)	9,400	4,911	251
France (1982)	3,640	1,950	250
England/Wales (1982)	5,300	1,200	16

Source: Blankenburg, 1996, 295. The German first instance adversarial rate includes procedures in administrative and labor courts, which Blankenburg included only in the note of his table.

frequently at the domestic level than the British or the French, it is not surprising that German courts are more frequently a source of access to the ECJ through Article 177 referrals.

Subnational Patterns of Transformation in French, German, and United Kingdom Courts

Within member states, references originate unevenly across different jurisdictions of national judiciaries.[6] Forty-six percent of all German references to the ECJ derive from tax courts. The ten German courts that have sent twenty or more references account for 64 percent of all ECJ referrals (Court of Justice 1994, 14–21). In France, the civil and commercial branch of the judiciary sent 56 percent of all references, and the four French courts that have sent twenty or more references account for 23 percent of all French referrals to the ECJ. The British concentration in references is situated in a single court system: the High Court of Justice, Queen's Bench Division, sends 41 percent of all British Article 177 references (see Table 6.5).

The distribution of French references between administrative courts (10 percent) and the judiciary courts (90 percent, from all other courts listed in Table 6.5) is consistent with national institutional traditions. French administrative tribunals are actually an extension of the executive: administrative adjudication formally belongs to the bureaucracy rather than the judiciary in France. Closely connected to the regime, administrative judges identify with state interests and are less likely to challenge government on the basis of European obligations. This has been particularly true of the highest administrative court, the Conseil d'État, which was among the most reluctant participants in the European legal system. This resistant orientation plausibly acts to discourage applicants from attempting to invoke European norms and request Article 177 referrals before administrative tribunals.

6. Referral rates vary across level of the judiciary as well: courts of last instance refer a minority of cases in most states, including France, Germany, and the United Kingdom. Many scholars attribute higher referral rates among lower courts to an interest in judicial empowerment (Alter 1996b; Burley and Mattli 1993; Slaughter, Stone Sweet, and Weiler 1998).

Table 6.5   Concentration of Article 177 references within German, French, and UK courts (in %)

German Courts		French Courts		UK Courts	
Tax	46	Civil and commercial	56	Civil Jurisdictions:	
				High Court of Justice,	41
				Queen's Bench Division	
				High Court of Justice,	3
				Chancery Division	
				County Courts	0.6
Civil and criminal	17	Criminal	11	Criminal Jurisdictions	13
				Crown, Magistrates Courts	
				House of Lords	10
Administrative	22	Administrative	10	Administrative Tribunals:	
				Taxation	6
				Insurance	4
Social	11	Social	23	Social Security	10
Labor	5			Industrial Tribunals,	7
				Employment Appeal Tribunal	
				Courts in Scotland and	
				Northern Ireland	6

Sources: Court of Justice of the European Communities 1994, 6–21, 35–37; and Alter 1996a, 204, for the division of cases at the Cour d'Appel and Cour de Cassation, which take all appeals from social, criminal, commercial, and civil courts. The percentages of references derive from each court system within the member state.

Other distributions of references among different court systems within individual member states reflect both the content of European law and the organizational resources that potential beneficiaries have to pursue multilevel litigation. Article 177 references derive overwhelmingly from civil jurisdictions that involve commercial disputes—references from German tax courts, French civil/commercial courts, and the United Kingdom's High Court of Justice, Queen's Bench division, which has a civil jurisdiction that includes a commercial court. European law overwhelmingly regulates economic activity, which would give rise to proportionately more conflicts with national law in this area. And in terms of access to legal arenas, "business and commercial interests are simply in a better position to purchase the leverage of due process" (Scheingold 1974, 127).

For instance, differences between domestic and European litigation rates in Germany are consistent with the narrow base of and costly access to European law. The rate of domestic litigation across different German jurisdictions is inverse to the pattern of Article 177 references across different German jurisdictions. Compare the litigation rates in Table 6.6 to the concentration of references in Table 6.5: labor courts hold the highest domestic litigation rate and refer the fewest Article 177 references, while tax courts hold the lowest domestic litigation rate and refer the greatest number of Article 177 references.

European law has a lot to say about duties and excise taxes that impede trade and much less to say about labor regulation. Germany, conversely, has a highly

Table 6.6   Domestic litigation rates across German courts

German courts	Litigation per 100,000 population
Labor	601
Social	275
Administrative	192
Civil and commercial	No comparable data available
Tax	70

Source: Blankenburg 1996, 278.

developed domestic system of labor law. Moreover, businesses pursuing tax claims have many more resources to pursue European litigation than the individual claimants before labor, social, and administrative courts. Multilevel litigation is more costly than standard domestic litigation, with delays for an Article 177 preliminary ruling averaging up to two years. Delays and costs only rise if litigants must appeal their questions through multiple levels of the national judiciary before obtaining references to the ECJ. A highly celebrated case of vindication of Community rights testifies to the incredible frustration that characterizes individual access to European justice: Helen Marshall spent sixteen years in court before she was able to receive financial compensation for gender discrimination that superseded national limits on damages awards. Outside of a small set of such "success" stories, Carol Harlow characterizes the citizen enforcement of Community law as a "fantasy" (Harlow 1996, 9, 13).

Evidence from the rates of references by subject matter provides a further indication that access to legal arenas is an important component of domestic transformation. The two fields with the greatest concentration of European litigation include the free movement of goods and agriculture, both the province of producer interests (see Table 6.7). National rates of European litigation in these fields are matched by the fields of social security and social provisions, generally the province of individuals, only in the United Kingdom. Particularly striking is the U.K. litigation rate for social provisions, which is more than four times the overall EU rate for social provisions and four times the general European litigation rate for the United Kingdom. United Kingdom litigation rates for social security also outpace the overall EU rate for social security and the general European litigation rate for the United Kingdom (see Tables 6.7 and 6.8).

I argue that this pattern of litigation derives from the interaction of two British institutional factors, where (1) substantive law involves significant conflict with European obligations, and (2) specialized public institutions facilitate individual access to European justice. Multiple discrepancies between equality measures in the United Kingdom and the EU inspire challenges to national law that are based on European social provisions. Universal welfare provisions in the United Kingdom, which often determine eligibility on the basis of residence or nationality conditions, can lead to conflict with European provisions designed to promote the free movement of people and prohibit nationality discrimination. Poor fit

Table 6.7 Percentage of Article 177 references from the United Kingdom, France, Germany, and the EU, by Field

Country	Free movement of goods	Agriculture	Social security	Social provisions
U.K.	14	17	14	17
France	18	16	8	1
Germany	24	30	9	4
EU	18	20	10	4

Source: Data base compiled by Alec Stone Sweet and the Research and Documentation Division of the ECJ. Data is available in Appendix A, Stone Sweet and Brunell 1998, 78–79. This table indicates litigation rates in each country across fields. These fields represent the only individual policy areas where percentages exceeded eleven percent for at least one of these three member states. Social Provisions (Articles 117–122 EEC) does not rank fourth in overall EU litigation rates by field. I have included it to illustrate the UK's position as an outlier in the field of equal pay between men and women (Article 119).

Table 6.8 Percentage of all Article 177 references by field in the United Kingdom, France, and Germany

Country	Free movement of goods	Agriculture	Social security	Social provisions	Percentage of total references in EU
United Kingdom	5	5	8	24	6
France	17	13	13	4	17
Germany	40	44	8	24	30

Source: Data base compiled by Alec Stone Sweet and the Research and Documentation Division of the ECJ. Data is available in Appendix A, Stone Sweet and Brunell 1998, 78–79. This table shows the extent to which each member state accounts for the share of all European litigation in these fields.

between substantive law in these two fields then yields elevated rates of European litigation due to the institutional activism of the British Equal Opportunities Commission (EOC) and the organization of British Social Security tribunals, which are designed to minimize costs for plaintiffs, and to a special form of legal aid unique to the United Kingdom (see Citizens' Advice Bureaux in Table 6.9).

With respect to social provisions and the EOC, the United Kingdom provides a particularly promising environment to pursue rights under European gender equality provisions. The British EOC is an independent public agency that collects and responds to complaints regarding gender equality and receives state funding to litigate cases. Its public advocacy role is rare in the EU and unusual with respect to its resource base and institutional aim. Carol Harlow attenuates the exceptionalism of the British EOC, labeling it a "statutory pressure group" (Harlow 1992, 344–48; 1993, 247; Harlow and Rawlings 1992, 285–87). A government legal adviser engaged in the promotion of equality in France found the British EOC to be "perverse," since it operates as one agent of the state bringing actions against the state itself.[7] Perverse or not, the EOC is an exceptionally

7. Interview at the Service for Women's Rights, Paris, 29 February 1996.

Table 6.9 Government legal aid expenditures in France, Germany, and the United Kingdom

	West Germany (1989)	France (1993)	England/Wales (1989)[a]
Civil and administrative legal aid	3.48	0.80	9.54
Citizens Advice Bureaux	No comparable institution	No comparable institution	1.24

Source: Blankenburg 1996, 298.

Note: The figures for funds spent on legal aid are European Currency Units (ecu) per capita.

[a] The UK changed rules to reduce the number of individuals who are eligible for regular legal aid in 1990 and 1993, thus substantially reducing access to public funds for litigation (Kritzer 1996, 141).

empowered institution to promote equality with legal strategies. Its only parallel in the EU is the Irish Employment Equality Agency.

With respect to social security, the organization of Social Security tribunals and British legal aid facilitate individual appeals to European rights. In the United Kingdom a set of Social Security tribunals handles the vast majority of appeals against negative decisions by agencies administering social benefit programs, keeping individual requests for benefits outside the normal court system. Individuals who take their cases before Social Security tribunals do not need representation by lawyers and can receive legal advice from a variety of sources, which reduces costs for claimants. Citizens' Advice Bureaux, typically financed by local governments, are the single most common source of representation before Social Security tribunals. Individuals who consider appeals to Social Security tribunals can access regular legal aid in order to get advice from an attorney before initiating a claim as well. Unions are a further source of advice, representing 6 percent of claimants before Social Security tribunals (Kritzer 1996, 133, 137–39).

The coincidence of both institutional factors is largely missing in the French and German cases. French law generates few substantive conflicts with European obligations in the field of gender discrimination, and disputes related to indirect discrimination in social security reach French social courts at roughly half the rate of those related to the concerns of producer interests, which is consistent with the lower availability of legal aid in the French system (see Tables 6.5, 6.7, and 6.9). Discriminatory gender provisions in German law do inspire some European litigation, but the measures do not generate the disproportionately high rate of challenges experienced in the United Kingdom (see Tables 6.7 and 6.8) because Germany lacks any institutional equivalent to the British EOC. German *Frauenbeauftragte* help women resolve conflicts and promote equal opportunities within particular organizational settings, but they do not actually litigate grievances as does the EOC. Conversely, German social courts are easily accessible to individuals, but the combination of contribution-based social insurance and means-tested schemes generate fewer conflicts with European obligations related to social security.[8]

Domestic Institutions and Structural Change: The Potential for Legal Transformation

This chapter demonstrates that the transformation of national legal structures through Europeanization remains incomplete and varies across member states in a pattern that is consistent with domestic institutional variation. In my concluding discussion, I summarize the correspondence between domestic institutions and structural adaptation, assess the variable potential for legal transformation across issue areas, and critique the competing transactionalist model.

Europeanization and Transformation: The Long Shadow of Domestic Institutions

This study suggests that preexisting domestic institutions account for variation in the impact of Europeanization: the general pattern of interaction between national courts and the ECJ in Germany, France, and the United Kingdom is consistent with variation in political structure across these states. German courts are the most active participants in the European judicial dialogue, and German political structure provides the best "institutional fit" with European political structure. The dispersion of power in both systems promotes the organization of societal interests into groups that can pursue strategic legal action. German society has long been prepared to seize the opportunities of Europeanization through judicial forums.

Conversely, lower British and French rates of participation in the European legal system are consistent with the lack of fit between domestic political structure and the European system. The centralized political structures of the French and British states create a less hospitable environment for the formation of societal groups that can instrumentalize courts to pursue political aims. Unusually low British referral rates, which coincide with much higher rates of citation to ECJ case law, are also consistent with the common law's acceptance of existing jurisprudence as a binding source of law.

Between Law and Leverage: The Role of Political Power in Litigation

France, Germany, and the United Kingdom share some patterns of judicial adaptation despite their distinctive domestic institutions: all three states experience concentration in Article 177 references among particular court systems. The con-

---

8. Discrepancies between European and domestic law also contribute to litigation at the Court of Human Rights in Strasbourg: European litigation has been virtually the only means to pursue human rights cases in the United Kingdom. Conversely, in Germany, where domestic law provides effective recourse, appeals to Strasbourg are much less frequent.

centration of references from courts that overwhelmingly deal with disputes of a commercial nature is a predictable consequence of the overwhelmingly commercial content of European law and its greater accessibility to producer groups. However, the distinctions that do exist among the issues referred in these three countries provide a further illustration of the impact of domestic institutions on the instrumentalization of European law. The United Kingdom has a disproportionately high number of references in the fields of social security and social provisions. Litigation in these fields is supported by state institutions (Social Security tribunals, Citizens' Advice Bureaux, and the EOC) that reduce the risks and costs of claims for individuals challenging discriminatory treatment.

Gradually, the dispersed authority of the EU polity should encourage societal interest organization that facilitates legal transformation. However, such change is likely only in the long term, since novel forms of collective action develop slowly and are extremely costly at the European and transnational level. Litigative onslaughts that exert significant pressures for adaptation do not yet regularly compel the transformation of domestic legal structures. Their potential to become a more common feature of European politics depends substantially on the mobilization of society into organized groups capable of concerted legal action. The divergent patterns of litigation across subject areas, where the experiences of organizationally and institutionally supported British men and women differs from those of the disparate individuals facing gender discrimination in most states, suggests that the incorporation of political factors is necessary to bridge the gap between legal pressures for Europeanization and actual transformations in national legal structures.

A Critique of the Competing Transactionalist Explanation

The competing transactionalist explanation cannot account for the currently large variation in reference patterns among France, Germany, and the United Kingdom. Alec Stone Sweet and Thomas Brunell support a transactionalist argument by correlating references with trade. The relatively high correlation, adjusted R2 = 0.73–0.77 (Stone Sweet and Brunell 1998), is hardly surprising: if most European law is trade related, then most appeals to the law should concern trade, and if the EU functions according to its rules, then trade should rise as well.

Yet, the United Kingdom is an outlier, with too few references for its trade profile (Golub 1996a; Stone Sweet and Brunell 1998, 68). An outlier with a small n (n = 12) is not particularly encouraging, especially given that the model includes much spurious correlation. Because Stone Sweet and Brunell do not disaggregate references by policy sector, they include references that have nothing to do with trade in their model. References clearly related to trade, that is, the free movement of goods (18%) and agriculture (20%), do not even constitute half of all references (see Table 6.7). Other fields with references can have indirect linkages to trade, but some areas that generate many references—social policy, social security, and the free movement of workers—have no connection to trade. Including non-trade-related references skews the results.

In particular, the United Kingdom would be a more extreme outlier if its disproportionately high share of gender discrimination cases (see Tables 6.7 and 6.8), which have no trade linkage, were excluded from the pool of references. The French originally insisted on the equal pay provision under Article 119 EEC in order to prevent French firms from facing a competitive disadvantage relative to other member-states' firms who might be able to exploit cheap female labor under domestic law. However, disputes in this field concern individual challenges to discriminatory laws and company policies and do not generate debates about international trade competitiveness.

This chapter demonstrates that preexisting patterns of state-society relations, which derive from variation in domestic political structure, remain consistent with the pace and extent of judicial adaptation to Europeanization. The findings have important implications for the nature of European governance: the variable transformation of national judiciaries provides a source of fragmentation for the European legal system, as courts engage European law at different rates and inconsistently invoke European legal norms. Long focused on the centralizing force of ECJ jurisprudence, research on legal integration must take account of factors that constrain domestic transformations. As we have seen, domestic institutional factors, including political structure, access to legal arenas, and substantive law, mediate patterns of judicial adaptation to Europeanization.

CHAPTER SEVEN

Adjusting to EU Environmental Policy:
Change and Persistence of
Domestic Administrations

Christoph Knill and Andrea Lenschow

Europeanization may occur in multiple ways and the domestic structures affected by it are manifold, as this volume shows. Here, we focus on the domestic impacts of European integration from the perspective of European Union (EU) regulatory policies.

Regulatory policies are particularly prone to have administrative impacts. Concrete administrative implications are transmitted via both substantive and procedural obligations defined in EU legislation. The challenges put to national administrations may be more or less fundamental. Hence, the question arises of what are the effects of the EU's increasing engagement in regulatory policy-making on well-established administrative patterns in the member states? Under which conditions can we expect administrative change on the national level?

To answer these questions, we draw on empirical results from the implementation of EU environmental policy in Britain and Germany. The comprehensive development as well as the broad variety of its regulatory requirements renders the environmental field a particularly appropriate area for the investigation of domestic impacts of EU regulatory policy (Knill in press[b]). To grasp the regulatory variety, we focus on four pieces of European legislation with distinct administrative implications—namely, the Drinking Water, Access to Environmental Information, and Environmental Impact Assessment (EIA) Directives, as well as the Environmental Management and Auditing Systems (EMAS) Regulation.[1] The selection of

We express our gratitude to the editors of this volume as well as all project participants who have provided very helpful comments. Special thanks go to Maria Green Cowles, Alberta Sbragia, Fritz W. Scharpf, Vivien Schmidt, and Amy Verdun. Furthermore, we would like to thank the participants of the ECPR Joint Session at Warwick, March 1998, for critical suggestions.

1. 80/778/EEC; 90/313/EEC; 85/337/EEC; Regulation (EEC) No. 1836/93.

Britain and Germany, with their considerable differences in terms of prevailing administrative structures and practices (Héritier, Knill, and Mingers 1996), on the one hand, and these four policies with their different kinds of administrative implications, on the other hand, allows us to compare the adaptation process.

To assess the domestic impact of EU environmental policy, we distinguish two dimensions—administrative structures and administrative styles. On the one hand, EU policies put pressure on national administrations because of the structural requirements they tend to imply. These requirements may address concrete institutional structures related to the presence, design, or integration of regulatory authorities in the overall system. For instance, a regulation may call for the creation of new structures (an environmental agency), the centralization or decentralization of regulatory processes (by introducing uniform reporting requirements to a central authority), or organizational change on the horizontal level (by requiring the coordination of previously distinct administrative tasks). On the other hand, European adaptation requirements may refer to the dimension of administrative style, including patterns of state intervention as well as administrative interest mediation. On the level of state intervention, two contrasting types are often distinguished: a hierarchical style of intervention imposing uniform, substantive standards, and a more flexible and discretionary style allowing for some level of self-regulation. Different forms of state intervention tend to go hand in hand with particular patterns of interest intermediation. These may range from formal and legalistic styles in the interaction between public authorities and the addressees of the regulation, to more informal and pragmatic patterns, with administrative actors playing a more mediating role between the different interests involved.

The empirical evidence presented below shows that the level of adaptation can neither be directly deduced from the respective policy (one regulation facilitating national adaptation in contrast to another), nor do systematic country differences exist with respect to their capability to adapt. To nevertheless explain the seemingly confusing patterns of national adaptation we adopt a historical institutionalist perspective. Based on the understanding that institutionally grown structures and routines prevent easy adaptation to exogenous pressure (Krasner 1988; March and Olsen 1989), we trace administrative adaptation to the "goodness of fit" between European policy requirements and existing national structures and procedures. In developing this argument, we suggest modifications to the frequently static historical-institutionalist framework; furthermore, we propose a link to an actor- or interest-centered analysis.

We proceed first, by developing the empirical question in detail: What are the institutional requirements that are implied in the four selected policies and what were the national responses? Then, we introduce the explanatory model: focusing on the aspect of institutional fit, clear patterns of adaptational behavior begin to emerge. A gray area that remains with respect to defining the boundaries between institutional fit or misfit points to the need for a modified, more dynamic and open, institution-based explanation. In the final section, we use empirical evidence to illustrate the explanatory model.

The Empirical Question

When investigating the administrative impact of the four pieces of EU environmental legislation under study, we find that different policy instruments may imply different administrative structures as well as patterns of administrative style. The analysis of corresponding forms of domestic adjustment to these varying European requirements indicates that patterns of domestic transformation follow no simple "country-based" or "policy-based" logic.

Administrative Implications of Environmental Legislation

The 1980 *Drinking Water Directive* specifies quality standards for water intended for human consumption. These standards apply to a range of substances that, at certain levels of concentration in the water, may pose a threat to human health. The Directive also establishes how often and by what means compliance with these standards should be monitored. The practical burden of compliance with the Directive therefore lies with the water providers, which may be public or private, national or local. Although not implying any direct institutional requirements, adaptational pressure may emanate from the distributional effects of the Directive. Are the existing water providers able and willing to carry the costs of implementation, or are organizational changes needed to facilitate compliant water provision? On the level of state-society relations, the Drinking Water Directive assumes hierarchical structures of intervention and quite formal and legalistic patterns of administrative interest intermediation. The substantive standards defined in the Directive are not negotiable and uniformly apply to all water providers. (Flexibility exists only with respect to some substances where guidance values rather than mandatory values are specified in the legislation.) Water providers and the superior health authority are also obliged to follow certain monitoring and reporting procedures.

The *Access to Environmental Information Directive* was adopted in 1990 and is part of the European Commission's attempt to make environmental information more easily available to the public in order to reduce enforcement and monitoring difficulties experienced with EU environmental policies. To make the activities of both public authorities and the regulated industries accountable to the public, the Directive requires that relevant authorities holding information on the environment make this information available to the persons requesting it. In short, the Directive establishes a "passive" regulatory procedure, as the immediately addressed public and private authorities are obliged to respond to requests, not to proactively engage in the provision of information. The explicit institutional implications of the Directive depend in magnitude on the information demand structure. Pressure for organizational changes may develop with regard to necessary increases in staff in order to effectively deal with information requests or to the need to facilitate a more regular exchange of data between organizational units. The procedural focus of the Directive affects patterns of administrative style and here, most notably, forms of administrative interest intermediation, as it demands open and transparent channels between the general public and the administration. The Directive strengthens the opportunities of third parties to control public and private economic actors; hence, it undermines images of an omnipotent administration.

The *EMAS Regulation* establishes a management tool helping European companies to evaluate the environmental impact of their activities. Companies voluntarily adopt an environmental policy and conduct an environmental review. An officially appointed, independent and accredited environmental auditor validates the environmental statement subsequently prepared by the company. The EMAS Regulation emphasizes industrial self-regulation by the voluntary introduction of an environmental management system. In other words, the level of direct state intervention is low. The state's role is to facilitate self-regulatory processes by providing and maintaining the institutional framework for the auditing process.

Finally, the 1985 *EIA Directive* obliges developers of formally specified kinds of public and private projects to provide information regarding the environmental impact of these projects to a designated public authority in the area of the environment. This environmental impact assessment must then be taken into consideration by those public authorities that are responsible for the authorization of the project(s) in question. The EIA Directive imposes a procedural requirement on public and private investors as well as regulatory authorities; it does not impose any substantive standards (specifying under what conditions a project should be denied authorization, for instance). Hence, the Directive mixes hierarchical elements, related to the requirement to carry out an EIA for a defined range of cases, with indirect procedural rules encouraging public participation and inducing awareness raising among investors. Considering institutional arrangements, the EIA Directive implies a concentration or at least coordination of administrative control responsibilities. Since an impact assessment will deal with the project's implications for air, water, and soil pollution as well as the threats for flora, fauna, and human health, the designated public authority ought to be able to evaluate these impacts in a comprehensive way, hence the need for integrating administrative structures. Table 7.1 summarizes the above considerations.

National Responses to EU Adaptation Pressure

In the following brief preview of the national responses to the policies' structural implications, we observe a seemingly unsystematic picture (see Table 7.2).

With some time delay, Britain managed to meet the requirements of the Drinking Water Directive not only through considerable investments but also by establishing new structures of hierarchical state control (Maloney and Richardson 1995). Its reaction to the Environmental Information Directive was more timely than the implementation of the Drinking Water legislation. Also, it was more proactive than the EU Directive explicitly called for; Britain established structures for the active provision of environmental information and departed from its for-

Table 7.1 Administrative implications of the policies under study

Policy type	Administrative style	Administrative structure
Drinking Water	*Intervention Patterns* hierarchical, uniform, substantive, low flexibility *Interest Intermediation* formal and legalistic	Indirect organizational implications
Access to Information	*Intervention Patterns* procedural *Interest Intermediation* transparency	Organizational implications
EIA	*Intervention Patterns* hierarchical, procedural *Interest Intermediation* (limited) public participation	Concentration and coordination of administrative competencies
EMAS	*Intervention Patterns* self-regulation, procedural, high flexibility *Interest Intermediation* not directly affected	Creation of facilitating structures

Table 7.2 National responses to EU adaptation requirements

Response	Britain	Germany
Drinking water	Delayed adaptation	Delayed adaptation
Access to information	Adaptation	Resistance
EIA	Resistance	Resistance
EMAS	Adaptation	Adaptation

EIA = Environmental Impact Assessment.
EMAS = Environmental Management and Auditing System.

merly rather secretive administrative procedures (Knill 1998). Britain reacted equally willingly to the institutional implications of the EMAS Regulation. Only in the case of the EIA Directive does Britain continue to resist adaptation (Knill 1998). The Directive would imply a shift toward a more formal regulatory framework as well as increases in hierarchical forms of coordination.

Turning to Germany, it long resisted the implementation of the Drinking Water Directive but in the end adapted to its requirements, taking advantage of technological innovations and using complementary economic instruments to deal with the redistributive implications of the legislation. Administrative resistance persisted in the cases of the Environmental Information and EIA Directives. In the former case, resistance became evident already on the level of formal transposition, which was based on an overly narrow interpretation of the EU Directive. Also on the level of practical application of the law, administrative actors frequently blocked rather than facilitated public information requests (Lenschow 1997; Scherzberg 1994). Legal proceedings already brought before the ECJ provide evi-

dence of the degree of German resistance. Legal proceedings are equally reveal-
ing with respect to Germany's reaction to the EIA Directive. Germany particularly resisted the integrative approach of the legislation, which would have implied
changes to its authorization procedures, which are separated by environmental
media such as air or water. Institutional adaptation was less of a problem in the
case of the EMAS Regulation. Germany willingly created the institutional structures that were needed (Lenschow 1997).

How do we explain these diverse national responses to EU-imposed adaptation
pressure? A clear pattern exists neither on the policy level nor on the national level.
Recalling the kinds of structural demands implicit in the four pieces of legislation,
it is difficult to detect systematic differences explaining the variance in the national
responses. For instance, while institutional reform pressure was resisted in the case
of the EIA Directive, Britain and Germany both responded positively to the institutional requirements of the EMAS Regulation. The demand to establish open
and transparent structures of administrative interest intermediation that is implicit
in the Environmental Information and EIA Directives resulted in only one case of
national adaptation, namely, in the British response to the Environmental Information Directive. Even a comparison of the responses to so-called new (bottom-
up) and old (command-and-control) instruments (Knill and Lenschow 2000;
Sabatier 1986) as represented by the EMAS Regulation and by the Drinking Water
Directive, does not reveal clearly distinct responses. Turning the comparative
perspective from the policy dimension to the national level, we observe similar
ambiguity. Neither Britain nor Germany produces a clear pattern of adaptation or
resistance.

It appears that "simple" explanations for national patterns of adaptation do not
suffice. One way to add depth to the analysis is to investigate the notion of adaptation pressure in more detail. In fact, one of the deficits in the previous account
has been the negligence of the relative nature of the concept. The pressure that is
felt on the domestic level is defined not only by the content of the respective EU
legislation but also by the already existing national structures. In short, the level
of adaptation pressure correlates with the degree of "fit" between EU structural
demands and domestic structures. In the following section we further develop the
explanatory value implicit in the institutionalist concept "goodness of fit."

The Impact of Europeanization on National Administrations:
An Institutional Perspective

We argue that the impact of European policies on national administrations can only
be fully understood when adopting a perspective that takes account of the institutional compatibility of European and domestic arrangements. The institutional
factors that may be relevant for adaptation processes are multiple, however, and
they are unlikely to fully determine the behavior of political actors. In order to
specify the institutional "fit or misfit" argument, we build on the actor-centered
institutionalist research strategy developed by Renate Mayntz and Fritz Scharpf

(1995). We develop their work further by specifying the conditions under which the institutional model needs to be complemented with an interest-based perspective and by introducing a new dynamic element to the analysis.

Actor-Centered Institutionalism as a Research Strategy

The institutional literature is a growing and quite diverse field. There is no consensus on how to explain processes of institutional transformation and stagnation under external adaptation pressure. There exist many theoretical variants (Hall and Taylor 1996), which, at a very general level, can be grouped into institution-based and rational choice or interest-based approaches, each with its distinct set of strength and weaknesses.

In short, the institution-based approaches, represented by sociological and for the most part historical institutionalism (Thelen and Steinmo 1992; March and Olsen 1989), provide us with clear expectations concerning the scope and mode of domestic administrative transformation in response to European pressures for adaptation. Given their emphasis on institutional stability and persistence, they lead us to expect domestic adaptation only if European policies imply incremental rather than fundamental departures from existing administrative arrangements at the domestic level. Those adaptations that will be undertaken, it is argued, will follow along historically prestructured paths.

In the practical application, this institution-based model suffers from three basic weaknesses, however. First, especially in the historical institutionalist literature, the analyst is left with little guidance with regard to *which* institutions matter. Institutional structures exist on the level of the political system, state, and legal traditions of the state as well as on the sectoral level. To which level is the analyst or policymaker supposed to turn in order to determine the boundaries for political and institutional change? This is left unspecified in the theoretical framework.

Second, although we are assured that institutions constrain and refract politics but never solely cause certain outcomes (Thelen and Steinmo 1992, 3), we receive little guidance with regard to the extent to which institutions prestructure the outcome, that is, *how much* institutions matter. Institution-based analyses conceive of institutions as affecting individual action and collective outcomes by conditioning the distribution of power and by reproducing particular world-views or routines to which the actors become accustomed. They remain silent with respect to the conditions under which and the degree to which other factors but institutions play a role. Given its exclusive focus on institutional prestructuring processes, it is difficult to avoid the taste of a deterministic flavor.

Third, the institution-based approach maintains a conservative view on institutional change. The "normal life" of institutions is characterized by continuity and persistence; change is confined to minor adaptations and fundamental reforms are restricted to highly exceptional cases of historical "shocks" or "crises" (Krasner 1988). Considering that there are instances in which institutional change goes beyond routine adaptation,[2] this conception seems too narrow and needs to be complemented with concepts that allow for more than incremental change from the "inside."

Turning to the rational choice variant of institutionalist explanations, this approach conceives of institutions basically as an opportunity structure, which constrains as well as enables the behavior of self-interested actors (Knight 1992). Such a perspective, taking account of different interests and strategic interactions, can equally well explain both institutional dynamics and persistence. Hence, it does not face the problems of institutional determinism and conservatism in the same way that institution-based approaches do. This analytical openness, however, constitutes at the same time a major weakness. A sound interest-based explanation would need to account for high empirical complexity. In practice, the challenge of an accurate attribution of resources to the diverse set of actors involved and hence, an accurate ex ante assessment of the conditions for institutional change, is enormous. In this respect, the more abstract and parsimonious institution-based model is superior.

Mayntz and Scharpf have developed a research strategy that fruitfully combines the interest-based and the actor-centered perspective, suggesting that models focusing on the independent impact of institutions on political outcomes should be supplemented by explanations that take account of the independent role of interests and actors (1995, 43). Recognizing the explanatory relevance of institutions both as independent and as intervening factors, they propose a pragmatic analytical solution to overcome the dilemma of encountering inappropriate determinism, on the one hand, and explanatory openness, on the other hand. Following the principle of "decreasing levels of abstraction" (Lindenberg 1991), explanations should take the more abstract and parsimonious institution-based approach as a starting point, considering strategic behavior as an independent factor only if institutions provide no sufficient explanation. In other words, the more indeterminate interest-based approach plays a subsidiary role in explaining political outcomes.

Mayntz and Scharpf do not further elaborate on the scope or boundary conditions of an institutional approach. What are the relevant institutions to be considered, and under which conditions will they provide no sufficient explanation? In what follows, we attempt to specify these boundary conditions of the institutionalist argument and thereby refine the research model proposed by Mayntz and Scharpf.

Which Institutions Do Matter? Distinguishing Institutional
Fit from Misfit

Political and institutional evolution takes place in a large context, ranging from the immediate institutional framework to the overall political, administrative, legal,

---

2. Examples are the numerous privatizations of public utilities taking place in many Western democracies.

and societal structures. Institutionalists take no position ex ante regarding which institutional structures will inform the particular research question at hand. For the identification of systematic patterns of change in a wider comparative research design, this is not very satisfactory. While realizing that in the end the decision which institutions matter remains an empirical question, we suggest narrowing the choices, at least for the environmental policy field.[3] We propose that administrative structures and procedures that are embedded in the member state's respective state, legal, and political traditions constitute the institutional core of *national administrative traditions*, which in turn represent the "deterministic" boundaries for adaptation processes. If European policy demands stand in violation to institutional core elements, that is, if they would require a change of the core in order to allow for effective policy implementation, we expect national resistance to such change. These contradictions of the core represent institutional "misfits" of such magnitude that, we argue, the institutional perspective alone allows us to predict the pattern—or rather absence—of domestic adaptation. Focusing the institutional perspective in such a way takes us also one step closer to specifying how much institutions matter. In short, in cases of institutional misfits on the level of core contradictions, they matter "very much." If European institutional demands remain "within the core," we are in the "undetermined" realm of the institutionalist model where other factors than institutional structures play an independent role in explaining the process of domestic change. It is at this point that we need to descend the ladder of abstraction to interest-based explanations. In these cases, the degree of "misfit" between European demands and domestic structures is not prohibitive, but adaptation to the European model depends on a supportive actor constellation that permits successful reform initiatives.[4] While actors move within the constraints of an institutional opportunity structure, their behavior cannot be predicted beforehand and needs to be investigated in detail ex post.

While we cannot pretend to have a theory for domestic adaptation under the impact of Europeanization that has full predictive capacities, we hope that this pragmatic but no longer entirely contingent explanatory model helps to sharpen our view of the nature and degree of institutional limits to change. Below, we add one more modification to the institutionalist framework that deals with its conservative bias.

Avoiding Conservatism: A Dynamic Perspective on Adaptation Pressure

So far, the modified actor-centered institutionalist model for domestic adaptation assumes, like all institutionalist models, a static concept of national adminis-

---

3. This specification of the model was derived from empirical analysis published elsewhere (Knill and Lenschow 1998). Here we show that "sectoral" institutions, such as regulatory standard operating procedures and structures, do not explain the processes of national adaptations to European pressures.

4. In cases of good fit or complete misfit, the presence or absence, respectively, of a supportive actor constellation is predetermined institutionally and does not need to be investigated separately.

trative traditions that constitute the institutional core for administrative structure and practice in the environmental field. The level of adaptation pressure varies with the compatibility of European policy implications and national administrative traditions. Holding administrative traditions constant, different national adaptation responses are explained by the challenge implied by different policies. Here, we argue that the level of adaptation pressure may vary not only across policies but also over time. Although a static institutional core should be considered the "normal case," given the general stability associated with macrolevel institutions, we will not completely preclude the possibility of core changes. The analytical admittance of institutional "core movements" does not contradict the previous institution-based argumentation. The scope of European adaptation requirements continues to be assessed in relation to domestic institutional structures, though now from a dynamic perspective.

Core changes may occur as the result of external shocks (Krasner 1988), such as the political and economic transition we have recently witnessed in Eastern Europe. More relevant for the cases examined in this chapter, core dynamics may also develop from within the system and, we suggest, are linked to the level of *administrative reform capacity*. While this concept does not allow for predicting if, when, and how such reforms will occur, it indicates the structural potential for changes within national administrative traditions, which may vary from country to country. In other words, the institutional framework in which policy-specific administrative arrangements are embedded is conceived of as a trajectory, along which—depending on the administrative reform capacity of the political system—more or less far-reaching developments may take place (Dobbin 1994).

The level of reform capacity is an inborn feature of the state tradition, the legal system, and the political system of a country. It is an aspect of the institutional core and therefore can be captured within our explanatory framework. To be precise, the structural capacity for national administrative reforms depends on the number of institutional veto points (Immergut 1992, 27) administrative actors have at their disposal in order to block and influence political and societal reform initiatives. The number and nature of veto points is linked to the country's institutional core in several ways. First, it is affected by aspects of the political system, including the party system (single party versus coalition governments) and the degree of political decentralization (unitary and centralized systems versus federal systems, with a strong linkage of policymaking at the federal and regional level). Second, the number of veto points increases with the extent to which administrative activity is based on legal and formal requirements. Each formal requirement creates the possibility that conflicting interests hinder reform and, hence, work against swift, single-handed institutional reorganization. Finally, the number of veto points increase, and administrative reform capacity decreases, the more comprehensive and fragmented are administrative structures, because reforms "from above" depend on the consensus and the coordination of a multitude of administrative actors (Benz and Götz 1996).

Linking Adaptation Pressure and Domestic Change

Following the above modifications of the institution-based approach, we are now able to identify different paths of domestic change and persistence in response to European influence.

Confirmation of the Core: Compliance without Change.   If the constellation of European requirements and national administrative traditions implies no or only negligible adaptations, EU policy can be seen as a confirmation of existing administrative arrangements at the national level. This holds especially true for cases where national arrangements exactly reflect or even go beyond the supranational provisions. In these cases we expect no administrative adaptation, as none is called for.

Contradiction of the Core: Administrative Resistance.   In cases where European policies conflict with the institutional core of national administrative traditions, resistance to change is expected. Following the propositions of sociological and historical institutionalism, well-established institutions and traditions persist, despite exogenous pressures for adaptation as posed by the process of Europeanization (Krasner 1988; March and Olsen 1989). Hence, we anticipate at most limited and symbolic adaptations in such constellations.

Change within a Static Core.   If European adaptation requirements can be achieved by changes *within* the boundaries defined by the domestic system's institutional core, an exclusive focus on institutional factors may render insufficient results. A satisfactory explanation of adaptation performance may require a lower level of abstraction, namely the independent analysis of the given interest constellations and the strategic interaction of domestic actors. These operate in the context of given institutional opportunities and constraints, but their behavior is not entirely prestructured by them.

Change within a Changing Core.   A variant of the just-discussed "indeterminate" path of adaptation refers to cases experiencing a core shift. Here, initially high adaptation pressure from core contradictions between national and European practices may be reduced in the context of independent national administrative reforms. These general national reform dynamics may alter the boundaries for policy-specific adaptation, so that adaptation to EU requirements can now be achieved within the (new) core. Similar to the above scenario of change within a stable core, a mere institution-based explanation is not sufficient to account for the actual occurrence and direction of domestic adjustments; it needs to be complemented by an interest-based account.

Empirical Evidence: The Implementation of EU Environmental Policy in Two Member States

Based on our theoretical considerations, we can now explain and interpret the empirical findings drawn from the implementation of EU environmental policy in Germany and Britain (also see Table 7.3).

Confirmation of the Core

EMAS in Britain.   Implementation of EMAS in Britain implied minimal institutional adaptation requirements and "confirms" national structures and procedures. This was because the adoption of the regulation coincided with the institutionalization of the British environmental management system and even used the British example as a reference point (Héritier, Knill, and Mingers 1996). The EU legislation merely demanded the introduction of few additional elements to the national system based on British Standard 7750. The standard did not need to be changed. Moreover, with respect to structural requirements, the UK could rely on administrative structures already in place to implement the national system as well as the ISO 9000 quality management (Knill 1998). This almost complete institutional "fit" resulted in easy implementation.

Contradiction of the Core: Administrative Resistance

By contrast, European policies severely contradicted the core of national administrative traditions in two of our eight empirical cases, namely the German implementation of the Environmental Information and EIA Directives. As argued above, the high degree of institutional misfit implied by core contradictions provides a sufficient basis to expect administrative resistance. In the two cases, such contradictions emerged from different sources. While the Environmental Information Directive challenged well-established patterns of administrative inter-

Table 7.3 Patterns of administrative transformation to European requirements in Britain and Germany

Requirement	Britain	Germany
Drinking Water	Change within a changing core (adaptation)	Change within a static core (adaptation)
Access to Information	Change within a changing core (adaptation)	Core contradiction (resistance)
EIA	Change within a static core (resistance)	Core contradiction (resistance)
EMAS	Confirmation of the core (adaptation)	Change within a static core (adaptation)

EIA = Environmental Impact Assessment.
EMAS = Environmental Management and Auditing System.

est intermediation, the EIA Directive required fundamental changes of administrative structures.

Access to Information in Germany.   The open and transparent form of administrative interest intermediation implied by the Environmental Information Directive was not compatible with the more closed practice to be found in Germany, where access to environmental information is generally restricted to parties directly affected by and involved in administrative activities and procedures (Scherzberg 1994). Following the principle of "restricted access to records," German authorities are only obliged to provide access to official documents if requesters can claim that access to "their records" is necessary to defend their legal interests in the context of administrative procedures (Winter 1996). This principle is strongly entrenched in the general institutional context of the German state and legal tradition. Within the German tradition of the state, the civil service is accountable to the state and to the law rather than to society, hence implying no particular necessity for administrative transparency (König 1996). Moreover, the *Rechtsstaat* principle places its emphasis on the protection of subjective individual rights rather than the participation of the public in administrative decision making. By contrast, rather than serving the protection of individual rights in the context of administrative procedures, the EU Directive aims at making administrative activities accountable to the public; hence, it instrumentalizes public access as a means of administrative control (Schwarze 1996, 172).

Given these fundamental differences in philosophy and procedure, the German implementation record is hardly surprising. The narrow interpretation of European policy requirements, circumventing an otherwise needed reorientation of administrative practice, corresponds with historical institutionalist expectations. Germany transposed the Directive in a way limiting the number of the affected administrative actors as well as the number of potential information requests, thereby minimizing the adaptive challenge at the risk of violating the Directive (Lenschow 1997).

EIA in Germany.   In the case of the EIA Directive, institutional misfit developed with respect to structural and organizational arrangements. The incompatibility of European and domestic arrangements emerges mainly from the integrated cross-media approach to environmental protection required by the Directive, which is in sharp contrast to corresponding core patterns in Germany.

The EIA Directive implied the concentration or at least intensified coordination of different consent procedures and structures with respect to different environmental media, such as air, water, and soil. By contrast, administrative processing in Germany of a project is medium specific both vertically and horizontally and, consequently, uncoordinated in legal terms and practical performance (Klöpfer and Durner 1997, 1082). These horizontally fragmented structures and procedures at the sectoral level are institutionally strongly entrenched by their tight linkage to a multitier hierarchical structure at the regional level. Individual consent procedures are embedded in vertically integrated but horizontally segmented procedures and structures of regional administrative arrangements, representing a rigid institutional structure (Seibel 1996; Benz and Götz 1996).

The resistance of the German administration to adjust to the requirements of the Directive is indicated by the EIA's integration into existing authorization procedures without adopting an integrative approach, hence avoiding an overhaul of administrative structures. As a consequence, the Directive makes not much difference for the German traditional authorization practice, which remains based on a single-media approach. German officials sometimes admit the desirability of a cross-media approach, but the difficulty of unraveling a complex system in the distribution of administrative responsibilities rooted in the German federal and horizontally fragmented structure stands in the way of pursuing such reform (Lenschow 1997).

Demands within a Static Core: Mixed Patterns of Adaptation

In contrast to the previous cases of contradictions, an exclusive focus on institutional factors may not be sufficient to account for cases where European requirements remain within the core of national administrative traditions. Here, an explanation may require the careful analysis of actor dynamics. The constellation where European adaptation requirements remain within a static core can be observed in three of our empirical cases under study, namely the German cases of Drinking Water and EMAS as well as the British EIA case. We find varying patterns of domestic adaptation, notwithstanding the similar level of institutional adaptation pressure.

Drinking Water in Germany.   The administrative implications of the Drinking Water Directive were basically in line with the hierarchical and interventionist administrative style traditionally characterizing German environmental policy. Legalistic and interventionist patterns of regulation are deeply rooted in the German state and legal tradition, which presupposes a superior role of the state vis-à-vis society and where obedience of the administration to the law (following the principle of the *Rechtsstaat*) traditionally serves as a substitute for democratic control. As a general rule, the scope and mode of administrative activity is specified by law; hence, the administration possesses comparatively little flexibility and discretion when implementing legal provisions (Peters 1995, 137).

Though not challenging this institutional core, the Drinking Water Directive implied some adaptational pressure in the form of stricter quality standards with regard to nitrate and pesticide pollution and, hence, either the imposition of control on the polluting actors (industry and farmers) or high investments in new abatement technologies. In Germany, it took considerable time to find a domestic solution to comply with the Directive that was acceptable for everybody.

Most other member states avoided domestic struggles by taking advantage of an inconsistency in the Directive. The measurement procedures prescribed by the

Directive were insufficient for detecting breaches of the assigned quality values and thus offered a loophole for ignoring these values and for avoiding significant costs on the part of either polluters or water providers. This easy or pragmatic solution was not feasible in Germany because it would have introduced a core contradiction after all. This "pragmatic" solution would have delegitimized the German regulatory practices by questioning the credibility of the law. Under the principle of the *Rechtsstaat*, however, the law represented the very basis for administrative action (Knill and Lenschow 1998).

The development of an alternative solution took considerable time because conflicts over the distribution of the costs of compliance had to be settled. Both water providers and environmental organizations pushed for stricter emission standards for the polluting actors, who naturally resented such proposal. The polluters, most notably farmers, have the advantage of being politically well represented, not only through their own associations but also through the federal and regional agriculture ministries. The farmers were only willing to change their production practices if they would be compensated for their anticipated financial losses. Water providers and environmentalists argued that this solution would violate the "polluter pays" principle. But the government was not prepared to engage in a major conflict with agricultural interests (Rüdig and Krämer 1994, 69).

In view of this constellation, reaching compliance with the European standards involved difficult and lengthy negotiations. They resulted in the introduction of consumption fees (Wasserpfennig) as well as voluntary agreements between the polluting industry and water providers. These instruments permitted the financing of the installation of new cleaning technologies, on the one hand, and some reduction of the overall level of water pollution, on the other hand—both at little cost for the polluters (Lenschow 1997).

EMAS in Germany.   While in the case of the Drinking Water Directive administrative adjustment took place after a considerable delay, Germany's implementation of the EMAS Regulation was characterized by a smooth adaptation to European implications. Although self-regulation and voluntary agreements as implied in the regulation were in sharp contrast to the legalist and interventionist style of German environmental policy, they correspond with other features of the German institutional core, namely, its tradition of corporatism. Corporatist arrangements are reflected in a whole range of intermediary organizations that partly assume public functions and partly represent private interests (Lehmbruch 1997; Benz and Götz 1996).

This case shows the need to apply a broad institutional perspective in the environmental policy field: given its horizontal nature, environmental policy is affected by various policy specific institutional structures; their relative importance depends on the degrees of embeddedness in the national state and legal traditions. In the EMAS case, both the identification of the relevant institutional core and the handling of adaptation requirements within this core requires a shift of the analysis to an actor-centered level.

Debates over the appropriate core context took place only during the EU decision-making period (Héritier, Knill, and Mingers 1996); by the time of the implementation phase, the "industrial relations perspective" had prevailed, allowing for adaptation within the (corporatist) core. The political arena was characterized by broad support for the regulation from both industrial and environmental organizations, which could be traced partly to the resonance of the legislation with national debates on deregulation and administrative reforms. The strong support from industry, in particular, resulted from its expectation that in the future authorization and inspection procedures might be "slimmed" for EMAS participants (Lenschow 1997).

As a consequence, domestic administrative arrangements were fully adapted to European legislation. The 1995 Environmental Audit Law lays down the basic regulatory structure for a national EMAS, which corresponds to the requirements spelled out in the regulation. As prescribed by European legislation, the law sets up a specific institution responsible for the accreditation and control of the so-called verifiers, which are in charge of the external evaluation of the company-internal auditing process. The professional criteria to be met by the verifiers are established by the Environmental Verifier Committee, which is a multipartite expert committee consisting of representatives of industry, the environmental administration from the federal and the Länder level, environmental verifiers, the economic administration from the federal and the Länder level, trade unions, as well as environmental associations.

EIA in Britain.   That administrative adaptation to only incremental European requirements must not be taken for granted, however, becomes obvious when considering the implementation of the EIA Directive in Britain. Although the Directive's procedural character and its structural requirements implied no particular adaptation problems, Britain resisted engaging in the marginal adaptive reforms.

The Directive departed from the British model only in requiring slightly more formal procedures and coordination, particularly between the planning procedures (which are the responsibility of local authorities) and industrial process authorizations (which for larger plants is conducted by the national Environment Agency). Apart from this, the Directive came close to British practice where

> . . . the developer already had to supply certain information; the public already had the chance to comment; the planning authority already went through a mental process in arriving at a decision which involves considering the information supplied by the developer and other; and when decisions were taken it was published. (Haigh 1996, chapter 11, 2–14)

Britain opted to integrate the EIA procedure merely in the local planning procedures without facilitating coordination. Furthermore, environmental impacts were given no priority compared to other considerations in the planning process. New prioritizing would have required a somewhat more formal regulatory framework to constrain the wide discretion traditionally given to the planning authorities; this was resisted (Alder 1993).

In view of the only moderate adaptational requirements of EU legislation, the negative response must be understood against the background of the particular policy context that was not supportive in the United Kingdom during the time of the EIA implementation in the mid-1980s. While both industry and the administration resisted any changes that would have increased the regulatory burden on project developers or complicated existing planning procedures (Haigh 1996, chapter 11, 2–3), environmental organizations did not mobilize much pressure to ensure effective implementation with the Directive. Their primary focus was on the debate about SO_2, a context in which Britain had been proclaimed the "dirty man of Europe." The EIA, which could not easily be linked to environmental disasters, was too "dull" to trigger similar public support (Knill 1998). In the light of this political constellation, Britain could afford to resist an effective response to adaptational requirements implied by the EIA Directive.

Change within a Changing Core

Looking closely at the implementation process of the Drinking Water and Information Directives in Britain, we observe that administrative adaptation to European requirements took place after the institutional scope of the European requirements had been reduced by far-reaching national administrative reforms. British compliance with these two Directives can be understood only when conceiving of national administrative traditions as a dynamic rather than a static phenomenon.

The Changing Core: National Dynamics.   In contrast to Germany, Britain has a high capacity for initiating and implementing administrative reforms. This characteristic is a result of the low number of institutional veto points and the strong position of the central government within the British political system: "Britain has . . . the fewest formal or codified restrictions on government action of any liberal democracy" (Dunleavy 1993, 5). Furthermore, the organization of public administration is not based on a comprehensive hierarchical system, as in Germany, but on a loosely coupled system of special authorities that evolved gradually over time (Peters 1995, 138). This structure implies relatively low institutional breadth, which makes administrative restructuring easier to achieve.

The structural potential for dynamic developments became evident in the reform policies of the Thatcher government, which had profound implications for British public administration. To improve efficiency and effectiveness of the public sector, policies were directed at administrative reorganization, management reforms, and privatization. All of these elements challenge existing administrative traditions. Important structural changes were introduced with the *Next Steps* initiative. It implied the creation of semi-autonomous agencies responsible for operational management, while policymaking functions remained the responsibility of the relevant departments. Private sector management and performance regimes were introduced in the new agencies. The performance drive—but also the need to compensate for lacking democratic control of the independent agencies—led to a tendency of making their activities more transparent and accountable to the public. A further feature of national reforms was the privatization of public utilities, including the nationalized energy and water supply industries. Regulatory regimes were created to control the market activities of these privatized utilities.

The dynamic developments at the national level implied important changes in administrative core characteristics in terms of administrative styles and structures. The establishment of performance-oriented regimes and the creation of independent regulatory bodies resulted in a shift toward more formal, legalistic but also open patterns of administrative interest intermediation. For instance, intra-administrative relations between the new agencies and their sponsoring departments are now defined in formal, contract-like documents. Moreover, the establishment of independent agencies implied a formalization of intra-administrative coordination. This, in turn, may reduce the leeway for informal interaction between administrative and private actors, at least in cases where the latter are now regulated by different (e.g., economic and environmental) agencies. Finally, both privatization and shifting political responsibilities to independent agencies have far-reaching structural implications, leading to a "trimmed down" but even more fragmented public sector (Hood 1991; Rhodes 1996).

The domestic reforms favored administrative adjustment to the requirements implied by the Drinking Water and Environmental Information Directives in two ways. First, as already hinted, domestic core changes reduced the scope for sectoral adaptation. Second, national reforms changed the institutional opportunity structures at the sectoral level and created a policy context favoring effective compliance with European requirements.

Drinking Water in Britain.   The national public sector reforms influenced water policy via the 1989 privatization of the water industry and the establishment of a fragmented regulatory structure. Privatization resulted in the separation of the regulatory and the water provision functions; both were previously fulfilled by the publicly owned water companies. The regulatory functions, in turn, were divided between three regulatory bodies responsible for economic and environmental regulation as well as the control of drinking water provision. A consequence of these reforms was a shift from industrial self-regulation toward a more formal, legalistic regulatory style based on substantive, performance-related criteria. These new structures and practices corresponded with the design of the EU Drinking Water Directive (Knill 1998).

Besides reducing the institutional scope of European adaptation pressures, domestic administrative reforms played a crucial role in providing a more favorable policy context for effective compliance. Privatization implied that the economic costs of compliance with European standards (which were considerable, given insufficient investment into control technologies up to that point) no longer interfered with the Conservative government's objective to reduce public spending, as the costs for retrofitting existing plants had to be borne by private companies. Political and administrative actors became less resistant toward long-standing public demands. The same holds true for the position of the water suppliers, given that the new regulatory regime provided new opportunities to finance technological retrofitting by increasing consumer charges within certain boundaries defined by the Office of Water Services, the economic regulator of the privatized water industry (Matthews and Pickering 1997). This constellation provided a favorable basis for the complete compliance with European requirements, notwithstanding the sometimes open conflicts on the balance between quality improvements and increases in water taxes between various regulatory bodies. To be specific, the Environment Agency, which is generally quite responsive to environmental interests, pushed in favor of stricter standards; the Office of Water Services, the economic regulator, fulfills the basic task of consumer protection, hence striving to restrict increases in water taxes. In the end, these conflicts were settled in negotiations between the various regulators involved, leading to a transparent regulatory regime in which the costs for improving water quality cannot be completely passed through to consumers. Instead, they have to be partly financed by more efficient and effective performance of the water providers (Maloney and Richardson 1995; Knill 1998).

In this context, the United Kingdom reached compliance with the Drinking Water Directive through a more substantive orientation in state intervention by relying on legally binding standards for drinking water quality, a shift toward more formal and legalistic patterns of administrative interest intermediation, and significant investment programs in order to meet the EU requirements (Knill 1998).

Access to Environmental Information in Britain.   In the context of domestic reforms directed at opening up government and increasing administrative transparency and accountability, the provision of access to environmental information, as required by the Environmental Information Directive, no longer reflected a core challenge to the traditionally secretive and closed patterns of administrative interest intermediation (Tant 1990; Knill 1998).

Strong support from domestic actor coalitions for public access to environmental information provided a favorable basis for administrative adjustment within a changing core already taking place. The institutional opportunities for domestic actors to successfully influence administrative change had significantly increased in the context of national reforms. The impact of the changed institutional environment can be inferred from previous domestic occurrences. The Royal Commission on Environmental Pollution as well as environmental organizations and the Campaign for the Freedom of Information had urged the adoption of more transparent environmental information and reporting practices in Britain already since the mid-1970s. But they were ignored in a national context still characterized by a secretive regulatory style. Similar resistance we would have expected had an EU Directive required more open practices at that time.

In fact, national reforms implied that British adaptations to the Environmental Information Directive have been far more proactive than expected. The British administration went even beyond the requirements of the Directive, which merely calls for the "passive" provision of information following public requests. British policy included, in addition, the proactive provision of environmental information in order to raise the general interest of the public in environmental information (Knill 1998).

In this chapter, we investigated the Europeanization of domestic structures, narrowly defined as administrative styles and structures. EU regulatory policies often imply concrete institutional requisites for successful implementation. Hence, depending on the nature of the respective national administrative structures and procedures, they may exert considerable administrative adaptation pressure in the EU member states. We asked what are the conditions under which adaptation pressure actually results in administrative change at the national level. For this purpose, we analyzed the process of administrative adaptation in Germany and Britain in the context of implementing EU environmental policy.

Three main arguments were advanced. First, the institutionalist perspective and, most notably, the concept of "goodness of fit" provide a useful analytical framework to explain patterns of national adaptation. In the empirical study we noted quickly that alternative perspectives, focusing either on "country-based" or "policy-based" logics, did not produce a systematic picture.

Second, in taking an institutionalist perspective as the analytical starting point, we suggest that it is useful to structure the analysis according to the principle of "decreasing level of abstraction" (Mayntz and Scharpf 1995), supplementing institution-based explanations by an interest-based perspective in cases where the former provides no sufficient results. This research strategy deals successfully with several weaknesses implied in the "pure" application of the institution- and the interest-based approaches, namely a tendency toward determinism in the former case and difficulties in developing ex ante hypotheses in the latter.

Third, while the actor-centered institutionalism proposed by Mayntz and Schapf represents a useful research strategy, it needs to be further elaborated to be effective as a theoretical framework to explain domestic structural change in response to Europeanization. We proposed two such elaborations, first, that the identification of the "institutional core" offers additional analytical leverage to distinguish cases where institutional factors sufficiently explain patterns of adaptation and resistance and second, cases where other factors need to be considered.

To be precise, in cases of "deep" institutional misfit—defined as contradictions with the institutional core of national administrative traditions—we expect administrative resistance to change. In three of the observed eight cases, we noted either such contradictions of the core or complete core confirmation; in both cases, the institutional constellation explained administrative resistance or adaptation, respectively. By contrast, if European requirements remain within the core of national administrative traditions, a mere institution-based focus is no longer sufficient to account for patterns of domestic adaptation. We are in the "undetermined" realm of the historical institutionalist framework, where other than institutional factors have to be considered. Here, national responses must be explained also in the light of underlying interest and actor constellations. In most of our empirical cases, the underlying actor constellation became, at least in the longer term, favorable to adaptational reforms; only in one case in the United Kingdom (specifically, Britain) did we observe a negative reaction.

Furthermore, our theoretical and empirical findings indicate the need for a more dynamic perspective on institutional core developments. Although a static core of national administrative traditions can be considered as the "normal case," we cannot preclude the possibility of core changes, which, in turn, alter the scope for domestic adaptation to European requirements. To grasp the structural potential for such developments, we introduced the concept of administrative reform capacity. We showed that the relatively high adaptation level in the United Kingdom (Britain) is linked to the country's overall high reform capacity, which has been responsible for core movements—that is, changing the level of adaptation pressure quite independent from European influences.

CHAPTER EIGHT

Europeanization and Territorial Institutional Change: Toward Cooperative Regionalism?

Tanja A. Börzel

T he Europeanization and regionalization of the nation-state are two of the most significant trends in the territorial organization of politics in postwar Western Europe. For a long time, supranational integration and subnational diversification were conceived and analyzed as two simultaneous but independent processes. This only changed in the early 1980s, when regional actors gained momentum in European politics. The increasing "regionalization" of European integration has given rise to a rich body of literature on the role of regions and other subnational authorities in European politics.

The link between Europeanization and regionalization of the nation-state is no longer contested. The concrete impact of European integration on the territorial structures of the member states, however, is still highly controversial. Whereas some authors suggest that regions might supersede the nation-state as the most important political entity of European integration, a series of comparative studies present rather "skeptical reflections" on such a "Europe of the Regions" (Anderson 1990). A third group of scholars does not expect either a withering away of the state or its obstinate resilience but a fundamental transformation of the state in terms of the emergence of a European system of multilevel governance where European, national, and subnational actors share rather than compete for political power. Although there is no consensus on the concrete outcome of the Europeanization of national territorial structures, most of these works share a common bias: they assume that Europeanization impacts the territorial structures of all member states in the same way, leading to some kind of

This chapter is derived from my forthcoming book (Börzel in press). For comments and criticisms, I am particularly thankful to David Cameron, Jeff Checkel, Maria Green Cowles, Michelle Egan, Adrienne Héritier, Yves Mény, Thomas Risse, Vivien Schmidt, and Fritz Scharpf.

convergence toward either a strengthening, a weakening, or a transformation of the nation–state.

In contrast, I argue in this chapter that the impact of Europeanization on national territorial structures is diverse and what I call "institution dependent." Domestic institutions mediate the impact of Europeanization in two fundamental ways: First, the "goodness of fit" between European and domestic institutions determines the institutional pressure for adaptation that a member state is facing. The more European rules and regulations challenge the domestic distribution of power between domestic actors, the higher the pressure for adaptation and the more likely domestic institutional change. Second, domestic institutions entail informal understandings about appropriate behavior within a given formal rule-structure. These collective understandings—the institutional culture—determine the dominant strategy of domestic actors by which they respond to adaptational pressure in order to redress the institutional balance of power and, thus, either prohibit or facilitate adaptation.

I demonstrate my argument empirically by comparing the effect of Europeanization on the territorial institutions of Germany and Spain. Europeanization caused similar pressure for adaptation on the territorial institutions of both member states by weakening the legislative and administrative powers of the regions vis-à-vis the national government. In the case of Germany, however, the informal institutions of "cooperative federalism" facilitated a cooperative strategy by the German Länder that allowed them to regain their competencies and, thus, to adjust existing German territorial institutions to Europeanization, reinforcing rather than fundamentally changing them. In contrast, the Spanish institutional culture of "competitive regionalism" privileged a confrontational strategy by the Spanish regions that proved ineffective in redressing the territorial balance of power. As a result, the Spanish regions changed their dominant strategy toward increasing cooperation with the central state in a multilateral framework. This strategy change resulted in a significant transformation of the existing Spanish territorial institutions, turning them away from competitive toward more cooperative forms of intergovernmental relations.

I proceed in the following steps. First, I develop my theoretical argument, which is centered on the three-step model outlined in the introductory chapter of this volume. Second, I analyze the effect of Europeanization on the territorial institutions of Germany and Spain. Finally, I summarize the theoretical argument in the light of the empirical findings and conclude with some considerations of to what extent Europeanization may cause a general shift toward cooperative regionalism and what implications this convergence would have for the future European polity.

Europeanization and Territorial Institutional Change: An Institution-Dependent Process

In the literature, the effect of Europeanization on the territorial institutions of the member states is controversial. One group of scholars suggests that European integration enhances the autonomy of national governments vis-à-vis the regions. Andrew Moravcsik, for instance, claims that the transfer of national policy competencies to the European level tends to reinforce the control of national executives over four crucial resources of domestic power, as the national executives can monopolize or "gate-keep" the access of domestic actors to the European policy-making arena (Moravcsik 1994, 1). This "paradox of weakness" (Grande 1996) is challenged by another group of scholars who turn Moravcsik's argument around. They suggest that European policymaking provides regions with additional resources that enable them to circumvent or bypass their national governments and to gain direct access to the European political arena (Marks 1993; Sandholtz 1996). Unlike in the early "Europe of the Regions" literature, many works on Europeanization and territorial institutional change no longer claim that European integration equally strengthens the role of subnational authorities in European politics (Keating and Hooghe 1996; Marks et al. 1996). But it remains unclear under which conditions subnational authorities are able to exploit European resources so that we can expect a change in the territorial institutions of a member state.

Finally, a third group of scholars does not share the zero-sum game conception of intergovernmental relations, in which Europeanization strengthens one level at the expense of the other(s). Rather, it is argued that the different levels of government become increasingly dependent on each other in European policymaking. Europeanization does not strengthen or weaken but transforms the state by fostering the emergence of cooperation between the actors at different levels of government (Kohler-Koch 1996; Rhodes 1997).

Despite a general disagreement on the concrete impact of Europeanization, most works seem to suggest that Europeanization will lead to some sort of convergence among the territorial institutions of the member states, a process either leading to more centralization, decentralization, or cooperation in the territorial systems of the member states. Yet, a series of comparative studies on the effect of Europeanization have not found much empirical evidence for any kind of convergence so far (Hooghe 1995; Jeffery 1997b). I argue in this chapter that the impact of Europeanization on the territorial institutions of the member states is indeed diverse and "institution dependent."

The Europeanization of Domestic Policy Competencies

The process of Europeanization as defined in the introductory chapter of this volume is largely driven by the transfer of policy competencies from the member state to the European level. In the European Treaties, the member states conferred the European Union's policymaking powers in a wide range of policy areas reaching from social regulation to macroeconomic stabilization. The shift of policy competencies to the European level does not only involve competencies of the central state. There is practically no area of regional responsibility in which the European Union has not intervened.

Obviously, regions in regionalized and federal member states are more affected by Europeanization than those in unitary or decentralized countries. The German,

Belgian, Spanish, Austrian, and Italian regions have considerably more competencies than their French, British, Portuguese, or Greek counterparts. At the same time, regions with strong legislative and administrative competencies have a larger role in the implementation of European policies. In countries like Germany, Belgium, or Spain, the regions implement the vast majority of European policies. In other words, the impact of Europeanization on the territorial institutions of the member states—driven by the transfer of competencies—increases with the degree of decentralization.

Institutional Misfit: The Uneven Distribution of "Say and Pay"

As a result of the increasing shift of policy competencies to the European level, Europeanization causes an uneven distribution of "say and pay" in strongly decentralized member states, thereby seriously challenging the institutional balance of power between the central state and the regions. Both the central state and the regions lose policymaking power ("say") when their competencies are transferred to the EU. Yet, unlike the central state, whose government is compensated for the loss of its competencies by decision-making powers in the Council of Ministers, the regions have no formal influence on the exercise of their former competencies at the European level. Moreover, by Europeanizing regional competencies, the central state gains access to areas of regional responsibility, which were removed from its reach by the national constitution. While the central state may be weakened vis-à-vis the EU, Europeanization strengthens its domestic position vis-à-vis the regions.

At the same time, the regions are the main implementers of EU policies. They often have to bear the lion's share of the implementation costs ("pay") of policies in whose decision making they do not formally participate.

The centralization of decision-making powers in the hands of the member states ("say") and the shifting of implementation costs onto the regions of the member states ("pay") causes a serious misfit between European decision-making rules and procedures, systematically privileging the central state executives over the regions and shifting the implementation costs to the domestic level, and the decision-making rules and procedures of highly decentralized states, where regions enjoy considerable co-decision-making powers and implementation costs are either shared or borne by the level of government that holds the decision-making power. In other words, Europeanization causes significant pressure for adaptation on the territorial institutions of regionalized and federal member states by seriously challenging the territorial balance of power to the detriment of the regions.

Regional Strategies: Facilitating or Prohibiting Adaptation?

The uneven distribution of "say and pay" causes a serious misfit between European institutions and the territorial institutions of strongly decentralized member states as the regions lose power. While facing similar pressure for adaptation, the regions have pursued different strategies in trying to redress the territorial balance of power. Regional authorities may pursue two basic strategies:

1. A cooperative strategy that aims at the compensation of regional losses of power through co-decision rights in the formulation and representation of the national bargaining position in European decision making as well as cooperation in the implementation of European policies at the domestic level. This strategy presupposes the cooperation of the regions with one another and the central state in a multilateral framework to coordinate a joint position. While this intrastate participation of the regions in European policymaking does not preclude direct contacts between the regions and the European institutions, such extrastate channels serve as a complement to rather than a substitute for access to the European policy arena provided by the central state.
2. A noncooperative or competitive/confrontational strategy that aims at "ring fencing" regional competencies against the intervention of both the European Union and the central state as well as at circumventing the central state through direct relations with European institutions. This strategy entails a zero-sum game type of competition for policy competencies between the different levels of government. In order to protect their competencies, the regions resort to constitutional litigation. They also minimize cooperation with the central state, as such cooperation is perceived as another attempt of the central state to intervene in their sphere of competencies. Rather than cooperating, the regions strive to circumvent or bypass the central state, establishing direct relations with European institutions to gain extrastate access to European policy-making.

The strategy choice of domestic actors is strongly influenced by the informal institutions or the "institutional culture" in which domestic actors are embedded (Börzel 1999). Domestic institutions entail informal understandings about appropriate behavior within a given formal rule-structure (March and Olsen 1989).

In states like Spain, Italy, or Belgium, ethnic, religious, and socioeconomic cleavages gave rise to an institutional culture of competitive regionalism, where the collective understanding of the regions about their behavior toward the central state is based on competition and confrontation rather than cooperation. The regions tend to protect their institutional autonomy by constitutional litigation and strive to deal with the central state on a bilateral rather than multilateral level. An institutional culture of confrontation, competition, and bilateralism favors a noncooperative strategy of "ring fencing" (i.e., fencing in) regional competencies by constitutional conflict and circumventing the state. On the contrary, in cooperative federalism, as we find it in Germany and Austria, the behavior of the regions toward the central state is based on a collective understanding that multilateral bargaining and consensus-seeking are the most appropriate way of dealing with intergovernmental problems. Such an institutional culture is far more conducive to a cooperative strategy of the regions that aims at redressing the territorial balance of power through the intrastate participation of the regions in European policymaking.

The initial strategy choice of the regions is institution dependent, but it is not necessarily conclusive. Whether the regions subsequently change their strategy is decisive for the degree of territorial institutional change. If the strategy of the regions succeeds in redressing the balance of power between central state and regions, it facilitates institutional adaptation, which ultimately reinforces rather than significantly changes territorial institutions. If, however, the initial strategy fails to redress the territorial balance of power and, thus, prohibits institutional adaptation, the regions can be expected to reconsider their strategy at some point. The change from a noncooperative to a cooperative strategy, or vice versa, is highly likely to result in some substantive institutional change, because existing institutions, formal and informal, will not be compatible with the new strategy.

To sum up, two features of domestic institutions determine the likelihood and the degree to which Europeanization leads to domestic institutional change. On the one hand, the formal rule structures determine the "goodness of fit" between European and domestic institutions. The higher the misfit, the higher the pressure for adaptation and the more likely domestic institutional change. On the other hand, the informal collective understandings of what is considered appropriate behavior within a given rule structure determine how domestic actors respond to pressure for adaptation in order to reduce adaptational costs.

It is hypothesized that domestic institutions which entail a cooperative institutional culture are more likely to induce actors to pursue a cooperative strategy that facilitates the accommodation of adaptational pressure by flexible adjustment, resulting in a reinforcement rather than fundamental change of domestic institutions (Katzenstein 1984).

The Effect of Europeanization on the Territorial Institutions of Germany and Spain

Germany and Spain were selected for this comparative case study because their formal territorial institutions faced similar pressure for adaptation, but the respective institutional cultures induced the regions to pursue very different strategies in responding to the adaptational pressure.[1]

Being strongly decentralized states, the territorial institutions of Germany and Spain faced very similar pressures of adaptation as a result of Europeanization. As we will see further on, the transfer of domestic competencies to the European level caused a significant misfit between formal European institutions that centralized decision-making powers in the hands of the member states on the one hand, and the domestic institutions of Spain and Germany, where the regions enjoy autonomous jurisdiction or co-determination rights in central-state decision making, respectively, on the other hand.

While facing similar pressures of adaptation from Europeanization in form of a

---

1. The following sections draw on Börzel 1999.

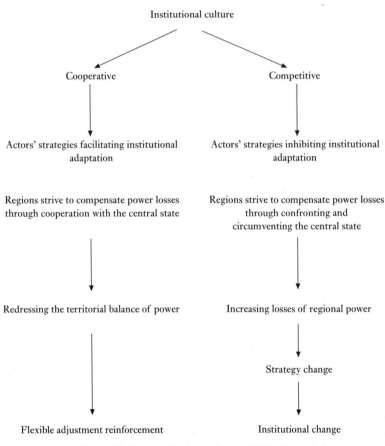

Europeanization

Transfer of policy competencies from the domestic to the European level

Misfit-pressure for adaptation

Shift in the territorial balance of power in favor of the central stage due to the regional losses of power and implementation costs: uneven distribution of "say and pay"

Domestic institutions facilitating and prohibiting adaptation

Institutional culture

Cooperative

Competitive

Actors' strategies facilitating institutional adaptation

Actors' strategies inhibiting institutional adaptation

Regions strive to compensate power losses through cooperation with the central state

Regions strive to compensate power losses through confronting and circumventing the central state

Redressing the territorial balance of power

Increasing losses of regional power

Strategy change

Flexible adjustment reinforcement

Institutional change

Figure 8.1   Europeanization and territorial institutional change

shift in the territorial balance of power in favor of the central state, the Spanish and German regions pursued very different strategies in trying to redress the balance of power. German cooperative federalism induced the Länder to pursue a strategy that aimed at constitutional participatory rights in the formulation and representation of the German bargaining position at the European level. Spanish competitive regionalism precluded such a strategy. The Comunidades Autónomas (CCAA)—the seventeen regions of Spain—strove to redress the balance of power by ring fencing their sphere of autonomous competencies through a strategy of confronting and circumventing the central state.

In the next two sections I explore further how far the different strategies of the German and the Spanish regions were able to redress the territorial balance of power in the two countries. I hypothesize that the cooperative strategy of the German Länder facilitates institutional adaptation, resulting in a reinforcement of cooperative federalism. The confrontational strategy of the Spanish CCAA, on the contrary, is expected to prohibit institutional adaptation because it is ineffective in redressing the territorial balance of power. As a result, the CCAA should reconsider their strategy, moving toward a more cooperative approach that might eventually result in some significant institutional change.

Europeanization and Territorial Change in Germany:
Reinforcing Cooperative Federalism

Europeanization and the Challenge to the German "Bundesstaat."   The territorial institutions of Germany were most affected by the transfer of regional policy competencies to the European level. This Europeanization process led to substantial change in the territorial balance of power, in favor of the central state.

First, when exclusive Länder competencies are Europeanized, the Länder are deprived of any formal influence on the exercise of these competencies at the European level. The central state, on the contrary, whose executive represents Germany in the Council of Ministers, is directly involved in the policy formulation and decision-making. As a result, the central state gains access to regional competencies at the European level, which the German constitution placed beyond its reach at the domestic level.

Second, when federal or shared competencies are transferred to the European level, the formal input of the Länder is reduced from a co-determination right in formulation and decision-making to the participation in the implementation of European policies. The central state, however, which also loses decision-making power, still has a major influence on policy formulation and decision making in the Council of Ministers.

There is hardly any policy area in which the exclusive or shared competencies of the Länder have not been affected by Europeanization. Fifty percent of all issues dealt with in the Bundesrat, the regional chamber of the national parliament, are related to European issues. The shift of competencies is most significant in culture, educational and vocational training, media (exclusive competencies), and in research and technology, transport, environment, regional and structural policy (shared competencies).

But the Länder do not only lose power on the "say" side (legislative competencies). Because the Länder have the responsibility for implementing the vast part of European policies, they have to bear the lion's share of implementation costs of European policies without participating in the formulation and decision making at the European level. Moreover, unlike in domestic policymaking, the Länder have little discretion in implementing European policies. Contrary to the principles of German legislation, European regulations and Directives do not allow the Länder to implement legislation as they see fit.

The uneven distribution of say and pay in favor of the central state seriously disturbs the institutional balance of power between central state and regions. The formal decision-making rules and procedures of the European Union are incompatible with the decision-making rules and procedures of German federalism. While European rules and procedures concentrate decision-making powers in the hands of the national governments, the German constitution mandates the sharing of decision-making powers between the national government and the regions. As a result, Europeanization leads to a centralization of regional competencies not only at the European but also at the central-state level.

Cooperative Federalism and the Strategy of Compensation through Participation: Facilitating Institutional Adaptation.   From the very beginning of European integration, the German Länder have been aware that Europeanization would cause them significant losses of power. In trying to redress the territorial balance of power, the Länder consequently pursued a strategy aimed at compensating their losses of formal decision-making powers through participation in European decision making mediated by the central state. This intrastate participation of the Länder in European decision making is based on the cooperation of the Länder with the central state in the formulation and representation of the German bargaining position at the European level. At no point did the Länder embrace a systematic strategy of confronting or circumventing the state. Only once, in more than forty years of European integration, did the Länder resort to means of constitutional conflict in order to protect their exclusive competencies against Europeanization. And although the Länder established strong direct and independent links with European institutions, they have never used such "extrastate" channels of access to European decision making in order to enhance their power vis-à-vis the central state (see below). Such a confrontational strategy is incompatible with the institutional culture of cooperative federalism.

The institutional culture of cooperative federalism is characterized by a strong sense of conflict avoidance and consensus seeking. The joint decisions of the national government and the Länder, which are necessary in most policy areas to bring about a policy outcome, are often based on informal decision-making rules approaching unanimity even where, by law, majority or unilateral decisions would be possible. More important, even those Länder that would also benefit from a particular policy outcome refrain from voting with the national government as long as there is no nearly unanimous agreement among all the Länder. A national government that can play off the interest of some Länder against the others is the exception rather than the rule. Rather, the Länder try to find a common position that accommodates the interests of all and is then negotiated with the national government. Horizontal self-coordination among the Länder is facilitated by certain unwritten rules, like the rule of nonintervention, according to which those Länder abstain whose interests are not directly affected. Multilateral bargaining and consensus seeking in German territorial politics is also favored by the general German political culture, which is traditionally averse to conflict (Sontheimer 1990).

The incompatibility of unilateral or bilateral action with the institutional culture of cooperative federalism has become most obvious since German unification. The Western German Länder complain about some of the New Länder, which "simply do not understand the rules of the game."[2] In particular, Sachsen repeatedly violated fundamental rules of cooperative federalism, for example, by striking unilateral deals with the national government, by refusing to facilitate a consensus with the other Länder on controversial issues, by taking a negative position on issues that concern the interests of other Länder rather than its own, or by officially voting against a proposal supported by the majority of the Länder.

The cooperative norms and practices embedded in the institutional culture of cooperative federalism determined the strategy by which the Länder strove to redress the territorial balance of power. The Länder started asking for codetermination powers of the Bundesrat in European affairs already in 1951. The federal government discarded these demands as an unconstitutional intervention into its foreign policy prerogative. Yet, the Länder were not completely left without any influence on European policymaking. In 1957, the federal government granted the Länder some initial possibilities of participating in European policymaking, which they successfully managed to expand over the following years. These intrastate channels of access to European institutions have been based on:

1. information to the Bundesrat regarding projects, initiatives, and proposals of the European Commission;
2. access to informal and formal European documents;
3. the right of the Bundesrat to make recommendations that the federal government is obligated to give due consideration;
4. the participation of the Länder observer and other Länder representatives in European decision-making bodies (e.g., Council of Ministers, Committee of Permanent Representatives, other committees) as members of the German delegation;
5. the ratification of European treaties revisions by the Bundesrat (veto power).

2. Interview with member of the Staatsministerium Baden-Württemberg, Abteilung Internationale Angelegenheiten und Europapolitik (State Ministry of Baden Württemberg, Department of International and European Affairs), Stuttgart, March 18, 1998.

In a continuous process of multilateral bargaining with the central state, the Länder subsequently succeeded in enhancing their intrastate participation in European decision making. But these intrastate channels of influence proved to be insufficient to compensate the Länder for their loss of domestic decision-making powers. Information and consultation in European decision making is not a substitute for self-determination and co-determination rights in domestic decision making.

In 1987, however, the Länder achieved substantial co-determination powers in European affairs by threatening to veto the ratification of the Single European Act (SEA) in the Bundesrat. A new intrastate procedure was introduced by the law ratifying the SEA. The so-called "Bundesratsverfahren" reinforced the obligation of the federal government to inform the Bundesrat comprehensively and as soon as possible of all European issues of interest for the Länder. The Bundesrat obtained the possibility of making formal recommendations on EC proposals that affected the exclusive jurisdiction or essential interests of the Länder, from which the Federal government could only depart for due reasons, which had to be justified before the Bundesrat. Finally, the Federal government was obliged to call in Länder representatives at the negotiation stage when important interests of the Länder were involved. These formal co-determination rights in European decision making provided a first step in effectively compensating the Länder for their losses of domestic power.

With the Maastricht Treaty, the Länder then definitively succeeded in redressing the territorial balance of power between them and the Federal government in European policymaking. Threatening again to veto ratification, the Länder finally got what they had always wanted: comprehensive, legally binding co-determination powers in EU policy-making. For the first time, the transfer of both national and regional competencies to the EU requires the consent of the Länder (Bundesrat). A two-thirds majority of Bundestag and Bundesrat has to ratify any changes in the EU Treaty, or similar regulations. When Länder interest are affected by a EU decision, the Federal government has to take into account the opinion of the Bundesrat, which is, however, ultimately not binding. But when former administrative or legislative Länder competencies are involved, the Bundesrat has the final decision on the German bargaining position in the Council of Ministers. And whenever exclusive legislative competencies of the Länder are concerned, a Länder minister represents Germany in the Council negotiations.

The Länder have successfully employed their "compensation-through-participation" strategy to continuously expand their participation in European policy-making mediated through the central state. This has given rise to a number of subsequent institutional changes culminating in an amendment of the German constitution granting the Länder comprehensive co-decision powers in the formulation and representation of the German bargaining position at the European level. The increasing intrastate participation of the Länder in European policy-making redressed the territorial balance of power, which had been disturbed by Europeanization, causing a double shift of competencies in favor of the central state. On the "say" side, the Länder losses of autonomous and shared competencies are compensated by co–determination rights in European policymaking. On the "pay side," the Länder are involved in the formulation and decision making of essentially every European policy that they have to later implement.

The coordination and cooperation necessary to make this intrastate participation of the Länder work is provided by the institutions of joint decision making and by interlocking politics. The national government and the Länder use the mechanisms of vertical and horizontal coordination that they have developed over more than forty years of German federalism, such as the Bundesrat and its committees, the interministerial conferences, or the (personal) contacts between the Länder representations in Bonn and Berlin, and the Ministry of Foreign Affairs and the Ministry of Economics. The federal–Länder cooperation in European affairs has proven quite efficient. It seems that the Länder and the federal government did not get caught in the dual joint decision-making trap. Hence, there are good reasons to argue that the compensation-through-participation strategy of the Länder successfully facilitated institutional adaptation to Europeanization by effectively leveling out the uneven distribution of say and pay.

Extrastate Channels of Influence: Complement Rather Than Supplement. Despite their considerable intrastate access to European policymaking, the Länder also established direct contacts with European institutions. The Länder opened offices in Brussels in the second half of the 1980s. The Länderbüros' main task is to inform their respective Länder government about all developments at the European level that could be of particular interest for the Land, to help public institutions and private enterprises of their Land to establish contacts with EU institutions, and to conduct public relations for the Land, especially with the European Commission.

Moreover, the Länder gained, together with the regions of the other member states, direct representation at the European level through various institutions, such as the Assembly of European Regions or the Committee of the Regions (CoR). The large number and strong heterogeneity of the regions and municipalities in these bodies, however, rendered it extremely difficult to arrive at common positions corresponding to the interests of the Länder. Because the Länder have ample possibilities for intrastate participation in EU policymaking, extrastate channels of access have always played a rather complementary role for the Länder. They have basically employed these European resources for two different purposes. Whereas intrastate channels serve very well to pursue common Länder interests, the individual Länder use their direct contacts with European institutions to realize particular interests, such as attracting foreign investments or Community subsidies. Moreover, the Länder instrumentalized their transnational relations with European and other regional actors to push their domestic agenda for co-determination powers in European policymaking at the intrastate level. In 1988, the Länder started to promote the idea of a "Europe of the Regions." Using their contacts with European and regional actors, such as the president of the European Commission, the European Parliament, the Assembly of European Regions, and the Conference "Europe of the Regions," the Länder mobilized political support inside and outside Germany for their claims of a strong role of the regions in European politics. In 1986, the demands of the Länder for intrastate participation in European policymaking had been largely considered hostile to European integration. In 1991–92, however, the Länder were able to legitimize their call for strong constitutional rights of intrastate participation by embedding their demands in the general concept of a Europe of the Regions, which was increasingly embraced by national and European politicians as a means to overcome the legitimacy crisis of European integration.

Extrastate channels of access to European policymaking have always been important to the Länder. Rather than circumvent or bypass the state, however, the Länder have been using their direct access to the European arena to complement and expand their intrastate channels of influence. The predominant interest of the Länder in using European resources and opportunities to pursue their "compensation-through-intrastate-participation" strategy has become most obvious in the negotiations for the Intergovernmental Conference of 1997. The Länder have not paid "more than lip-service to the Third Level ambitions trumpeted during the Maastricht process" (Jeffery 1997a, 73). This may be partly due to the Länders' sobering experience with the newly established CoR. The Länder had to realize that they could not simply control this body the way they had initially thought. Moreover, the Länder have diverging opinions on the future role of the regions in Europe. The New Länder especially are very skeptical toward enhancing the political weight of the Third Level. Most important, however, the Länder have real intrastate decision-making powers in European policymaking by effectively cooperating with the federal government—a compensation for adaptational costs neither the CoR, nor direct contacts with European institutions can provide.

Europeanization and the Reinforcement of German Territorial Institutions.   All in all, cooperative federalism has clearly favored a cooperative strategy of the Länder in trying to redress the territorial balance of power disturbed by Europeanization. Constitutional litigation and bilateral contacts with the central state have hardly been employed by the Länder. They have always pursued a joint position vis-à-vis the federal government that has aimed at cooperating with rather than confronting and circumventing the central state. The compensation-through-intrastate-participation strategy proved very effective in redressing the balance of power, facilitating institutional adaptation. It resulted in an externalization of cooperative federalism to European policymaking by which the German central state has been neither strengthened nor weakened nor transformed. Even if the German Länder may now officially sit on the Council of Ministers, this has not changed either the formal rules of joint decision making or the institutional culture of multilateral bargaining and consensus seeking on which German cooperative federalism rests. Rather, Europeanization has led to incremental adjustments of the system of interlocking politics, extending it to the European level, which has ultimately reinforced rather than fundamentally changed the institutions of cooperative federalism.

Europeanization and Territorial Change in Spain:
Toward Cooperative Regionalism

Europeanization and the Challenge to the Spanish "Estado de Autonomías". As in Germany, Europeanization led to an uneven distribution of say and pay by centralizing regional competencies at the central-state level. Because the Comunidades Autónomas (CCAA) do not have any co-determination powers in central-state decision making, the CCAA have been more affected in the area of their exclusive legislative and executive competencies (Montoro Chiner 1989).

The Spanish central state has not only gained access to the exclusive jurisdiction of the CCAA by the participation of the Spanish government in the European decision-making process. The Spanish government also used the transposition of European Directives into national law to intervene in the area of exclusive regional competencies for the legal and administrative execution of European policies in many policy areas. The central state has been able to take on exclusive competencies of the CCAA by subsuming the implementation of European policies under its exclusive responsibility for "external relations" or the setting of national framework legislation so as to ensure a uniform and effective application of European law. The CCAA have been particularly affected by centralization in the areas of agriculture, fishing, cattle rearing, dairy production, research and technology, transport, environment, regional and structural policy, and culture and education.

While Europeanization constrains the CCAA in their legislative and administrative autonomy, they remain central in the implementation of European policies, especially when it comes to practical application and enforcement. Like the German Länder, the CCAA often have to bear the political and material costs of implementation without being involved in the formulation and decision-making process. Their discretion in implementation is not only reduced by European regulations but also by an often very detailed transposition of European policies into domestic law at the central-state level.

The uneven distribution of say and pay caused by Europeanization upset the already fragile balance of power between the central state and the CCAA. Decentralization and Europeanization of the Spanish state largely coincided with each other and introduced two contradictory trends in Spanish territorial politics. On the one hand, the CCAA strove to enhance their decision-making powers striving to minimize the intervention of the central state into their own affairs. On the other hand, the formal rules and procedures of European decision making enabled the central state to increasingly interfere with the autonomous decision-making powers of the CCAA.

Competitive Regionalism and the Strategy of "Confronting and Circumventing the State": Prohibiting Institutional Adaptation.   The CCAA have been aware of the centralizing effect of Europeanization since Spain joined the European Community in 1986. But unlike the Länder, the CCAA did not attempt to redress the territorial balance of power by pushing for intrastate participation in European policymaking. Rather, the CCAA pursued a strategy of confronting and circumventing the central state, restricting relations with the central state to the level of bilateral, mostly informal, bargaining.   ·

The choice for a confrontative strategy results from the institutional culture of competitive regionalism, which has traditionally dominated the center-periphery relations in Spain. For historical, political, cultural, and socioeconomic reasons, the relationship between the central state and its regions has always been characterized by competition, conflict, and imposition rather than cooperation and mutual understanding. Cooperation with the central state is perceived to be a threat to regional autonomy. Intergovernmental conflicts tend to be solved before the Constitutional Court rather than by political agreement. Spain is facing the highest number of constitutional conflicts between the central state and its regions in Europe. The CCAA strive to minimize their institutional relationship with the central government, as a result of which intergovernmental relations are non-formalized, ad hoc, and usually bilateral. Institutionalized cooperation with the central state and other CCAA is not only rare, it requires public justification. When, for instance, the Catalan government struck a formal coalition agreement with the ruling national government in 1996, it faced strong public criticism for "betraying" the Catalan cause. This institutional culture of competition and conflict rendered a cooperative strategy (like that of the Länder) in striving to redress the territorial balance of power more than unlikely for the CCAA. Rather, they pursued a twofold strategy of confronting and circumventing the central state in the first place. Any offer of the Spanish government to establish some form of intergovernmental coordination with the CCAA in order to facilitate the implementation of EU policies was turned down by the CCAA.

A first proposal for intergovernmental cooperation had been made by the national government even before Spain entered the EC. The agreement should regulate the participation of the CCAA both in the decision-making and implementation of European legal acts. For the implementation stage, the Spanish government suggested a distribution of responsibilities in which the central state, notwithstanding the internal distribution of competencies, would legally transpose and the CCAA practically apply EU policies. The CCAA would not be allowed to have any direct contact with European institutions. But if the central government decided that a European proposal could affect autonomous competencies, it would inform the CCAA. And the central government would consider the concerns of the CCAA in the formulation of its bargaining position. The CCAA rejected this proposal, interpreting it as an attempt by the central state to establish a general competence to legally implement EU law. They also criticized the low level of influence that they would have on European decision making.

The Spanish government prepared a second proposal in April 1986, taking into account some of the concerns that the CCAA had raised against the first proposal. The CCAA would participate in the implementation of European law according to their domestic competencies. In addition, the CCAA should create an interregional coordination body through which the central government would inform the CCAA on European issues and the CCAA could formulate joint positions that the central government would give due consideration. Finally, the CCAA could nominate an observer of the Comunidades Autónomas, who would be a member of the Spanish permanent representation in Brussels. Again, the CCAA rejected this proposal because of the lax obligation of the central state to consider their preferences in the formulation of the Spanish positions and the restricted role of the observer, on whose selection procedure the CCAA had not been able to agree, either.

A year later, the central government drafted a third agreement, which, however, never reached the status of a formal proposition, owing to the opposition of the CCAA.

The heterogeneity among the CCAA with regard to their resources and historical self-understanding has made it extremely difficult to find a modus operandi of intergovernmental cooperation to accommodate the interests and claims of all CCAA. The insistence of the regions of Catalunya and el País Vasco on privileged rights because of their status as historical nationalities has precluded any effective horizontal coordination of interests among the CCAA; such coordination is the prerequisite for both the agreement on and the effective functioning of regional intrastate participation in European decision making.

Moreover, multilateral intergovernmental coordination in European policymaking between the central state and the CCAA has also been difficult to achieve. Most of the CCAA have had a strong preference for bilateral and informal contacts with the central government (Bustos Gisbert 1995). They perceived the proposals for intergovernmental cooperation in European affairs organized in a formal multilateral framework as yet another attempt by the central state to centralize their competencies.

During the first years of Spain's EC membership, the CCAA appeared unwilling to cooperate either among one another or with the central state on European affairs. Rather, the CCAA pursued a twofold strategy of circumventing and confronting the state. First, they strove to bypass the gatekeeping position of the Spanish government by establishing extrastate channels of access to European institutions, exploiting European resources and thus, "outflank[ing] the central authorities" (Morata 1995). Second, they litigated against the central state before the Constitutional Court every time they perceived an intrusion of the central state in their sphere of competencies in European policymaking.

Most of the CCAA maintain regular contacts with EU institutions at the informal level. Regional politicians and delegations travel to Brussels more often than to any other foreign country (Cuerdo Pardo 1995), although the Spanish government was able to suppress most attempts of the CCAA to establish official contacts with EU institutions (Dalmau i Oriol 1997).

To be present at the European level, thirteen of the seventeen CCAA have opened information offices in Brussels. They enable the CCAA to collect information, maintain regular contact with EU institutions, and promote their economic and cultural interests. Until 1994, the offices were not allowed to have official status.

Only then, a ruling of the Constitutional Court enabled the CCAA to integrate the offices into their government structure.

The CCAA have been also participating in the various bodies of regional representation at the European level. The Spanish regions held and hold several leading positions in the Assembly of the Regions in Europe, the Committee of the Regions, and the Council of European Municipalities. Most CCAA have also been involved in transregional and interregional forms of cooperation, such as the conferences Europe of Regions, the Four Motors of Europe, the Pyrenean Working Group, or the Transpyrenean Euro-region.

All in all, the CCAA have exploited European resources to establish several extrastate channels of access to the European level. Especially those CCAA that have been critical of the multilateral framework of intrastate participation (above all el País Vasco and Catalunya) have made intensive use of their direct contacts with European institutions.

Increasing Losses of Power: The Strategy Change of the CCAA.   The twofold strategy of the CCAA of confronting and circumventing the state in order to redress the territorial balance of power proved largely ineffective. Rather than compensating the domestic losses of power of the CCAA, their confrontational strategy tended to promote even further centralization of regional competencies.

First, extrastate channels of access to European policymaking have considerable limits. Some of the smaller CCAA have lacked the organizational capacity to establish direct contacts with the EU. More important, there are also significant legal and political constraints to the establishment of such extrastate channels of access. All official contacts with European institutions have to be mediated through the central state. And the European institutions are very careful in dealing with the regions without the involvement or at least the consent of central state authorities. The CCAA increasingly became aware that extrastate channels of influence, which are essentially reduced to lobbying activities, do not compensate for the loss of formal decision-making powers.

Second, the strategy of the CCAA to fight any intrusion of the central state in their autonomous sphere of competencies before the Constitutional Court proved equally ineffective in redressing the territorial balance of power. In an attempt at ring fencing their competencies, the CCAA initiated a whole series of constitutional conflicts over competencies in the area of European policymaking. But a ruling of the Constitutional Court usually takes up three to five years and requires considerable administrative resources. The jurisdiction of the court indeed helped to clarify the delimitation of competencies between the central state and the CCAA in European policymaking. But in most cases, the Constitutional Court sided with the central state, allowing it to use its exclusive competencies for external relations to intervene in areas of regional competencies (Pérez González 1989).

Toward the end of the 1980s, the CCAA started to realize that their twofold strategy of circumventing and confronting the state had failed in redressing the balance of power. Their refusal to cooperate with the central state in European policymaking as well as most of the rulings of the Constitutional Court tended to further centralization instead of counterbalancing it. Moreover, by refusing to cooperate with the central state, the CCAA were deprived of systematic access of European funding to pay off some of the costs for implementing European policies.

The Piece-Meal Approach toward Intergovernmental Cooperation.   The strategy change of the CCAA was facilitated by the Spanish government, which initiated an "institutionalized dialogue" in which specific problems were to be tackled and the participation of the CCAA in European policymaking could be discussed. An ad hoc Interministerial Conference on European Affairs was established. The conference, which was convened once per year on a strictly informal level, mainly served for the mutual exchange of information on issues on the agenda of the European Council. It also produces two important partial agreements in 1990. One provides for the participation of the CCAA in infringement procedures of the European Commission against the Spanish state. And another regulates the obligatory announcement of public subsidies to the European Commission. Finally, the Commission of Coordinators in European Affairs, comprising one representative of each regional administration, was created. The major task of this "second order body" is to prepare the meetings of the conference and to implement its decisions.

In 1992, the Spanish government made the suggestion to formally institutionalize the Conference on European Affairs. For the very first time, the CCAA accepted a formal agreement made by the central state government.

Europeanization and Territorial Change in Spain: The Institutionalization of Intrastate Participation.   In the two years after its institutionalization, the Conference on European Affairs negotiated a general agreement on a formal intrastate participation of the CCAA in European policymaking, which was adopted in November 1994. The only region that initially did not sign the agreement of 1994 was el País Vasco.[3] The 1994 procedure strongly resembles the German model. The participation of the CCAA in European policymaking is based on the intergovernmental cooperation of CCAA and central state. But unlike in Germany, the sectoral conferences and not the Second Chamber of the national legislature, serve as the mechanism to coordinate the interests of the regions and the central state.[4] The Spanish government informs the CCAA in the various sectoral conferences about all European issues relevant to their competencies or interests throughout the whole decision-making process. The CCAA formulate joint positions on specific issues and coordinate them with the central state administration. As in the German procedure, the binding character of the CCAA joint position for the

3. In 1995, el País Vasco finally abandoned its strategy of exclusive bilateralism and signed all the multilateral agreements reached between the central state and the other sixteen CCAA.

4. The by now more than twenty sectoral conferences bring together the ministers of the CCAA and the central state in one particular policy area.

Spanish government varies according to the degree to which the competencies of the CCAA are affected. With regard to the implementation of EU policies, the central state and regional administrations inform the respective sectoral conference about the legal and administrative measures taken in the transposition and practical application. The sectoral conferences are also the place to settle any conflict over competencies or other implementation problems.

In 1997, the Conference on European Affairs agreed to establish a Counselor of Autonomous Affairs, a representative of the CCAA who is associated with the Spanish permanent representation in Brussels and who may be allowed to participate in European decision-making bodies. In the same year, the conference reached also an informal agreement that allows for the participation of regional representatives in fifty-five advisory committees and working groups of the European Commission. Finally in 1998, the conference produced a resolution that provides the CCAA with the right to ask the central state to appeal before the European Court of Justice if Community action infringes their competencies.

All in all, the central state and the CCAA finally reached a comprehensive agreement providing for an intrastate participation of the CCAA in both the formulation and implementation of EU policies. The procedure does not provide the CCAA with the same co-determination powers that the Länder have. Yet, for the first time ever, the CCAA do have the right to participate in central-state decision making. Co-decision rights can never be a full substitute for self-determination powers. But the intrastate participation of the CCAA in European policymaking prevents the central state from further centralizing regional competencies, particularly in the implementation of European policies.

The formal intrastate participation of the CCAA in European policymaking constitutes the very first institutional framework in Spain that provides for a systematic, multilateral participation of the CCAA in central-state decision making. Spain had so far lacked any effective institutional structure that could have provided the intergovernmental coordination both among the CCAA and between the CCAA and the national government necessary to make intrastate participation work. In order to participate in European policymaking, the CCAA have for the first time ever committed themselves to a certain degree of formal intergovernmental coordination based on the principle of multilateral cooperation. The importance of this new decision-making model in European policymaking must not be underestimated. Being already an accomplishment by itself given the conflictual and competitive institutional culture of Spanish intergovernmental relations, it also serves as a test case for a new form of intergovernmental coordination, which, if successful, might be transferred to areas outside European policymaking (Bustos Gisbert 1995). The next years will show whether Europeanization triggered a change in Spanish territorial institutions that will go beyond the—though quite substantial—area of European policymaking, leading to an overall shift from competitive toward some form of cooperative regionalism (cf. Börzel, 2000).

Conclusion: Toward Cooperative Regionalism in Europe?

This paper argued that the impact of Europeanization on the territorial institutions of the member states is institution dependent. Domestic institutions matter in two ways. First, the formal territorial institutions define the degree of pressure for adaptation that Europeanization exercises. The greater the misfit between European and domestic institutional rules and procedures, the greater the potential change in the domestic distribution of power and the higher the pressure for institutional adaptation. Second, the informal institutional culture strongly influences the strategies by which domestic actors respond to adaptational pressure facilitating or prohibiting institutional adaptation. It was hypothesized that Europeanization is most likely to trigger domestic institutional change if there is significant pressure for adaptation to which domestic actors respond by a noncooperative strategy that prohibits rather than facilitates institutional adaptation.

I demonstrated my institutionalist argument empirically in comparing the effect of Europeanization on the territorial institutions of Germany and Spain. Europeanization caused similar pressure for adaptation on the territorial institutions of both member states by changing the territorial balance of power, to the detriment of the regions. But the German and Spanish regions pursued very different strategies in trying to redress the balance of power due to the different institutional cultures in which they are embedded. Cooperative federalism induced the German Länder to pursue a cooperative strategy that aimed at the compensation of the centralization of their powers through the intrastate participation in European policymaking. This strategy proved successful in redressing the balance of power, facilitating institutional adaptation, which reinforced rather than changed the formal and informal institutions of cooperative federalism. In Spain, on the contrary, competitive regionalism favored a confrontational strategy of the CCAA of confronting and circumventing the central state. This strategy, however, did not prevent the progressive centralization of their powers, nor did it provide a compensation for it. Instead of reducing adaptational costs, it increased them, prohibiting institutional adaptation. As a result, the CCAA finally changed their strategy toward a more cooperative approach, which resulted in the very first formal institutional framework, providing for a participation of the CCAA in central-state decision making. This intrastate participation, which is based on the multilateral cooperation between the central state and the regions, constitutes a significant change in the territorial institutions of Spain, at least at the formal level, where joint decision making had never existed before. Whether these changes of the formal institutions will also change the institutional culture of competitive regionalism, is too early to assess.

While Spain finally adopted the German model of intrastate participation in adapting its territorial institutions to the challenges of Europeanization, other member states with a high degree of decentralization have moved in the same direction. Facing similar pressure of adaptation, the Austrian, Belgian, and Italian regions pursued the same strategy as the German Länder, aiming at redressing the territorial balance of power by demanding co-decision rights in the formulation and representation of the national bargaining position (Börzel 1999). The territorial institutions of the regionalized and federal member states appear to converge around a model of regional participation in European policymaking that is predominantly mediated through the central states.

Paradoxically, those regions with the necessary resources to exploit direct channels of access to the European policy arena increasingly rely on cooperation with the central state government to project their interests in the European policymaking process. Even institutionally well-entrenched regions realized that the status of an albeit powerful interest group is no substitute for formal decision-making powers. The shift toward cooperative federalism, even in member states like Belgium, Spain, and Italy, where a competitive institutional culture had prevented any effective multilateral cooperation between the central state and the regions, does not only constitute a major change in the (formal) territorial institutions of some member states. It has also important implications for the future European polity.

First, the prevailing or maybe even increasing relevance of intrastate participation of the regions in European policy-making is undercutting the prospects of a "Europe of the Regions," where the regions are to constitute a "Third Level," next to the member states and the European institutions. There appears to be a certain disenchantment with the idea of a "Europe of the Regions," particularly among the institutionally well-entrenched regions, which are increasingly skeptical about the effectiveness of the collective representation of regional interests at the European level. The regions, which have the necessary resources, rely on their offices in Brussels rather than the CoR for direct access to the European policy arena. The support of the stronger regions, however, is crucial for promoting the institutionalization of the Third Level (e.g., by strengthening the rights of the CoR) because those regions have the domestic resources (veto power) to push the issue onto the European agenda.

Second, intrastate participation of the regions promotes executive dominance in European policymaking, raising additional problems of legitimacy. The compensation of regional losses of competencies caused by Europeanization through co-decision rights in the formulation and representation of the national bargaining position may prove effective in redressing the territorial balance of power between the central state and the regions. Yet, these compensatory co-decision powers are exercised by the regional governments, which usually merely inform their parliaments on European issues. Unlike in domestic policymaking, the regional parliaments do not have any formal decision-making powers with respect to the intrastate participation of the regions in European policymaking. The erosion of the political power of regional parliaments reinforces the general trend of deparliamentiarization at the domestic level as a consequence of Europeanization. With the exception perhaps of the Danish Parliament, the power of the national legislatures relative to their executives is rather small in European policymaking. The uneven distribution of "say and pay" at least partly holds for the relationship between the executive and the legislature, too. But unlike the regions, the national parliaments have been less effective in asking for a compensation of their losses of power resulting from the transfer of domestic policy competencies to the European level.

All in all, cooperative regionalism appears to be effective in redressing the territorial balance of power between the central state and the regions. But by dealing with one major challenge of Europeanization (domestic centralization), cooperative regionalism appears to reinforce another—the lack of transparency and accountability. Cooperative regionalism does not only undermine the prospects of a "Europe of the Regions," which has been celebrated as a potential remedy against the legitimacy problems of the EU. Cooperative regionalism also tends to exacerbate these legitimacy problems by promoting regional deparliamentiarization.

CHAPTER NINE

The Transatlantic Business Dialogue and Domestic Business-Government Relations

Maria Green Cowles

Since the 1980s, the nature of business mediation or "lobbying" has changed dramatically in Brussels (Greenwood, Grote, and Ronit 1992; Mazey and Richardson 1993; Cowles 1996a). It is not merely who and how many groups are in Brussels, but *the nature and composition of the relationship between business groups and European institutions* that have significantly changed. Once shunned by European Commission officials (Feld 1966; Sidjanski 1967), multinational firms and key industry groups now enjoy strong working relationships, particularly during the drafting stage of European Union (EU) legislation. In certain EU cabinets, seconded representatives of major companies work with Commission officials to forge industrial policies. Captains of industry in the European Round Table of Industrialists (ERT) meet regularly with the Commission president and heads of state (Cowles 1995). The same chief executive officers or company board directors attend carefully planned news conferences with EU officials to declare their support for various EU programs, thus allowing Commissioners an opportunity to demonstrate their own "business constituency" vis-à-vis the member states.

In effect, there has been a Europeanization of business-government relations. The creation of a distinct form of business-government relationship at the European level is in itself a form of political institution, albeit an informal one. Significant to this relationship is the fact that oftentimes, individual firms have similar if not more privileged links to European authorities than European "peak" industry associations.

I thank Tanja Börzel, Jim Caporaso, Michelle Egan, Thomas Risse, Fritz Scharpf, Vivien Schmidt, Volker Schneider, Mitchell Smith, Martin Stangeland, and Bastian van Apeldoorn for their comments on earlier versions of this chapter.

How does this Europeanization process impact domestic structures—namely, business-government relations at the national level? Do the emerging transnational systems of interest mediation at the European level have any consequences for the national systems of interest formation, aggregation, and mediation? More specifically, what impact does the Europeanization of business-government relations have on the traditional relationship between the national "peak" industry associations and their respective governments?

While studies point to EU-level business-government relations or the actions of national groups in Brussels (Van Schendelen 1993), very little attention has been paid to how this EU development impacts business-government relations at the domestic level in member states.[1] Perhaps one reason for the paucity of literature is the relative newness of European-level business-government relations. Perhaps another is the difficulty in separating the European and domestic levels when discussing business activity and relationships. As I discuss later in the chapter, national business groups act at both the European and domestic level. Moreover, they may interact with their respective governments at the supranational as well as national level in the EU's multilevel system of governance.

The purpose of this chapter is to examine the impact of the Europeanization of business-government relations on business-government relations at the national level through a case study of the Transatlantic Business Dialogue (TABD). In particular, the case study focuses on the changing relationship of national industry associations (NIAs) vis-à-vis their respective governments in France, Germany, and the United Kingdom, as well as the large companies they represent. The national industry associations are emphasized because they have historically held a special position in most European countries. NIAs are generally recognized as "the voice of industry" in EU member states. Unlike the United States, where there is no single umbrella business organization, European countries have one, sometimes two, "peak" industry associations. The Confederation of British Industry (CBI) in the United Kingdom, the Bundesverband der Deutschen Industrie (BDI) in Germany, and the Mouvement des Entreprises de France (MEDEF) in France are thus considered to be the most representative organizations of industry in their respective countries.

The TABD serves as an important case study in that it represents a clear example of the Europeanization of business-government relations in common commercial policy. Prior to the TABD, domestic business-government relations served as the focal point of European business mediation in external trade matters. For example, most NIAs (as well as national sectoral associations) held an important bargaining position with their governments in shaping European policy in the General Agreement on Tariffs and Trade (GATT) negotiations. The TABD, however, created a new form of business-government relationship at the European

---

1. However, some works have focused on the Europeanization of business. Kassim and Menon (1996) focus on how the EU impacts the substance of national policies—and not on business-government relations per se. V. Schmidt (1996a, 1996b) examines the EU's impact on business-government relations in a single country—France.

level that ultimately challenges the primordial position of the NIAs in external trade matters. The TABD—while a business-to-business dialogue—is also a quadrilateral forum in which European companies, the European Commission, American firms, and the U.S. government seek to eliminate nontariff barriers to trade. Thus, large European firms have organized themselves at the European level to provide input into the TABD process. They have sought to influence U.S.-EU TABD negotiations through the development of lobbying and close consultation procedures with the European Commission. By promoting this new European business-government relationship, large companies have moved the locus of EU commercial policy lobbying activity from the domestic to the European level.

As I discuss in this chapter, the Europeanization of business-government relations in the TABD process impacts domestic business-government relations in a number of ways. First, the domestic relationships become less important given that the largest economic actors have demonstrated their willingness to work directly through the Commission—and not through the NIAs or national governments. Second, the authoritative voice of NIAs vis-à-vis their respective governments is often challenged, given that large firms are effectively bypassing the industry associations. Moreover, the same firms are meeting directly with the national governments to discuss their positions, thus further altering the position of NIAs at the domestic level. Finally, the participation of these large European companies in the TABD represents a breakdown of the traditional "separation of responsibilities" between firms and industry associations in Europe. By devoting the resources to develop their own expertise in external trade policy, the firms have demonstrated their willingness to play a leading role in future common commercial policy matters. In short, the Europeanization of business-government relations in the TABD process will continue to impact the domestic business-government relationship in EU common commercial policy.

I begin this chapter with a discussion of "goodness of fit" between the European form of business-government relationship adopted in the TABD and the traditional business-government relationship found at the domestic level. In the second section, I explore the creation of the TABD and the European business-government relationship in common commercial policy. I then analyze in the third part of the chapter the impact of this Europeanization on domestic business-government relations in the United Kingdom, Germany, and France, and the mediating factors that allowed for domestic institutional change. The final section examines issues such as convergence and shifting loyalties, as well as limits to domestic structural change.

Europeanization and the Goodness of Fit

As discussed in the introduction of this book, one means of analyzing these pressures from, impact of, and responses to the Europeanization of business-government relations is to examine how closely the structure of domestic business-government relations is related to that found at the European level in common commercial policy matters. What is the institutional fit? If the institutional relationship is similar to that of Europe, one would expect little difficulty in adapting to the situation—if adaptation is even necessary. But if the domestic relationship does not resemble that found at the European level, one might expect problems in adaptation.

In examining the institutional relationship, I will focus on two dimensions. The first is the bargaining relationship between the government and industry associations. How exclusive is the bargaining relationship between government and industry associations in common commercial policy? Do the associations engage in a close partnership with the government, or do the associations bring pressure to bear on state authorities in a more arms-length fashion?

The second dimension concerns the authoritative nature of the associations vis-à-vis the firms that they represent. To what extent are the associations recognized as the "voice" of business interests in society on common commercial policy matters? How organized or centralized are these associations that bargain with governments?

The European Commission and the TABD

Before the TABD, there was no significant business-government relationship at the European level in external trade matters. In some respects, this absence is surprising, given the European Commission's visible role in trade negotiations. The Commission, for example, has competence for making proposals for any negotiating platform while the General Affairs Council has the right to approve the platform based on a qualified majority vote. Historically the Commission also serves as the sole spokesperson and negotiator during trade negotiations.[2] The Article 133 Committee, a group of senior member-state officials, advises the Commission throughout the negotiating process (Woolcock and Hodges 1996; Meunier 1998).

Despite the Commission's leadership in producing the negotiating mandate and serving as key spokesperson/negotiator, there were no formal procedures for consultation between the Commission and business groups during recent Uruguay GATT rounds. Thus, while the Union of Industrial and Employers' Confederations (UNICE)—the European peak business association—provided official comments on the GATT negotiations, it did not have any significant consultations with the European Commission (Woolcock and Hodges 1996, 305). The industry coordination that did take place occurred at the domestic level. National industry associations served as the key coordinators of business interests on common

---

2. Recently the sole competence of the Commission has been challenged. A 1994 ECJ ruling allowed the Commission and member states to share competence in the new trade issues of services and intellectual property. The 1997 Amsterdam Treaty further restricted the Commission's power by "allowing member states to decide what competence to delegate on a case-by-case basis at the outset of a negotiation" (Meunier and Nicolaïdis in press).

commercial policy and expressed business interests with national government authorities who, in turn, informed the Commission of government and industry preferences.

As discussed below, the TABD changed this business-government dynamic. With the creation of TABD, a new business-government relationship emerged in Brussels in common commercial policy. However, instead of UNICE serving as the key adviser on European business interests, large European companies became the primary interlocutors and partners with the European Commission. Thus, UNICE, the representative of the national industry associations and "logical" partner of the Commission in external trade matters, was not accorded a primary role in the TABD business-government relationship. In terms of bargaining vis-à-vis the Commission, therefore, UNICE became but one of many voices in TABD policymaking. Moreover, its self-proclaimed authority as "the voice of European business" was further weakened by the importance of individual companies in the TABD relationship. Thus, the TABD business-government relationship transformed the traditional government-industry association model of interest representation found at both the national and European levels.

With the multiple actors expressing their interests to the government, the TABD process might be characterized as "pluralist" (see Truman 1951; Dahl 1961; Lowi 1969). However, the creation of close linkages between the European Commission and large firms in the TABD process might be better captured by what other scholars have called "elite pluralism" (Coen 1997a). Large multinational corporations lobbied Commission officials and developed close working relations with top-tier Eurocrats to promote their interests. While these large firms are not the only business groups to express their concerns to the Commission, they did have privileged access.

In examining the impact of Europeanization on domestic-business government relations, we can evaluate how closely this elite pluralist relationship "fits" with business-government relations at the domestic level. What is the institutional goodness of fit? To answer this question, we now examine the domestic business-government relationships in the United Kingdom, Germany, and France.

The United Kingdom and the CBI

Business-government relations, and the role of the Confederation of British Industry (CBI) in those relations, have evolved considerably over the past thirty years. Part of the reason for this evolution is that the state itself has changed during this period. Indeed, political scientists have often disagreed on how to characterize business-government relations in the United Kingdom. The close consultation between the state and peak associations between 1964-79, for example, prompted some scholars to characterize the United Kingdom as having a weak corporatist model. Since 1979, the United Kingdom has been characterized as a pluralist system in which pressure groups lobby and compete for access to both policy formulation and implementation (Jordan and Richardson 1987). More recently, however, scholars have noted the rising role of firms in business–government relations (Grant 1987).

Historically, the bargaining relationship between business and government was rather consensual. The CBI serves on a number of government advisory bodies, tribunals, and committees, thus creating a close relationship between the NIA and government departments (Norton 1991, 175). This consensual relationship suffered, however, during the Thatcher years, when the CBI leadership openly questioned the government's strict monetary policy that negatively impacted the CBI's manufacturing members. In response, Thatcher limited the CBI's access to government committees, and promotion-minded civil servants cut back on their consultation with business (Wilson 1990, 81–82). That the CBI also tended to be more pro-European than the prime minister further exacerbated the business–government relationship.

When the CBI lost some standing with the government, large companies stepped in to increase contacts with state officials, thus bypassing the organization. Ministers and civil servants welcomed the opportunity to speak with "real businessmen" instead of CBI officials. While business–government relations improved during the tenure of Prime Minister John Major and now Tony Blair, the United Kingdom has increasingly become a "company state," relying on contacts with individual firms as much if not more than with the CBI (Grant 1987). In this regard, the British model of business–government relations shares a number of similarities with the European "elite pluralism" model found in the TABD.

The CBI's authority vis-à-vis its membership also allows for individual firms to play a greater role in British business–government relations. The CBI is unique in that it is not a "confederation of federations," like most continental European industry associations, but rather an organization that allows both association as well as direct firm membership. The British NIA represents 250,000 firms and 200 trade, commercial, and employer associations (Greenwood and Stancich 1998, 151).

Moreover, the CBI is sometimes regarded as a big business club. While more than 90 percent of the member firms are small- and medium-sized companies, more than half of the CBI's income comes from large firms—that is, those with more than one thousand employees (Norton 1991, 174). Given that the UK has more large multinational firms—many of which are non-British in origin—than any other European country, the role of these companies is highly visible within the NIA.

Finally, because it is first and foremost a lobbying organization, the CBI cannot speak authoritatively on all policy issues. While its mandate is based on regular surveys of and direct consultations with its membership (Greenwood and Stancich, 151), its positions are not binding on its members. The weak nature of British sectoral trade associations further complicates the matter. With poor budgets and relatively weak staffs, these associations are "unimpressive when compared to continental European counterparts" (Wilson 1990, 74). Thus, large

United Kingdom corporations often bypass their sectoral trade associations and meet directly with government departments.

This pluralist—indeed, elite pluralist—business-government relationship in the United Kingdom was evident throughout the GATT negotiations. The CBI, with its "privileged position" as the primary peak association, met regularly with the British government. At the same time, British firms opted not only to work through their national association but also to hold regular discussions with the government. Given that the United Kingdom's "company state" model resembles the elite pluralist TABD relationship in common commercial policy, there is an "institutional fit" between the two. Therefore, one might expect there to be little problem for the CBI to adapt to the new European business-government relationship.

Germany and the BDI

Business-government relations in Germany are quite different. There, the national industry association, the Bundesverband der Deutschen Industrie (BDI, or German Federation of Business), plays a central role.[3] Unlike the CBI, the BDI has a very close relationship with the German government. The corporatist tradition in Germany (Cawson 1986; Katzenstein 1985; Schmitter 1985) makes the state coequal with organized interests such as the BDI and its union counterpart, the Deutscher Gewerkschaftsbund (DGB—German Trade Union Federation). In this sense, German industry groups like the BDI are not disinterested lobbying organizations, but strategic economic actors within the state. The BDI is not a traditional "pressure group" found in pluralist societies such as the United Kingdom; rather, it is a body with which the state consults on a regular basis to develop and carry out policies.

Moreover, the BDI carries a particular authority vis-à-vis its membership not found in the U.K. model. In the first place, the BDI is a "confederation of federations," comprised of thirty-nine sectoral industry associations/federations. It represents more than 85 percent of all German firms, both large and small (Allen 1992, 295). Consequently, the German industry organization enjoys "a high degree of acceptance" as the sole representative of business in dealings with other groups and with government (Wilson 1990, 94; see also Katzenstein 1987, 23).

Equally important, however, is the highly organized, centralized, and authoritative nature of the BDI. While the various sectoral associations may work on their respective issues, they ultimately work through the national association on general trade matters. Through the BDI, therefore, German industry is fairly successful in "speaking with one voice."

That is not to say, however, that individual German firms—large multinational corporations such as Siemens, DaimlerChrysler, BMW, BASF, Hoechst, Bayer, and

---

3. There are two peak industry associations in Germany. The Bundesvereinigung der Deutschen Arbeitgeberverbände (BDA, or National Association of German Employers) participates in labor matters. The BDI is the trade association that represents Germany industry on most industrial matters (Braunthal 1965).

ThyssenKrupp—do not have strong links to government officials. Indeed, they meet with ministry officials on a regular basis. In recent years, fueled by the dual concerns of growing competition and a growing German welfare state, companies have emerged as more visible actors in business–government relations (Allen 2000). More often than not, however, the firms speak out on positions coordinated through their respective sectoral industry associations or deliver their opinions as a member of the BDI presidential board (a CEO group representing major German companies).[4] The reason for the firms' discretion is largely cultural (Egan 1997). As Kohler-Koch points out: "Direct lobbying by private firms and the use of professional lobbyists are uncommon in national politics and can raise suspicions of inappropriate political manipulation by capital interests" (1993, 27).

The BDI plays a central role in this corporatist arrangement as the primary representative of business interests and as a partner with the German government in matters of external trade policy. In the past, while working with its European counterparts in UNICE to develop European-level positions, the BDI focused much of its energy on discussions with the German federal government. During the GATT Uruguay Round, for example, the BDI was a "normal partner" to the government, meeting with the Foreign Section of the Economics Ministry on a regular basis for consultation. The BDI's Trade Policy Committee served as the primary voice for German industry's position on the GATT negotiations.[5] While individual companies and branch federations also participated in the discussions when their particular expertise was needed, the BDI remained the dominant industrial representative.

The corporatist business–government relationship in Germany, therefore, contrasts sharply with the elite pluralist relationship developed in TABD policymaking. In other words, there is a "misfit" between the German and European business–government relationships, and one can expect there to be some difficulty for the BDI to adapt to the new European situation in the TABD negotiations.

France and the MEDEF

The business–government relationship in France is quite different from that found in the United Kingdom and Germany (Kesselman 1992). As Schmidt points out, France comes from a "statist tradition" in which

> government decision-makers and decision-making organizations take a leadership role in policymaking and have primary control over structuring the "state-society relationship," meaning that they are for the most part able to dictate the pattern of interest representation and to resist the pressures of interests, whether organized or not, where they choose. A statist policy, as a result, is one in which government has the power and authority to take unilateral action at the policy formulation stage, without prior consultation with those most interested in the policy (V. Schmidt 1996a, 47).

4. Interview with industry official, February 18, 1998.
5. Interview with BDI official, February 11, 1998.

Where French interest organizations can and do have a greater voice in French policy is at the implementation stage, when special exemptions and procedural reforms are made.

While numerous government committees consult with the French NIA, the Mouvement des Entreprises de France (MEDEF), the "consultation" can be largely one-sided.[6] At times, for example, the government will simply inform the MEDEF of its independently formulated policy (V. Schmidt 1996a, 19) or, indeed, tell the MEDEF what position it should take on a particular issue.[7] Thus, the bargaining relationship of the MEDEF to the French state is quite weak—especially if one compares it to that of the BDI in Germany.

In terms of its authority to speak out on behalf of its membership, the MEDEF is weaker than the BDI but stronger than the CBI. Like its German counterparts, the MEDEF is also a "confederation of federations" that comprises eighty-five trade federations and six hundred professional groups (*syndicats*), and represents more than 1.5 million companies. Yet, the MEDEF does not have the same centralized authority as the BDI. French sectoral trade associations, for example, are more independent from their peak association and do not seek to coordinate their positions to the same degree as their German counterparts do with the BDI. Moreover, the bulk of firms' expenditure on business representation in France goes to the sectoral trade associations; only a fraction goes to the MEDEF (Wilson 1990, 134).

Moreover, the MEDEF is part of two different logics of business representation in France. On one hand, there is the formal role of the MEDEF: developing industry platforms, discussing business views with the press, and meeting informally but frequently with ministers and cabinet members, as well as with members of the National Assembly and French Senate. On the other hand, there are the informal activities of large French companies that interface with the highest-level government officials. There is some overlap and, indeed, synergism between the two logics of representation. Leading officials (though not necessarily the CEOs) from large French firms, for example, often chair MEDEF commissions and working groups (V. Schmidt 1996a, 32).

The French statist form of business-government relationship was evident during the GATT Uruguay Round. While the MEDEF met monthly with the Direction de l'Economie Exterieure, it was disappointed with the government's lack of initiative in industry matters.[8] Government officials were preoccupied with other issues (notably agriculture and audio visual matters). One MEDEF representative put the situation more succinctly: "The [MEDEF's] influence on French negotiating power internationally is peanuts."[9] Aware that the French state would do as it pleased, MEDEF officials ended up focusing most of their energy working on European industry's policy position through

6. The MEDEF was established on October 27, 1998, and superceded the Conseil National du Patronat Français (CNPF), which was created on June 12, 1946.
7. Interview with MEDEF official, February 25, 1998.
8. Interview with MEDEF official, February 18, 1998.
9. Interview with MEDEF official, February 25, 1998.

UNICE. Large French companies also expressed their interests at the European level, even though the European Commission's negotiating mandate came from the national governments.

The statist model business–government relationship is also diametrically opposed to the elite pluralist form of business–government ties found in the TABD process. There is a misfit between the traditional French and European model in common commercial policy. Consequently, one can also expect significant adaptational pressures on the MEDEF to respond to the Europeanization of business–government relations in the TABD.

In looking at the three case studies, it is clear that there is a "fit" between the European and national model (the United Kingdom and the CBI), and two cases of misfit (Germany and the BDI, and France and the MEDEF). One would expect both the German and French industry associations, therefore, to undergo considerable adaptational pressures as a result of the Europeanization of business–government relations in the TABD. Below, I explore these "goodness of fit" hypotheses further, following the discussion of the TABD and the emergence of the new form of business–government relationship in common commercial policy.

The Transatlantic Business Dialogue: A New Business-Government Relationship

The TABD concept was formally launched by the late U.S. Commerce Secretary Ronald Brown at a speech in Brussels in 1994 (Cowles in press[a]). While the U.S. government initially proposed the idea for largely economic reasons— encouraging greater industry participation in global economic activity—the European Commission as well as major European companies were interested in the proposal for more political reasons. Specifically, European government and business leaders were concerned that the United States was "drifting apart" from Europe in the post–Cold War era and was more interested in developing economic links with East Asia.

Following lengthy discussions with U.S. government officials, EU Commissioners and officials from Directorate Generals of External Relations and Industry gave their support to the TABD idea. As one European Commission official noted, "In the initial stages, there was a certain amount of skepticism because we thought transnational relations was best done between governments . . . but the advantages of business involvement soon became apparent" (Cowles in press[a]).

The Commerce Department and the European Commission each recruited two leading businessmen who, in turn, brought transatlantic industry leaders together to discuss regulatory reform and the elimination of nontariff barriers to trade. The process was well underway when U.S.-EU business leaders, along with U.S. and EU government officials, met in Seville, Spain, on November 10, 1995, to hammer out more than seventy specific recommendations that were later presented in a formal document for U.S.-EU government consideration. By most accounts, the

conference was a great success—not only in terms of the overall transatlantic negotiation agenda that was proposed but also in terms of the cooperative working environment between the two sides. For the next four years, Commission officials and
European company representatives worked closely in TABD issue groups and standards committees to identify impediments to trade and to suggest ways in which
the U.S. and EU governments could resolve trade problems. Between 1996 and
1999, four summits following the Seville model were held in Chicago, Rome, Charlotte (N.C.), and Berlin, where CEOs and top-level government officials met to
discuss and, at times, negotiate trade and regulatory issues. Beginning in June 1996,
the CEOs who served as the TABD co-chairs met directly with and presented
TABD concerns to President Clinton and Commission President Santer, as well
as to the head of government presiding over the U.S.-EU biannual transatlantic
summits. The TABD also began to produce tangible success, such as a telecommunications agreement (that led to the World Trade Organization telecommunications agreement), as well as a U.S.-EU Mutual Recognition Agreement (MRA)
in five areas, including pharmaceuticals, medical devices, and electromagnetic
equipment (Peterson and Cowles 1998, 266). The companies also worked to
develop a united front on key issues at the ill-fated 1999 World Trade Organization ministerial in Seattle, Washington.

The Europeanization of Business-Government Relations

A large part of TABD's success can be attributed to the new relationship between
the European companies and the European Commission. The Commission had
agreed with the U.S. government that the business dialogue should be driven by
CEOs from major firms, and not traditional industry associations such as the
National Association of Manufacturers (NAM) in Washington, D.C., or UNICE
in Brussels. Commission officials, for example, believed that UNICE's institutional
format (requiring the consensus of all national industry associations) would not
provide the dynamism for TABD to be successful. They also feared that UNICE
and the NIAs would focus too much on technical details instead of seeking broader
political initiatives. Of course, as numerous NIA officials pointed out, Commission officials were also interested in developing closer ties with CEOs from major
European companies whose support would enhance the Commission's positions
vis-à-vis the member states.

An important outcome was that the European business-government relationship
emerged not along the lines of any American model of business-government relationship, but in a manner similar to that in which large firms had organized vis-à-
vis the Commission during the early years of the Single Market Program. Many
of the TABD firms, for example, were members of the European Roundtable of
Industrialists, a key group of CEOs and chairmen of the board who had organized
to promote the creation and development of the 1992 project (Cowles 1995). In
this sense, the Europeanization of business-government relations in the TABD was

influenced not so strongly by any transatlantic or global factors, but by earlier examples of such Europeanization.

The new relationship, however, did not form overnight. Both sides had to address some initial difficulties in working with one another. First, many of the CEOs and their company representatives had little experience lobbying on international trade issues. The NIAs had carried out this role at the domestic level over the years. Therefore, company representatives had to learn about various international agreements and procedures and work with their American counterparts to find "political solutions" to historically intractable problems.[10]

Second, the Directorate General (DG) for External Relations had to moderate its "global approach" to trade negotiations: developing a negotiating platform that it believed was based on the interests of society at large, including labor and environmental groups. Commission officials had to adapt to the TABD process in which the interests of companies were taken into consideration upfront in the trade negotiation process.

A strong Commission-business relationship was forged following the Seville conference. As firms developed better expertise in the issues, the DG for External Relations developed a TABD "points-of-contact list." The list allowed firms to immediately identify the Commission officials in charge of specific TABD matters, and to meet with these officials on a regular basis. Over time, the meetings between the companies and the Commission became routine and the Europeanization of business-government relations well established (Cowles in press[b]).

The NIAs' Discontent

The new European business-government relations did not please UNICE or the NIAs. The business associations were upset with the TABD process for a simple reason: the CEO-driven format defied the traditional business-government relationship long established in Europe, notably continental Europe, in external trade policy matters. In the belief that the CEO-only format would minimize the role of sectoral, national, and European associations, UNICE officials held frank conversations with Commission officials, arguing that a transatlantic industry dialogue already existed between it and American associations. They also questioned the representativeness of the TABD process, maintaining that TABD must be representative of European business as a whole, and not a handful of companies.[11] Finally, UNICE officials pointed out that the TABD required individuals with specific technical expertise on trade and investment matters—an expertise usually found in the industry associations themselves.

The European Commission and TABD firms slowly loosened their restrictions on the NIAs over the next two years. UNICE and NIA officials were invited, for example, to participate in TABD working groups. Confindustria, the Italian NIA,

10. Interview with EU business representative, Brussels, June 26, 1996.
11. Interviews with UNICE official, July 1, 1996.

was co-host of the 1997 Rome conference. Improved relations were attributable to a number of factors. First, the companies found the NIAs' expertise to be valuable in certain situations. Thus, they could rely on the NIAs for information and other data. Second, the companies recognized that they needed to address the criticism that the TABD process only benefited large European firms. Allowing the NIAs—who purportedly represent all European industry—to participate in TABD working groups would demonstrate that the TABD was open to all companies. Third, the European firms recognized that allowing NIA participation would help them in persuading the national governments to support the TABD and its proposals.

While accommodating some of the industry associations' concerns, the TABD remained a company-driven process. Moreover, the strong linkage between the large companies and the European Commission continued.

The Impact on Domestic Business-Government Relations

The TABD challenged the NIAs' role not only at the European level but at the domestic level as well. While the TABD Commission–big business relationship brought new dynamics to the EU commercial policymaking process, it also created adaptational pressures for change on the domestic business-government relations in the member states. These pressures are found not only between business groups and national governments but also within the NIAs themselves.

Simply put, the Europeanization of business-government relations in the TABD altered the traditional privileged relationship between the NIAs and their member states in external trade policy. It did so in a number of ways. First, by working closely together, the companies and the European Commission presented the member states with a negotiating strategy "pre-approved" by European industry. As a result, the traditional consultation process between governments and the NIAs at the domestic level became much less important.

Second, the Europeanization of business-government relations signaled the willingness of companies to enter into negotiations not only with the Commission on EU common commercial policy but with the member states as well. A German, French, or British firm that met regularly with Commission officials on the U.S.-EU MRA agreement, for example, would also meet directly with its own government officials. In other words, large firms were bypassing the NIAs at both the European and national levels. Thus, the traditional leadership role of the NIAs vis-à-vis the states as well as within national industry itself was considerably weakened.

Third, the Europeanization of business-government relations in the TABD irrevocably altered the traditional roles of firms and NIAs in external trade policy. Whereas the EU common commercial policy was once the sole domain of the NIAs, large companies have devoted considerable resources to developing their own expertise in this area. Moreover, they show no sign of returning these responsibilities to the NIAs. Indeed, a significant part of the TABD agenda is focused on developing U.S.-EU positions regarding the WTO and the Organization for Economic Cooperation and Development (OECD). In certain respects, the TABD relationship has served as a Pandora's box, opening up and allowing firms direct access to trade negotiations both now and in the future.

As I discuss below, these pressures impact the NIAs in different ways depending, in part, on the "fit" between the European model of business–government relations and the existing domestic relations.

The Institutional Fit/Misfit and Mediating Factors

Looking at the case of the United Kingdom and the CBI, one did not expect there to be many problems adapting to the Europeanization of business–government relations in the TABD. There was, after all, a "fit" between the elite pluralist model of business–government in the TABD and the "company state" model in the United Kingdom. Indeed, this proved to be the case. While questioning the "representativeness" of a process promoted by individual firms, the CBI has not been overly concerned with the new relationship between the European Commission and the large companies. CBI officials recognize that similar linkages already exist with large firms and the British government at the domestic level. The CBI adapted rather readily to the situation by becoming involved in the TABD working groups and meeting directly with Commission officials in Brussels.[12] Thus, instead of continuing to focus at national-level bargaining, the CBI has opted to play a more active role by participating in the European business–government relationship surrounding the TABD. Indeed, in recent years, the British NIA has demonstrated its willingness to go "the European route" quite often on any number of issues. In 1998, the CBI recorded twice as many meetings with EU Commissioners as with U.K. ministers (Greenwood and Stancich 1998, 152).

Unlike the British case, there was not an institutional fit between the pluralist European relationship and the corporatist relationship between BDI and the German government. Not surprisingly, the Europeanization of business–government relations in the TABD posed problems for the German NIA and its relationship with the state. As one BDI official who had been very active in Uruguay Round discussions noted: "I would admit that the TABD is a challenge to the federation. It is a challenge for industrial organizations if individual companies take such a visible interest in a specific topic."[13] While several leading German companies participate in TABD, at least two have taken active leadership roles. The first European chair of TABD, Jürgen Strube, was CEO of BASF; a later EU chair, Jürgen Schrempp, is chairman and CEO of DaimlerChrysler. These

12. Interview with CBI official, February 25, 1998.
13. Interview with BDI official, February 11, 1998. One BDI official interviewed argued that the TABD had little or no impact on his organization, because TABD had no legal standing in the EU treaties (interview with BDI official, February 25, 1998). However, his was the lone viewpoint among German business and government officials interviewed.

German CEOs and their companies not only chaired the European side of the TABD process, they also led discussions with business groups and the German government.

The companies' leadership challenged not only the BDI's relationship with the German state but also its authoritative structure and the membership. With the Europeanization of business-government relations in the TABD process, however, the BDI plays a secondary role at the domestic level. While firms like BASF and DaimlerChrysler still discuss TABD developments with the BDI, it is clearly the firms and not the NIA that are in the leadership position.

That business and the Commission secure the negotiating mandate upfront in the TABD process also impacts domestic business-government relations in Germany. During the Uruguay Round, the BDI had significant input into the policymaking process at the domestic level—arguably more input than either the CBI or MEDEF. However, under the TABD, the relative loss of state power to the European level also signals a relative loss of BDI power as a partner of the state. Therefore, in order to represent the interests of German industry in the TABD process, the BDI must participate at the European level to shape the EU's negotiating mandate.

So how did the BDI adapt, if at all, to the Europeanization of business-government relations in the TABD? On one hand, the BDI could have resolved to maintain its representational activities at the national level without getting involved in the TABD business-government relationship in Brussels. A decision to have remained focused on national business-government relations would make sense, given the BDI's power at the domestic level. On the other hand, however, the BDI faced a considerable loss of influence if it chose to remain focused on the national business-government relationship. Most of the TABD decision making—agenda-setting, negotiating postures, and so forth—was taking place in Brussels. If the BDI wanted to have any significant input into the European business-government bargaining process, it would have to refocus its activities on Brussels.

In the end, the BDI chose to become more involved in TABD policymaking in Brussels. Unlike the CBI, however, it did not seek to become involved directly in the TABD committee work itself. Instead, the BDI association official responsible for TABD matters opted to work through UNICE to express German industry views.

What accounts for this change, albeit a cautious one, on the part of the BDI? What were the mediating factors? In the case of Germany, the answer appears to be found in the lessons learned from the Single Market program, when large companies also mobilized at the European level to press their interests on European Commission officials. During the 1992 program's legislative phase, when "pluralism ran riot" (Wallace 1996, 33), firms recognized that they could no longer rely on the "national route" to influence EU policymaking—particularly with the end of the unanimous voting for much of the Single Market legislation. Instead, they developed new European business-government relations to ensure their interests were known.

As with the TABD, the BDI also had to respond to similar developments during the Single Market building phase. While in strong support of the 1992 program, the BDI was initially reluctant to change its national approach. That German companies were slow to mobilize in Brussels and "play the European game" meant that the BDI's authoritative role was not challenged early on (Cowles 1996b). However, once large firms like DaimlerChrysler (then Daimler-Benz) opened up offices in the European capital, pressures were placed on the BDI to respond.

Initially, high-level BDI officials, while upset that the firms would "break tradition" and bypass their NIA, refused to change the federation's structure and create a "European department" to respond more efficiently to the Single Market legislation. In Brussels, the BDI office was unwilling to appoint German companies to UNICE policy groups and working committees as means to prevent further corporate encroachment on its authority (Cowles 1996b, 94).

The BDI's position began to change after 1991, with new leadership in the organization. The new head of the Brussels office, for example, appointed firms to the UNICE committees and, with "permission" from the headquarters, instituted monthly meetings with four German sectoral federations and twenty-some company representatives. These developments represented a major sea change in the organization. Instead of serving as the source of information for the federations and companies, the BDI used the monthly meetings to gather data from and coordinate views with the large German firms (Cowles 1996b, 95).

Thus, having learned from its experience in the Single Market Program, the BDI adapted to the Europeanization of business-government relations in the TABD. To "recapture" some of the influence lost at the domestic level, the BDI became more involved in TABD matters at the European level. In a sense, however, the BDI's involvement in TABD has remained rather "German" in orientation by choosing to work through the traditional hierarchical European channel of UNICE.

As noted earlier, there was also a "misfit" between the statist French model and the pluralist European model. One might expect this misfit to also pose considerable problems for the French NIA and its relationship with the state. Interestingly, in the French case, although there is a "misfit," the MEDEF actually benefits from the new business-government relationship in Brussels. Whereas the BDI loses some of its authority in the TABD process, the exact opposite is true for the MEDEF and French business in general. In other words, the MEDEF becomes empowered as a result of the Europeanization of business-government relations.

This empowerment, and the resulting ease with which the MEDEF adapted to the new TABD situation, is evident if one looks at the domestic business-government relationship in France. Because the MEDEF had little or no voice under the statist model of business-government relations, the MEDEF found that adapting to the European TABD process—becoming involved in the European business-government relationship—gives it greater influence vis-à-vis the French government. Whereas in the past, the government informed the MEDEF of its policy decisions, the government now must often rely on the MEDEF to inform it of TABD developments, especially those not generally reported in the Article 133 Committee. Moreover, government officials have been told that they are not to "give instructions" on what position French industry should undertake. As one MEDEF official noted, "[The MEDEF] doesn't accept censorship any longer. We consult, but I refuse to take orders."[14] Indeed, the MEDEF talks more often with European Commission officials than it does with those from the French government on TABD issues. The change in the MEDEF's position is not lost on the French government, which views the NIA as "allies, partners of the Commission to help it transfer decision-making from Paris."[15]

Because the MEDEF does not have a hierarchical structure or a close relationship with sectoral associations like the BDI, it has few problems with the involvement of French companies in the TABD process. The participation of large firms in the European business-government relationship does not threaten the MEDEF's domestic role per se. Indeed, the MEDEF's TABD representative has recruited a number of French firms to become involved in the TABD.

In addition to being empowered in relation to the French state, the MEDEF was also able to adapt to the Europeanization of business-government relations because of lessons learned during the Single Market Program. Like the BDI, the MEDEF also responded to the Europeanization of business-government relations in the 1992 project rather slowly. While a number of French firms were active in Brussels early on in the Single Market Program, the MEDEF was not. Internal MEDEF divisions between pro-liberalization forces on the one hand, and state-run enterprises on the other, kept the MEDEF in its traditional "statist" relationship with the French government. Pressure on the MEDEF to play a more prominent role in Brussels began to rise in the 1990s. The turning point was the success of the Uruguay Round, "where previously assured national interests were now seen to be increasingly subservient to the EU trade liberalisation goals and the need for national economies to converge" (Coen 1997b, 17). Leading firms knew that French industry and, in turn, the MEDEF, had to adapt. In the words of one MEDEF official, "*L'Europe nous fait bouger*" (Europe makes us move).[16]

Of course, the GATT Uruguay Round had also demonstrated the French government's willingness to overlook industry concerns and focus on agricultural and cultural matters. Moreover, the MEDEF was unimpressed with the caliber of the French officials involved in the negotiations and believed the Uruguay Round had significantly weakened the position of France in comparison to the European Commission and other member states. It didn't make sense for the MEDEF to continue the traditional relations with the French government, especially when the concerns of French industry were not being aired. As one MEDEF official summed up the situation, "We took our interests to Europe."[17]

14. Interview with MEDEF official, February 25, 1998.
15. Interview with MEDEF official, February 25, 1998.
16. Interview with MEDEF official, June 27, 1996.
17. Interview with MEDEF official, June 27, 1996.

By the mid-1990s, the MEDEF had taken considerable steps to strengthen its office in Brussels. Additional staff was hired to improve relations with European institutions and French firms involved in EU policymaking. In addition, the director of the Brussels office, who had held the position for over a decade, was encouraged to retire. The new director heads both the Brussels as well as Parisian MEDEF European office to ensure stronger communication with headquarters.

Convergence and the Limits to Change

The Europeanization of business-government relations in the common commercial policy area challenged the traditional role of the NIAs in the United Kingdom, Germany, and France. It has placed pressures on domestic relations and prompted NIAs to adapt by participating more fully in the Brussels policymaking process. The NIAs have become participants along with large European companies in promoting the TABD agenda. In effect, there was a convergence in the NIAs' new roles and relationships in common commercial policy. At both the European and domestic levels, the NIAs became one of several pressure groups attempting to influence TABD policy.

While there is evidence of convergence, it is also clear that the adaptation to the Europeanization of business-government relations is both cautious and incomplete, particularly in the German case. For now, the German BDI has not chosen to participate directly in the TABD working parties (unlike the CBI and MEDEF) but has, instead, opted to focus its energies on UNICE. Moreover, despite these changes, the TABD has not prompted a complete disintegration of the basic NIA-government model in the member states. There have not been any calls to dismantle the "peak associations" of the member states. Thus, the Europeanization of business-government relations has prompted evolutionary, as opposed to revolutionary change, in domestic structures.

The historically entrenched ties between the state and peak association is one reason why the relationship continues so strongly. The Europeanization of business-government relations in common commercial policy matters has only taken place over the past five years. While big business–European Commission relations have developed in other policy areas over the past two decades, this pales in contrast to the century-old relations between most continental NIAs and their respective governments.

Another reason why the NIAs remain important interlocutors vis-à-vis the governments is because of their "representativeness." In general, the NIAs represent all of industry. And while peak associations may sometimes develop bland position papers because they are wrestling with the competing demands of its membership, the notion of "representativeness" is important in the cultures of all three countries examined. Indeed, as multinational firms become more politically active in Brussels, concerns have been raised over the dominant role of large firms in the EU policymaking process (Cowles 1997). The role of "organized capital" in

Europe helps legitimize business interests in comparison to other societal interests, even in countries such as the United Kingdom.

Yet another reason for the evolutionary—as opposed to revolutionary—change in domestic structures is the veto power held by member states in common commercial policy. During an April 27, 1998, meeting of European foreign ministers, for example, France blocked the Commission's proposal for a New Transatlantic Marketplace (NTM) between the United States and the EU ("New Transatlantic Marketplace," 1998). French president Jacques Chirac noted that the NTM proposal ran counter to French vital interests with regard to audiovisual, agriculture, and "intellectual creativity" sectors. While the NTM is not a TABD matter per se, parts of the proposal do involve the liberalization of transatlantic trade—one of the key TABD aims. The Europeanization of business-government relations in common commercial policy, therefore, does not prevent France from "being France" on certain external trade matters.

At the same time, however, one should not dismiss pressure on the Elysée from the French business elite who have now organized themselves in the TABD (as well as the pressure from other member states). The 1999 European TABD chair, for example, was Jérome Monod, head of Lyonnaise des Eaux, and former head of the ERT. To date, there has been little opposition from France on TABD matters in the Article 133 Committee. Moreover, U.S. and EU officials believe that a package similar to the NTM can still be negotiated—albeit under a different name—so that France can save face and trade liberalization will still take place.

In this chapter I have explored the Europeanization of business-government relations in the Transatlantic Business Dialogue and its impact on domestic structure—namely, the relationship between NIAs and governments in France, Germany, and the United Kingdom. The new relationship between large European firms and the European Commission has challenged the dominant role traditionally played by NIAs and member states in the development of common commercial policy. In doing so, it has also challenged the authority of the NIAs as the primary interlocutors in external trade matters.

The influence of the Europeanization process on domestic business-government relations depends, in part, on the "fit" between the domestic and European models. When there is a fit between the two, the Europeanization of business-government relations poses few problems for the NIA in its relations with its membership as well as with the government. This was the case in the United Kingdom, where the CBI was familiar with the pluralist lobbying style of TABD firms vis-à-vis the European Commission, given that a similar system already existed at the domestic level. Where there is a "misfit," the European model can pose serious challenges to the domestic model. In corporatist Germany, for example, the BDI was reluctant to give up its status as a "normal partner" with the German state. The Europeanization process challenged not only its privileged ties with the government but also its authoritative status in German industry. Sometimes when there is a misfit, as in the case of the French statist system, the Europeanization of business-government relations actually provides a window of opportunity for the NIA. When its interests were not taken seriously by the French state, the MEDEF could participate in the TABD at the European level and, thus, ignore the domestic business-government relationship.

The impact on these domestic structures was not revolutionary but evolutionary. Changes in the domestic business-government relationship as well as within the NIAs themselves were limited in nature. The historical ties between governments and peak associations, the importance of organized capital as a legitimate force in European society, as well as the traditional power of member states in common commercial policy mitigated the impact of the Europeanization process. Moreover, these same historical, cultural, and political factors ensured that there was no wholesale homogenization of domestic business-government relations across countries in light of the Europeanization process in the Transatlantic Business Dialogue.

The TABD is not the only example of the Europeanization of business-government relations and its impact on domestic structures. Domestic business-government relations also came under pressure in the early 1980s, with the mobilization of large firms both to promote and participate in the Single Market Program. As large companies discredited the "national route" of EU policymaking in favor of direct negotiations with European institutions, domestic business-government relations were challenged. Interestingly, in both the TABD and the Single Market initiative, the NIAs responded to the Europeanization process by participating more actively at the European level—whether to maintain its voice in industrial matters (the CBI), to recapture part of its voice (the BDI), or to find its voice (the MEDEF).

This chapter provides a first cut in understanding the Europeanization of business-government relations and its impact on NIA-government relations at the domestic level through a case study of the TABD. Of course, the Europeanization of business-government relations does not influence domestic relations equally across policy areas. Rather, as Ted Lowi pointed out, "Policy makes politics" (Lowi 1964). Different policies forge different relationships among business groups and government. Whereas the TABD and the single market Program can be described as "pluralist" in nature, other EU policies may be better characterized as "corporatist," "neo-corporatist," or "other" in terms of business-government relationships. Thus, one might expect the Europeanization of business-government relations in telecommunications R&D (i.e., the Advanced Communications Technologies and Services [ACTS] program) to pose more difficulty in the United Kingdom than in France.

One might also expect that the impact of the Europeanization of business changes depending on the various phases of the policymaking process. For example, while the Europeanization of business-government relations places adaptational pressures on the NIAs during the agenda-setting and negotiation phases of the TABD, it is not clear that this relationship will have the same influence during the implementation phase of TABD-related legislation (see Aguilar 1993).

The impact of the Europeanization process and the willingness of domestic business groups to adapt might also be more problematic given the NIAs' support for the issue at hand. Oftentimes, as one BDI official noted, the NIAs are more in agreement with the European Commission's policies than they are with their own governments' opinions (notably those of the Länder in Germany).[18] In the case of the TABD and the Single Market Program, for example, the BDI's willingness to adapt to the Europeanization process (albeit slowly) was facilitated by the NIA's agreement with the Commission on liberalized trade. The position of the BDI regarding the nascent Social Dialogue, however, may prompt a more divisive adaptation process—if one is to be made.

Finally, the Europeanization process does not only impact the relationship between the NIAs and governments at the domestic level. It also alters relationships among public and private companies, sectors, small firms, and universities. In short, the agenda for studying the Europeanization of business-government relations and its impact on domestic structure is wide open.

18. Interview with BDI official, February 18, 1998.

CHAPTER TEN

The Europeanization of Citizenship?

Jeffrey T. Checkel

In this chapter, I define Europeanization as the development of new norms regarding citizenship and membership at the European level. These collective understandings can have two quite different effects within states: (1) they may provide domestic agents and actors with new understandings of interests and identities (constitute them); or (2) they may simply constrain the choices and behaviors of self-interested agents with given identities (Klotz 1995, chapter 2). The first possibility is premised on a constructivist or "thick" understanding of the role norms and institutions play in social life, whereas the second is based on a "thin" or rationalist conception.

I test these competing institutional assumptions against evidence taken from contemporary German debates over citizenship and membership. Drawing upon historical institutionalism, I claim that the structure of state-society relations predicts the likely effect—constructivist or rationalist—of regional norms in particular countries. In terms of the book's theoretical themes, I thus explore the connection between Europeanization and changes in national collective identities. Substantively, despite the many important changes of recent years, I argue that it is still premature to speak of an unambiguous Europeanization of German national identity.

Before proceeding, two comments are in order. First, my dependent variable—responses of particular domestic agents to European-level processes—is more

The financial support of the Alexander von Humboldt-Stiftung, German Marshall Fund of the United States, and Norwegian Research Council is gratefully acknowledged. For detailed comments on earlier versions, I thank Albrecht Funk, Peter Katzenstein, Andy Moravcsik, Thomas Risse, Fritz Scharpf, Antje Wiener and, especially, Jim Caporaso. Portions of this chapter build upon an earlier essay (Checkel 1999a).

narrow than that found in the other chapters of this book, in which a broader time frame is invoked. I do so because my interest is in how Europeanization affects and feeds into the politics of agenda-setting in the domestic arena. Second, the arguments and results presented below are in a very important sense preliminary. European-level work on citizenship/membership is quite recent. Thus, in terms of national-level effects, the implementation phase is just beginning.

Citizenship and Membership in the Federal Republic of Germany

As in many European states, recent years saw a heated debate over citizenship and broader issues of membership (rights of national minorities, immigration) in Germany. Although such debates had occurred before, those of the 1990s were qualitatively different in two respects. Domestically, it was broad ranging and included a wide array of actors: elite decision makers, Bundestag deputies, representatives from the church and trade unions, members of nongovernmental organizations (NGOs), and immigrants themselves. As is seen below, this broad political mobilization is key in allowing for a test of the argument I advance here.

Internationally, Germany was debating fundamental reforms to its citizenship/membership laws at a time when regional institutions—in particular, the European Union (EU) and the Council of Europe (CE)—had taken a renewed interest in such questions. Thus, if it was ever possible to analyze national debates over membership in isolation, this is certainly not the case today (Soysal 1994). Put differently, one might a priori suspect Europeanization to be at work in this policy area as well.

Within these new domestic and international contexts, the German discussion has centered on two questions. First and at a practical level, the issue was how and to what degree the country's citizenship laws should be reformed. While most politicians, analysts, and activists were in agreement that change was needed, the devil has been in the details. For example, should German law incorporate greater elements of jus soli, where citizenship is based on birthplace and not blood? Should immigrants be allowed to retain their former nationality when they acquire German citizenship? Opinion has been sharply divided on these and other matters.

Second, underlying and, indeed, motivating this practical legal debate has been a more basic one, which addresses fundamental notions of how Germans collectively view their nation-state. Conceptions of citizenship, by their very nature, create boundaries. Who is a member of the national collectivity? Who is not? At core, answers to these questions revolve around degrees of inclusion or exclusion. Do Germans view the boundaries of their collectivity/state in terms more ethnic (blood) or civic (territorial)? In a crucial sense, then, the recent debate was about much more than changes to law and administrative practice; it was also about the dominant shared understandings—norms—of what it means to be German and whether these needed to be changed.

Europeanization and Diffusion Dynamics

So, norms matter. In itself, such a statement is of little use, for everything can matter. The challenge is to think systematically about scope conditions: the mechanisms and processes that link European norms—my cut at Europeanization—with the domestic arena. In other words, how does the norm get from "out there" (the European level) to "down here" (the domestic arena) and have possible effects?

A review of the broader political science, sociology, and international law literatures reveals two different diffusion mechanisms that empower regional norms domestically: one is a "bottom-up" process, whereas the other is "top-down." In the first case, non-state actors and policy networks are united in their support for norms; they then mobilize and coerce decision makers to change state policy. Norms are not internalized by the elites. The activities of Greenpeace exemplify this political pressure mechanism (Keck and Sikkink 1998; Risse, Ropp, and Sikkink 1999).

A second, top-down diffusion mechanism has received less attention from scholars. Nonetheless, it is represented in the literature, albeit often implicitly. In this case, political learning, not political pressure, leads agents—typically, elite decision makers—to adopt prescriptions embodied in norms, which become internalized and constitute a set of shared intersubjective understandings that make behavioral claims (Finnemore 1996; Soysal 1994).

Thus, two dominant diffusion mechanisms appear to be empowering norms domestically. The challenge is to explain this variation, with the argument here being that historically constructed domestic political institutions account for a good bit of it. Specifically, I argue that the mechanisms of norm diffusion vary as a function of domestic structure, with four ideal-typical categories identified: liberal, corporatist, statist, and state-above-society. From these, I deduce and predict cross-national variation in the mechanisms through which norms are empowered.

The argument is summarized in Table 10.1. The diffusion mechanisms—societal pressure and elite learning—are those highlighted in recent empirical work on norm diffusion. However, I go a step beyond this research by incorporating historically constructed domestic political institutions as an intervening variable, one that predicts which mechanism will prevail (Checkel 1999a, 87–91).

As my empirical case concerns a corporatist polity, I should explain the theoretical logic for cell two in Table 10.1 in more detail. Here, state decision makers

Table 10.1   Domestic structure and norm diffusion

	Liberal	Corporatist	Statist	State-above- society
Domestic mechanisms empowering international norms	Societal pressure on elites	Societal pressure on elites (primary) and Elite learning (secondary)	Elite learning (primary) and Societal pressure on elites (secondary)	Elite learning

play a greater role in bringing about normative change than in the liberal case (cell one), where social forces have more access/influence, thus generating the societal pressure that empowers norms. At the same time, normative change is not simply a function of the newly learned preferences of policymakers, who then impose them on a pliant populace (cells three and, especially, four). Rather, a hallmark of corporatism is the policy networks connecting state and society, with the latter still accorded an important role in decision making. In this setting, it is thus both societal pressure (primary) and elite learning (secondary) that lead to norm empowerment (see also Risse-Kappen 1994).

For the study of Europeanization as a process of norm diffusion, the foregoing helps distinguish between rationalist and constructivist logics for the way in which European-level norms connect to domestic agents. The mobilization of pressure from below is largely consistent with rationalist accounts: norms constrain the behavior and options of decision makers. In contrast, elite learning is more consistent with a sociological understanding of norms, where their effects reach deeper.[1]

A final point concerns not particular diffusion mechanisms but the norms generating them in the first place. Simply put, how does one identify a European-level norm? Drawing upon accumulating empirical work and sociological theoretical logic, I argue that a norm's existence can be inferred from two properties: its degree of prescriptive guidance and of shared consensus (Legro 1997, 33–35; Meyer and Strang 1993). For a norm to exist, it thus must embody clear prescriptions, which provide guidance to agents as they develop preferences and interests on a issue. In turn, clear prescriptions imply some degree of shared consensus at the European level. Thus, high levels of both specificity and intersubjective agreement are indicators of a norm's existence.

Case Selection

In a larger work in progress, I demonstrate the utility of the foregoing argument to explain cross-national variation in the diffusion mechanisms linking European norms to processes of domestic change in independent Ukraine and unified Germany, two countries with different domestic structures. Here, I focus only on Germany, and for two reasons. First, it is a most likely case for international-regional norms to have a domestic impact; given my interest in the role of norms at the national level, the German focus thus makes sense. The theoretical logic, in brief, is that Germany sits within the most densely institutionalized environment in the post–Cold War world—Western Europe; high levels of international institutionalization promote transnational normative processes (Risse-Kappen 1995, chapter 1; Weber 1994).

---

1. For the pressure-from-below argument, I say "largely" because it is possible that norms, initially adopted for instrumental reasons, get locked-in to a polity, thus reshaping underlying preferences and interests. However, my focus on near-term implementation allows this issue to be bracketed.

Methodologists may find this case selection strategy problematic. Good theory-testing standards suggest that one pick "tough cases," where the theory is likely to be shown true, only if it really is true. Such a strategy works best where the extant body of literature is relatively mature and advanced; however, theoretical work on the diffusion mechanisms linking norms to domestic polities is at an early stage. Thus, I have purposely chosen a case (Germany in post–Cold War Europe) where normative diffusion should be at work; this more readily allows me to establish the plausibility of my framework linking the structure of domestic political institutions with important aspects of this process (see also George 1979 on "plausibility probes").

Second, given my process-tracing method and its attendant data requirements, it simply would not be possible to fit four cases (two countries, plus the evolution of two sets of European-level norms) into one chapter. The resulting analysis would be stretched too thin, leading readers to question the validity of my results.

All research designs involve trade-offs, and mine is no exception. The present chapter, lacking a cross-national focus, cannot demonstrate the utility of my institutional argument for explaining variance in normative diffusion mechanisms (see, however, Checkel 1997). However, by considering two different arenas of Europeanization (Brussels and Strasbourg) and their possible effects in a country (Germany) that popular and scholarly wisdom hold to be thoroughly Europeanized, I simultaneously establish the plausibility of my theoretical argument while contributing to an ongoing debate over German identity.

Citizenship and Membership in Europe: Post-Maastricht and Post–Cold War

Below, I discuss the pressures for domestic change—in my case, those emanating from emerging European-level norms. Next, I assess the degree of fit between these norms and German conceptions of identity. Finally and most important, I document how historically constructed political institutions are structuring the interaction between these European and national arenas.

Pressures for Change

When examining the development of European understandings on citizenship and membership, one is immediately struck by their tentative, incipient nature. Indeed, at best one can speak of emergent norms and understandings on these issues. Moreover, Brussels-centered students of Europeanization might be surprised to know it, but much of the more substantive and interesting work in this area has occurred elsewhere, in Strasbourg (Council of Europe).

I begin by considering recent Council of Europe (CE) work on membership and then examine the Maastricht treaty's provisions for a European citizenship. While the CE treaties contain minimal normative guidance, Maastricht's conception of citizenship is nearly devoid of such prescriptions. The difference is explained by the ability of member states to dominate the agenda-setting and negotiation that led to Maastricht's concept of European citizenship, while in Strasbourg, activists and entrepreneurs, at least initially, were able to dominate the European-level process.

Post–Cold War: Council of Europe.   Questions of membership—rights of immigrants and ethnic minorities—have become central to the construction of national identity in post–Cold War Europe. In recent years, such issues have been matters of public debate in a wide range of European countries (Brubaker 1989; Hayden 1992).

In contrast with the EU's work on citizenship, much of the impetus behind this debate, as well as specific proposals for change, came from the scholarly community and nongovernmental organizations (NGOs) with interests in citizenship and immigrant/minority rights. These discussions have advanced to the point where specific propositions—for example, on the desirability of dual citizenship—have gained wide backing (Bauboeck 1994; Bauboeck and Cinar 1994; Miller 1989).

Moreover, proponents of such arguments have linked them to the norms of the European human rights regime centered on the Council of Europe. Far from being a passive player in this process, the Council has sought actively to influence it, seeking to create shared understandings of citizenship and the rights of immigrants and minorities—the common social categories that are a prerequisite for the creation of norms. Indeed, the European rights framework and the Council are considered to be one of the clearest examples of an effective international regime (Donnelly 1986, 620–24; Moravcsik 1995).

Since the early 1990s, the CE has devoted increasing attention to minority rights and citizenship. In December, 1994, it adopted the Framework Convention for the Protection of National Minorities (Council of Europe 1994); in May 1997, the CE approved a new convention on nationality that addresses issues of citizenship and immigrant rights (Council of Europe 1997). The former promotes shared understandings regarding the legitimacy of minority rights and identities; until now, such a consensus had never existed at the European level.

The convention on nationality revises norms on citizenship that were embodied in a 1963 CE-sponsored treaty. On the question of multiple nationality (often referred to as dual citizenship), this earlier treaty had taken a negative view. It privileged state interests; from the vantage point of the state, dual citizenship was bad news, leading to split loyalties and complicating military service obligations.

Seeking to exploit a growing scholarly, NGO, and European consensus that multiple nationality is often necessary and desirable, the CE secretariat drafted a new European Convention on Nationality that privileges individual over state interests and takes a neutral view on dual citizenship. In reality, however, this neutrality, by removing the earlier explicit negative sanction, is designed to pressure states to be more open to multiple nationality.

Do the Framework Convention and the Convention on Nationality promote European norms favoring new, more inclusive conceptions of national membership? The methodological challenge is to establish the existence of these norms independently of their putative effects (at the national level, in my case). Here, I used two techniques. One is textual, which meant a careful reading of the various draft treaty texts and, for the nationality convention, a comparison with its 1963 predecessor. Textual analysis of this sort uncovered areas where shared understandings have emerged.

A second, more important, technique is discursive. Interviewing in Strasbourg and in the various capitals revealed that key aspects of both treaties have acquired a prescriptive, taken-for-granted status as normative understandings. For example, those involved in the negotiations—CE bureaucrats and national negotiators—no longer question the legitimacy of minority/group rights in Europe, a concept that is still deeply contested in the broader international arena. Exploitation of this second method was only possible due to extensive fieldwork, which involved four rounds of interviewing over three years.

By the definition given earlier, these treaties—and the process that led to their promulgation—indeed promote norms, which embody both specific prescriptions and intersubjective agreement. At the same time, their scope should not be overstated. For example, the shared understanding on minority rights is limited to the cultural sphere; on the more contentious issue of political rights (territorial autonomy, say), no normative understanding exists.

The particular negotiating process that led to these two CE treaties explains why, in contrast to the EU citizenship case, they embody tentative areas of normative agreement. Both treaties were discussed for several years in special "committees of experts" (one on national minorities; the other on nationality) that consisted of CE secretariat officials and national-level representatives (state officials as well as independent analysts). Thus out of the limelight, these groups debated issues extensively. Moreover, at early stages, key CE secretariat officials—for example, former CE Secretary General Laluminiere—were able to exploit windows of opportunity to promote new normative understandings within the groups (Checkel 1999b, 18–20).

In sum, recent years have witnessed the development of an emergent and tentative set of European understandings on questions of membership; these norms are reflected in the two CE treaties discussed above. Given the existence of these norms, one should expect to see normative diffusion dynamics at the national level, with the German case exemplifying the predicted combination of societal mobilization and elite learning.

Post-Maastricht: European Union.   For all the scholarly attention devoted to the European citizenship provisions of the Treaty on European Union (TEU, or Maastricht Treaty), it is surprising just how little is there, either in terms of substantive content or prescriptive guidance. Indeed, much of the academic writing is explicitly normative in nature—complaining of the provisions' limited scope (Twomey 1994; and, for background, Wiener 1998).

The citizenship provisions of the TEU (Part 2, Article 8) articulate minimal political rights (voting in local and European Parliament [EP] elections), while glossing over social and fundamental rights. Moreover, the Treaty language on citizenship is devoid of prescriptive guidance on such key issues as the relation between EU citizenship and member-state nationality or fundamental rights (Treaty on European Union 1993).

Conceptually, of course, nationality can be distinguished from citizenship. However, as a practical matter, the latter is inextricably bound up with nationhood and national identity. Maastricht thus presented an opportunity to address this relationship, one that is changing in contemporary Europe. Yet, the TEU's citizenship provisions are silent on nationality, except to say that European citizenship is available only to individuals who are nationals of EU member states; the latter is defined by member-state nationality laws, which the TEU decisively leaves as a state-level prerogative (O'Leary 1992; Rea 1995, 179–81).

Regarding fundamental rights, the European Commission and the European Parliament had been hoping to include them in Maastricht's conception of EU citizenship. This inclusion would have corrected what they saw as the EU's long-standing neglect of basic rights, most notably its refusal to ratify the European Convention of Human Rights (ECHR). Once again, however, member-state preferences dominated, and Commission proposals to include fundamental rights in Maastricht's citizenship provisions were rejected (O'Leary 1995; Neuwahl and Rosas 1995).

In sum, despite persistent agenda-setting efforts by the Commission and the EP, the member states maintained firm control over development of the TEU's citizenship provisions—perhaps not surprising given how national conceptions of citizenship are such a deeply rooted part of state identity in contemporary Europe. The informal deliberative processes that were key for generating shared understandings in Strasbourg were absent in Brussels. Given these trends, it comes as no surprise that the June 1997 Amsterdam EU summit (and subsequent Amsterdam Treaty), despite its mandate to revise the TEU, had nothing to say about extensions to or modifications of Maastricht's citizenship provisions; it also failed to change the status-quo regarding the ECHR ("EU Lowers" 1997; Lemke 1997, 2–3; "A Protection" 1998).

To put the above somewhat differently, Maastricht's citizenship provisions lack any normative dimension (see also O'Leary 1995, 548–49, 553). Rather than embodying prescriptive guidance, they are a list of minimal rights and information, which essentially codify (but do not further develop) what was already extent in Community law. At the national level, one would therefore expect few noticeable diffusion effects, be they through societal mobilization or social learning.

Goodness of Fit

The foregoing suggests that European norms on citizenship and membership are evolving. Especially in the case of the Strasbourg-based process, they are moving in a more inclusive direction, with emphasis on broadened understandings of both citizenship and the rights of national minorities; in particular, these CE norms promote inclusion by facilitating dual citizenship. In Germany, dual citizenship would promote the assimilation of the large foreigner population. Through the mid-1990s, however, German law required immigrants and foreigners to give up their original citizenship if they wished to seek it in Germany; this was an obstacle to integration, since many did not wish to sever all ties to their homeland. The importance of dual citizenship for large parts of the foreigner community was so great that they acquired it through illegal methods that contravene German law (Keller 1997, Sen 1994).[2]

The lack of fit—or, better said, mismatch—between these changing regional norms and German understandings of identity and citizenship was significant. While there were clear historical reasons why these understandings took hold in Germany, the important point is that they were reinforced over time and became rooted in domestic laws and institutions (Brubaker 1992, chapters 3–4, 6; Kanstroom 1993).

Legal and bureaucratic indicators as well as textual analysis and interview data all suggested the institutionalized nature of these domestic norms. Most important, as of spring 1999, the German citizenship statute continued to be based on the Law on Imperial and State Citizenship, which dates from 1913, and an ethnic conception of identity was maintained throughout the German legal system, notably in Article 116 (1) of the Basic Law (the postwar German constitution). Indeed, the ethnic core of the 1913 citizenship law is reproduced in the Basic Law via a so-called Nationalstaatsprinzip (nation-state principle), which makes very clear that there is a material core (that is, blood ties) connecting a citizen with his or her nation (Hailbronner 1989, 77; "Halb und halb" 1995; Kanstroom 1993).

Developments in German jurisprudence also promoted the institutionalization of historically constructed understandings of citizenship and identity. Most notably, the Federal Constitutional Court (Bundesverfassungsgericht) elaborated what German analysts call the "evil doctrine": the dictum that "dual nationality is an evil from the national as well as the international viewpoint, and it should be avoided in the interests of citizens and states." Likewise, in a 1989 ruling that struck down a Länder law on local voting rights for immigrants, the court insisted it "would be incorrect to claim that the concept of the 'people' in the German constitution had undergone a change due to the drastic rise of the aliens population" (Bauboeck 1994, 116; Kreuzer 1997, 1, respectively).

In terms of this book's institutional foci, my brief review suggests that to explain the goodness of fit between German and regional norms on citizenship a combination of sociological and historical institutionalism is necessary. The former, with its focus on the constitutive nature of institutions, alerts one to the presence of

---

2. Interviews with Kennan Kolat, president, and Safter Cinar, speaker, Tuerkischer Bund in Berlin/Brandenburg, May 1996.

this normative dimension to the German debate. The latter, with its stress on processes of (long-term) institutionalization, demonstrates how "fuzzy variables" like norms gain political saliency and influence (Katzenstein 1987, 382–85). Put differently, the German state institutionalized myths about the national community and its requirements. These myths, or, better said, domestic norms, and their effect on elite preferences should erect barriers in Germany to the diffusion of regional norms on membership.

Germany and the Europeanization of Membership—I: Strasbourg

Scholars typically characterize Germany as possessing a decentralized state and centralized society, with a dense policy network connecting the two parts. These features have endowed it with a corporatist domestic structure: both state and society are participants in policymaking, and the latter is consensual and incremental (Katzenstein 1985; Risse-Kappen 1991; Thelen 1993).

Given this coding, Table 10.1 predicts societal pressure (primary) and elite learning (secondary) as the mechanisms empowering CE norms in Germany. Recall that the mobilization of societal pressure from below is largely consistent with rationalist accounts, while elite learning is more consistent with a constructivist understanding of norms. Thus, I should expect to uncover agent-level evidence of both dynamics at work, but with rationalist processes dominating. Moreover, the presence of institutionalized and countering domestic norms should hinder and slow these diffusion dynamics. The empirical record supports these predictions.

Societal Pressure.   The 1990s witnessed an explosion of societal interest in questions of citizenship and the situation of foreigners in Germany, with key roles being played by the liberal media, churches, grass-roots citizens' initiatives, and the commissioners for foreigners' affairs (Kanstroom 1993, Part 3; Katzenstein 1987, chapter 5; Klusmeyer 1993).

One force helping to mobilize pressure from below has been the liberal German press, especially the Hamburg-based *Die Zeit*. During the mid-1990s, its analyses of foreigners in Germany shifted from neutral reporting to near advocacy. Of interest here, the paper's reporters forcefully promoted dual citizenship as a way to better integrate immigrant groups such as the Turks. In making such arguments, they often pointed to broader European understandings favoring it (Leicht 1994; Sommer 1995).

A second societal actor is the churches. In recent years, the governing bodies of the Protestant, Evangelical, and Catholic denominations have called for Germany to adopt an immigration and integration policy for its resident foreigners, including acceptance of dual citizenship and a move to greater elements of *jus soli* in German law. In Berlin, the Evangelical church has produced flyers on dual citizenship; these make the case for it by referring, among other factors, to emerging European norms and recent work by the Council of Europe. In the best corporatist tradition, the churches also sought to make their views known by participating in conferences and policy networks on issues of foreigners' rights (Buchsteiner 1994).[3]

The broader public, in the form of a grass-roots citizens' initiative, has been a third social force present in the debate. Seizing upon a policy window created by the surge in anti-foreigner violence that accompanied German unification, a group of activists based in Berlin orchestrated, beginning in 1992, one of the largest mass campaigns seen in Germany for a number of years. The initiative, which was specifically focused on the need for dual citizenship in German law, gathered more than 1 million signatures from a broad array of public figures.[4]

The existence of European understandings favoring inclusive conceptions of citizenship played an important role in the campaign. Signature collectors pointed to the presence of such norms, and, more generally, the initiative distributed an information sheet noting that Germany's refusal to recognize multiple nationality made it "an international exception."

A fourth actor playing a role at the societal level is a unit nominally a part of the government: the various commissioners of foreigners' affairs. While there are dozens of such commissioners in Germany, two stand out for their importance: the Office of the Federal Government's Commissioner for Foreigners' Affairs, established in 1978 and headed until late 1998 by Cornelia Schmalz-Jacobsen; and the Commissioner of Foreigners' Affairs of the Berlin Senate, created in 1981 and directed by Barbara John (Auslaenderbeauftragte des Senats 1994, 1995).[5]

Both units, but especially the one in Berlin, have significant influence at the local level, for example, working with foreigners' councils and furthering the social integration of immigrants into communities. The office in Berlin, in contrast to the federal one, is also involved in politics, seeking to build policy networks that can advance the rights of immigrants. In playing this political role, John's office makes use of the liberal citizenship policies of several neighboring countries, as well as European norms. On the latter, a brochure distributed by the Berlin office is entitled *Double Citizenship—A European Norm* (Auslaenderbeauftragte des Senats 1995, 21).

In sum, societal pressure and groupings have played a major linking role in the process of norm-induced change, seeking to empower European norms on citizenship in the German domestic arena. This mechanism and dynamic are consistent with my theoretical expectations. Moreover, interviewing and fieldwork reveal that the majority of these societal agents were using the CE norms to pursue given ends; they were an additional tool that could be used to generate pressure on government policymakers. Thus, the domestic impact of CE norms is here better captured by rationalist arguments.

3. Interview with Thomae-Venske, Commissioner for Foreigners' Affairs, Evangelical Church of Berlin-Brandenburg, May 1996.

4. Interviews with Ismail Kosan, Member of the Berlin Parliament, Buendnis 90/Die Gruenen Fraction, May 1996; Andreas Schulze, Staff Member, Office of F.O. Wolf, German Member of the European Parliament, Berlin, May 1996.

5. Interview with Barbara John, Commissioner of Foreigners' Affairs of the Berlin Senat, November 1995, May 1996.

Elite Learning.   There is evidence of learning from norms among several elites and decision makers. Consider Cornelia Schmalz-Jacobsen, former head of the federal commissioner's office, and Richard von Weizsaecker, who held the post of federal president until May 1994. Both spoke out forcefully for a new understanding of the place of foreigners and minorities in the German state—in some cases, well before the worst of the anti-foreigner violence occurred. In particular, they called for an easing of naturalization rules, a revocation of laws prohibiting dual nationality, and for a more inclusive, civic conception of German citizenship (Peel 1992).

With Schmalz-Jacobsen, there is clear evidence of a learning process driven by exposure to broader European understandings. Her office has extensive contacts with governmental units and NGOs addressing citizenship-nationality issues in Great Britain, the Netherlands, and several Scandinavian countries. She is aware of Council of Europe work in this area, often making reference to it in Bundestag debates or other public appearances. Germany, Schmalz-Jacobsen argues, must develop a "concept" for immigration and citizenship that is "integrated on a European and international level" (Federal Republic of Germany 1994, 87–88).[6]

More specifically, two types of data support a learning argument. First, there is the change over time in Schmalz-Jacobsen's understanding of the citizenship/dual citizenship issue. While she has long campaigned for foreigners' rights in Germany, Schmalz-Jacobsen now explicitly connects this concern with a broader and changing European context (compare Dempsey 1993 with Federal Republic of Germany 1994). Second, interviews with two advisers confirm that exposure to international/CE work on citizenship has influenced her views.[7]

Below these top levels, there is additional evidence of learning among other elites, in particular, the so-called young, wild ones in the ruling CDU. This is a group of younger Christian Democratic Bundestag deputies who advocated, contra the wishes of party elders, major reforms to German citizenship laws. In particular, they favored granting dual citizenship, for a limited period of approximately eighteen years, to children born in Germany of foreigner parents (Altmaier and Roettgen 1997; Heims 1997).

Why this behavior? As they are politicians, an obvious explanation would be instrumental self-interest: it is a way of advancing their political careers within the party. However, throughout 1997–98, leading CDU figures vehemently opposed any move toward dual citizenship, with former Chancellor Kohl at one point declaring that "if we were to yield on the question of double citizenship, then in a short time we would have not three million, but four, five or six million Turks in our land" (Loelhoeffel 1997). Tellingly, the chancellor made this angry statement at a meeting of the CDU Youth Union, where the young, wild ones enjoy a measure of support. Career advancement thus does not seem to explain their actions.

6. Interview with Dr. Camelia Sonntag-Volgast, Bundestag Deputy, SDP, August 1995.

7. Interviews with Georgios Tsapanos and Michael Schlikker, Office of Federal Government's Commissioner for Foreigners' Affairs, March, August 1995.

A more likely explanation is learning from emerging norms. In their own writings and interviews, the wild ones and their supporters in the party argued that they are seeking to bring German policy into line with "European standards"; in a similar fashion, they claim to be "fitting German citizenship law to the European context." Altmaier and Roettgen, two of the group's leaders, refer to extensive discussions with foreigners' organizations and churches and how these exchanges have influenced their views on DC. And, as noted earlier, it is precisely immigrant NGOs and churches who have played key roles in diffusing changing European norms on DC to the Federal Republic (Eylmann 1997; "Schnellere" 1996).

Yet, for each instance of learning of this sort at the state level, one found—through late 1998—many cases of "non-learning" as well. That is, other elite players had a radically different conception of German identity, a much more exclusive one that appeared heavily shaped by dominant domestic norms; in turn, these hindered and slowed any learning process. For example, opponents of change often cast their arguments in terms of "Germanness" and "national identity," sometimes explicitly referring to the 1913 citizenship statute. Some might claim this was simply political posturing, where notions of identity are invoked as a cover for self-interest. In this case, there are problems with such an argument. It is not at all clear whose economic or electoral interests were being served, given the growing public consensus on the need to integrate the large foreigner population. These opponents also made use of the broader European context to buttress their arguments, often pointing to the norms of the earlier, 1963 Council of Europe treaty that essentially prohibited dual nationality (Buchsteiner 1996).[8]

This active resistance and "non-learning" of governmental elites, led to a situation where, despite the societal mobilization documented above, there was not rapid or wide-ranging policy change, particularly on the issue of dual citizenship. With the exception of some minor changes to citizenship statutes enacted in 1993 that affected children of foreigners (Weidlener and Hemberger 1993), the pace of change was slow and contested, with five rounds of Bundestag debate over a three-year period that ended in deadlock and recrimination ("Zwei Paesse" 1995; "Auslaenderrechts-Tango" 1996; "Debatte zur Neuregelung" 1997; "Die Koalition" 1998).

Europeanization Triumphant?   At this point, the knowledgeable reader may exclaim, "Wait a minute"! Surely, this deadlocked state of affairs changed dramatically after the September 1998 federal elections, when the CDU–CSU coalition was replaced by a Social Democratic Party (SPD)–Green one. Indeed, during the spring of 1999, the new government legislated far-reaching changes to Germany's nationality laws. Among other liberalizing provisions, these allow for dual citizenship, albeit for a limited period, after which immigrants must choose

8. Interviews with Cem Oezdemir, Bundestag Deputy, Green Party, March 1995; Dr. Camelia Sonntag-Volgast; German Ministry of Interior, March, August 1995; Dr. Jens Meyer-Ladewig and Detlef Wasser, German Ministry of Justice, August 1995.

German nationality or that of their "home" country (Koalitionsvertrag 1998; "Der Kampf" 1999; "Deutsche und Auchdeutsche" 1999; "Ambitious Plans" 1999).

Interpreting these changes drives home the importance of systematically integrating both institutional and counterfactual analysis into studies of Europeanization. On the former, recent events confirm the relevance of my earlier discussion of the "goodness of fit" between German and regional norms, with historically constructed conceptions of German identity clashing with new understandings. The SPD–Green citizenship reform proposals both intensified this clash and revealed its deeper normative dimension. The result has been a wide-ranging debate in Germany unlike any seen in many years, with the exception of those over the Holocaust. It is a heated, impassioned, and very public disagreement over what it means to be German. For sure, much of the rhetoric is just that: rhetoric employed strategically in an ongoing political contest.

In many other cases, however, behavior seems driven not by politics and strategizing, but by more fundamental identity conceptions—to what Free Democratic Party (FDP) general secretary Westerwelle has called "immigration policies from the gut." The results of the Hesse state election in February 1999, where the CDU–CSU scored an upset victory by exploiting deep popular concern over dual citizenship and its impact on German identity, vividly confirm the importance of this normative dimension in the current debate. As former Hesse governor Hans Eichel noted, the question of double citizenship "became so emotional that it mobilized the opposition" ("Germany: Dual Nationality Change" 1999; "Kampagne gegen Doppel-Staatsbuergerschaft" 1999; Schmid 1999).

Given these emotional/normative realities, it comes as no surprise that when the Bundestag eventually passed the revised citizenship statute in May 1999, nearly 40 percent of its deputies voted against or abstained ("Germany: Option Model Approved" 1999).

This said, one must still ask, Are not the recent changes compelling evidence of the power of Europeanization, in this case, of a regional norm's ability to reshape fundamental German identity constructs? After all, there is a striking correlation between the content of the SPD–Green proposals, on the one hand, and the prescriptions embedded in emerging European norms and the reforms earlier advocated by numerous groups and movements in Germany, on the other. Yet, correlation is not causation, and I am skeptical of any strong claims along these lines. For one, the shift in policy also correlates with a dramatic changeover at the elite level. SPD Chancellor Schroeder is not simply a "third way," Blairite social democrat. Equally important, he signals the arrival in power of a truly postwar generation of German politicians. And generational change of this sort is often a key causal variable behind radical policy shifts, especially at the ideational/normative level highlighted here (Stein 1994, 162–63, *passim*).

Methodologically, however, it is important to ask the counterfactual: Absent any Europeanization in this policy area (the development of new regional norms) and absent domestic social pressure, would liberalizing changes to conceptions of citizenship in any case be occurring in a modern industrial democracy such as

Germany? That is, would it look like Europeanization when, in fact, something else was at work? While it is beyond the limits of this chapter to conduct a thorough analysis of this sort, there are reasons to expect the answer might be "yes." For example, it has been persuasively argued that immigration and nationality policy in liberal states has an in-built bias toward becoming more expansionist and inclusive over time: it is dominated by client politics, where small and often well-organized employer, human-rights, and ethnic groups work with state officials outside public view to promote more inclusive membership policies. While the sentiment of the general public is typically anti-immigration, this interest is diffuse. In contrast, the interests of immigrant advocacy groups tend to be concentrated. Collective action problems thus explain (a) the public's inability to bring about more restrictive change; and (b) why the preferences of the better organized liberal interest groups tend to prevail (Freeman 1998, 101–104; Joppke 1998).

Indeed, the very process of exploring the counterfactual sharpens my argument. In particular, I would reconcile the three causal strands identified above—Europeanization in the form of societal pressure spurred by regional norms, generational turnover, and client politics—in the following manner. For one, it is very likely that the SPD election victory and accompanying generational shift simply accelerated a process of change that was already under way, due to the Europeanization/mobilization dynamics sketched earlier. Moreover, the "concentrated interests" of the advocacy groups engaged in client politics were likely more "mobilizeable" due to the existence of new regional norms and, in some cases, learned in the first place via exposure to them.

My more general point is that institutional analysis along with careful consideration of counterfactuals are crucial components of any argument about Europeanization. Use of the two techniques allowed me to produce a more nuanced argument regarding the influence of regional norms. Moreover, as the German case demonstrated, both rationalist and, to a lesser extent, constructivist toolkits are needed to explain the domestic empowerment of European understandings. The value added of historical institutionalism was to disentangle and model, in a systematic manner, the scope of application of these differing approaches.

Germany and the Europeanization of Membership—II: Brussels

Precisely because the TEU's citizenship provisions lack any prescriptive guidance, the German debate over their implementation has lacked the mobilization or learning dynamics seen in the CE case. Indeed, the EU's democratic deficit is being replicated within the Federal Republic, as few societal actors or groups have even taken notice of Maastricht's Union citizenship provisions. Instead, the debate (if one can even refer to it as such), has been largely confined to elites (Länder officials, judges) as they calculate strategies for carrying out the TEU's citizenship injunctions.

I use the phrase "calculate strategies" purposely, as the evidence indicates that the adoption of EU citizenship in Brussels has led to no fundamental reconceptualization of German membership; rather, domestic agents view it as a constraint on their behavior. This is not to argue that Maastricht's European citizenship provisions are not having effects in the Federal Republic. Far from it: various Länder have been required to make changes to their electoral laws and, to take just one example, French nationals are now voting in local elections in Baden-Württemberg. However, in terms of the central concerns of this chapter—how and whether Europeanization is leading to the erosion of national collective identities—these changes are of little interest. The overwhelming conclusion one can infer from media coverage and the specialist literature is that European citizenship in Germany has been a dry and technocratic affair, where agents (mainly elites) have engaged in a self-interested game of strategic adaptation to a new external constraint (Bauer and Kahl 1995; Degen 1993; Engelken 1995; "Gericht: EU-Auslaender" 1997; "Kein Konkurrenzschutz" 1997).

Two caveats to this analysis are in order, however, with both oriented to the future. First, it may be too early to tell whether EU citizenship will have deeper, identity-shaping effects in the Federal Republic. After all, new laws are now on the books, and when or if they become institutionalized and locked-in, a slow, long-term process may occur whereby domestic agents come to rethink fundamental interests and perhaps conceptions of German identity. This is an argument historical institutionalists have made in other contexts (Hattam 1993).

Yet, I am skeptical. The new laws are limited to EU nationals. They also continue to view such individuals precisely as foreign nationals who are temporarily resident on German soil.

Second, evidence from other countries and the European level suggests that the mobilizational, norm-creating dynamics present in the Strasbourg/CE case are intensifying in Brussels as well. Key here was the failure of the 1997 Amsterdam Treaty to move forward the citizenship agenda begun in Maastricht. More and more, transnational and domestic NGOs and activists are adopting—and simultaneously seeking to modify—European citizenship as a cause of their own (Favell 1998). As these groups multiply, create links to the European Parliament ("Call to Strengthen" 1997) and perhaps begin to work with like-minded organizations in countries such as Germany, the debate over EU citizenship could move to a more conceptual, norm-promoting level.

Conclusion: Implications for Studies of Europeanization and for German Identity

Regarding Europeanization, my concern has not been to dismiss rationalist conceptions of institutions employed in research on the EU. Rather, I have sought to expand the disciplinary foundations for understanding how they have effects. To this end, I developed and demonstrated the empirical plausibility of a constructivist or thick institutionalist account of institutions in European integration. This argument itself incorporated a thin institutional element: the empowerment of

European norms via societal pressure—one of the hypothesized diffusion mechanisms—is best explained by rational choice.

Thus, both thick and thin institutions matter in European integration. Some may find this a trivial insight, but it has crucial importance for one of this book's central research questions: is Europeanization eroding historically constructed national collective identities? The addition of a thick, normative element significantly complicates—and, I would argue, enriches—debate surrounding this issue. At the European level, taking norms seriously suggests yet another "actor" challenging state identity. Domestically, however, the existence of identity norms that filter or hinder European understandings (my German study) indicates the hard shell of the state is anything but hollow when viewed from this nonmaterialist and nonrationalist perspective. A complete understanding of how Europeanization affects state identity thus requires not only a debate over which institutions matter, but how they work their effects on those states. Ontological assumptions about the latter influence our substantive answers to the former.

In an important sense, students of Europeanization, in making their European-to-domestic linkages, need to follow the same path taken by international relations and international political economy scholars exploring the international sources of domestic politics—the so-called second-image reversed. Early second-image work adopted a rationalist and materialist understanding of how international effects constrained the choices of domestic agents with given interests (Gourevitch 1986). Much of the existing EU literature, including that which explicitly attacks (rationalist) intergovernmentalism, makes similar assumptions in exploring the domestic impact of EU institutions (Checkel 2000).

Only more recently, with the constructivist turn in international relations theory, have IR scholars taken seriously the possibility that the international sources of domestic politics include such factors as norms and culture (Finnemore 1996; Katzenstein 1996). The latter, instead of acting as behavioral constraint, provide domestic agents with basic understandings of interests. While there are growing hints of such a turn in studies of the European Union, they have yet to consolidate themselves and still await rigorous empirical application and testing (Christiansen, Joergensen, and Wiener 1999; Olsen 1996; Risse-Kappen 1996, 68–72; see also Pollack 1998).

Among other issues, this book asks whether Europeanization, in a particular policy area or sector, is leading to the "incorporation of Europeanness into nationally constructed identities." For this chapter, where I define Europeanization as the development of new collective understandings on citizenship and membership at the European level, the answer—for Germany—is contested and ambiguous. German policy on citizenship has indeed changed in important ways since the SPD–Green coalition assumed office in late 1998; yet, as indicated earlier, endogenous demographic and domestic political factors—and not Europeanization—likely explain much of this outcome (see also Gurowitz 1999, 416–17). Moreover, whatever the source of change, it is highly contested, with continuing normative disputes, especially over the issue of dual citizenship.

Two factors account for this state of affairs. First, Europeanization of nationality or citizenship, be it in Brussels or Strasbourg, is at best emergent and tentative. Second, Germany's historically constructed identity, for some domestic agents, has acted as a filter or block vis-à-vis more civic and inclusive European-level norms.

My results are therefore partly at odds with accounts that depict the emergence of a postnational membership model in Western Europe or with arguments that assert a thorough Europeanization of German national identity in the postwar era. On the former, differences arise because previous work (Soysal 1994) employed a theoretical apparatus that brackets the process through which European and international discourses favoring postnational membership actually play out in particular national settings (see also Joppke 1998, 293). For the latter, my empirical focus—the hard case of fundamental conceptions of nationhood (citizenship, membership)—explains why I see less Europeanization of German identity.[9]

9. Katzenstein and collaborators (1997a, 24–33, *passim*) argue for a Europeanization and internationalization of German national identity but neglect the issues of citizenship and membership addressed here.

CHAPTER ELEVEN

A European Identity? Europeanization and the Evolution of Nation-State Identities

Thomas Risse

An effectively functioning polity requires that its members attach legitimacy to it. Political systems need the diffuse support of their members in order to be able to carry out and implement authoritative decisions that might otherwise meet resistance. Those theorizing about an emerging European polity have always been interested in questions of collective identity formation. The founding fathers of regional integration theory, such as Ernst Haas and Karl W. Deutsch, were also pioneers of the literature on nation-building and nationalism (Deutsch et al. 1957, 5–6, 129; Haas 1958, 16). "Euro-pessimists" challenge the evolutionary logic of European integration on precisely these grounds. They argue that a European polity is impossible, because integration in terms of collective identity cannot be achieved (see Kielmansegg 1996; Smith 1992).

The impact of Europeanization on collective identities and shifting loyalties is not only controversial but also poorly understood. In this chapter I explore how Europeanization has influenced nation-state identities in France, Germany, and the United Kingdom over the past fifty years. I argue that individuals and social groups

This chapter reports findings from a research project on "Ideas, Institutions, and Political Culture: The Europeanization of National Identities" funded by the German Research Association (Deutsche Forschungsgemeinschaft). The empirical research was carried out by Daniela Engelmann-Martin, Hans-Joachim Knopf, Martin Marcussen, and Klaus Roscher. I am most grateful for their input. I thank the participants and discussants in the transatlantic project on "Europeanization and Domestic Change" for their comments on the various drafts, particularly Jim Caporaso, Mark Pollack, Yasemin Soysal, and Fritz Scharpf.

hold multiple identities and the real question to be asked concerns, therefore, how much space there is for "Europe" in collective nation-state identities. I concentrate empirically on discourses among political elites, in particular the major political parties of the three countries. I claim that five distinct identity constructions with regard to the nation-state were available in the transnational European discourses and promoted by various transnational groups during the 1950s. These identity constructions can be distinguished along two dimensions, first, ideas about how "Europe" relates to given nation-state identities, and second, visions about the European political and economic order. The degree to which these identity constructions were represented in the political discourses in the three countries varied considerably. Moreover, different identity constructions carried the day and became consensual.

In the *British* case, notions of "Englishness" have been largely constructed as distinct from "Europe" and have remained so since the 1950s. The prevailing English nation-state identity still perceives Europe as the (friendly) "other." The distinctive nationalist English identity is incompatible with federalist or supranationalist visions of European political order. It explains why British governments, whether Conservative or Labour, have consistently been reluctant to support a deepening of European integration.

In contrast, the (West) *German* nation-state identity was thoroughly reconstructed during the 1950s, when purely nationalist visions were less and less available after the catastrophe of Nazi Germany and World War II. A "European Germany" was seen as overcoming the German nationalist past. By 1960, this new German nation-state identity had become consensual and has remained so ever since. The European German nation-state identity survived the end of the Cold War and German unification and explains why German political elites, whether Christian Democrats or Social Democrats, have supported further steps toward European integration.

While Britain and Germany are thus cases of continuity since at least the late 1950s, there have been substantial changes in the *French* collective nation-state identities. In contrast to Germany, a distinct nationalist vision of French identity carried the day in the late 1950s. President de Gaulle's Fifth Republic combined the French history of a centralized state, of enlightenment, and of Republicanism in a vision of *grandeur* and *indépendence*. De Gaulle's successors found out, however, that these visions of France were increasingly inconsistent with the reality of European integration. As a result, the political elites, starting with the center-left during the 1980s and continuing on the center-right, incorporated "Europe" into the French collective identity by adopting a vision of Europe as the French nation-state writ large.

This chapter proceeds in the following steps. First, I adjust the conceptual framework of this book to my particular question and clarify theoretical concepts. Second, I discuss the empirical evolution of nation-state identities in the three cases and the extent to which they were influenced by Europeanization. Third, I try to explain the variation among the cases.

Europeanization, Nation–State Identities, and Perceived Instrumental Interests: Conceptual Clarifications

The theoretical framework of this book is primarily suited to study the adaptation of domestic formal institutions—political, administrative, and societal—to pressures emanating from European-level rules and regulations. With regard to collective identities and other informal understandings, however, the term "adaptational pressure" does not make a lot of sense. While the preambles of the Rome, Maastricht, and Amsterdam treaties routinely invoke references to a collective European identity to justify the process toward "an ever closer union" (Preamble to the European Union Treaty 1992), there is, of course, no contractual obligation to develop a common European identity. There are no formal or informal norms requiring European Union (EU) citizens to transfer their loyalties to the EU instead of or in conjunction with the nation-state.

At the same time, people need to make sense and develop collective understandings of political processes in the EU. If more and more competences are transferred to the EU level and made subject to joint decision-making involving supranational institutions, we should expect that this emerging European polity impacts upon the way individuals and social groups view themselves and the nation-state. When EU developments more and more erode national sovereignty as traditionally defined, one would at least assume challenges to given nation-state identities. In sum, it is a relevant question to ask how Europeanization influences collective understandings and loyalties toward the nation-state.

The first conceptual task is to define those EU-level developments that might challenge and impact given collective nation-state identities. In this chapter, I look at two such processes:

1. *Transnational European discourses* and the emergence of a European public space. These transnational activities predate the EC/EU. Several European movements promoting European integration emerged, for example, during the interwar period. They also advocated specific identity constructions, overcoming purely nationalist conceptions. Ideas of these groups became particularly salient during the 1950s and, apart from influencing the first steps toward European integration, found their way into the domestic discourses of various European countries. During the 1970s and 1980s, in conjunction with the increasing significance of the European Parliament, transnational links among political parties were formalized, leading to European-level transnational party organizations. While the influence of these groups on European policymaking has been rather limited, they served the exchange of ideas about European unity (Kuper and Jun 1997; Neßler 1997).

2. *European integration* and the emergence of a European polity. The continuous transfer of competences from the nation-state to the European level and the Europeanization of more and more issue-areas is expected to have repercussions for the perceptions and collective understandings of individuals and social groups, in this case political elites. While other chapters in this volume focus on the domes-

tic impact of the rules and regulations emanating from the EU level, I concentrate on the intersubjective meanings that people attach to the Europeanization process as a whole and their influence on collective identities.

I then investigate how these two developments impact upon collective identities pertaining to the nation-state. I use social identity and self-categorization theories to clarify the concept of collective identity (see Abrams and Hogg 1990; Turner 1987). I emphasize the term "collective" here in the sense of intersubjective, shared understandings of identity that have become consensual among social groups. While political elites are almost constantly in the business of identity constructions, only some of these constructions are consensual at any given point in time. In this chapter I investigate how Europeanization affects such consensual identity constructions. But how can we conceptualize collective identities pertaining to the nation-state?

Social identities contain, first, ideas describing and categorizing an individual's membership in a social group including emotional, affective, and evaluative components. Groups of individuals perceive that they have something in common, on the basis of which they form an "imagined community" (Anderson 1991). Second, this commonness is accentuated by a sense of difference with regard to other communities. Individuals frequently tend to view the group with which they identify in a more positive way than the "out-group." This does not mean, however, that the perceived differences between the "in-group" and the out-group are necessarily based on value judgements and that the "other" is usually looked down at (Eisenstadt and Giesen 1995). Third, *national* identities construct the "imagined communities" of (mostly territorially defined) nation states and are therefore closely linked to ideas about sovereignty and statehood (Bloom 1990). National identities often contain visions of just political and social orders. Fourth, individuals hold multiple social identities, and these social identities are context bound (Oakes, Haslam, and Turner 1994, 100). The context-boundedness of national identities also means that different components of national identities are invoked depending on the policy area in question. National identities with regard to citizenship rules might look different from national identities concerning understandings of the state and political order. Because I am concerned with the latter rather than with the former, I use the term *nation-state identity* to delineate the differences with other components of national collective identities.[1] The multiplicity, context-boundedness, and contestedness of collective identities has led many authors to conclude that social identities are fluid and subject to frequent changes (for example, Neumann 1996). But the latter does not follow from the former. Cognitive psychology and self-categorization theory argue that self/other categorizations change the more gradually, the more they are incorporated in institutions, myths, and symbols, as well as in cultural understandings (Fiske and Taylor 1984; Oakes, Haslam, and Turner 1994). This should be particularly relevant for collective identities pertaining to the nation-state, which usually take quite some time

---

1. I owe this point to Yasemin Soysal. For identity constructions concerning citizenship rules, see chapter 10, this volume.

and effort to construct and are then embedded in institutions and a country's political culture.

Having clarified the concepts of Europeanization and of collective nation–state identities as used in this chapter, I now turn to the equivalent of "goodness of fit" (see also Marcussen et al. 1999). Cultural sociology and sociological institutionalism (Jepperson and Swidler 1994; Lepsius 1990; Powell and DiMaggio 1991) suggest that ideas about European order and identity constructions about Europe and the nation–state emanating from the transnational level will interact with given collective nation–state identities. Such political visions and identity constructions are the more likely to impact upon and to be incorporated in collective nation–state identities, the more they resonate with the ideas about the nation and political order embedded in these collective understandings. The same holds true for the effects of the European integration process itself on collective nation–state identities. Thus, for this chapter, the degree of resonance resembles the goodness of fit.

It follows that some collective nation–state identities resonate more with Europeanization than others and are expected to incorporate understandings of Europe and of European order earlier. The very content of a "European" collective nation–state identity might also vary, depending on how various ideas about Europe resonate with nationally constructed identities. One would expect different interpretations with regard to what is understood as "European" in the various national contexts and how Europe's "others" are defined. Finally, social groups are unlikely to give up their nation–state identity altogether in favor of a collective European identity; rather, "Europe" is incorporated in and coexists with given nation–state identities, depending on the degree of resonance. While a convergence toward a unified European identity is not to be expected, several versions of European nation–state identities are possible, depending on how much ideational space there is for "Europe" in given collective identity constructions.

The resonance of ideas and visions about Europe with given collective nation–state identities explains which ideas and identity constructions are considered legitimate and appropriate in a given political setting. However, the "resonance" argument does not explain that sometimes several concepts of political order and European visions might be compatible with historically emerged nation–state identities. How can we explain that some identity constructions prevail over time and carry the day by ultimately becoming consensual and being incorporated in a new, collective nation–state identity?

Two additional explanatory factors come to mind that represent the functional equivalent of facilitating institutions and actor strategies as the third part of the adaptational "three-step" process described in the other chapters of this volume. First, political elites in general and party elites in particular continuously pursue perceived instrumental interests. Parties want to gain power or remain in government. They need to sell their political ideas to a larger public opinion in order to be (re-)elected. At the same time, political power is the precondition for them to be able to pursue other, including ideational, goals. We can, therefore, assume that political elites (including party leaders) try to promote ideas (including identity constructions) with an eye on gaining power or remaining in government. Many of the internal programmatic controversies center on the question of which ideas are more likely to win elections than others. Thus, political elites select those identity constructions among the ones considered legitimate that suit their perceived instrumental interests. In a sense then, instrumental interests explain which identity constructions are selected and promoted among a given group of actors, in this case political parties.

Second, we need to account for the consensuality and stickiness of collective nation-state identities, once they have been successfully selected by political elites. Here, one can make a socialization argument. Ideas and identity constructions become consensual when actors thoroughly internalize them, perceive them as "their own," and gradually take them for granted (Finnemore and Sikkink 1998). Socialization might then explain why collective nation-state identities do not change frequently and are likely to be challenged only in times of perceived severe crises ("critical junctures").

In sum, the *resonance* argument explains which identity constructions are considered appropriate and legitimate in a given political arena and discourse. The *interest* hypothesis then accounts for which of these constructions are being selected and promoted by political elites. Finally, the *socialization* assumption explains how collective nation-state identities assume their "taken for grantedness" over time. Below, I demonstrate this argument with regard to the evolution of nation-state identities in the three countries.

Europe and the Evolution of Nation-State Identities in Britain, Germany, and France

The Early 1950s: Five Nation-State Identity Constructions

My empirical argument starts with the 1950s (for the following, see also Marcussen et al. 1999; Jachtenfuchs, Diez, and Jung 1998). At the time, five ideal-typical identity constructions can be differentiated from one another in the various national debates on Europe and the nation-state. Their origins can be found in the interwar period (and earlier), and these ideas were hotly debated in various transnational European movements and organizations during the 1950s:

1. *Nationalist* concepts of nation-state identity whereby the "we" is restricted to one's own nation and "Europe" constitutes part of the "others": These ideas were compatible with a *Europe of nation-states* in an intergovernmentalist sense. Such a concept prevailed in Great Britain among both major parties, dominated among the French Gaullists, and was also supported by an elite minority in Germany.
2. A *Europe as a community of values* "from the Atlantic to the Urals," embedded in geography, history, and culture: This concept gained some supporters during the early years of the Cold War, particularly in France and Germany. Its most prominent advocate was Charles de Gaulle.

3. *Europe as a "third force,"* as a democratic socialist alternative between capital-ism and communism, thus overcoming the boundaries of the Cold War order: This concept originated in the transnational socialist movement, particularly among resistance circles against the Nazis. This identity construction prevailed among French Socialists and German Social Democrats during the early 1950s.
4. A *modern Europe as part of the Western community* based on liberal democracy and social market economy, in sharp contrast to communist ideas: This identity construction originated partly among transnational European movements of the interwar period. During the 1940s and 1950s, U.S. leaders strongly promoted this particular concept of European identity. It then became salient among German and French Christian Democrats as well as among a minority of the German Social Democratic Party (SPD).
5. A *Christian Europe (Abendland)* based on Christian, particularly Catholic values, including strong social obligations: This identity construction also originated in transnational European movements of the interwar period. Such ideas were widespread among Christian Democratic parties in France and Germany during the 1950s but then became increasingly amalgamated with modern, Western-ized ideas of Europe.

While these five conceptions of "we as a nation-state" were heavily contested during the 1950s, only two competitors remain in the three countries during the 1990s: The *nationalist* idea of nation-state identity and the *modern Western* concept of Europe as a liberal community. However, the latter concept comes in distinct national colors, particularly in France and Germany.

Europe as Britain's "Other"

Probably the most remarkable feature of British elite attitudes toward European integration is their stability and lack of change (for the following, see Knopf 1997). The fundamental orientations toward the European Community have remained essentially the same since the end of World War II and have survived the ups and downs in British policies toward the EC/EU. More than twenty years after entry into the European Community, Britain is still regarded as "of rather than in" Europe; it remains the "awkward partner" and "semi-detached" from Europe (Bailey 1983; George 1994). This is also true for the major divisions among and within the two main parties, the Conservatives and Labour. British views on Euro-pean integration essentially range from those who objected to British entry into the EC in the first place and who now oppose further Europeanization (right wing of the Conservatives, Labour's far left and far right) to a mainstream group within both main parties supporting a "Europe of nation-states." European federalists remain a minority in the political discourse, both among the Tories and within Labour. The mainstream of the two leading parties shares a consensual vision of European order (see Labour Party 1997; Conservative Party 1997). This general attitude has not changed since the 1950s: "Where do we stand? We are not members of the European Defence Community, nor do we intend to be merged in a Federal

European system. We feel we have a special relation to both, expressed by prepositions: by the preposition 'with' but not 'of'—we are with them, but not of them. We have our own Commonwealth and Empire" (Churchill 1953).

British attitudes toward the European project reflect collectively held beliefs about British, particularly English identity, since "Britishness" has been identified with "Englishness" throughout most of the post–World War II era. Among the five ideal typical identity constructions presented above, the nationalist identity clearly prevailed in the British political discourses. There is still a feeling of "them" vs. "us" between Britain and the continent. "Europe" continues to be identified with the continent and perceived as "the other" in contrast to Englishness. The social construction of "Englishness" as the core of British nation-state identity comprises meanings attached to institutions, historical memory, and symbols. Each of these components is hard to reconcile with a vision of European political order going beyond intergovernmentalism (see Lyon 1991; Schauer 1996; Schmitz and Geserick 1996). It is not surprising that parts of English nation-state identity are often viewed as potentially threatened by European integration. Institutions such as the Parliament and the Crown form important elements of a collective nation-state identity. The identity-related meanings attached to these institutions center on a peculiar understanding of national sovereignty. The Crown symbolizes "external sovereignty" in terms of independence from Rome and the Pope as well as from the European continent since 1066. Parliamentary or "internal" sovereignty represents a most important constitutional principle relating to a 700-year-old parliamentary tradition and hard-fought victories over the king. English sovereignty is, thus, directly linked to myths about a continuous history of liberal and democratic evolution and "free-born Englishmen." British objections against transferring sovereignty to European supranational institutions are usually justified on grounds of lacking democratic—meaning parliamentary—accountability. Identity-related understandings of parliamentary sovereignty are directly linked to the prevailing visions of a European order comprising independent nation-states. This is demonstrated by the following quotes from 1950 and from the 1990s:

Labour Chancellor of the Exchequer Sir Stafford Cripps, 1950: "It does not, however, seem to us—as at present advised—either necessary or appropriate . . . to invest a supra-national authority of independent persons with powers for overriding Governmental and Parliamentary decisions in the participating countries. (. . .) Certainly this Parliament has always exercised the greatest caution as to agreeing to any removal from its own democratic control of any important element of our economic power or policy" (Cripps 1950).

Prime Minister Margaret Thatcher, 1990: "But—and it is a crucial but—we shall never accept the approach of those who want to see the EC as a means of removing our ability to govern ourselves as an independent nation. The British Parliament had endured for 700 years and had been a beacon of hope to the peoples of Europe in their darkest days" (Thatcher 1990).

Prime Minister John Major, 1993: "It is clear now that the Community will remain a union of sovereign national states. That is what its peoples want: to take decisions through their own Parliaments. That protects the way of life, the cultural differences, the national traditions. . . . It is for nations to build Europe, not for Europe to attempt to supersede nations" (Major 1993).

These and other statements show a remarkable continuity of British attitudes toward the European Union and related identity constructions from the 1950s (and earlier) until today. They also demonstrate that nation-state identities supersede ideological orientations among the two major parties.

How do British collective identity constructions relate to general attitudes toward the EC/EU? In this regard, the picture is fairly consistent. In the 1950s, Britain did not join the European Economic Community (EEC) and instead created European Free Trade Area (EFTA), because it opposed the political project of European integration. It nevertheless applied for membership later, but for pragmatic rather than principled reasons (George 1992, 40). This pragmatism also characterized British policies in the EU after it had joined. It is not surprising, therefore, that London remained "semi-detached" and on the sidelines whenever the EU took major steps toward further integration. The Single European Act is the one and only exception, while the decision not to join the European Monetary System (EMS) at first, the Maastricht opt-outs, and so forth, fit the bill. It is also consistent with this reluctance that the new Labour government sticks to John Major's "wait and see" attitude with regard to the Euro.

In sum, British nation-state identity seems to be hardly affected by European integration, and "Europe" is still largely constructed as the—albeit friendly— "other." While the British case is one of nonadaptation to the European Union, German nation-state identity transformed toward Europe before the integration process could have left its mark. In other words, Britain is a case of strong incompatibility between Europe and the nation-state, while Europe resonates well with contemporary German nation-state identity.

The Past as European Germany's "Other"

The German case is one of thorough and profound reconstruction of nation-state identity following the catastrophe of World War II (for the following, see Engelmann-Martin 1998; Risse and Engelmann-Martin forthcoming). Thomas Mann's dictum that "we do not want a German Europe, but a European Germany" quickly became the mantra of the postwar (West) German elites.[2] Since the 1950s, a fundamental consensus has emerged among the political elites and has been shared by public opinion that European integration is in Germany's vital interest (see Bulmer 1989; Katzenstein 1997a).

In contrast to Britain, all five ideal typical identity constructions mentioned above were represented in the German political debates of the 1950s. At the time, the Christian Democratic Party (CDU) promoted both the Christian-Catholic

2. In the following, I use "Germany" routinely for the Federal Republic, including the pre-unification period.

Abendland vision of Europe and the modern, Westernized concept. The first chancellor, Konrad Adenauer, amalgamated both identity constructions into one. He regarded the integration of the German state and society in the West as the best means of overcoming the German past. Adenauer's thinking about Europe was heavily influenced by ideas and visions of the interwar period (Baring 1969; Schwarz 1966). The *Abendland* vision of Europe was related to identity constructions around the concept of a *Christian (i.e., Catholic) Occident*, wherein the Slavic and Islamic *Orient* constituted "the other." After 1945, the Soviet Union and communism easily replaced religiously oriented perceptions of the "other."

After 1945, the newly founded Christian Democratic Party (CDU) immediately embraced European unification as the alternative to the nationalism of the past. As Ernst Haas put it, "In leading circles of the CDU, the triptych of self-conscious anti-Nazism, Christian values, and dedication to European unity as a means of redemption for past German sins has played a crucial ideological role" (Haas 1958, 127). Christianity, democracy, and (later) social market economy became the three pillars on which a collective European identity was to be based. It was sharply distinguished from both the German nationalist and militarist past and, during the late 1940s and early 1950s, from Soviet communism and marxism. In other words, Germany's own past as well as communism constituted the "others" in this identity construction.

But throughout the early 1950s, there was no elite consensus on German nation-state identity. Within Adenauer's own party, Jacob Kaiser, CDU leader in Berlin and later chairman of the German trade unions, embraced the notion of Europe as a "third force" between East and West. He favored a German policy of "bridge-building" between East and West, including neutrality between the two blocs (see Pfetsch 1993, 139). Party elites of Adenauer's coalition partner, the Free Democratic Party (FDP), also endorsed this concept, while FDP chairman Thomas Dehler remained a supporter of a nationalist, albeit liberal and democratic vision of German nation-state identity (Glatzeder 1980).

The Social Democrats (SPD) were the main opposition party to Adenauer's policies at the time. In the interwar period, the SPD had been the first major German party to embrace the concept of a "United States of Europe" in its 1925 Heidelberg program. When the party was forced into exile during the Nazi period, the leadership fully embraced the notion of a democratic European federation that would almost naturally become a socialist order. As in the case of the CDU, "the 'European idea' was primarily invoked as a spiritual value in the first years of the emigration. . . . What Europe would be like after Hitler was a second-order question, though it was taken as self-evident that it would be socialist. In this period Europe was seen as an antithesis to Nazi Germany" (Paterson 1974, 3). Consequently, when the SPD was refounded in 1946, its first program supported the "United States of Europe, a democratic and socialist federation of European states. [The German Social Democracy] aspires to a Socialist Germany in a Socialist Europe" (Sozialdemokratische Partei Deutschlands 1946). Thus, Europe, Germany, democracy, and socialism were perceived as identical.

The SPD's first postwar leader, Kurt Schumacher, a survivor of Nazi concentration camps, strongly promoted the "Europe as a third force" concept for the new German nation-state identity. He argued vigorously against the politics of Western integration, since it foreclosed the prospects of rapid reunification of the two Germanies (Paterson 1974; Rogosch 1996). Schumacher denounced the Council of Europe and the European Coal and Steel Community (ECSC) as "un-European," as "mini-Europe" (*Kleinsteuropa*), as conservative-clericalist and capitalist. At the same time, the SPD went to great pains to argue that it did not oppose European integration as such, just this particular version.

Two major election defeats later (1953 and 1957), the SPD changed course. There had always been an internal opposition against Schumacher's policies. Party officials such as Ernst Reuter (the legendary mayor of Berlin), Willy Brandt (who later became party chairman and, in 1969, chancellor), Fritz Erler, Herbert Wehner, and Helmut Schmidt (Brandt's successor as chancellor in 1974) supported closer relations with the United States as well as German integration into the West. Influenced by the Socialist Movement for the United States of Europe, founded in 1947, and by Jean Monnet's Action Committee, these party elites supported the identity construction of a modern European Germany as part of the Western community of liberal and democratic states. By the late 1950s, this group took over the party leadership. The German Social Democrats thoroughly reformed their domestic and foreign policy program. With regard to the latter, they revisited the 1925 Heidelberg program and became staunch supporters of European integration. The changes culminated in the 1959 Godesberg program (Bellers 1991; Rogosch 1996).

The SPD's turnaround can partly be explained by perceived instrumental interests. The party needed to attract new voters who apparently supported Adenauer's policies, while Schumacher's opposition did not pay off. The party's new ideological orientation resulted from a leadership change that brought the Europeanist and Atlanticist faction into power. Thus, instrumental interests explain that "something" had to be done. The political goals and collective identity of the new party leaders account for the content and substance of the change.

From the 1960s on, a federalist consensus ("United States of Europe") prevailed among the German political elites comprising the main parties from the center-right to the center-left. This consensus outlasted the changes in government from the CDU to the SPD in 1969, from the SPD to the CDU in 1982, and the recent change toward a coalition between the SPD and the Green Party in 1998. It also survived a major foreign policy change of West German policy toward Eastern Europe, East Germany, and the Soviet Union. When Chancellor Willy Brandt introduced *Ostpolitik* in 1969, he made it very clear that European integration was untouchable and had to be continued.

Even more significant, German unification twenty years later did not result in a reconsideration of German European policies. With the unexpected end of the East-West conflict and regained German sovereignty, a broad range of foreign policy opportunities emerged, creating a situation in which the German elites could have redefined their national interests. But Germany did not reconsider its fundamental foreign policy orientations, since Germany's commitment to European integration had long outlived the context in which it had originally emerged (see Banchoff 1997, 1999; Hellmann 1996; Katzenstein 1997a). In the aftermath of unification, the German government accelerated rather than slowed its support for further progress in European integration. German support for a single currency and for a European political union was perfectly in line with long-standing attitudes toward integration and the country's European nation-state identity.

This German federalist consensus went hand in hand with a peculiar identity construction in the aftermath of World War II. The German notion of what constitutes the "other," the non-European, is related to European and German nationalist history. German nationalism came to be viewed as authoritarianism, militarism, and anti-Semitism. Germany's nationalist and militarist past constituted the "other" in the process of "post-national" identity formation, whereby Europeanness replaces traditional notions of nation-state identity. All federal governments, from Konrad Adenauer onward, were determined to render the European unification process irreversible because they were convinced that the concept of a unified Europe was the most effective assurance against the renaissance of nationalism and disastrous conflicts. Nowadays, a "good German" equals a "good European" supporting a united Europe. "Europe," in this identity construction, stands for a stable peace order overcoming the continent's bloody past, for democracy and human rights (in contrast to European—and German—autocratic history), as well as for a social market economy, including the welfare state (in contrast to both Soviet communism and Anglo-Saxon "laissez-faire" capitalism; see Bellers and Winking 1991; Katzenstein 1997a).

This European German nation-state identity explains to a large extent German elite attitudes toward European integration, as exemplified by the single currency, the euro (see Risse et al. 1999). The majority of the German political elite views the euro as a cornerstone of European political integration, despite a legitimacy crisis in German public opinion. Chancellor Kohl framed the single currency as the symbol of European integration, and he labeled 1997—the reference year for the fulfillment of the convergence criteria—as the "key year of Europe," as essential for further integration. He even framed the success of the euro as a "question of war and peace" ("Kohl" 1994).

In sum and in contrast to Great Britain, the German case is one of comprehensive transformation of post–World War II nation-state identity. German Europeanness as a particular identity construction was contested throughout the 1950s but became consensual afterward, partly because it suited perceived instrumental interests of political elites. The European integration process did not create this identity. It rather reinforced and stabilized it by demonstrating that Germany can prosper economically and regain political clout in Europe through a policy of "self-binding" in European institutions. German Euro-patriotism deeply affected elite perceptions of the country's national interests and attitudes toward European integration. This Euro-patriotism remained stable despite various challenges that might otherwise have led to changes in instrumental interests.

Europeanization and the Transformation of French Exceptionalism

In contrast to Britain and Germany, attitudes toward Europe shared by the French political elites underwent considerable changes over time (for the following, see Roscher 1998). Policymakers of the Third Republic, such as Aristide Briand and Eduard Herriot, were among the first who embraced a federalist vision of *"les Etats Unis d'Europe"* during the interwar period (Bjøl 1966, 172–73). However, their visions did not become consensual within their own parties until after World War II. As in the German case, all five nation-state identity constructions were represented in the French political discourses during the 1950s. Quite a few French parties embraced federalist visions of Europe, including the predecessors of today's center UDF (Union pour la Démocratie Française, the successor party of the Christian Democratic Mouvement Républicain Populaire—MRP) and of the French Socialists (Section Française de l'Internationale Ouvrière— SFIO, now Parti Socialiste Français—PSF). As in the case of the German CDU, the MRP promoted both the Christian vision of Europe and the modern Westernized concept. And similarly to the German SPD under Schumacher, the French Socialists favored the idea of Europa as a "third force" between capitalism and communism. Finally, the French Gaullists supported a nationalist identity construction and a "Europe of nation-states," while de Gaulle himself sometimes embraced the concept of Europe as a geopolitical community of values "from the Atlantic to the Urals."

During the 1950s and in conjunction with the first efforts toward European integration, a national debate took place that concerned French identity and basic political orientations in the postwar era. World War II and the German occupation served as traumatic experiences, as a result of which French nation-state identity became deeply problematic and contested. Many controversies centered on how to deal with Germany as the most significant French "other" of the time. Supporters of European integration argued in favor of a "binding" strategy, of creating supranational institutions in order to contain German power once and for all, while opponents favored traditional balance-of-power strategies to deal with the German problem:

> Socialist Leader Guy Mollet: "The only means to disinfect the German people from Nazism and to democratize it is to surround Germany in a democratic Europe" (Mollet 1947).
>
> MRP Leader Alfred Coste-Floret: "There is no Europe without Germany and there is no solution for the German problem without Europe" (Coste-Floret 1952).
>
> RPF Leader Michel Debré: "Our policy must, first of all, anchor Germany. Thus, one observes that the European army does not only not anchor Germany, but that it increases the German threat" (Debré 1953).

These policy prescriptions correlated with nation-state identity constructions prevailing in the respective parties at the time. There was no consensus among the French political elites about European integration as a solution to the German problem. The defeat of the treaty on the European Defense Community in the French National Assembly in 1954 showed the deep divisions among the political elites.

The next "critical juncture" for French nation-state identity was the war in Algeria and the ongoing crisis of the Fourth Republic. When the Fifth Republic came into being in 1958, its founding father, President Charles de Gaulle, reconstructed French nation-state identity and managed to reunite a deeply divided nation around a common vision of the French role in the world:

> When one is the Atlantic cape of the continent, when one has planted one's flag in all parts of the world, when one spreads the ideas, and when one opens oneself to the environment, in short, when one is France, one cannot escape the grand movements on the ground. (De Gaulle 1950)
>
> We are the people made to establish and to help international cooperation. This is our national ambition today. . . . It is for the good of mankind and for the future of humanity. Only France can play this game and only France plays it. (De Gaulle 1965)

De Gaulle's identity construction related to historical myths of Frenchness and combined them in a unique way. As the leader of the French *résistance* during World War II, he overcame the trauma of the Vichy regime and related to understandings of the French nation-state that combined a specific meaning of sovereignty with the values of enlightenment and democracy (Furet, Juillard, and Rosanvallon 1988; Nicolet 1982; Saint-Etienne 1992). The notion of sovereignty, understood as national independence from outside interference together with a sense of uniqueness (*grandeur*), was used to build a bridge between postrevolutionary Republican France and the prerevolutionary monarchy. The understanding of the French *l'état-nation* connoted the identity of the nation and democracy as well as the identity of French society with the Republic. Finally, de Gaulle reintroduced the notion of French exceptionalism and uniqueness in terms of a civilizing mission for the world (*mission civilisatrice*) destined to spread the universal values of enlightenment and of the French Revolution. None of these nation-state identity constructions was particularly new, but de Gaulle combined them in a special way and managed to use them in order to legitimize the political institutions of the Fifth Republic.

Of course, these understandings were hard to reconcile with federalist visions of European order. Rather, "*l'Europe des nations*" (Europe of nation-states) became the battle cry during de Gaulle's presidency. But the specific Gaullist nation-state identity construction only remained consensual among the political elites for about another ten years after de Gaulle's resignation. Beginning in the late 1970s, Europeanization gradually transformed French nation-state identity among the elites in conjunction with two critical junctures: the failure of President Mitterrand's economic policies in the early 1980s, and the end of the Cold War in the late 1980s (Flynn 1995; V. Schmidt 1997).

When Mitterrand and the Socialist Party came into power in 1981, they initially embarked upon a project of creating democratic socialism in France based on leftist

Keynesianism. This project bitterly failed when the adverse reactions of the capital markets hit the French economy, which in turn led to a severe loss of electoral support for Mitterrand's policies. In 1983, Mitterrand had practically no choice other than changing course dramatically, if he wanted to remain in power (Bauchard 1986; Uterwedde 1988). This political change led to a deep crisis within the Socialist Party (Parti Socialiste—PS), which then gradually abandoned the socialist project and moved toward ideas once derisively labeled "social democratic." In changing course, the party followed President François Mitterrand, who had defined the construction of the European Community as a central issue of his time in office: "We are at the moment where everybody unites, our fatherland, our Europe, Europe our fatherland, the ambition to support one by the other, the excitement of our land and of the people it produces, and the certainty of a new dimension is expecting them" (Mitterrand 1986, 15, 104).

The reorientation of the French Socialists toward neoliberal economics—in "French colors," of course—went hand in hand with a change in attitudes toward European integration as a whole, which had hitherto often been denounced as a "capitalist" project. The Socialists now saw the European future in a more or less federal model. They were willing to share larger amounts of sovereignty in various domains, for example, security, economic, and social policies, because national sovereignty in its traditional understanding was regarded as an illusion in an interdependent world. The commitment to European integration had reached consensual status in the PS by the mid-1980s.

The PS's move toward Europe included an effort to reconstruct French nation-state identity. The French Socialists started highlighting the common European historical and cultural heritage. They increasingly argued that the French future was to be found in Europe: "France is our fatherland, Europe is our future" (Mitterrand 1992). The French left started embracing the notion of a "European France," extending the vision of the French "*mission civilisatrice*" toward Europe writ large. The peculiar historical and cultural legacies of France were transferred from the "first nation-state" in Europe to the continent as a whole, because all European states were seen as children of enlightenment, democracy, and republicanism. France should imprint its marks on Europe. This identity construction uses traditional understandings of Frenchness and the French nation-state and extends them to Europe. In contrast to English identity constructions, where Europe is still the "other," this understanding incorporates Europe into one's own collective identity and its understandings about sovereignty and political order. French identity is transformed, but only to the degree that ideas about Europe can be incorporated into and resonate with previous visions of the state.

Similar changes in the prevailing visions of European order and reconstructions of French nation-state identity took place on the French right, albeit later. The heir of Charles de Gaulle's visions, the Rassemblement pour la République (RPR), provides another example of the French political elite changing course. The end of the Cold War was the decisive moment constituting another "critical juncture" and crisis experience for French identity. When the Berlin Wall came down,

Germany united, and the post–Cold War European security order was constructed, France—*la grande nation*—remained largely on the sidelines. French diplomatic efforts failed miserably. As a result, large parts of the political elite realized the grand illusion of *grandeur* and *indépendence*. The way out was Europe (see Flynn 1995). The political debates surrounding the referendum on the Maastricht treaties in 1992 represented identity-related discourses about the new role of France in Europe and the world after the end of the Cold War. As in the 1950s, fear of German power dominated the debates. Supporters of Maastricht and EMU, particularly on the French right, argued in favor of a "binding" strategy, while opponents supported a return to traditional balance of power politics. This time, supporters of European integration prevailed in all major parties.

Competing visions about European order held by RPR leaders correspond to differing views of Frenchness and French identity. President Jacques Chirac expressed similar ideas about Europe and French distinctiveness as his counterparts among the French left: "The European Community is also a question of identity. If we want to preserve our values, our way of life, our standard of living, our capacity to count in the world, to defend our interests, to remain carriers of a humanistic message, we are certainly bound to build a united and solid bloc. . . . If France says yes [to the treaty of Maastricht], she can better reaffirm in what I believe: French exceptionalism" (Chirac 1992).

In sum, the majority of the French political elite gradually incorporated Europe in notions of French distinctiveness and started identifying the future of France as a nation-state within the European order. But a distinct minority sticks to the old Gaullist concepts of French "grandeur" and "indépendence." Of the three countries considered in this chapter, France is the only one in which a major reshaping and reshuffling of the elite discourse on nation-state identity took place in the past two decades. The failure of the Socialist program in the early 1980s and the turnaround of Mitterrand's economic policies served as a catalyst for an identity crisis among the French left, as a result of which the Parti Socialiste became a modern European social democratic party. This identity change was initially triggered by the desire to remain in power. Perceived political interests led to a thorough alteration of preferences about European order and, subsequently, to identity changes. But the reconstruction of French identity by the Socialists was profound and outlasted subsequent changes in instrumental interests. The stubbornness with which the French Socialists continuously supported austerity policies in order to fulfill the Maastricht convergence criteria supports the argument that collective identities stick, once they have become consensual. While French Socialist leaders attacked neoliberalism, European integration and the euro remained taboo.

The end of the Cold War served as a similar catalyst for identity changes, in particular on the French right. France's irrelevance during this earthquake in world politics directly challenged the French nation-state identity, its notion of *grandeur*, and the like. The meaning of these events, not perceived instrumental interests, called into question prevailing identity constructions.

The empirical cases confirm that nation-state identities are rather sticky and only slowly subject to change. In the case of the United Kingdom, Englishness is still defined in contrast to Europeanness, whereby "Europe" constitutes the "other" of nation-state identity. Almost twenty years of EC/EU membership do not seem to have made much difference. In contrast, the German case is one of thorough reconstruction of nation-state identity in the post–World War II period. Once German Europeanness became consensual among the political elites in the early 1960s, this nation-state identity remained stable ever since. German Europeanness preceded rather than followed progress in European integration. But European integration made a difference in the French case in terms of transforming Gaullist nation-state identity. Since the 1980s, the French elites, from the center-right to the center-left, have started identifying with European rather than strictly French distinctiveness.

How can these different developments be explained? As argued in the theoretical section of this chapter, new ideas about political order and identity constructions have to resonate with the given notions embedded in collective identities. Classic British notions of political order, for example, emphasize parliamentary democracy and external sovereignty, which is why only intergovernmentalist versions of European political order resonate with internal and external sovereignty. A European identity is not compatible with these deeply entrenched notions of sovereignty in the British political discourse. The "misfit" between a European nation-state identity and historically entrenched notions of Englishness was too great.

In the French case, state-centered republicanism—the duty to promote values such as brotherhood, freedom, equality, and human rights, in short, "civilization"—constitutes a continuous element in the French discourse about political order. Therefore, any European idea that resonates with French exceptionalism and that does not violate the state-centered concept of republicanism can legitimately be promoted in France, including a European rather than solely French exceptionalism.

The situation was similar in Germany. German concepts of a social market economy, democracy, and political federalism were central elements in the discourse of German exiled elites during the war and among the entire political class after World War II. Ideas about European political order that resonated with these concepts were, therefore, considered legitimate in the German political debate. In addition, militarism and Nazism had thoroughly discredited a nationalist notion of Germany. Europe provided an alternative identity construction and, thus, a way out.

In short, the "resonance hypothesis" seems to account for the variation between Great Britain, on the one hand, and France as well as Germany, on the other. European identity constructions were incompatible with Englishness, while French and German elites could easily embrace these notions and incorporate them in their political discourse. But this argument cannot explain why very different identity constructions carried the day in the two latter countries toward the end of the 1950s and why it took France thirty years more than Germany to integrate Europe in its nation-state identity and its exceptionalism. Several different identity constructions were considered legitimate and appropriate in the German and French political discourses of the 1950s. Each of them originated in transnational arenas during the interwar period and were promoted among exile and resistance groups during World War II. But the "resonance hypothesis" does not explain why Gaullist nationalism carried the day in France in the late 1950s, while a modern Western concept of Europeanness prevailed in the German debates.

Perceived crisis situations or "critical junctures," together with perceived instrumental interests, account for the variation. In the Federal Republic of Germany, the SPD reached its critical juncture in the mid- to late 1950s, when members of the party leadership realized that Kurt Schumacher's vision of Europe as a third force was no longer a viable option given the realities of the European Coal and Steel Community, the Treaty of Rome, and two severe federal election defeats in a row. At the same time, the modern Western concept of European identity resonated well with the domestic program of the party reformers who supported liberal democracy, market economy, and the welfare state while giving up more far-reaching socialist visions. The desire to gain political power facilitated the ideological change of the Social Democrats' party program and their thorough reconstruction of German nation-state identity.

In the French case, the war in Algeria and the ensuing crisis of the Fourth Republic ultimately brought President Charles de Gaulle into power. His notions of French *grandeur* and *mission civilisatrice* complemented and legitimized the institutions of the Fifth Republic by supplying the public with a consistent and comprehensive identity construction that resonated well with French traditions of republicanism and the état-nation.

Thus, the resonance argument explains in both cases which identity constructions and visions about European order became salient in the political discourse and were considered legitimate and appropriate. Perceived crises in conjunction with instrumental interests can account for the fact that different identity constructions carried the day in the two countries and became consensual.

But what explains the "stickiness" of the German European nation-state identity since the late 1950s? We can see socialization effects at work here. Over time, the political elites thoroughly internalized the new German nation-state identity and acted accordingly. German Europeanness survived both the turn toward *Ostpolitik* in the late 1960s and, more significant, the end of the Cold War and German unification. There was no need to challenge or reconstruct German Europeanness, since progress in European integration constantly confirmed it. Thus, Europeanization and the gradual emergence of a European polity did not cause a change in German nation-state identity but reinforced and confirmed it. Over time, then, German political elites reconfigured their perceived instrumental interests in line with their European identity. German elite enthusiasm for the single currency confirms the point for the 1990s (Risse et al. 1999).

The French case followed a different path. It was only a question of time when the French-Gaullist nation-state identity would become incompatible with the Europeanization process and the overall French support for it. While German Europeanness and European integration went hand in hand, the gap between a French nationalist nation-state identity and the reality of European integration widened over time. When President Mitterrand's economic policies bumped up against the European Monetary System (EMS) in 1982–83, he was forced to choose between Europe and his French Socialist goals. Mitterrand readily opted for Europe to remain in power but then set in motion a process that the German Social Democrats had experienced twenty-five years earlier: the parallel social democratization and adjustment to Europe in the French Socialists' nation-state identity. By the end of the decade, Frenchness and Europeanness had been reconciled among the French center-left. The French Gaullists underwent a similar process after the end of the Cold War, when they gradually realized that French exceptionalism and its *mission civilisatrice* could only be preserved within a European identity construction. Thus, French Europeanness became consensual among a majority of the political elites from the center-right to the center-left during the early 1990s. Perceived instrumental interests—the desire to remain in power for Mitterrand and the attempt to succeed him for the Gaullists—largely explain these changes in collective nation-state identities. Socialization effects again account for their stickiness during the 1990s, in particular with regard to French support for the Euro (see Risse et al. 1999).

In conclusion, the different evolutions of nation-state identities and the varying degrees to which Europe entered collective identity constructions can be well accounted for by a combination of three explanatory factors. The "resonance" hypothesis taken from sociological institutionalism and constructivist reasoning explains which identity constructions have a chance to be considered as legitimate and appropriate in a given political discourse. Perceived instrumental interests then select the successful ones among the available identity constructions. Once selected, socialization effects explain their stickiness through gradual internalization processes.

Thus, more than forty years of European integration had different effects on the collective nation-state identities in the three countries. Supranationalism remains largely incompatible with deeply entrenched notions of Englishness and concepts of British sovereignty. In contrast, the emergence of a European polity reinforced and strengthened the German postwar Europeanness. Finally, Europeanization gradually contributed to changing the French nation-state identity. Frenchness and Europeanness are no longer incompatible.

CHAPTER TWELVE

Transforming Europe: Conclusions

Maria Green Cowles and Thomas Risse

This book investigates how the process of European integration and Europeanization in general affect the domestic structures of the member states in the European Union (EU). We define Europeanization as the emergence and development at the European level of distinct structures of governance, that is, of political, legal, and social institutions associated with political problem solving that formalize interactions among the actors, and of policy networks specializing in the creation of authoritative rules.

We asked the contributors to this volume to embrace a three-step approach to their material. First, we identify the Europeanization process relevant to their empirical domain. Second, we examine the "goodness of fit" between these EU rules, regulations, and practices, on the one hand, and national institutional settings, rules, and practices, on the other. This degree of fit constitutes "adaptational pressures." When there is a fit or match between Europeanization and domestic structures, little if any adaptational change is necessary. European rules and regulations can simply be incorporated into the given domestic institutional arrangements. But when there is a misfit between the two structures, change will be necessary.

Third, we analyze the domestic institutional factors and actors' strategies facilitating or impeding structural change. We want to understand the conditions under which domestic institutional adaptation in response to Europeanization pressures occurs. Whether or not a country adjusts its institutional structures to Europe depends on the presence or absence of these mediating factors.

We are grateful to Jim Caporaso, Peter Katzenstein, several anonymous reviewers, and to the contributors of the empirical chapters for their insightful comments on earlier versions of these conclusions.

This chapter summarizes the empirical findings of this book in light of the conceptual framework (see the introduction) and draws out some of the broader findings and implications of this study. We begin by reexamining Europeanization as a force for domestic change. We then discuss the goodness of fit highlighted in the case studies as well as the domestic institutional factors and actors' strategies that mediate change in the member states. We explore the degree of convergence or divergence across policy and system-wide structures in the countries examined. We also highlight the effects of Europeanization on loyalty and collective identities. Finally, we examine whether Europeanization actually matters in changing domestic institutional structures—and in transforming the nation-state.

Europeanization

Processes of Europeanization

The ten case studies in this book reveal that Europeanization can be found in a number of sources. Sometimes the pressures for domestic structural change do not come from a single European rule or policy but from a combination of various Europeanization processes.

The emergence of a *formal EU legal structure* is one example of Europeanization. As Conant notes in chapter 6, the Article 177 preliminary ruling enables national judiciaries to participate in the European legal system, thus adding another layer to their own national legal institutions. Most of our empirical contributions (chapters 2, 3, 4, 5, 7, and 10) understand Europeanization as the *development of EU policies* in particular, issue-areas embodying new rules, norms, regulations, and procedures. As the authors of these chapters demonstrate, the introduction of new policies prompted national governments to respond to these new requirements. Where national gender, transport, environmental, telecommunications, and monetary policies were not in alignment with the EU policies, pressures were thus placed on the governments to adapt to the new EU policies. In the case of citizenship, Checkel demonstrates the influence of Europeanization not on national policy per se, but on the constitutive norms of citizenship.

The development of European policies in specific issue-areas implies the *transfer of decision making or policy competences to the European level*, another important feature of Europeanization that places considerable pressure on domestic institutional structures. As Börzel (chapter 8) points out, the shifting of regional competences to the European level is significant not only due to the resulting EU policies (though they may, in fact, create pressures for domestic change as well), but also due to the resulting change in domestic opportunities for the actors involved (see also, chapter 6, for a similar argument). Europeanization originally strengthened the national executives and disempowered the regions, which then had to regain their competences. Cowles (chapter 9) reveals a similar story in examining the role of national industry associations in the Transatlantic Business

Dialogue (TABD). When multinational firms decided to work directly with European Commission officials who have primary competence in external trade matters, national industry associations were faced with changing political opportunities. The German Bundesverband der Deutschen Industrie (BDI) found itself losing its political initiative and prestige in negotiations with national officials. On the other hand, the Mouvement des Entreprenses de France (MEDEF), which was previously denied a significant role in external trade matters by the French state, could enhance its political standing domestically.

Europeanization also consists of *constructing systems of meanings and collective understandings*, including social identities. European citizens, and the political actors among them, need to make sense of the European integration process. While this aspect implicitly informs many of the contributions to this volume, Risse (chapter 11) directly explores the impact of Europeanization on collective nation-state identities (see also chapter 10, on citizenship identities).

Europeanization, Positive and Negative Integration, and Globalization

Most chapters in this book look at Europeanization in terms of positive integration: the development of European policies, the enactment of legal procedures, the transfer of competences, and the creation of norms and identities. Yet European integration also encompasses negative integration, such as trade liberalization and the freeing up of market forces. (On the distinction between positive and negative integration, see Scharpf 1996.) In chapters 3 and 4, Héritier and Schneider deal explicitly with negative integration, while case studies by Sbragia (chapter 5), Conant (chapter 6), Börzel (chapter 8), and Cowles (chapter 9), contain more implicit instances of negative integration. The distinction between positive and negative integration raises two questions.

First, can we observe different patterns of how Europeanization impacts domestic institutional change, depending on the type of integration? One could argue, for example, that adaptational changes in response to market liberalization are more likely to occur than adjustments to instances of positive integration, because negative integration usually mobilizes domestic constituencies, such as multinational corporations and pro-liberalization parties and elites.

Our findings disconfirm this expectation in terms of both process and outcome. Our three-step framework applies to instances of both negative and positive integration. While the facilitating institutions and actors' strategies vary across cases, this variation is unrelated to the type of integration. In the case of Italy, Schneider (chapter 4) reports that Europeanization as negative integration successfully liberalized the Italian telecommunications market. In the transport sector, however, another case of negative integration, the Italian government was unable to overcome a multitude of veto players until very recently (chapter 3). Finally, the most profound changes in the Italian political and administrative structure in recent years—the reform of public finances that included a major institutional overhaul—occurred in response to pressures largely emanating from positive integration, the desire to be part of "Euro-land" (chapter 5).

The second question concerns alternative explanations. Do Europeanization pressures primarily result from larger global developments? Liberal intergovernmentalist theory, after all, emphasizes that domestic preferences are the result of exogenous changes in the international economic, ideological, and geopolitical realm—and are not formed in response to Europeanization per se (Moravcsik 1998).

Schneider's case study (chapter 4) is a clear example of how global market forces influenced the EU telecommunications policy and, in turn, domestic change in telecommunications services in the member states. In this case, globalization is the dominant explanation for what triggered the privatization of telecommunication services in France, Germany, and Italy. Cowles's study (chapter 9) of the TABD and Héritier's analysis of transport (chapter 3) also can be attributed in part to these global forces. We must question, therefore, whether globalization is simply an alternative explanation for Europeanization.

Most chapters in this book suggest that Europeanization plays an important distinct role in addressing exogenous change. Globalization alone, for example, cannot explain why a country such as Italy would agree to liberalize its telecommunications systems when it did. As Schneider points out, institutional change without Brussels was unthinkable. Europeanization served to significantly reinforce change at the domestic level in Italy—and to amplify this change in both Germany and France.

Europeanization also allows member states and their firms to take advantage of global economic changes. One reason for the creation of the Transatlantic Business Dialogue was to develop transatlantic regulatory policies that would allow European companies to more effectively compete in the global economy (chapter 9). Another rationale for the TABD was to play a greater role in shaping the World Trade Organization (WTO) agenda.

Of course, Europeanization can also work to fend against these forces. The European Economic and Monetary Union (EMU), for example, was created in part to protect "Euro-land" against the fluctuations of global currency markets. The Common Agricultural Policy (CAP) is probably the most prominent example of this protective shield. While CAP policies have been under attack in the General Agreement on Tariffs and Trade (GATT) for more than two decades, member states were able to deflect any significant changes by presenting a united front in early GATT negotiations (Moyer and Josling 1990; Ingersent, Rayner, and Hine 1998). When the Uruguay Round did produce a significant CAP reform, the resulting MacSharry plan was due more to changes in member states' preferences as a result of CAP membership—differences between net importers and net exporters of food—than to any "external" force (Paarlberg 1997; Patterson 1997; for an opposing view, see Coleman and Tangermann 1999). The recent CAP reform, for example, did not address issues of market access and export subsidies, which were central to the GATT negotiations (Meunier 2000).

Whether Europeanization reinforces, takes advantage of, or fends against these globalization forces, the independent effects of Europeanization can be shown through careful process-tracing and comparisons. Héritier, for example, clearly distinguishes between global forces (United Kingdom and the Netherlands) and Europeanization (Germany and Italy) in her case studies of railways and road haulage. Schneider is also careful to highlight these differences in telecommunications reform in Germany, France, and Italy.

Global market forces are not the only exogenous factors that might influence domestic institutional change. As evidenced by Checkel (chapter 10), norms and ideas can also develop outside the European Union. Transnational human rights groups and historical events like the end of the Cold War influence the discourse on citizenship and identity within the European Union. They may even "trigger" domestic responses. However, the creation of norms at the European level serves as important focal points around which these discourses and identities are fashioned. Membership in the EU matters (Sandholtz 1996).

Of course, we must also distinguish between Europeanization pressures and those emanating from the member states themselves. As Knill and Lenschow demonstrate in chapter 7, the neoliberal turn in Britain and the subsequent changes in political-administrative structures only reflected Europeanization pressures to some extent, but were largely driven by domestic politics (see also, chapter 4). In Sbragia's case study (chapter 5), changes in domestic political coalitions account in part for Italy's ability to meet the EMU convergence criteria. In chapter 9, Cowles notes changes in domestic business-government relations in Germany over the past decade that provide insights into why large German firms have emerged as more important societal actors in domestic matters. Recent elections and the subsequent change in government partly account for Germany's embrace of dual citizenship in Checkel's case study (chapter 10).

While globalization and domestic processes exert independent effects on domestic structural change, the empirical findings of this book demonstrate that Europeanization matters as a reference point through which these processes can be channeled—and domestic change addressed. Our contributors show through careful process-tracing and comparisons that processes at the European level have a distinct impact on both the scope and the timing of domestic transformation.

Adaptational Pressures and "Goodness of Fit"

To understand the impact of Europeanization, we examine the goodness of fit between the EU institutions and domestic institutions. The empirical case studies confirm our expectation that the adaptational pressures vary widely, since Europeanization encounters very different domestic institutional structures.

Our authors use several indicators to establish the degree of fit between Europeanization and domestic institutions. Several chapters identify a *policy misfit* between EU policies and regulations and domestic practices. Caporaso and Jupille (chapter 2) used pay disparities as indicators for the match between EU equal pay rules and domestic policies in France (fit) and the United Kingdom (misfit). Héritier and Schneider (chapters 3 and 4) chose the policy misfit in the transport and the telecommunications sectors, respectively, to establish the initial pressures for adaptation. In transport, the United Kingdom and the Netherlands are cases of policy fit and agreement, whereas Germany and Italy are cases of mismatch. In telecommunications, Italy represents a strong misfit. Sbragia (chapter 5) also uses a policy mismatch—the EMU convergence criteria versus Italian public finances—as her main indicator for adaptational pressures. In each of these chapters, however, policy misfit exerts adaptational pressures on domestic institutional structures:

Europeanization → policy misfit → adaptational pressures on domestic structures

Yet, Knill and Lenschow (chapter 7) demonstrate that too narrow an emphasis on policy misfits does not explain the actual adaptational pressures and leads to mispredictions concerning the outcome. They argue that it is the degree of fit between the EU approach in the respective area, on the one hand, and core elements of national administrative traditions, on the other, which establishes the adaptational pressures emanating from Europeanization.

Conant (chapter 6) also examines the degree of fit between EU and core elements of national structures. She identifies the difference between national legal traditions and institutions, on the one hand, and the EU legal structure, on the other, as the primary source of adaptational pressure. The French centralization of political power in the executive branch in combination with limited constitutional reviews by the Constitutional Council contrasts with the dispersal of power in the EU's political structure. Germany, however, represents a case of institutional fit, given its horizontal and vertical dispersal of political power. The high number of Article 177 references to the European Court of Justice (ECJ) by German courts versus the low number of referrals by French courts confirm her point.

Similarly, Börzel and Cowles (chapters 8 and 9) focus on the misfits formed when established institutions at the domestic level are challenged by new European ones. Börzel demonstrates how the Spanish and German regions lose policymaking responsibilities to their national governments with the transfer of former regional competencies to the European level. She argues that this creates an "unequal distribution of say and pay," since the Spanish and German regions were still required to implement regulations emanating from the EU. Cowles examines how the traditional linkages between national industry associations, member states, and large firms are altered when major corporations form new relationships with the European Commission in the Transatlantic Business Dialogue.

Finally, for Checkel and Risse (chapters 10 and 11), the constitutive effects of Europeanization create adaptational pressures. The Council of Europe's citizenship norms directly contradicted the historical understandings of citizenship in Germany (jus sanguinis), thus creating a serious misfit. Concerning collective nation-state identities, the emergence of a European polity resonates to diverging degrees with given nation-state identities in Britain (misfit), Germany (fit), and France (partial misfit).

In sum, these chapters measure adaptational pressures directly as the degree of compatibility between European rules, policymaking styles, and the collective understandings accompanying them, on the one hand, and national institutions and their administrative styles, legal cultures, state-society relationships, and collective identities, on the other:

Europeanization → misfit with domestic structures → adaptational pressures on domestic structures

Table 12.1 summarizes these findings concerning the goodness of fit between Europeanization and domestic institutional structures according to the countries investigated. Can we draw any general conclusion from this picture? We disregard the cases of Spain and the Netherlands, since they are only treated in one empirical chapter each. Among the remaining cases in our sample, Italy is the only country where Europeanization exerted considerable adaptational pressures in each issue-area investigated. But these Italian policy areas all concerned market liberalization or deregulation to one degree or another. Since Italy has traditionally been one of the most protected European markets with a rather clientelist domestic structure, our finding is not too surprising.

Thus, we focus our analysis on the goodness of fit between Europeanization and the domestic structures of the "big three"—France, Germany, and the United Kingdom. Since our empirical chapters cover a wide variety of issue-areas, we can treat them as a representative sample of the Europeanization pressures exerted on the three countries. Two findings stand out:

1. Each of the big three faced considerable adaptational pressures in some areas, while in others, there was some institutional fit.
2. There is no easily identifiable pattern of fits or misfits.

The first result is significant insofar as it implies that Europeanization has led to the emergence of a new and distinct structure of governance, which is not structurally isomorphic to any of the individual EU member states, not even the big three. If France, Germany, and the UK face considerable adaptational pressures on their domestic ways of doing things, what about the smaller European countries? Our sample does not cover southern European or Scandinavian countries in a systematic way, but we can deduce from our findings that they should face even more serious pressures to adjust their domestic institutions. The Italian case points in this direction.

Furthermore, our findings challenge liberal intergovernmentalism as a general theory of European integration. If Europeanization mostly results from "grand bargains" among the three leading members and entails "lowest common denominator solutions" (Moravcsik 1998), we would not expect strong adaptational pressures when Europe hits home, at least not in Germany, France, and the United

Table 12.1 "Goodness of fit," by country

Country	Fit	Misfit
France	• Equal pay	• Equal treatment • Industry association • Legal structure • Nation-state identity • Telecommunications
Germany	• Environment (partly) • Legal structure • Nation-state identity	• Citizenship norm • Environment (partly) • Industry associations • Railways • Road haulage • Telecommunications • Territorial structure
United Kingdom	• Environment (partly) • Industry associations • Railways • Road haulage	• Environment (partly) • Equal pay • Equal treatment • Legal structure • Nation-state identity
Italy		• Public finances (EMU) • Railways • Road haulage • Telecommunications
Netherlands	• Railways • Road haulage	
Spain		• Territorial structure

Kingdom. Yet, our sample recorded serious cases of misfit for each of these countries and across a wide variety of issue-areas.

But several arguments derived from sociological institutionalism and pointing to structural isomorphism do not fare much better. The alleged European "top of the class," Germany, faces as much adaptational pressure across a variety of issue-areas as the European "laggard," Britain. Our findings challenge, in part, the arguments by Peter Katzenstein and Simon Bulmer (Katzenstein 1997a, b; Bulmer and Paterson 1987; Bulmer 1997) that the German institutional structure of cooperative federalism, "semi-sovereignty," and democratic corporatism fits well with the EU structure of dispersed power. Such structural isomorphism implies a rather low degree of adaptational pressures. This assertion holds true for some of our cases (legal structure, nation–state identity, and environment to some extent), but is definitely wrong in others (citizenship norms, territorial structure, industry associations, transport, telecommunications, and other environmental policies). In each of the latter cases, the degree of misfit between Europeanization and the German institutional structure is considerable. While some of our chapters (particularly chapters 3 and 8) show that particular features of German institutions and culture facilitated adaptational changes (see below), the initial misfit is quite striking.

As for the United Kingdom, two of the "fit" cases (road haulage and railways) concern market liberalization and deregulation, where Britain has been the front-runner in the EU for quite some time and, thus, did not face much adaptational pressure. Two mismatches (equal pay and equal treatment) concern social policy and gender; here, the United Kingdom has been among the European "laggards." The same holds true for British (mostly English) nation-state identity, which has not resonated well with ideas of Europe. But these explanations do not account for the only partial fit regarding environmental regulations and the "misfit" in legal structure (see chapters 6 and 7). While the British common-law tradition of citing cases as "precedents" serves as a functional equivalent to the Article 177 referrals in other countries, there are still strong differences between the British and European legal systems.

This points to our second overall finding that there is no easily discernible pattern of "fits" or "misfits" in the three large member states. How can we account for this? Two explanations are possible. First, one could argue that domestic institutions vary significantly depending on the policy area. Countries do not display the same institutional arrangement in every policy area. Yet, our empirical chapters by and large find similar institutional structures across policy areas and, thus, confirm what has been written about the institutions and embedded domestic structures of the EU member states. German cooperative federalism, consensual decision-making culture, and strong societal peak associations show up in a number of case studies. The same holds true for France's centralized state institutions, weak peak associations, statist ideology, and strong nationalist collective identity, which also are mentioned in several chapters.

Second, the mixture of fits and misfits found in the empirical chapters could result from the Europeanization process itself. Indeed, our finding of "no discernable pattern" when it comes to adaptational pressures appears to follow from the enormous variation in Europeanization processes across and even within single issue-areas. As Knill and Lenschow demonstrate in chapter 7, there is no single "European" regulatory style concerning various environmental directives, but several. Our case studies therefore, confirm across policy areas what Héritier et al. have called a "regulatory patchwork" of EU rules and regulations (Héritier, Knill, and Mingers 1996; Héritier 1996). The particular European policymaking processes include package deals, issue linkages, and "decision-making by subterfuge" (Héritier 1997, 1999). They, in turn, lead to a complex variety of institutional features and regulatory styles depending on which member state can "upload"—or which part of the European Commission can push—its preferences on the European level. It is not surprising that individual member states face very different degrees of adaptational pressures when they have to "download" these EU policies, rules, and regulations into their domestic institutional structures. In sum, the variation among Europeanization patterns appears to explain the variation in adaptational pressures faced by individual member states across and even within specific issue-areas (cf. also Börzel in press).

But how do countries respond to these pressures? How can we explain successful adaptation to Europeanization pressures, and what accounts for failure or continuous resistance to adjust? What is the impact of mediating institutions or actor strategies? In answering these questions, we will exclusively focus on the cases of misfit as specified in Table 12.1.

Adaptational Results and the Impact of Mediating Factors

A closer look at cases of considerable adaptational pressures reveals mixed results. Adaptational pressures emanating from Europeanization do not necessarily lead to domestic institutional change. Some countries experienced sustained resistance to change over considerable periods of time. France did not adjust to the Equal Treatment Directive for quite a long time (chapter 2). Some member states did not change at all, which led to compliance problems with EU rules and regulations. Germany needed more than ten years to fully comply with the EU Drinking Water Directive and still resists change concerning other environmental regulations (see chapter 7). The disposition toward adaptational change varies even within countries. Italy faced adaptational pressures in all four issue-areas investigated here (chapters 3–5). Institutional transformation occurred in two of these areas: telecommunications and public finance. Concerning the latter, the change was particularly dramatic, since the Prodi coalition succeeded where previous Italian governments had failed. In general, no single EU member state investigated in this volume is more likely than others to change its institutional structure in response to Europeanization pressures. The possible exeption is Germany. As we argue below, the German institutional structure and political culture exhibits many factors that we identify as facilitating adaptational change.[1]

In the introduction to this book, we identified five mediating factors inhibiting or facilitating domestic reform in response to adaptational pressures. Table 12.2 documents our empirical findings with regard to these factors.

Multiple Veto Points

The existence of multiple veto points in a country's institutional structure (Tsebelis 1995), which allows actors to resist change effectively, turns out to be one of the most important causes for a lack of institutional adaptation. Three of the six cases of "resistance" to Europeanization pressures—Italian road haulage and railways and German environmental policies—explain the failure to adapt on the basis of this factor (cf. chapters 3 and 7). Both Italy and Germany feature domestic political institutions allowing a multitude of societal and political actors to block reform.

---

1. Note that this argument differs substantially from the Katzenstein and Bulmer claims concerning structural isomorphism between the German domestic structure and features at the European level. Germany faces as much adaptational pressures as the other member states. The capacity for institutional change does not result from structural isomorphism but from the presence of facilitating factors.

Table 12.2   Cases of "misfit," adaptational results, and mediating factors

Country	Issue area of "misfit"	Adaptational result	Mediating factors
France	Equal treatment	Resistance	Centralized structure, statist system
	Industry associations	Change	Empowerment of domestic interests vis-à-vis the state
	Legal structure	Resistance	Centralized structure, statist system
	Nation-state identity	Change	Empowerment of pro-European interests and elite learning
	Telecommunications	Change	Empowerment of pro-liberalization interests (and global forces)
Germany	Citizenship norm	Slow change	Empowerment of "liberal interests" and elite learning
	Environment (partly)	Resistance	Multiple veto points
	Industry associations	Slow change	Elite learning
	Railways	Change	Cooperative culture
	Road haulage	Change	Empowerment of pro-liberalization interests and cooperative culture
	Telecommunications	Change	Empowerment of pro-liberalization interests (and global forces)
	Territorial structure	Change	Cooperative culture
Great Britain	Legal structure	Partial change	Centralized structure
	Equal pay and equal treatment	Partial change	Facilitating institutions and empowerment of domestic interests
	Environment (partly)	Initial resistance, then change	(Change in government)
	Nation-state identity	Resistance	Europe as "the other"
Italy	Public finances (EMU)	Change	Empowerment of the government and elite learning
	Railways	Resistance	Multiple veto points
	Road haulage	Resistance	Multiple veto points
	Telecommunications	Change	Empowerment of the government (some elite learning)
Spain	Territorial structure	Initial failure, then partial change	Elite learning

While the reasons for this differ (decentralization in Germany, clientelism in Italy), the outcome is similar: it is difficult to build "winning coalitions" in favor of reform in either country. Multiple veto points can be overcome, however, as indicated by the Italian telecommunications and public finance cases, and the German transport cases. In these cases, however, other mediating factors are necessary to contend with the multiple veto points.

Mediating Formal Institutions

Both France and the United Kingdom are centrist systems in which power is focused on the state. Several of our case studies suggest that resistance to

Europeanization pressures is found not in "multiple veto points" but in the centralized structure of the state itself. Yet the differences in state structure between France and the United Kingdom also explain why different mediating factors facilitate adaptational change. France, for example, is a statist system in which the government largely determines state-society relationships and often resists societal pressures. As Conant notes, it is precisely the lack of power dispersal in and formal access to the French domestic structure that prevents actors from exploiting the opportunities provided by the European legal system.

The United Kingdom, by contrast, is a pluralist system that allows societal interests to be regularly represented by formal or informal means. Thus, the presence of facilitating formal institutions provides actors with resources to induce change. This explains the successful adaptation in the British equal pay and equal treatment cases (see chapter 2) and, by extension, the British legal structure (see chapter 6). The British Equal Opportunities Commission (EOC), for example, provided women's organizations with the means to use EU equal pay directives in furthering gender equality. As Caporaso and Jupille point out, the absence of such facilitating institutions in the French case largely accounts for the resistance to implement the EU equal treatment policies.

Not every issue area has or can benefit from facilitating institutions. It is likely that the future of nation-state identity in the United Kingdom, for example, will have little to do with facilitating institutions or formal access to political processes. The emphasis of identity on the state means that people will continue to view Europe as "the other."

Political and Organizational Cultures

The third structural factor that affects the ability of actors to induce institutional changes in response to Europeanization concerns informal collective understandings of appropriate behavior embedded in national political and organizational cultures. The Spanish regions and the German Länder rarely used the opportunities provided by Europeanization to circumvent their national governments (chapter 8). Circumventing the nation-state was simply not considered appropriate behavior. There was little attempt by British political or economic elites to adjust the English collective nation-state identity to the reality of the EU, even though this could have legitimized their actual policies (chapter 11). In contrast, the enthusiastic support for Europe enabled Italian elites to meet the Maastricht convergence criteria for the single currency (chapter 5).

Collective understandings about appropriate behavior embedded in a country's political culture not only define the realm of interests that actors can legitimately pursue, they also provide actors with the means and strategies to act. Our authors identify a consensus-oriented and cooperative political culture as the most important factor overcoming multiple veto points. In the cases of transport, the German tradition of cooperative decision making made it possible to overcome the veto points through "integrated political leadership," while the Italian confrontational culture further reinforced them. The German cooperative culture also explains why the Länder managed to compensate for the loss of competences unto the European level by gaining co-decision powers with the federal government concerning European affairs (chapter 8). In contrast and in accordance with their own understanding of appropriate behavior vis-à-vis Madrid, the Spanish regions initially embarked on a confrontational course against their national government. Only when this strategy failed, did they emulate the German Länder and tried to use cooperative federalism.

These findings confirm Peter Katzenstein's argument that the "taming of German power" (Katzenstein 1997a, b) through Europeanization is reinforced by the German consensual culture. While there is little indication for institutional isomorphism between German and European institutions across the board, Germany more easily adjusts to Europe because of its political culture and facilitating institutions.

Differential Empowerment of Actors

As argued in the introduction, institutions do not change institutions, actors do. Europeanization not only leads to adaptational pressures, it also empowers domestic interests in a differential way. European policies, rules, and institutionalized relationships have distributional consequences and, thus, are likely to affect the preferences of domestic actors. This is probably the most important agency-centered factor conducive to structural adaptation. In the cases of road haulage and telecommunications (chapters 3 and 4), Europeanization strengthened those forces and interest groups in France, Germany, and Italy that favored liberalization and deregulation. The EU's Equal Pay and Equal Treatment Directives provided an opportunity for women's organizations in Britain to appeal to local, national, and European courts (chapter 2). NGOs and churches in Germany used the Council of Europe's citizenship norm to advocate citizenship rights to foreigners (chapter 10). French political elites pushed a European French identity construction to legitimize a fundamental change in economic policies during the early 1980s (chapter 11). Core executives in the Italian government used the enthusiastic support for "Europe" and European integration among the elites and public opinion against the domestic opposition to the reform of public finances (chapter 5). The French industry association promoted a novel European business-government relationship in order to find its "voice" to address the French state in trade matters (chapter 9).

Indeed, Europeanization has impacted different domestic interests since the early years of the European Community. CAP, for example, has historically strengthened farmers' groups in relation to their member governments. While the "agricultural power" of farmers is related to a number of factors (Keeler 1996), the relationship forged between the European Commission and farm organizations has given farmers an additional influence on agriculture policy that they willingly use in discussions with their national governments. For example, French farmer groups—

who recognized that future price increases would be agreed to in Brussels, not Paris—were upset when the government withdrew from the Council of Ministers in 1965 (the infamous empty chair crisis) over differences on agricultural pricing (Neville-Rolfe 1984, 117). The farmers' reaction prompted the French government to avoid any serious confrontation over the CAP ever since (143).

Thus, domestic actors whose interests are positively affected by Europeanization, and who command the capacity and the resources to act within a domestic context, tend to use the adaptational pressures in their favor to bring about institutional change. In the absence of such interests, change is unlikely to occur, as the cases of transport in Italy and of some environmental directives in Germany demonstrate (see chapters 3 and 7).

But sometimes, the dynamics of change are also set in motion because actors' interests are negatively affected by Europeanization. The Spanish regions and the German Länder lost competences to the central government and the European level, as a result of which they mobilized in favor of structural adjustment (chapter 8). Similarly, the German industry association, whose privileged position vis-à-vis the government was weakened in international trade matters, opted to pursue a different strategy of interest representation (chapter 9).

Learning

Several chapters point to elite learning as a final mediating factor explaining structural change. The Spanish Comunidades Autonómas apparently learned from the failure of their initial strategy of confrontation and then adopted the German model (chapter 8). Checkel and Risse argue in chapters 10 and 11 that elite learning in France and Germany played a role in changing the interests of German political elites with regard to citizenship norms. Learning also explains the incremental change by which the German industry association adjusted to the fact that individual firms are directly involved in the Transatlantic Business Dialogue on the European level (chapter 9).

But we should not overemphasize the degree of elite learning. "Elite learning" meant in two cases (chapters 8 and 9) that actors changed their strategies to pursue their goals as a result of previous failures ("simple or single-loop learning"; see Argyris and Schön 1978). We have only a few examples of "complex learning" whereby elites not only adjusted their strategies but also changed their interests and identities (see chapters 10 and 11). In these cases of German citizenship norms and of French nation-state identity, however, the transformations are profound and reach core features of the polity.

In sum, the five mediating factors largely explain the variation in the degree to which domestic structural change occurred in response to adaptational pressures from Europeanization. Taken together, they combine insights from rationalist and from sociological institutionalism. Emphasizing multiple veto points, the existence of facilitating institutions, and the differential empowerment of domestic actors, is largely compatible with a "logic of consequentialism" whereby actors hold fixed interests and preferences. Pointing to political and organizational culture as well as to complex elite learning conforms to the "logic of appropriateness" identified by sociological institutionalism (on the two logics, see March and Olsen, 1998). We need both logics in order to understand the conditions under which structural change in response to Europeanization pressures occurs. Moreover, the five factors also combine structural features and the properties of actors (see the introduction). Thus, our approach also fits the framework of "actor-centered institutionalism" proposed by Mayntz and Scharpf (1995; see also Scharpf 1997).

Our empirical findings do not point to a particular order of significance among these five factors. They do suggest, however, that different factors may be more or less appropriate depending on the core structures of the states. For example, a cooperative and consensus-oriented political culture can overcome the negative effects of multiple veto points in the case of Germany (Héritier, chapter 3, and Börzel, chapter 8) while the empowerment of domestic core government elites explain this phenomenon in Italy (Schneider, chapter 4, and Sbragia, chapter 5). Similarly, centralized structures can be addressed by mediating formal institutions in the case of the United Kingdom (chapter 2), and the empowerment of domestic interests in statist France (chapter 4; chapter 9; and chapter 11).

Convergence and Divergence

A primary goal of this book is to evaluate the overall pattern of domestic institutional responses to Europeanization. We are interested in knowing the outcome of that change—whether or not there is a convergence or continued divergence of domestic institutions across countries and issue areas, both in terms of policy structures or "system-wide" domestic structures.

The results of the case studies are quite clear. First, domestic institutional change resulted in some form of structural convergence across countries in most of our cases. Indeed, as indicated in Table 12.3, we find evidence of at least partial convergence in eight of the ten policy areas investigated in this book.

Table 12.3 Convergence and divergence

Convergence	Mixed	Divergence
Telecommunications	Environment	Equal pay/treatment
	Industry associations	Legal structure
	Nation-state identity	
	Railways	
	Road haulage	
	Territorial structure (slow convergence)	

Note: The citizenship case by Jeffrey Checkel is omitted here because it only focuses on one country.

Second, however, most of our empirical cases fall in the "mixed" category, whereby some countries converged toward similar policy or system-wide structures, while others retained their specific institutional arrangements, state society relations, or cultural understandings. Convergence does not mean the homogenization of domestic structures. There is no evidence that domestic institutional change means the complete rejection of national administrative styles, legal cultures, societal relationships, and/or collective identities. As Risse points out, France did not shed its national identity per se when adopting a European one. The meanings of "Europe" differ in the German and French political discourses, even though the elites in both countries have incorporated Europeanness into their collective nation-state identities. The traditional tensions between the Spanish regions and central government did not disappear as a result of a more cooperative arrangement in territorial matters (see chapter 8). Moreover, there is no general convergence toward cooperative federalism in Europe, just a movement toward such structures among federal states such as Germany and Spain. As to "Euroland," the policy convergence among the eleven EMU members with regard to inflation and budget restraints has not led to similar institutional arrangements in the economic and fiscal policy area. Rather, structural convergence is confined to the independence of central banks. Even in telecommunications—the only case of strong convergence in policy structures across a wide variety of countries— Schneider (chapter 4) reveals that each country adopted a slightly different institutional setup, thus reflecting variation in administration traditions.

Third, there are some indications that convergence is largely confined to policy—rather than to system-wide domestic structures. The two cases of continuing strong divergence concern century-old and deeply embedded legal structures (chapters 2 and 6). Regarding the environmental sector, Knill and Lenschow (chapter 7) do not observe an increasing similarity of the broader regulatory frameworks in the United Kingdom and Germany. Börzel's finding of slow convergence concerns two countries with federal traditions (chapter 8). Moreover, Cowles notes, in chapter 9, that national industry associations still retain distinctly national business-government relations in other areas such as corporate or industry benefits negotiations.

Our findings disconfirm those schools of thought discussed in the introduction of this book that expect strong structural convergence. According to the economic convergence school, we would expect increasing similarities in institutional arrangements in areas exposed to global market forces. While the case of telecommunications confirms the argument, the EMU case does not. The difference between positive and negative integration does not explain the variation in the degree of convergence, either.

But sociological institutionalism does not fare much better. According to DiMaggio and Powell (1991), convergence can be expected when there is frequent interaction among institutions, for example, among European and domestic structures. Yet, in the environment, railways, road haulage, and nation-state identity cases, we find evidence of divergence as well as convergence.

Even our own qualifications to the "isomorphism hypothesis" merit closer review. We argued in the Introduction that structural convergence was unlikely where European institutions meet domestic institutions that are historically and culturally well entrenched. Yet, as numerous case studies of well-entrenched institutions suggest—public finance, industry associations, railways, road haulage, nation-state identity, and territorial structure, among others—some structural convergence did take place, albeit slowly and often with considerable difficulty.

We also argued that Europeanization often leaves considerable discretion to countries as to how they should adapt their institutional arrangements. Thus, the extent of institutional discretion would explain the variation in the degree of convergence. This argument holds true for telecommunications, the independence of central banks in "Euro-land," and for some of the environmental directives investigated in this book. But it fails to account for the partial convergence in the case of industry associations, territorial structures, and transport, let alone nation-state identity. In each of these cases, Europeanization does not prescribe specific forms of institutional adaptation. Yet, we find partial convergence.

So, how do we account for this general finding? While our case studies do not allow us to draw any firm conclusion, they offer a point of departure for further inquiry. One important factor that might explain convergence is institutional emulation resulting from both imitation of "best practice" and elite learning.[2] This is evident in the chapters on transport, territorial structure, industry associations, and nation-state identity. Héritier (chapter 3) suggests that regulatory competition accounts for the partial convergence in both road haulage and railways. Similarly, Börzel (chapter 8) demonstrates that the Spanish regions tried to emulate German cooperative federalism after their confrontational strategy had failed. Both arguments are compatible with a logic of efficiency whereby actors imitate those practices that have been proven successful in reaching their goals. But they also point to what DiMaggio and Powell (1991) call mimetic processes, whereby institutions emulate others to reduce uncertainty and complexity. Here, the micromechanism is learning. For example, Cowles (chapter 9) points out that after initial reluctance, the German industry association opted to accept a model of interest mediation in trade matters similar to that of the British. Risse (chapter 11) argues that the French Socialists looked to Germany in an effort to reconstruct their nation-state identity. In other words, actors evaluate existing models and determine which one is most successful. They then adopt the model irrespective of its national origin.

The same factor might also explain our cases of divergence. There is little evidence of learning and institutional emulation taking place in the court systems. In her chapter on the national courts (chapter 6), Conant debunks transactionalist accounts of court behavior—that strong societal demand for European law enforcement as such transforms domestic legal structures (Stone Sweet and Brunell 1998; Stone Sweet and Sandholtz 1998; Golub 1996a). She argues

2. We thank Mitchell Smith for initially raising this argument.

that strong societal demand is diluted by institutional constraints that vary greatly from country to country. This also applies to Caporaso and Jupille's discussion (chapter 2) of the equal treatment cases in the United Kingdom and France. In the United Kingdom, the existence of public agencies and related complementary institutions empower societal actors to take action in the court. In France, however, these agencies and institutions simply do not exist in the statist French system. Nor is there any indication that Article 177 referrals would lead to the adoption of such agencies and institutions in the French legal system. Thus, as Conant reminds us, "independence and resistance" remain key characteristics of domestic legal structures.

Of course, a word of caution is in order. Europeanization itself is still a relatively recent phenomenon and continues to evolve. Thus, we cannot exclude the possibility that it will lead to further and stronger structural convergence than that found in this book, maybe even in the legal area.

Loyalty and Collective Identity

So far, we have largely treated the domestic impact of Europeanization in terms of institutional adaptation of formal organizational arrangements. But Europeanization also entails systems of meanings and collective understandings. Although our empirical chapters (except for chapters 10 and 11) did not deal with this question systematically, they nevertheless yield some insights on the effects of Europeanization on political cultures and collective identities.

The first finding is rather sobering. Early integration theories, in particular neofunctionalism (Haas 1958), assumed that Europeanization leads to a gradual shift in elite loyalties from the national to the European levels. This would be particularly relevant for those domestic elites who benefit from European integration. But we only have limited evidence for such a shift in loyalties. In the cases of transport and telecommunications (chapters 3 and 4), Europeanization empowered proliberalization interests in the respective countries. But whether the new private service providers hold more pro-European attitudes, let alone identities, is an altogether different question. British women who clearly benefit from the EU's equal pay regulations and ECJ rulings (chapter 2), are in fact more Euro-skeptical than British men (Liebert 1998). Only in the case of the French industry association was a strong shift of loyalty from the French government to European institutions observable, as Cowles argues in chapter 9.

But our empirical findings reveal that Europeanization did not leave collective identities completely unaffected either. Just the neofunctionalist logic of "shifting loyalties" appears to be incorrect. Actors hold multiple social identities, and these loyalties appear to be context dependent. As a result, individuals may hold strong nation-state identities and, at the same time, identify with Europe. Even more significant, the distinction between one's nation-state identity and one's European identity might blur over time. As Risse argues (chapter 12), this was the case in both Germany and France. Since the German nation-state identity became problematic after Hitler and World War II and a purely nationalist identity was no longer available, political elites gradually integrated Europe into their collective identities during the 1950s. In the French case, European integration had a more direct effect on identity changes on the elite level. When Mitterrand's nationalist economic policies bumped against European integration during the early 1980s, the French elites, beginning with the Socialists, started revamping their political outlook, including their nation-state identities. Frenchness and Europeanness increasingly blurred.

Such a process of complementary loyalties toward both the nation-state and toward Europe is also observable among national judges in various countries, as Conant (chapter 6) implies. National judges assume both national and European roles simply by participating in both legal systems, sometimes simultaneously. When European law is incorporated in the British common-law tradition, the distinction between national and supranational law starts blurring. A similar blurring of identities might be underway among national industry associations as they attempt to restate or regain their role in international trade matters by operating in Brussels and on the national level (cf. chapter 9). Thus, loyalties toward one's nation-state (or region, for that matter) and European identity need not contradict each other but might become rather supplementary.

There is an even more subtle and more implicit way by which collective identification with and diffuse support for Europe and European integration might affect adaptational change in many of our empirical cases. Let us consider the case of Italy, EMU, and the reform of public finances. As Sbragia points out in chapter 5, the Prodi government used references to Europe in order to silence the considerable domestic opposition against the reforms. She argues that this legitimizing strategy was successful because of strong support for and identification with Europe and the European order among the elites and public opinion. The Italian government successfully framed the reform of public finances as the entry ticket to "Europe" and the single currency. A similar process silenced the German opposition against giving up the cherished *Deutsche Mark* (Risse et al. 1999). In these cases, collective identification with Europe enabled the national governments to carry out their preferred policies and to silence the considerable domestic opposition.

Neofunctionalists probably got it wrong by assuming that domestic interests empowered by Europeanization would shift their loyalties toward Brussels. But this empowerment itself might be a function of collective identification with Europe. The argument in domestic discourses that "Europe made me do it," which puts the blame on Brussels for tough domestic decisions, works only if people take this "Europe" for granted, be it the European legal structure or rules and regulations emanating from the European Commission. The differential empowerment of domestic interests by Europeanization could ultimately result from an underlying collective attitude that takes "Europe" for granted as a normal part of political life. If so, Europeanization leads to domestic institutional change, because there is a functioning European polity that coexists with national polities and includes collective identification. This point is largely speculative and has not been dealt with explicitly in our case studies. But it is at least a plausible hypothesis meriting further research.

Transforming Europe? Does Europeanization Matter?

The larger goal of this book is to explore the degree to which Europeanization transforms the nation-state. How significant is the resulting domestic institutional change? Does Europeanization matter?

As our empirical chapters demonstrate, domestic adaptation occurred in response to Europeanization pressures in eight of the ten cases studied. In all but one case, the transformation of domestic structures was directly linked to Europeanization, as opposed to global or domestic pressures. Europeanization can even lead to relatively quick and dramatic changes in domestic structures, as Schneider and Sbragia indicate in their case studies of the telecommunications and public finance sectors in Italy (chapters 4 and 5). Other examples of domestic change were more "evolutionary than revolutionary" (cf. chapter 9). Yet, these slower-paced changes should not be discounted. The core structures of member states are often resistant to Europeanization. It is not surprising, therefore, that it may take several years or decades to overcome multiple veto points in German society or the statist system in France.

But Europeanization does not result in the homogenization of domestic structures. Member states face varying degrees of adaptational pressures to the "regulatory patchwork" of EU rules and regulations. Different factors restrain or facilitate their adaptation to these Europeanization pressures. Yet, the transformation of domestic structures takes place all the same, oftentimes in rather fundamental ways. In chapter 3 Héritier, for example, not only outlines the complete revamping of domestic institutions in the railways and road haulage sectors in Germany but also implies the tremendous political changes that occurred in these sectors at the same time. Knill and Lenschow (chapter 7) review changes in institutional arrangements for carrying out environmental policy but emphasize the challenges posed to hallowed administrative traditions. Schneider (chapter 4) points to a shift in Italian telecommunications policy that ultimately transcends party politics and reshapes market activity. Caporaso and Jupille (chapter 2) discuss changes in domestic institutions that modify the fundamental rights of women in the United Kingdom. Cowles (chapter 9) explores new forms of interest intermediation that alter fundamental relationships between state and society in continental Europe. Börzel (chapter 8) discusses the transformation not only of Spanish territorial structures but also decades of confrontational history.

As Sbragia (chapter 5) notes, the transformation of the Italian public finance system is not simply a matter of taxing and spending; rather, it impacts the "heart of the nation state." Changing norms of citizenship, as Checkel (chapter 10) points out, are essential in determining who is a member of a nation-state or Europe, and what it means to be German or European. Moreover, as Risse argues (chapter 11), changes in collective identities are fundamental in understanding support for the European polity itself. Given that these changes have occurred after only forty-five years of Europeanization, the significance of these transformations are all the more noteworthy.

To be certain, the discussion of Europeanization and domestic change has just begun. Whether or not Europeanization will ultimately lead to structural convergence is open to debate. Whether or not it will finally transcend the nation-state is also a matter of contention. This book marks an important starting point for these discussions. As we demonstrate, Europeanization transforms the domestic structures of the nation-state and the meanings attached to them. In short, Europeanization matters.

REFERENCES

Abrams, Dominic, and Michael A. Hogg, eds. 1990. *Social Identity Theory*. London: Harvester Wheatsheaf.

Aguilar, Susana. 1993. "Corporatist and Statist Designs in Environmental Policy: The Contrasting Roles of Germany and Spain in the European Community Scenario." *Environmental Politics* 2, no. 2: 223–47.

Alder, John. 1993. "Environmental Impact Assessment: The Inadequacy of English Law." *Journal of Environmental Law* 5: 203–20.

Allen, Christopher S. 1992. "Germany." In *European Politics in Transition*, 2d ed., edited by Mark Kesselman, Joel Krieger, Christopher S. Allen, Joan Debardeeben, Stephen Hellman, and Jonas Pontusson. Lexington, Mass.: D. C. Heath.

———. 2000. "The Politics of Adapting Organized Capitalism: United Germany, the New Europe, and Globalization." In *Breakdown, Breakup, Breakthrough: Germany's Modernity in State and Society*, edited by Carl F. Lankowski and Andrei S. Markovits. New York: Berghahn.

Alter, Karen J. 1996a. "The Making of a Rule of Law in Europe: The European Court and the National Judiciaries." Ph.D. dissertation, Massachusetts Institute of Technology.

———. 1996b. "The European Court's Political Power: The Emergence of the European Court as an Influential Actor in Europe." *West European Politics* 19: 458–87.

———. 1998a. "Who Are the Masters of the Treaty? European Governments and the European Court of Justice." *International Organization* 52: 121–47.

———. 1998b. "Explaining National Court Acceptance of European Court Jurisprudence: A Critical Evaluation of Theories of Legal Integration." In *The European Court and the National Courts—Doctrine and Jurisprudence: Legal Change in Its Social Context*, edited by Anne-Marie Slaughter, Alec Stone Sweet, and Joseph Weiler, 227–52. Oxford: Hart.

Alter, Karen J., and Jeannette Vargas. 2000. "Explaining Variation in the Use of European Litigation Strategies: EC Law and UK Gender Equality Policy." *Comparative Political Studies* 32, no. 4: 452–82.

Altmaier, Peter, and Norbert Roettgen. 1997. "Die Uhr läuft: Das Staatsangehörigkeitsrecht muss noch bis zur Bundestagswahl 98 reformiert werden." *Die Zeit*, August 15.

239

"Ambitious Plans for Reform Run into Trouble." 1999. *Financial Times*, June 1.

Anderson, Benedict. 1991. *Imagined Communities: Reflections on the Origin and Spread of Nationalism.* New York: Verso.

Anderson, Jeffrey. 1990. "Sceptical Reflections on a Europe of the Regions: Britain, Germany, and the ERDF." *Journal of Public Policy* 10, no. 4: 417–47.

Andersen, Sven S., and Kjell A. Eliassen, eds. 1993. *Making Policy in Europe: The Europeification of National Policy-making.* Thousand Oaks, Calif.: Sage.

Argyris, Chris, and Donald A. Schön. 1978. *Organizational Learning.* Reading, Mass.: Addison-Wesley.

Ausländerbeauftragte des Senats. 1994. *The Commissioner Foreigners' Affairs of the Berlin Senat: Principal Duties.* Berlin: Ausländerbeauftragte des Senats, April.

―――. 1995. Bericht zur Integrations und Ausländerpolitik: Fortschreibung 1995. Berlin: Ausländerbeauftragte des Senats, October.

"Ausländerrechts-Tango im Bundestag." 1996. *Süddeutsche Zeitung*, November 14.

Bailey, R. 1983. *The European Connection: Implications of EEC Membership.* Oxford: Pergamon Press.

Banchoff, Thomas. 1997. "German Policy Towards the European Union: The Effects of Historical Memory." *German Politics* 6, no. 1: 60–76.

―――. 1999. "German Identity and European Integration." *European Journal of International Relations* 5 (3): 259–89.

Baring, Arnulf. 1969. *Aussenpolitik in Adenauers Kanzlerdemokratie: Bonns Beitrag zur Europäischen Verteidigungsgemeinschaft.* München-Wien: Oldenbourg.

Bashevkin, Sylvia. 1996. "Tough Times in Review: The British Women's Movement During the Thatcher Years." *Comparative Political Studies* 28: 525–52.

Bauboeck, Rainer, ed. 1994. *From Aliens to Citizens: Redefining the Status of Immigrants in Europe.* Aldershot: Avebury Publishers.

Bauboeck, Rainer, and Dilek Cinar. 1994. "Briefing Paper: Naturalization Policies in Western Europe." *West European Politics* 17: 192–96.

Bauchard, Philippe. 1986. *La Guerre des Deux Roses.* Paris: Grasset.

Bauer, Hartmut, and Wolfgang Kahl. 1995. "Europäische Unionsbürger als Träger von Deutschen-Grundrechten?" *Juristen Zeitung* 50, no. 22: 1077–85.

Baumol, W. J., J. C. Panzar, and R. D. Willig. 1982. *Contestable Markets and the Theory of Industry Structure.* New York: Harcourt Brace Jovanovich.

Bellers, Jürgen. 1991. "Sozialdemokratie und Konservatismus im Angesicht der Zukunft Europas." In *Europapolitik der Parteien: Konservatismus, Liberalismus und Sozialdemokratie im Ringen um die Zukunft Europas*, edited by Jürgen Bellers and Mechthild Winking, 3–42. Frankfurt/Main: Lang.

Bellers, Jürgen, and Mechthild Winking, eds. 1991. *Europapolitik der Parteien: Konservatismus, Liberalismus und Sozialdemokratie im Ringen um die Zukunft Europas.* Frankfurt am Main: Lang.

Benz, Arthur. 1994. *Kooperative Verwaltung.* Baden-Baden: Nomos.

Benz, Arthur, and Klaus H. Götz. 1996. "The German Public Sector: National Priorities and the International Reform Agenda." In *A New German Public Sector? Reform, Adaptation and Stability*, edited by Arthur Benz and Klaus H. Götz, 1–26. Aldershot: Dartmouth.

Bermann, George, Roger Goebel, William Davey, and Eleanor Fox. 1993. *Cases and Materials on European Community Law.* St. Paul, Minn.: West Publishing.

Bjøl, Erling. 1966. *La France devant l'Europe.* Copenhagen: Munskgaard.

Blankenburg, Erhard. 1996. "Changes in Political Regimes and Continuity of the Rule of Law in Germany." In *Courts, Law, and Politics in Comparative Perspective*, edited by

Herbert Jacob, Erhard Blankenburg, Herbert Kritzer, Doris Marie Provine, and Joseph Sanders, 249–314. New Haven: Yale University Press.

Blitz, James. 1999. "Contradictions Trigger Uncertainty." *Financial Times* survey, "Euro-Zone Economy," September 10.

Blitz, James, and Tony Barber. 1999. "Weak Output Raises Doubts over Italy." *Financial Times*, July 16, p. 2.

Blom, Judith, et al. 1995. "The Utilization of Sex Equality Litigation Procedures in the Member States of the European Community: A Comparative Study." Brussels: Report of the Commission of the European Union, DG V.

Bloom, William. 1990. *Personal Identity, National Identity and International Relations.* Cambridge: Cambridge University Press.

Boissieu, Christian de, and Jean Pisani-Ferry. 1998. "The Political Economy of French Economic Policy in the Perspective of EMU." In *Forging an Integrated Europe*, edited by B. Eichengreen and J. Frieden, 49–90. Ann Arbor: University of Michigan Press.

Börzel, Tanja A. 1999. "Towards Convergence in Europe? Institutional Adaptation to Europeanisation in Germany and Spain." *Journal of Common Market Studies* 37, no. 4: 573–96.

———. 2000. "From Competitive Regionalism to Cooperative Federalism." *Publius, the Journal of Federalism* 30, no. 3.

———. In press. *Shaping States and Regions: The Domestic Impact of Europe.* Cambridge, UK.: Cambridge University Press.

Bretherton, Charlotte, and Liz Sperling. 1996. "Women's Networks and the European Union: Towards an Inclusive Approach?" *Journal of Common Market Studies* 34: 487–508.

Braunthal, Gerard. 1965. *The Federation of German Industry in Politics.* Ithaca: Cornell University Press.

Brubaker, Rogers, ed. 1989. *Immigration and the Politics of Citizenship in Europe and North America.* Lanham, Md: University Press of America.

———. 1992. *Citizenship and Nationhood in France and Germany.* Cambridge: Harvard University Press.

Buchsteiner, Jochen. 1994. "Konzepte, die erst reifen muessen." *Die Zeit*, November 18.

———. 1996. "Am liebsten abschirmen." *Die Zeit*, February 2.

Bulmer, Simon. 1989. *The Changing Agenda of West German Public Policy.* Aldershot: Dartmouth.

———. 1997. "Shaping the Rules? The Constitutive Politics of the European Union and German Power." In *Tamed Power: Germany in Europe*, edited by Peter J. Katzenstein, 49–79. Ithaca: Cornell University Press.

Bulmer, Simon, and William Paterson. 1987. *The Federal Republic of Germany and the European Community.* London: Allen and Unwin.

Burley, Anne-Marie, and Walter Mattli. 1993. "Europe Before the Court: A Political Theory of Legal Integration." *International Organization* 47: 41–76.

Burrows, Noreen, and Jane Mair. 1996. *European Social Law.* New York: John Wiley and Sons.

Bustos Gisbert, Rafael. 1995. "Un paso mas hacia la participación autonómica en asuntos europeos: El acuerdo de 30 de noviembre de 1994." *Revista Española de Derecho Constitucional* 15, no. 45: 153–72.

"Call to Strengthen Rules on Human Rights and Democracy." 1997. *Financial Times*, February 11.

Cawson, Alan. 1986. *Corporatism and Political Theory.* Oxford: Basil Blackwell.

Chamoux, J.-P. 1993. *Télécoms: La fin des privilèges.* Paris: Press Universitaires de France.

Checkel, Jeffrey T. 1997. "International Norms and Domestic Politics: Bridging the Rationalist-Constructivist Divide." *European Journal of International Relations* 3, no. 4: 473–95.

———. 1999a. "Norms, Institutions and National Identity in Contemporary Europe." *International Studies Quarterly* 43, no. 1: 83–115.

———. 1999b. *Why Comply? Constructivism, Social Norms and the Study of International Institutions.* Working Paper No. 99/24. August. Oslo: ARENA.

———. 2000. "Constructing European Institutions." In *The Rules of Integration: The Institutionalist Approach to European Studies*, edited by Mark Aspinwall and Gerald Schneider. Manchester: Manchester University Press.

Chiorazzo, Vincenzo, and Luigi Spaventa. 1999. "The Prodigal Son or a Confidence Trickster? How Italy Got into EMU." Manuscript.

Chirac, Jacques. 1992. "Le Choix de l'Europe." *Liberation*, September 11.

Christiansen, Thomas, Knud Erik Joergensen, and Antje Wiener, eds. 1999. "The Social Construction of Europe." *Journal of European Public Policy* 6, special issue.

Churchill, Winston. 1953. "Speech on 11 May." *House of Commons* 513: 895.

Clarke, Linda. 1983. "Proposed Amendments to the Equal Pay Act 1970—II." *New Law Review* December 23: 1129–32.

———. 1984. "Equal Pay for Work of Equal Value." *New Law Review* February 24: 177.

Coen, David. 1997a. "The Evolution of the Large Firm as a Political Actor in the European Union." *Journal of European Public Policy* 4, no. 1: 91–108.

———.1997b. "The Role of Large Firms in the European Public Policy System: A Case Study of European Multinational Political Activity." Paper presented at the European Community Studies Association, Seattle, May 29–June 1.

Cohen, E. 1992. *Le Colbertisme "High Tech": Économie des Télécoms et du Grand Projet.* Paris: Hachette.

Cohen, Jeffrey. 1996. "The European Preliminary Reference and U.S. Supreme Court Review of State Court Judgments: A Study in Comparative Judicial Federalism." *American Journal of Comparative Law* 44: 421–61.

Coleman, William D., and Stefan Tangermann. 1999. "The 1992 CAP Reform, the Uruguay Round and the Commission: Conceptualizing Linked Policy Games." *Journal of Common Market Studies* 37, no. 3: 385–405.

Coll, S. 1986. *The Deal of the Century: The Breakup of AT&T.* New York: Atheneum.

Commission of the European Communities (CEC). 1979. *Report of the Commission to the Council on the Application as at 12 February 1978 on the Principle of Equal Pay for Men and Women.* COM (78) 711 final, 16 January.

———. 1981. *Report from the Commission to the Council on the situation at 12 August 1980 with regard to the implementation of the principle of equal treatment for men and women.* COM (80) 832 final, 11 February.

———. 1995a. *Handbook on Equal Treatment for Men and Women in the European Community.* Luxembourg: Office for Official Publications of the European Communities.

———. 1995b. *Towards Fair and Efficient Pricing in Transport Policy: Options for Internalizing the External Costs of Transport in the European Union.* COM (95) 691 final. Luxembourg: Office for Official Publications of the European Communities.

———. 1996. *White Paper: A Strategy for Revitalizing the Community's Railways.* COM (96) 421 final. Luxembourg: Office for the Official Publications of the European Communities.

———. 1997. *Equal Opportunities for Women and Men in the European Union, 1996.* Luxembourg: Office for Official Publications of the European Communities.

———. 1998a. *Equal Opportunities for Women and Men in the European Union: Annual Report, 1997.* Luxembourg: Office for Official Publications of the European Communities.

————. 1998b. *Third Report on the Implementation of the Telecommunications Regulatory Package*. Communication from the Commission to the Council, the European Parliament, the Economic and Social Committee, and the Committee of the Regions. http://www.ispo.cec.be/infosoc/telecompolicy/en/Imp3.doc.

Conservative Party. 1997. *Our Vision for Britain. Election Manifesto*. London: http://www.conservative-party.org.uk/manifesto.

Coste-Floret, Alfred. 1952. "Bilan et Perspectives d'une Politique Européenne." *Politique Etrangère* November: 328.

Council of Europe. 1994. *Framework Convention for the Protection of National Minorities and Explanatory Report*. Strasbourg: Council of Europe, Document H (94) 10, November.

————. Directorate of Legal Affairs. 1997. *European Convention on Nationality and Explanatory Report*. Strasbourg: Council of Europe, Document DIR/JUR (97) 6, 14 May.

Court of Justice of the European Communities. 1994. "List of Courts." In *Index A-Z Numerical and Alphabetical Index of Cases before the Court of Justice of the E uropean Communities since 1953: Situation on 31 August 1994*. Luxembourg: Research, Documentation and Library Directorate, Legal Data-Processing Service.

————. 1995. *Report of Proceedings, 1992–1994: Synopsis of the Work of the Court of Justice and of the Court of First Instance of the European Communities*. Luxembourg: Office for Official Publications of the European Communities.

Cowles, Maria Green. 1995. "Setting the Agenda for a New Europe: The ERT and EC 1992." *Journal of Common Market Studies* 33, no. 4: 501–26.

————. 1996a. "The EU Committee of AmCham: The Powerful Voice of American Firms in Brussels." *Journal of European Public Policy* 3, no. 3: 339–58.

————. 1996b. "German Big Business: Learning to Play the European Game." *German Politics and Society* 14, no. 3: 73–107.

————. 1997. "Organising Industrial Coalitions." In *Participation and Policymaking in the European Union*, edited by Helen Wallace and Alasdair Young. London: Oxford University Press.

————. In press[a]. "The Transatlantic Business Dialogue: The Private Face of TransAtlantic Relations." In *Policy-Making in the U.S.-EU Relations: the New Transatlantic Agenda Revisited*, edited by Eric Philippart and Pascaline Winand. Manchester: Manchester University Press.

————. In press[b]. "The Transatlantic Business Dialogue: Transforming The New Transatlantic Dialogue." In *The New Transatlantic Dialogue*, edited by Mark Pollack and Gregory Schoffer. Lanham, Md.: Rowman and Littlefield.

Craig, P. P. 1998. "Report on the United Kingdom." In *The European Court and the National Courts—Doctrine and Jurisprudence: Legal Change in Its Social Context*, edited by Anne-Marie Slaughter, Alec Stone Sweet, and Joseph Weiler, 195–226. Oxford: Hart.

Cripps, Sir Stanford. 1950. "Speech on 26 June." *House of Commons*, pp. 1946–50.

Crisham, C. A. 1981. "The Equal Pay Principle: Some Recent Decisions of the European Court of Justice." *Common Market Law Review* 18: 601–12.

Cuerdo Pardo, José Luis. 1995. *La Acción Exterior de las Comunidades Autónomas: Teoría y Práctica*. Madrid: Escuela Diplomática.

Cyert, R. M., and J. G. March. 1992. *A Behavioral Theory of the Firm*. 2d ed. Oxford: Blackwell.

Dahl, Robert. 1961. *Who Governs*. New Haven: Yale University Press.

Dalmau i Oriol, Casimir de. 1997. "Propuestas y aspiraciones de las Comunidades Autónomas sobre la articulación de mecanismos para garantizar la participación autonómica en la toma de decisiones en el seño de la Unión Europea." *Autonomies* 22: 87–99.

Davies, P. L. 1987. "European Equality Legislation, U.K. Legislative Policy and Industrial Relations." In *Women, Employment, and European Equality Law*, edited by Christopher McCrudden, 23–51. England: Eclipse Publications.

"Debatte zur Neuregelung des Staatsangehörigkeitsrechts am 30. Oktober 1997." 1997. *Das Parlament* November 7.

Debré, Michel. 1953. "Speech at the Conseil de la République." October 27. In *Journal Officiel Conseil de la République Débats*, p. 1642.

De Gaulle, Charles. 1950. "Speech in Lille." December 11. *Discours et Messages* 2: 393.

———. 1965. "Television Interview." December 14. *Discours et Messages* 4: 432.

Degen, Manfred. 1993. "Die Unionsbürgerschaft nach dem Vertrag über die Europäische Union unter besonderer Berücksichtigung des Wahlrechtes." *Die Oeffentliche Verwaltung* 46: 749–58.

Della Sala, Vincent. 1997. "Hollowing out and Hardening the State: European Integration and the Italian Economy." *West European Politics* 20: 14–33.

Dempsey, Judy. 1993. "A Change Foreign to Her Nature." *Financial Times*, February 8.

Denkhaus, I. 1997. "Competition for Co-operation: The EC Commission and the European Railway Reforms of the 1990s." Paper presented at the HCM Network Meeting, Dublin. May.

"Der Kampf um die Pässe." 1999. *Der Spiegel*, January 11.

Derthick, M., and P. J. Quirk. 1985. *The Politics of Deregulation*. Washington, D.C.: Brookings Institution.

"Deutsche und Auchdeutsche." 1999. *Die Zeit*, February 4.

Deutsch, Karl W. et al. 1957. *Political Community and the North Atlantic Area*. Princeton: Princeton University Press.

"Die Koalition lehnt die erleichterte Einbürgerung von Ausländerkindern ab." 1998. *Frankfurter Allgemeine Zeitung*, March 28.

DiMaggio, Paul J., and Walter W. Powell. 1991. "The Iron Cage Revisited: Institutional Isomorphism and Collective Rationality in Organizational Fields." In *The New Institutionalism in Organizational Analysis*, edited by Walter W. Powell and Paul J. DiMaggio, 63–82. Chicago, London: University of Chicago Press.

Dobbin, Frank. 1994. *Forging Industrial Policy: The United States, Britain, and France in the Railway Age*. Cambridge: Cambridge University Press.

Donnelly, Jack. 1986. "International Human Rights: A Regime Analysis." *International Organization* 40, no. 3: 599–642.

Duina, Francesco G. 1999. *Harmonizing Europe. Nation-States within the Common Market*. New York: State University of New York Press.

Dunleavy, Patrick. 1993. "Introduction: Stability, Crisis or Decline?" In *Developments in British Politics* edited by Patrick Dunleavy, Andrew Gamble, Ian Holliday, and Gillian Peele, 1–18. London: Macmillan

Dyson, Kenneth, and Kevin Featherstone. 1996. "Italy and EMU as a 'Vincolo Esterno': Empowering the Technocrats, Transforming the State." *South European Society and Politics* 1: 272–99.

Egan, Michelle. 1997. "Modes of Business Governance: European Management Styles and Corporate Cultures." *West European Politics* 20, no. 2: 1–21.

Eisenstadt, Shmuel N., and Bernhard Giesen. 1995. "The Construction of Collective Identity." *European Journal of Sociology* 36: 72–102.

Ellis, Evelyn. 1996. "Equal Pay for Work of Equal Value: The United Kingdom's Legislation Viewed in the Light of Community Law." In *Sex Equality Law in the European Union*, edited by Tamara K. Hervey and David O'Keeffe, 7–19. New York: John Wiley and Sons.

Engelken, Klaas. 1995. "Einbeziehung der Unionsbürger in kommunale Abstimmung (Bürgerentscheide, Bürgerbegehren)?" *Neue Zeitschrift für Verwaltungsrecht* 5: 432–36.

Engelmann-Martin, Daniela. 1998. "Arbeitsbericht für die Länderstudie Bundesrepublik Deutschland" (Fünfziger Jahre). Unpublished manuscript. Florence: European University Institute. August.

Epstein, Lee, and C. K. Rowland. 1986. "Interest groups in the courts: do groups fare better?" In *Interest Group Politics*, 2d ed., edited by Allan Cigler and Burdett Loomis, 275–88. Washington, D.C.: Congressional Quarterly Press.

Erdmenger, J. 1981. *EG unterwegs: Wege zur Gemeinsamen Verkehrspolitik.* Baden-Baden: Nomos.

"EU Lowers its Sights over Sensitive Goals." 1997. *Financial Times.* June 17.

European Industrial Relations Review (EIRR). 1989. "Employment Equality Law to Be Mended." No. 185: 3.

European Parliament (EP). 1995. *Les organismes chargés de la promotion de l'égalité des chances entre les femmes et les hommes dans les États membres et les institutions de l'Union européenne.* Série Droits des Femmes, Working Document W-1/rév. 3, November.

Evangelista, Matthew. 1997. "Domestic Structure and International Change." In *New Thinking in International Relations Theory*, edited by Michael Doyle and G. John Ikenberry. Boulder Colo.: Westview.

Eylmann, Horst 1997. "Es gibt keine nationale Blutgruppe." *Die Zeit*, April 18.

Fabbrini, Sergio. 1995. "Italy: The Crisis of an Oligarchical State." In *Disintegration or Transformation? The Crisis of the State in Advanced Industrial Societies*, edited by Patrick McCarthy and Erik Jones, 65–84. New York: St. Martin's Press.

———. 1998a. "Due anni di governo Prodi. Un primo bilancio istituzionale." *Il Mulino*, no. 4: 657–72.

———. 1998b. "A Changing Democracy: The Italian Experience with Consensualism." Manuscript.

Favell, Adrian. 1998. "The European Citizenship Agenda: Emergence, Transformation and Effects of a New Political Field." Paper presented at the Eleventh International Conference of Europeanists. February.

Federal Republic of Germany. 1994. *Report by the Federal Government's Commissioner for Foreigners' Affairs on the Situation of Foreigners in the Federal Republic of Germany in 1993.* Bonn: Federal Government's Commissioner for Foreigners' Affairs, March.

Feld, Werner. 1966. "National Economic Interests Groups and Policy Formation in the EEC." *Political Science Quarterly* 81, no. 3: 392–411.

Felsen, David. 1999. "Changes to the Italian Budgetary Regime: The Reforms of Law n. 94/1997." In *The Return of Politics—Italian Politics. A Review*, edited by David Hine and Salvatore Vassallo. New York: Berghan.

Fenwick, Helen, and Tamara K. Hervey. 1995. "Sex Equality in the Single Market: New Directions for the European Court of Justice." *Common Market Law Review* 32: 443–70.

Finnemore, Martha. 1996. *National Interests in International Society.* Ithaca: Cornell University Press.

Finnemore, Martha, and Kathryn Sikkink. 1998. "International Norm Dynamics and Political Change." *International Organization* 52, no. 4: 887–917.

Fiske, Susan, and Shelley Taylor. 1984. *Social Cognition.* New York: Random House.

Fitzpatrick, Barry. 1993. *Sex Equality Litigation in the Member States of the European Community: A Comparative Study.* European Commission DG V/A/3, Equal Opportunities Unit, document number V/407/94-EN. October.

Flynn, Gregory, ed. 1995. *The Remaking of the Hexagon: The New France in the New Europe.* Boulder, Colo.: Westview.

Forbes, Ian. 1989. "Unequal Partners: The Implementation of Equal Opportunities Policies in Western Europe." *Public Administration* 67: 19–38.

Fratianni, Michele, and Franco Spinelli. 1997. *A Monetary History of Italy.* Cambridge: Cambridge University Press.

Freeman, Gary. 1998. "The Decline of Sovereignty? Politics and Immigration Restriction in Liberal States." In *Challenge to the Nation-State: Immigration in Western Europe and the United States,* edited by Christian Joppke. New York: Oxford University Press.

Frieden, J. A., and R. Rogowski. 1996. "The Impact of the International Economy on National Policies: An Analytical Overview." In *Internationalization and Domestic Politics,* edited by R. O. Keohane and H. V. Milner. Cambridge: Cambridge University Press.

Furet, François, Jacques Juillard, and Pierre Rosanvallon. 1988. *La République du centre: La fin de l'exception française.* Paris: Calmann-Levy.

Galanter, Marc. 1974. "Why the 'Haves' Come Out Ahead: Speculations on the Limits of Legal Change." *Law and Society Review* 9: 95–160.

Garrett, Geoffrey. 1992. "International Cooperation and Institutional Choice: The European Community's Internal Market." *International Organization* 46: 533–60.

———. 1998a. "The Transition to Economic and Monetary Union." In *Forging an Integrated Europe,* edited by B. Eichengreen and J. Frieden, 21–48. Ann Arbor: University of Michigan Press.

———. 1998b. "Global Markets and National Politics: Collision Course or Virtuous Cycle?" *International Organization* 52, no. 4: 787–824.

Garrett, Geoffrey, R. Daniel Kelemen, and Heiner Schulz. 1998. "The European Court of Justice: Master or Servant? Legal Politics in the European Union." *International Organization* 52: 149–76.

George, Alexander. 1979. "Case Studies and Theory Development: The Method of Structured, Focused Comparison." In *Diplomacy: New Approaches in History, Theory and Policy,* edited by Paul Lauren. New York: Free Press.

George, Stephen, ed. 1992. *Britain and the European Community: The Politics of Semi-Detachment.* Oxford: Clarendon Press.

———. 1994. *An Awkward Partner: Britain in the European Community.* 2d ed. Oxford: Oxford University Press.

"Gericht: EU-Ausländer darf in Bayern nicht Bürgermeister werden." 1997. *Agence France Presse,* November 6.

"Germany: Dual Nationality Change," 1999. *Migration News,* March 6.

"Germany: Option Model Approved." 1999. *Migration News,* June 6.

Giuliani, Marco. 1999. "Europeanization and Italy." Paper prepared for the Biennial Conference of the European Community Studies Association, June 2–5.

Glatzeder, Sebastian J. 1980. *Die Deutschlandpolitik der FDP in der Ära Adenauer.* Baden-Baden: Nomos.

Goetz, Klaus. 1995. "National Governance and European Integration: Intergovernmental Relations in Germany." *Journal of Common Market Studies* 33: 91–116.

Golub, Jonathan. 1996a. "Modeling Judicial Dialogue in the European Community: The Quantitative Basis of Preliminary References to the ECJ." EUI Working Paper, RSC 96/58.

———. 1996b. "The Politics of Judicial Discretion: Rethinking the Interaction between National Courts and the European Court of Justice." *West European Politics* 19: 360–85.

Gourevitch, Peter. 1978. "The Second Image Reversed: The International Sources of Domestic Politics." *International Organization* 32, no. 4: 881–912.

———. 1986. *Politics in Hard Times: Comparative Responses to International Economic Crises.* Ithaca: Cornell University Press.

Grande, E. 1994. "The New Role of the State in Telecommunications: An International Comparison." In *West European Politics* 17: 138–57.

———. 1989. *Vom Monopol zum Wettbewerb? Die neokonservative Reform der Telekommunikation in Großbritannien und der Bundesrepublik Deutschland.* Wiesbaden: Deutscher Universitäts-Verlag.

———. 1996. "The State and Interest Groups in a Framework of Multi-level Decision-making: The Case of the European Union." *Journal of European Public Policy* 3: 318–38.

Grande, E., and V. Schneider. 1991. "Reformstrategien und staatliche Handlungskapazitäten: Eine vergleichende Analyse institutionellen Wandels in der Telekommunikation." *Politische Vierteljahresschrift* 32: 452-78.

Grant, Wyn. 1987. "The Organization of Capitalists in Britain's Company State: A Comparative Perspective." Paper presented to the Annual Convention of the American Political Science Association, Washington, D.C.

Greenwood, Justin, and Lara Stancich. 1998. "British Business: Managing Complexity." In *Britain for and against Europe*, edited by David Baker and David Seawright. Oxford: Oxford University Press.

Greenwood, Justin, Jürgen R. Grote, and Karsten Ronit, eds. 1992. *Organized Interests and the European Community.* London: Sage.

Gurowitz, Amy. 1999. "Mobilizing International Norms: Domestic Actors, Immigrants and the Japanese State." *World Politics* 51, no. 3: 413–46.

Haas, Ernst B. 1958. *The Uniting of Europe: Political, Social, and Economic Forces, 1950–57.* Stanford, Calif.: Stanford University Press.

Haigh, Nigel. 1996. *The Manual of Environmental Policy: The EC and Britain.* London: Catermill Publishing.

Hailbronner, Kay. 1989. "Citizenship and Nationhood in Germany." In *Immigration and the Politics of Citizenship in Europe and North America*, edited by Rogers Brubaker. Lanham, Md.: University Press of America.

"Halb und halb." 1995. *Der Spiegel*, no. 12.

Hall, Peter A. 1990. "Pluralism and Pressure Politics." In *Developments in French Politics*, edited by Peter A. Hall, Jack Hayward, and Howard Machin, 77–94. New York: St. Martin's Press.

Hall, Peter A., and Rosemary C. R. Taylor. 1996. "Political Science and the Three New Institutionalisms." *Political Studies* 44, no. 5: 936–57.

Hallerberg, Mark. 1999. "High Debt Countries in an Integrating World: Why Belgium and Italy Qualified for EMU." Paper prepared for the Annual Meeting of the American Political Science Association.

Harlow, Carol. 1992. "A Community of Interests? Making the Most of European Law." *Modern Law Review* 55: 331–50.

———. 1996. "'Francovich' and the Problem of the Disobedient State." Florence: EUI Working Paper, RSC No. 96/62.

Harlow, Carol, and Richard Rawlings. 1992. *Pressure through Law.* New York: Routledge.

Hartley, T. C. 1994. *The Foundations of European Community Law*, 3d ed. Oxford: Clarendon Press.

Hattam, Victoria. 1993. *Labor Visions and State Power: The Origins of Business Unionism in the United States.* Princeton: Princeton University Press.

Haverland, Markus. 1999. *National Autonomy, European Integration, and the Politics of Packaging Waste.* Amsterdam: Thela Thesis.

Hayden, Robert. 1992. "Constitutional Nationalism in the Formerly Yugoslav Republics." *Slavic Review* 51, no. 4: 654.

Hayward, Jack. 1995. "Organized Interests and Public Policies." In *Governing the New Europe*, edited by Jack Hayward and Edward Page, 224–56. Durham, N.C.: Duke University Press.

Heims, Hans-Joerg. 1997. "Beruhigungspillen fuer die jungen Wilden: Der Streit um die doppelte Staatsangehoerigkeit spaltet die CDU." *Süddeutsche Zeitung*, April 23.

Hellmann, Gunther. 1996. "Goodbye Bismarck? The Foreign Policy of Contemporary Germany." *Mershon Review of International Studies* 40: 1–39.

Hellman, Steven and Gianfranco Pasquino. 1993. "Introduction." In *Italian Politics: A Review*, edited by Steven Hellman and Gianfranco Pasquino, 1–12. London: Pinter.

Hennion-Moreau, Sylvie. 1992. "L'influence du droit social communautaire sur le droit interne." *Droit Social* 7–8: 736–43.

Héritier, Adrienne. 1996. "The Accommodation of Diversity in European Policy-Making and Its Outcomes: Regulatory Policy as a Patchwork." *Journal of European Public Policy*. 3, no. 2: 149–76.

———. 1997. "Policy-making by Subterfuge: Interest Accommodation, Innovation and Substitute Democratic Legitimation in Europe—Perspectives from Distinct Policy Areas." *Journal of European Public Policy* 4: 171–89.

———. 1999. *Escape from Deadlock: Shifting Patterns in European Policy-Making*. Cambridge: Cambridge University Press.

Héritier, Adrienne, Christoph Knill, and Susanne Mingers. 1996. *Ringing the Changes in Europe: Regulatory Competition and the Transformation of the State—Britain, France, Germany*. New York: Walter de Gruyter.

Høj, J., Toshiyasu Kato, and D. Pilat. 1995. "Deregulation and Privatization in the Service Sector." *OECD Economic Studies* 25: 37–74.

Hood, Christopher. 1991. "A Public Management for All Seasons?" *Public Administration* 69: 3–19.

Hooghe, Liesbet. 1995. "Subnational Mobilisation in the European Union." In *The Crisis of Representation in Europe*, edited by Jack Hayward. London: Frank Cass.

Hoskyns, Catherine. 1996. *Integrating Gender: Women, Law, and Politics in the European Union*. London: Verso Publications.

Humphreys, P. 1990. "The Political Economy of Telecommunications in France: A Case Study of 'Telematics.'" In *The Political Economy of Communications. International and European Dimensions*, edited by K. Dyson and P. Humphreys, 198–228. London: Routledge.

———. 1992. "The Politics of Regulatory Reform in German Telecommunications." In *The Politics of German Regulation*, edited by K. Dyson, 105–36. Aldershot: Dartmouth.

Ikenberry, J. G. 1990. "The International Spread of Privatization Policies: Inducements, Learning, and Policy Bandwagoning." In *The Political Economy of Public Sector Reform and Privatization*, edited by E.N. Suleiman and J. Waterbury, 88–110. Boulder, Colo.: Westview Press.

Immergut, Ellen M. 1992. *Health Politics: Interests and Institutions in Western Europe*. Cambridge, UK: Cambridge University Press.

Ingersent, K. A., A. J. Rayner, and R. C. Hine, eds. 1998. *The Reform of the Common Agricultural Policy*. New York: St. Martin's Press.

Jachtenfuchs, Markus, Thomas Diez, and Sabine Jung. 1998. "Which Europe? Conflicting Models of a Legitimate European Political Order." *European Journal of International Relations* 4, no. 4: 409–45.

Jeffery, Charlie. 1997a. "Farewell to the Third Level? The German Länder and the European Policy Process." In *The Regional Dimension of the European Union: Towards a Third Level in Europe?*, edited by Charlie Jeffery, 56–75. London: Frank Cass.

———, ed. 1997b. *The Regional Dimension of the European Union: Towards a Third Level in Europe?* London: Frank Cass.

Jepperson, Ronald L., and Ann Swidler. 1994. "What Properties of Culture Should We Measure?" *Poetics* 22: 359–71.

Joppke, Christian. 1998. "Why Liberal States Accept Unwanted Immigration." *World Politics* 50, no. 2: 266–94.

Jordan, Grant, and J. J. Richardson. 1987. *Government and Pressure Groups in Britain.* Oxford: Oxford University Press.

"Kampagne gegen Doppel-Staatsbürgerschaft: FDP Lässt die Union allein." 1999. *Süddeutsche Zeitung*, January 5–6.

Kanstroom, Daniel. 1993. "Wer Sind Wir Wieder? [Who Are We Again?]: Laws of Asylum, Immigration and Citizenship in the Struggle for the Soul of the New Germany." *Yale Journal of International Law* 18 (Winter) 155–211.

Kassim, Hussein, and Anand Menon, eds. 1996. *The European Union and National Industrial Policy.* London: Routledge.

Katzenstein, Peter J., ed. 1978. *Between Power and Plenty: Foreign Economic Policies of Advanced Industrial States.* Madison: Wisconsin University Press.

———. 1984. *Corporatism and Change: Austria, Switzerland, and the Politics of Industry.* Ithaca: Cornell University Press.

———. 1985. *Small States in World Markets: Industrial Policy in Europe.* Ithaca: Cornell University Press.

———. 1987. *Politics and Policy in West Germany: The Growth of a Semisovereign State.* Philadelphia: Temple University Press.

———, ed. 1996. *The Culture of National Security: Norms and Identity in World Politics.* New York: Columbia University Press.

———, ed. 1997a. *Tamed Power: Germany in the European Union.* Ithaca: Cornell University Press.

———. 1997b. "United Germany in an Integrating Europe." In *Tamed Power: Germany in Europe*, edited by Peter J. Katzenstein, 1–48. Ithaca: Cornell University Press.

Katzenstein, Peter J., and Nobuo Okawara. 1993. *Japan's National Security.* Ithaca: Cornell University Press.

Keating, Michael, and Liesbet Hooghe. 1996. "By-Passing the Nation-State? Regions and the EU Policy Process." In *European Union. Power and Policy Making*, edited by Jeremy J. Richardson, 216–29. London: Routledge.

Keck, Margaret, and Kathryn Sikkink. 1998. *Activists Beyond Borders: Transnational Advocacy Networks in International Politics.* Ithaca: Cornell University Press.

Keeler, John T. S. 1985. "Situating France on the Pluralism-Corporatism Continuum." *Comparative Politics* 17: 229–49.

———. 1996. "Agricultural Power in the European Community: Explaining the Fate of CAP and GATT Negotiations." *Comparative Politics* 28, no. 2: 127–49.

"Kein Konkurrenzschutz an der Urne." 1997. *Süddeutsche Zeitung*, February 28.

Keller, Martina. 1997. "Einbürgern, Ausbürgern, Einbürgern." *Die Zeit*, March 27.

Kenney, Sally J. 1992. *For Whose Protection: Reproductive Hazards and Exclusionary Policies in the United States and Britain.* Ann Arbor: University of Michigan Press.

———. 1995. "Pregnancy Discrimination: Toward Substantive Equality." *Wisconsin Women's Law Journal* 10: 351–402.

Keohane, Robert O., and Helen V. Milner, eds. 1996. *Internationalization and Domestic Politics.* Cambridge, UK: Cambridge University Press.

Kerwer, D. In press. "The Dynamics of EC and EU Transport Policies." In *Differential Europe: EU Impact on National Policymaking,* edited by A. Héritier et al. Lanham, Md.: Rowman and Littlefield.

Kesselman, Mark. 1992. "France." In *European Politics in Transition,* 2d ed., edited by Mark Kesselman, Joel Krieger, Christopher S. Allen, Joan Debardeleben, Stephen Hellman, and Jonas Pontusson. Lexington, Mass.: D. C. Heath.

Kielmansegg, Peter Graf. 1996. "Integration und Demokratie." In *Europäische Integration,* edited by Markus Jachtenfuchs and Beate Kohler-Koch, 47–71. Opladen: Leske and Budrich.

Kilpatrick, Claire. 1997. "Effective Utilisation of Equality Rights: Equal Pay for Work of Equal Value in France and the UK." In *Sex Equality Policy in Western Europe,* edited by Frances Gardiner, 25–45. New York: Routledge.

Kingdon, J. W. 1984. *Agendas, Alternatives, and Public Policies.* Boston: Little, Brown.

Kitschelt, Herbert P. 1986. "Political Opportunity Structures and Political Protest: Anti-Nuclear Movements in Four Democracies." *British Journal of Political Science* 16: 57–85.

Klöpfer, Michael, and Wolfgang Durner. 1997. "Der Umweltgesetzbuch-Entwurf der Sachverständigenkommission." *Deutsches Verwaltungsblatt* 112: 1081–107.

Klotz, Audie. 1995. *Norms in International Relations: The Struggle Against Apartheid.* Ithaca: Cornell University Press.

Klusmeyer, Douglas. 1993. "Aliens, Immigrants and Citizens: The Politics of Inclusion in the Federal Republic of Germany." *Daedalus* 122, no. 3: 81–115.

Knight, Jack. 1992. *Institutions and Social Conflict.* Cambridge, UK: Cambridge University Press.

Knill, Christoph. 1998. "European Policies: The Impact of National Administrative Traditions" *Journal of Public Policy* 18: 1–28.

———. In press[a]. "Reforming British Transport Policy: Separate but Concurrent Change." In *Differential Europe: EU Impact on National Policymaking,* edited by A. Héritier et al. Lanham, Md.: Rowman and Littlefield.

———. In press [b]. *The Transformation of National Administrations in Europe: Patterns of Institutional Change and Persistence.* Cambridge, UK: Cambridge University Press.

Knill, Christoph, and Andrea Lenschow. 1998. "Compliance with Europe: The Implementation of EU Environmental Policy and Administrative Traditions in Britain and Germany." *Journal of European Public Policy* 5: 597–616.

———. 2000. "On Deficient Implementation and Deficient Theories: The Need for an Institutional Perspective in Implementation Research." In *Implementing EU Environmental Policy: New Approaches to an Old Problem,* edited by Christoph Knill and Andrea Lenschow. Manchester: Manchester University Press.

Knopf, Hans-Joachim. 1997. "English Identity and European Integration: A Case of Non-Europeanization?" June paper and Ph.D. proposal, European University Institute, Florence.

"Kohl: Bei der Europäischen Währung ist Stabilität Wichtiger als der Kalender." 1994. *Frankfurter Allgemeine Zeitung,* May 28.

Kohler-Koch, Beate. 1993. "Germany." In *National Public and Private EC Lobbying,* edited by M. P. C. M. Van Schendelen. Aldershot: Dartmouth.

———. 1996. "The Strength of Weakness: The Transformation of Governance in the EU." In *The Future of the Nation State: Essays on Cultural Pluralism and Political Integration,* edited by Sverker Gustavsson and Leif Lewin, 169–210. Stockholm: Nerenius and Santerus.

————, ed. 1997. *Interaktive Politik in Europa: Regionen im Netzwerk der Integration*. Opladen: Leske and Budrich.

Kohler-Koch, Beate, and Rainer Eising, eds. 1999. *The Transformation of Governance in the European Union*. London: Routledge.

König, Klaus. 1996. "Unternehmerisches oder exekutives Management: Die Perspektive der klassischen öffentlichen Verwaltung." *Verwaltungs-Archiv* 87: 19–37.

Krasner, Stephen D. 1988. "Sovereignty: An Institutional Perspective." *Comparative Political Studies* 21: 66–94.

Kreuzer, Christine. 1997. "Reforming Germany's Citizenship Law." Paper presented at the conference "Managing Migration in the twenty-first Century," University of California at Davis, October.

Kritzer, Herbert. 1996. "Courts, Justice, and Politics in England." In *Courts, Law, and Politics in Comparative Perspective*, edited by Herbert Jacob, Erhard Blankenburg, Herbert Kritzer, Doris Marie Provine, and Joseph Sanders, 81–176. New Haven: Yale University Press.

Kuper, Ernst, and Uwe Jun, eds. 1997. *Nationales Interesse und integrative Politik in transnationalen parlamentarischen Versammlungen*. Opladen: Leske and Budrich.

Labour Party. 1997. *Britain Will Be Better with New Labour: Election Manifesto*. London: http://www.labourwin97.org.uk/manifesto/index.

Ladeur, Karl-Heinz. 1995. "Supra- und transnationale Tendenzen in der Europäisierung des Verwaltungsrechts—eine Skizze." *Europarecht* 30: 227–46.

Lanquetin, Marie-Thérèse, and Hélène Masse-Dessen. 1989. "Les Droits Particuliers Pour les Femmes Dans les Conventions Collectives." *Droit Social* 7–8: 551–54.

Lanzara, G. F. 1998. "Self-Destructive Processes in Institution Building and Some Modest Counterveiling Mechanisms." *European Journal of Political Research* 3, no. 2: 3–39.

Legro, Jeffrey. 1997. "Which Norms Matter? Revisiting the 'Failure' of Internationalism." *International Organization* 51, no 4: 1251–89.

Lehmbruch, Gerhard. 1997. "From State of Authority to Network State: The German State in a Comparative Perspective." In *State and Administration in Japan and Germany: A Comparative Perspective on Continuity and Change*, edited by Michio Muramatsu and Frieder Naschold, 39–62. Berlin: De Gruyter.

Lehmbruch, Gerhard, and Manfred G. Schmidt. 1988. "Institutionelle Bedingungen ordnungspolitischen Strategiewechsels im internationalen Vergleich." In *Staatstätigkeit. International und historisch vergleichende Analysen*, edited by M. G. Schmidt, 251–83. Opladen: Westdeutscher Verlag.

Lehmkuhl, D. In press. "Reforming Dutch Transport Policy: From Regulation to Stimulation." In *Differential Europe: EU Impacts on National Policymaking*, edited by A. Héritier et al. Lanham, Md.: Rowman and Littlefield.

Leicht, Robert. 1994. "Scheinangebot." *Die Zeit*, December 2.

Lemke, Christiane. 1997. "Citizenship and European Integration." Paper presented at the Annual Meeting of the American Political Science Association, September.

Lenschow, Andrea. 1997. "The Implementation of EU Environmental Policy in Germany." In *The Impact of National Administrative Traditions on the Implementation of EU Environmental Policy*, edited by Christoph Knill. Research report. Florence: European University Institute.

Lepsius, M. Rainer. 1990. *Interessen, Ideen und Institutionen*. Opladen: Westdeutscher Verlag.

Levitsky, Jonathan E. 1994. "The Europeanization of the British Legal Style." *American Journal of Comparative Law* 42: 347–80.

Levy, Jack. 1994. "Learning and Foreign Policy: Sweeping a Conceptual Minefield." *International Organization* 48, no. 2: 279–312.

Liebert, Ulrike. 1998. "Der 'gender gap' in der europäischen Öffentlichkeit als Problem der international vergleichenden Meinungsforschung." In *Europa der Bürger? Voraussetzungen, Alternativen, Konsequenzen——Mannheimer Jahrbuch für Europäische Sozialforschung*, edited by T. König, E. Rieger, and H. Schmitt, 177–200. Frankfurt/Main: Campus.

Lindenberg, Siegwart. 1991. "Die Methode der Abnehmenden Abstraktion: Theoriegesteuerte Analyse und Empririscher Gehalt." In *Modellierung Sozialer Prozesse*, edited by Hartmut Esser and Klaus G. Troitsch, 29–78. Bonn: Informationszentrum Sozialwissenschaften.

Locke, Richard. 1995. "Eppure Si Tocca: The Abolition of the Scala Mobile." In *Italian Politics: Ending the First Republic*, edited by Carol Mershon and Gianfranco Pasquino, 185–96. Boulder, Colo.: Westview.

Lölhöffel, Helmut. 1997. "Koalition vertagt ihren Streit." *Frankfurter Rundschau*, October 31.

Lovenduski, Joni. 1990. "Feminism and West European Politics: An Overview." In *Politics in Western Europe Today: Perspectives, Policies, and Problems since 1980*, edited by D. W. Urwin and W. E. Paterson, 137–61. New York: Longman.

———. 1997. "Sex Equality and the Rules of the Game." In *Sex Equality Policy in Western Europe*, edited by Frances Gardiner, 91–108. New York: Routledge.

Lowi, Theodore. 1964. "American Business, Public Policy Case Studies and Political Theory." *World Politics* 16, no. 4: 677–715.

———. 1969. *The End of Liberalism: Ideology, Policy, and the Crisis of Public Authority*. New York: W. W. Norton.

Lyon, David. 1991. "British Identity Cards: The Unpalatable Logic of European Membership?" *Political Quarterly* 62, no. 3: 377–85.

Major, John. 1993. "Raise Your Eyes, There Is Land Beyond." *The Economist* 328, no. 7830: 27–30.

Maloney, William A., and Jeremy Richardson. 1995. *Managing Policy Change in Britain: The Politics of Water*. Edinburgh: Edinburgh University Press.

Mancini, G. Federico. 1991. "The Making of a Constitution for Europe." In *The New European Community: Decisionmaking and Institutional Change*, edited by Robert O. Keohane and Stanley Hoffman, 177–94. Boulder, Colo.: Westview Press.

Mann, M. 1986. "The Autonomous Power of the State: Its Origins, Mechanisms and Results." In *States in History*, edited by J. A. Hall, 109–36. Oxford: Basil Blackwell.

March, J. G. 1981. "Footnotes to Organizational Change." *Administrative Science Quarterly* 26: 563–77.

March, James G., and Johan P. Olsen. 1989. *Rediscovering Institutions*. New York: Free Press.

———. 1998. "The Institutional Dynamics of International Political Orders." *International Organization* 52, no. 4: 943–69.

Marcussen, Martin, Thomas Risse, Daniela Engelmann-Martin, Hans-Joachim Knopf, and Klaus Roscher. 1999. "Constructing Europe: The Evolution of French, British, and German Nation-State Identities." *Journal of European Public Policy* 6, no. 4: 614–33.

Marks, Gary. 1993. "Structural Policy and Multilevel Governance in the European Community." In *The State of the European Community II: Maastricht Debates and Beyond*, edited by Alan Cafruny and Glenda Rosenthal, 391–410. Boulder, Colo.: Lynne Rienner.

Marks, Gary, Francois Nielsen, Leonard Ray, and Jane Salk. 1996. "Competencies, Cracks and Conflicts: Regional Mobilization in the European Union." In *Governance in the European Union*, edited by Gary Marks, Fritz W. Scharpf, Philippe C. Schmitter, and Wolfgang Streeck, 40–63. Thousand Oaks, Calif.: Sage.

Matthews, Duncan, and John Pickering. 1997. "Corporate Responses to European Environmental Law: The Case of the Water Industry and the Drinking Water Directive." *International Journal of Biosciences and the Law* 1: 265–99.

Mattli, Walter, and Anne Marie Slaughter. 1998. "Revisiting the European Court of Justice." *International Organization* 52: 177–209.

Mayntz, Renate, and Fritz W. Scharpf. 1995. "Der Ansatz des Akteurszentrierten Institutionalismus." In *Gesellschaftliche Selbstregelung und Politische Steuerung*, edited by Renate Mayntz and Fritz W. Scharpf, 39–72. Frankfurt/Main: Campus.

Mazey, Sonia. 1988. "European Community Action on Behalf of Women: The Limits of Legislation." *Journal of Common Market Studies* 27: 63–84.

———. 1998. "The European Union and Women's Rights: From the Europeanization of National Agendas to the Nationalization of a European Agenda?" *Journal of European Public Policy* 5: 131–52.

Mazey, Sonia, and Jeremy Richardson, eds. 1993. *Lobbying in the European Community*. Oxford: Oxford University Press.

Mazur, Amy G. 1995a. *Gender Bias and the State: Symbolic Reform at Work in Fifth Republic France*. Pittsburgh: University of Pittsburgh Press.

———. 1995b. "Strong State and Symbolic Reform: The 'Ministère des Droits de la Femme' in France." In *Comparative State Feminism*, edited by Dorothy McBride Stetson and Amy Mazur, 76–94. Thousand Oaks, Calif.: Sage.

McCann, Michael. 1994. *Rights at Work: Pay Equity Reform and the Politics of Legal Mobilization*. Chicago: University of Chicago Press.

McCrudden, Christopher. 1983. "Equal Pay for Work of Equal Value: The Equal Pay (Amendment) Regulations 1983." *Industrial Law Journal* 12: 197–219.

Meehan, Elizabeth, and Evelyn Collins. 1996. "Women, the European Union, and Britain." *Parliamentary Affairs* 49: 221–34.

Mény, Yves, Pierre Muller, and Jean-Louis Quermonne, eds. 1996. *Adjusting to Europe: The Impact of the European Union on National Institutions and Policies*. London: Routledge.

Muenier, Sophie. 1998. "Europe Divided But United: Institutional Integration and EC-U.S. Trade Negotiations since 1962." Ph.D. dissertation. Massachusetts Institute of Technology.

———. 2000. "What Single Voice? European Institutions and EU-U.S. Trade Negotiations." *International Organization*, 54 no. 1: 103–35.

Muenier, Sophie, and Kalypso Nicolaïdis. In press. "EU Trade Policy: The 'Exclusive vs. Shared' Competence Debate." In *The State of the European Union: Risks, Reform, Resistance, and Revival*, 5th ed., edited by Maria Green Cowles and Michael Smith. Oxford: Oxford University Press.

Meyer, John, and David Strang. 1993. "Institutional Conditions for Diffusion." *Theory and Society* 22, no. 4: 487–511.

Miller, Mark. 1989. "Conference Report: Dual Citizenship—A European Norm?" *International Migration Review* 23, no. 4: 945.

Milner, Helen. 1988. *Resisting Protectionism: Global Industries and the Politics of International Trade*. Princeton: Princeton University Press.

Milner, Helen, and Robert O. Keohane. 1996. "Internationalization and Domestic Politics: A Conclusion." In *Internationalization and Domestic Politics*, edited by R. O. Keohane and H. V. Milner. Cambridge: Cambridge University Press.

Mitterrand, François. 1986. *Réflexions Sur la Politique Extérieure de la France: Introduction à Vingt-cinq Discours*. Paris: Fayard.

———. 1992. *Le Monde*, September 4.

Moe, Terry. 1990. "The Politics of Structural Choice: Toward a Theory of Public Bureaucracy." In *Organization Theory*, edited by Oliver Williamson, 116–53. Oxford: Oxford University Press.

Mollet, Guy. 1947. *Le Populaire*. September 18.

Montoro Chiner, Maria Jesus. 1989. "Rechtliche Konsequenzen aus dem Beitritt Spaniens zu den Europäischen Gemeinschaften." In *Aspekte der öffentlichen Verwaltung und Verwaltungswissenschaften in Spanien*, edited by Carl Böhret, 49–61. Speyer: Hochschule für Verwaltungswissenschaften Speyer.

Moore, Sarah. 1996. "Enforcement of Private Law Claims of Sex Discrimination in the Field of Employment." In *Sex Equality Law in the European Union*, edited by Tamara K. Hervey and David O'Keeffe, 139–60. New York: John Wiley and Sons.

Morata, Francesc. 1995. "Spanish Regions in the European Community." In *The European Union and the Regions*, edited by Barry Jones and Michael Keating, 115–34. Oxford: Clarendon Press.

Moravcsik, Andrew. 1993. "Preferences and Power in the European Community: A Liberal Intergovernmentalist Approach." *Journal of Common Market Studies* 31, no. 4: 473–524.

———. 1994. *Why the European Community Strengthens the State: Domestic Politics and International Cooperation*. Working paper no. 52. Cambridge: Harvard University.

———. 1995. "Explaining International Human Rights Regimes: Liberal Theory and Western Europe." *European Journal of International Relations* 1, no. 2, 157–89.

———. 1998. *The Choice for Europe: Social Purpose and State Power from Rome to Maastricht*. Ithaca: Cornell University Press.

Morgan, K., and D. Webber. 1986. "Divergent Paths: Political Strategies for Telecommunications in Britain, France and West Germany." In *The Politics of the Communications Revolution in Western Europe*, edited by K. Dyson and P. Humphreys, 56–79. London: Frank Cass.

Morganti, Franco. 1994. "I Vincoli Imposti dalla Normativa Italiana." Unpublished manuscript, Milan.

———. et al. 1988. *Le Telecomunicazioni*. Rome: Pubblicazioni Internazionali.

Morris, Anne E., and Susan M. Nott. 1991. *Working Women and the Law: Equality and Discrimination in Theory and Practice*. London: Routledge/Sweet and Maxwell.

Moyer, Wayne H., and Timothy E. Josling. 1990. *Agricultural Policy Reform*. Ames, Iowa: Iowa State University Press.

Mullen, Paul Fabian. 1998. "Legitimate Options: National Courts and the Power of the European Court of Justice." *ECSA Review* 11: 2–7.

Muller, Pierre. 1992. "Entre le Local et l'Europe: La Crise du Modèle Français de Politiques Publiques." *Revue Française de Science Politique* 42: 275–97.

Neßler, Volker. 1997. *Europäische Willensbildung: Die Fraktionen im Europaparlament zwischen nationalen Interessen, Parteipolitik und Europäischer Integration*. Schwalbach: Wochenschau Verlag.

Neumann, Iver B. 1996. "Self and Other in International Relations." *European Journal of International Relations* 2, no. 2: 139–74.

Neuwahl, Nanette, and Allan Rosas, eds. 1995. *The European Union and Human Rights*. The Hague: Martinus Nijhoff.

Neville-Rolfe, Edmund. 1984. *The Politics of Agriculture in the European Community*. London: Policy Studies Institute.

"New Transatlantic Marketplace: France Keeps Brittan's Ship at Bay." 1998. *International Trade Reporter*, April 29.

Nicolet, Claude. 1982. *L'idée républicaine en France*. Paris: Gallimard.

Norton, Philip. 1991. *The British Polity*, 2d ed. New York: Longman.

Notermans, Ton. 1993. "The Abdication from National Policy Autonomy: Why the Macro-economic Policy Regime Has Become So Unfavorable to Labor." *Politics and Society* 21, no. 2: 133–67.

Oakes, Penelope J., S. Alexander Haslam, and John C. Turner. 1994. *Stereotyping and Social Reality*. Oxford: Oxford University Press.

O'Keeffe, David. 1996. "Judicial Protection for the Individual by the ECJ." *Fordham International Law Journal* 19: 901–14.

O'Leary, Siofra. 1992. "Nationality Law and Community Citizenship: A Tale of Two Uneasy Bedfellows." *Yearbook of European Law* 12: 353–84.

———. 1995. "The Relationship between Community Citizenship and the Protection of Fundamental Rights in Community Law." *Common Market Law Review* 32: 519–54.

Olsen, Johan P. 1995a. *European Challenges to the Nation State*. Working Paper no. 14, September. Oslo: ARENA.

———. 1995b. *Europeanization and Nation-State Dynamics*. Working Paper no. 9, March. Oslo: ARENA.

———. 1996. "Europeanization and Nation-State Dynamics." In *The Future of the Nation State: Essays on Cultural Pluralism and Political Integration*, edited by Sverker Gustavsson and Leif Lewin. Stockholm: Nerenius and Santerus Publishers.

Olson, Mancur. 1965. *The Logic of Collective Action: Public Goods and the Theory of Groups*. Cambridge: Harvard University Press.

Olson, Susan. 1990. "Interest-group Litigation in Federal District Court: Beyond the Political Disadvantage Theory." *Journal of Politics* 52: 854–82.

Paarlberg, R. 1997. "Agricultural Policy Reform and the Uruguay Round: Synergistic Linkage in a Two-Level Game?" *International Organization* 51, no. 3: 413–44.

Pasquino, Gianfranco. 1989. "Unregulated Regulators: Parties and Party Government." In *State, Market, and Social Regulation: New Perspectives on Italy*, edited by P. Lange and M. Regini, 29–50. Cambridge: Cambridge University Press.

Paterson, William E. 1974. *The SPD and European Integration*. Glasgow: Glasgow University Press.

Patterson, L. A. 1997. "Agricultural Policy Reform in the European Community: A Three-Level Game Analysis." *International Organization* 51, no. 1: 135–66.

Peel, Quentin. 1992. "German President Urges Easier Citizenship Laws." *Financial Times*, December 24.

Pérez González, Manuel. 1989. "Die Rolle der Comunidades Autonomas im Spanischen Staat und Ihre Rechtlichen Einflußmöglichkeiten auf die Nationale Gemeinschaftspolitik." In *Die Bundesrepublik Deutschland und das Königreich Spanien 1992—Die Rolle der Länder und der Comunidades Autonomas im Europäischen Integrationsprozeß*, edited by Harry Andreas Kremer, 51–71. Munich: Bayerischer Landtag.

Perrons, D. 1994. "Measuring Equal Opportunities in European Employment." *Environment and Planning A* 26: 1195–220.

Pescatore, Pierre. 1983. "The Doctrine of 'Direct Effect': An Infant Disease of Community Law." *European Law Review* 8: 155–77.

Peters, B. Guy. 1995. *The Politics of Bureaucracy*. New York: Longman.

Peterson, John, and Maria Green Cowles. 1998. "Clinton, Europe and Economic Diplomacy: What Makes the EU Different?" *Governance* 11, no. 3: 251–71.

Pettiti, Christophe. 1988. "Le Travail de Nuit des Femmes: Aspects Nationaux et Internationaux." *Droit Social* 4: 302–10.

———. 1989. "La France Condamnée par la Cour de Justice des Communautés Européennes." *Gazette du Palais*, April 11: 162–65.

Pfetsch, Frank. 1993. *Die Aussenpolitik der Bundesrepublik Deutschland, 1949–1992: Von der Spaltung zur Wiedervereinigung*. Munich: UTB.

Pierson, Paul. 1994. *Dismantling the Welfare State? Reagan, Thatcher, and the Politics of Retrenchment*. Cambridge: Cambridge University Press.

———. 1996. "The Path to European Integration: A Historical Institutionalist Analysis." *Comparative Political Studies* 29, no. 2: 123–63.

Pollack, Mark. 1998. "Constructivism, Social Psychology and Elite Attitude Change: Lessons from an Exhausted Research Program." Paper presented at the eleventh International Conference of Europeanists. February.

Pourtaud, Danièle. 1997. *Egalité entre hommes et femmes. Délégation du Sénat pour l'Union Européenne*. Information Report no. 293, March 27.

Powell, Walter W., and Paul J. DiMaggio, eds. 1991. *The New Institutionalism in Organizational Analysis*. Chicago: University of Chicago Press.

"A Protection of Fundamental Rights in the Union." 1998. http://europa.eu.int. March 16.

Provine, Doris Marie. 1996. "Courts and the Political Process in France." In *Courts, Law, and Politics in Comparative Perspective*, edited by Herbert Jacob, Erhard Blankenburg, Herbert Kritzer, Doris Marie Provine, and Joseph Sanders, 177–248. New Haven: Yale University Press.

Rea, Andrea. 1995. "Social Citizenship and Ethnic Minorities in the European Union." In *Migration, Citizenship and Ethno-National Identities in the European Union*, edited by Marco Martiniello. Aldershot: Avebury Publishers.

Rhodes, R. A. W. 1996. *The New European Agencies. Agencies in British Government: Revolution or Evolution?* EUI Working Papers, RSC No. 96/51. Florence: European University Institute.

———. 1997. *Understanding Governance: Policy Networks, Governance, Reflexivity and Accountability*. Philadelphia: Open University Press.

Rhodes, R. A. W., and Patrick Dunleavy, eds. 1995. *Prime Minister, Cabinet, and Core Executive*. New York: St. Martin's Press.

Risse, Thomas, et al. 1999. "To Euro or Not to Euro: The EMU and Identity Politics in the European Union." *European Journal of International Relations* 5, no. 2: 147–87.

Risse, Thomas, and Daniela Engelmann-Martin. Forthcoming. "Identity Politics and European Integration: The Case of Germany." In *The Idea of Europe*, edited by Anthony Pagden, Cambridge: Cambridge University Press.

Risse, Thomas, Stephen Ropp, and Kathryn Sikkink, eds. 1999. *The Power of Human Rights: International Human Rights Norms and Domestic Change*. Cambridge: Cambridge University Press.

Risse-Kappen, Thomas. 1991. "Public Opinion, Domestic Structures and Foreign Policy in Liberal Democracies." *World Politics* 43, no. 4: 479–512.

———. 1994. "Ideas Do Not Float Freely: Transnational Coalitions, Domestic Structures and the End of the Cold War." *International Organization* 48, no. 2: 313–45.

———, ed. 1995. *Bringing Transnational Relations Back In: Non-State Actors, Domestic Structures and International Institutions*. Cambridge: Cambridge University Press.

———. 1996. "Exploring the Nature of the Beast: International Relations Theory and Comparative Policy Analysis Meet the European Union." *Journal of Common Market Studies* 34, no. 1: 53–80.

Rogosch, Detlef. 1996. *Vorstellungen von Europa: Europabilder in der SPD und der belgischen Sozialisten, 1945–1957*. Hamburg: Kraemer.

Rogowski, Ronald. 1989. *Commerce and Coalitions: How Trade Affects Domestic Political Alignments*. Princeton: Princeton University Press.

Rometsch, Dietrich, and Wolfgang Wessels, eds. 1996. *The European Union and the Member States: Towards Institutional Fusion?* New York: Manchester University Press.

Roscher, Klaus. 1998. "Arbeitsbericht zur Fallstudie Frankreich." Manuscript. European University Institute, Florence. August.

Rosenau, James N. 1966. "Transforming the International System: Small Increments along a Vast Periphery." *World Politics* 18: 525–45.

Rubsamen, V. 1989. "Deregulation and the State in Comparative Perspective: The Case of Telecommunications." *Comparative Politics* 22: 105–20.

Rüdig, Wolfgang, and R. Andreas Krämer. 1994. "Networks of Cooperation: Water Policy in Germany." *Environmental Politics* 3: 52–79.

Sabatier, Paul A. 1986. "Top-Down and Bottom-Up Approaches to Implementation Research." *Journal of Public Policy* 6: 21–48.

Sabatier, Paul A., and H. C. Jenkins-Smith, eds. 1993. *Policy Change and Learning: An Advocacy Coalition Approach.* Boulder, Colo.: Westview.

Saint-Etienne, Christian. 1992. *L'exception française.* Paris: Colin.

Sandholtz, Wayne. 1996. "Membership Matters: Limits of the Functional Approach to European Institutions." *Journal of Common Market Studies* 34, no. 3: 403–29.

Sandholtz, W., and J. Zysman. 1989. "1992: Recasting the European Bargain." *World Politics* 42: 95–128.

Savatier, Jean. 1990. "Travail de nuit des femmes et droit communautaire." *Droit Social* 5: 466–71.

Sbragia, Alberta. 1992. "Thinking about the European Future: The Uses of Comparison." In *Euro-politics: Institutions and Policymaking in the "New" European Community*, edited by Alberta Sbragia, 257–92. Washington, D.C.: Brookings Institution.

Scharpf, Fritz W. 1985. "Die Politikverflechtungsfalle: Europäische Integration und deutscher Föderalismus im Vergleich." *Politische Vierteljahresschrift* 26, no. 4: 323–70.

————. 1996. "Negative and Positive Integration in the Political Economy of European Welfare States." In *Governance in the European Union*, edited by Gary Marks, Fritz W. Scharpf, Philippe C. Schmitter, and Wolfgang Streeck, 15–39. Thousand Oaks, Calif.: Sage.

————. 1997. *Games Real Actors Play: Actor-Centered Institutionalism in Policy Research.* Boulder, Co: Westview.

Scharpf, Fritz W., Bernd Reissert, and Fritz Schnabel. 1976. *Politikverflechtung, Theorie und Empirie des kooperativen Föderalismus in der Bundesrepublik Deutschland.* Kronberg/Ts.: Scriptor.

Schauer, Hans. 1996. *Europäische Identität und demokratische Tradition.* Munich: Olzog.

Scheingold, Stuart. 1974. *The Politics of Rights: Lawyers, Public Policy, and Political Change.* New Haven: Yale University Press.

Schermers, Henry, and Denis Waelbroeck. 1987. *Judicial Protection in the European Communities.* 4th ed. Deventer: Kluwer.

Scherzberg, Arno. 1994. "Freedom of Information—deutsch gewendet: Das neue Umweltinformationsgesetz." *Deutsches Verwaltungsblatt*: 733–45.

Schmid, John. 1999. "Germany Searches Soul with Debate on Citizenship." *International Herald Tribune*, February 4.

Schmidt, S. K. 1991. "Taking the Long Road to Liberalization: Telecommunications Reform in the Federal Republic of Germany." *Telecommunications Policy* 15, no. 3: 209–22.

————. 1996. "Privatizing the Federal Postal and Telecommunications Services." In *A New German Public Sector? Reform, Adaptation and Stability*, edited by A. Benz and K. H. Goetz, 45–70. Aldershot: Dartmouth.

————. 1997. *Behind the Council Agenda: The Commission's Impact on Decisions*. MPI discussion paper no. 97/4.

Schmidt, Vivien. 1990. *Democratizing France: The Political and Administrative History of Decentralization*. New York: Cambridge University Press.

————. 1995. "The New World Order, Incorporated: The Rise of Business and the Decline of the Nation-State." *Daedalus* 124: 75–106.

————. 1996a. *From State to Market? The Transformation of French Business and Government*. Cambridge, UK: Cambridge University Press.

————. 1996b. "Loosening the Ties That Bind: The Impact of European Integration on French Government and Its Relationship to Business." *Journal of Common Market Studies* 34, no. 2: 223–54.

————. 1997. "A New Europe for the Old?" *Daedalus* 126, no. 3: 167–97.

Schmitter, Philippe C. 1974. "Still the Century of Corporatism?" *Review of Politics* 36: 85–131.

————. 1985. "New-Corporatism and the State." In *The Political Economy of Corporatism*, edited by Wyn Grant. New York: St. Martin's.

Schmitz, Petra L., and Rolf Geserick. 1996. *Die Anderen in Europa: Nationale Selbst- und Fremdbilder im europäischen Integrationsprozeß*. Bonn: Europa-Union.

Schneider, V., and T. Vedel. 1999. "Franco-German Relations in Telecommunications." In *The Franco-German Relationship in the European Union*, edited by D. Webber, 75–92. London: Routledge.

Schneider, V., and R. Werle. 1990. "International Regime or Corporate Actor? The European Community in Telecommunications Policy." In *The Political Economy of Communications: International and European Dimensions*, edited by K. Dyson and P. Humphreys, 77–106. London: Routledge.

————. 1991. "Policy Networks in the German Telecommunications Domain." In *Policy Networks: Empirical Evidence and Theoretical Considerations*, edited by B. Marin, and R. Mayntz, 97–136. Frankfurt am Main: Campus.

Schneider, V., G. Dang Nguyen, and R. Werle. 1994. "Corporate Actor Networks in European Policy-Making: Harmonizing Telecommunications Policy." *Journal of Common Market Studies* 32: 473–98.

"Schnellere Beratungen gefordert: Jüngere Abgeordnete zur Novellierung des Staatsangehörigkeitsrechts." 1996. *Frankfurter Allgemeine Zeitung*, April 16.

Schumpeter, Joseph. 1954. "The Crisis of the Tax States." *International Economic Papers* 4: 5–38.

Schwarz, Hans-Peter. 1966. *Vom Reich zur Bundesrepublik: Deutschland im Widerstreit der Aussenpolitischen Konzeptionen in den Jahren der Besatzungsherrschaft 1945 bis 1949*. Neuwied: Luchterhand.

Schwarze, Jürgen. 1993. "Tendances vers un droit administratif commun en Europe." *Revue Trimestrielle de droit Européen* 29: 235–45.

————. 1996. "Deutscher Landesbericht." In *Administrative Law under European Influence*, edited by Jürgen Schwarze, 123–227. Baden-Baden: Nomos.

Sciarra, Silvana. 1996. "Dynamic Integration of National and Community Sources: The Case of Night-work for Women." In *Sex Equality Law in the European Union*, edited by Tamara K. Hervey and David O'Keeffe, 97–108. New York: John Wiley and Sons.

Seibel, Wolfgang. 1996. "Administrative Science as Reform: German Public Administration." *Public Administration Review* 56: 74–81.

Sen, Faruk. 1994. "Links und stumm." *Die Zeit*, September 30.

Sidjanski, Dusan. 1967. "The European Pressure Groups." *Government and Opposition* 3: 397–416.

Simon, J. P. 1994. "Vers une Réglementation Européene Unifiée? Généalogie de la Réglementation des Télécommunications, 1973–1992." *Réseaux* 66: 119–36.

Skocpol, Theda. 1985. "Bringing the State Back In: Strategies of Analysis in Current Research." In *Bringing the State Back*, edited by Peter Evans, Dietrich Reuschemeyer, and Theda Skocpol. Cambridge, UK: Cambridge University Press.

Slaughter, Anne-Marie, Alec Stone Sweet, and Joseph Weiler. 1998. *The European Court and the National Courts—Doctrine and Jurisprudence: Legal Change in Its Social Context.* Oxford: Hart.

Smith, Anthony D. 1992. "National Identity and the Idea of European Unity." *International Affairs* 68, no. 1: 55–76.

Sommer, Theo. 1995. "Diese Türkei zählt nicht zu Europa." *Die Zeit*, April 7.

Sontheimer, Kurt. 1990. *Deutschlands politische Kultur.* Munich: Piper.

Soysal, Yasemin. 1994. *Limits of Citizenship: Migrants and Postnational Membership in Europe.* Chicago: University of Chicago Press.

Sozialdemokratische Partei Deutschlands. 1946. "Politische Richtlinien." *Parteitag Hannover*, May.

Spotts, Frederic, and Theodor Wieser. 1986. *Italy: A Difficult Democracy. A Survey of Italian Politics.* Cambridge, UK: Cambridge University Press.

Stein, Eric. 1981. "Lawyers, Judges, and the Making of a Transnational Constitution." *American Journal of International Law* 75: 1–27.

Stein, Janice. 1994. "Political Learning by Doing: Gorbachev as Uncommitted Thinker and Motivated Learner." *International Organization* 48, no. 2: 155–83.

Steiner, J. M. 1983. "Sex Discrimination Under UK and EEC Law: Two Plus Four Equals One." *International and Comparative Law Quarterly* 32: 399–423.

Sterett, Susan. 1997. *Creating Constitutionalism? The Politics of Legal Expertise and Administrative Law in England and Wales.* Ann Arbor: University of Michigan Press.

Stone, Alec. 1992. *The Birth of Judicial Politics in France.* New York: Oxford University Press.

———. 1994. "What Is a Supranational Constitution? An Essay in International Relations Theory." *Review of Politics* 56: 441–74.

Stone Sweet, Alec, and Thomas Brunell. 1998. "Constructing a Supranational Constitution: Dispute Resolution and Governance in the European Community." *American Political Science Review* 92: 63–81.

Stone Sweet, Alec, and Wayne Sandholtz, eds. 1998a. *Supranational Governance: The Institutionalization of the European Union.* Oxford: Oxford University Press.

Stone Sweet, Alec, and Wayne Sandholtz. 1998b. "European Integration and Supranational Governance." In *Supranational Governance: The Institutionalization of the European Union*, edited by A. Stone Sweet and W. Sandholtz. Oxford: Oxford University Press.

Strange, Susan. 1996. *The Retreat of the State: The Diffusion of Power in the World Economy.* Cambridge: Cambridge University Press.

Szyszczak, Erika. 1995. "Future Directions in European Union Social Policy Law." *Industrial Law Journal* 24: 19–32.

Szyszczak, Erika, and John Delicostopoulos. 1997. "Intrusions into National Procedural Autonomy: The French Paradigm." *European Law Review* 22: 141–49.

Tant, A. P. 1990. "The Campaign for Freedom of Information: A Participatory Challenge to Elitist British Government." *Public Administration* 68: 477–91.

Teutsch, Michael. In press. "Reforming German Transport Policy: Overcoming Multiple Veto Points." In *Differential Europe: EU Impact on National Policymaking*, edited by A. Héritier et al. Lanham, Md.: Rowman and Littlefield.

Thatcher, Margaret. 1990. "Speech at the Conservative Party Conference." *Financial Times*, October 13–14: 7.

Thelen, Kathleen. 1993. "West European Labor in Transition: Sweden and Germany Compared." *World Politics* 46, no. 1: 23–49.

Thelen, Kathleen, and Sven Steinmo. 1992. "Historical Institutionalism in Comparative Politics." In *Structuring Politics. Historical Institutionalism in Comparative Analysis*, edited by Kathleen Thelen, Sven Steinmo, and Frank Longstreth, 1–32. Cambridge: Cambridge University Press.

Toth, A. G. 1990. *The Oxford Encyclopaedia of European Community Law*. Vol. 1. Oxford: Clarendon Press.

Treaty of Rome (European Economic Community). 1957. March 25.

Treaty on European Union. 1993. Brussels.

Truman, David. 1951. *The Governmental Process*. New York: Knopf.

Tsebelis, George. 1995. "Decision Making in Political Systems: Veto Players in Presidentialism, Parliamentarism, Multicameralism and Multipartyism." *British Journal of Political Science* 25, no. 3: 289–325.

Turner, John C. 1987. *Rediscovering the Social Group: A Self-Categorization Theory*. Oxford: Blackwell.

Twomey, Patrick. 1994. "The European Union: Three Pillars without a Human Rights Foundation." In *Legal Issues of the Maastricht Treaty*, edited by David O'Keeffe and Patrick Twomey. London: Chancery Law Publishing.

Unger, Brigitte, and Frans van Waarden. 1995. "Introduction: An Interdisciplinary approach to convergence." In *Convergence or Diversity? Internationalization and Economic Policy Response*, edited by Brigitte Unger and Frans van Waarden, 1–35. Aldershot: Avebury.

Ungerer, H. 1988. *Télécommunications in Europe*. Luxembourg: Office des Publications Officielles des Communautés Européennes.

Uterwedde, Henrik. 1988. *Die Wirtschaftspolitik der Linken in Frankreich: Programme und Praxis, 1984–87*. Frankfurt am Main: Campus.

Vanhamme, Jan. 1994/95. "Comment on Case C-158/91, 'Ministère public et Direction du travail et de l'emploi v. Jean-Claude Levy.'" *Columbia Journal of European Law* 1: 116–20.

Van Schendelen, M. P. C. M., ed. 1993. *National Public and Private EC Lobbying*. Aldershot: Dartmouth.

Vassallo, Salvatore. 2000. "La Politica di Bilancio: Le Condizioni e gli Effetti Istituzionali della Convergenza." In *Condannata al Successo? L'Italia Nell-Europa Integrata*, edited by Giuseppe Di Palma, Sergio Fabbrini, and Giorgio Freddi, 287–325. Bologna: Il Mulino.

Vedel, T. 1988. "La Déréglementation des Télécommunications en France: Politique et jeu Politique." *In Les Déréglementations: Etude comparative*, edited by Institut Français des Sciences Administratives, 281–312. Paris: Economica.

———. 1991. "La réforme de P et T." *Universalia 1991*, 273–76. Paris: Encyclopaedia Universalis.

Vogel, S. K. 1996. *Freer Markets, More Rules: Regulatory Reform in Advanced Industrial Countries*. Ithaca: Cornell University Press.

Wallace, Helen. 1996. "Politics and Policy in the EU: The Challenge of Governance." In *Policy-Making in the European Union*, edited by Helen Wallace and William Wallace. Oxford: Oxford University Press.

Webber, D. 1986. "Die Ausbleibende Wende bei der Deutschen Bundespost. Zur Regulierung des Telekommunikationswesens in der Bundesrepublik Deutschland." *Politische Vierteljahresschrift* 27: 397–414.

Weber, Steven. 1994. "Origins of the European Bank for Reconstruction and Development." *International Organization* 48, no. 1: 1–38.

Weidlener, Helmut, and Frotz Hemberger, eds. 1993. *Deutsches Staatsangehörigkeitsrecht*, 4th ed. Munich: Jehle.

Weiler, Joseph. 1994. "A Quiet Revolution: The European Court of Justice and Its Interlocutors." *Comparative Political Studies* 26: 510–34.

Weiler, Joseph, and Renaud Dehousse. 1992. "Primus Inter Pares. The European Court and the National Courts: Thirty Years of Cooperation." Unpublished report, European University Institute, Florence.

Weiner, Merle H. 1990. "Fundamental Misconceptions about Fundamental Rights: The Changing Nature of Women's Rights in the EEC and Their Application in the United Kingdom." *Harvard International Law Journal* 31: 565–610.

Werle, R. 1999. "Liberalisation of Telecommunications in Germany." In *European Telecommunications Liberalisation*, edited by Kjell A. Eliassen and M. Sjøvaag. London/New York: Routledge.

Wiener, Antje. 1998. *"European" Citizenship Practice: Building Institutions of a Non-State.* Boulder, Colo.: Westview Press.

Wilson, Frank L. 1982. "Alternative Models of Interest Intermediation: The Case of France." *British Journal of Political Science* 12: 173–200.

Wilson, Graham K. 1990. *Business and Politics: A Comparative Introduction*, 2d ed. Chatham, N.J.: Chatham House Publishers.

Wilson, James Q. 1973. *Political Organizations*. New York: Basic Books.

Winter, Gerd. 1996. "Freedom of Environmental Information." In *European Environmental Law. A Comparative Perspective*, edited by Gerd Winter, 81–94. Aldershot: Dartmouth.

Woolcock, Stephen. 1996. "Competition among Forms of Corporate Governance in the European Community: The Case of Britain." In *National Diversity and Global Capitalism*, edited by Suzanne Berger and Ronald Dore, 179–96. Ithaca: Cornell University Press.

Woolcock, Stephen, and Michael Hodges. 1996. "EU Policy in the Uruguay Round." In *Policy-Making in the European Union*, edited by Helen Wallace and William Wallace, 301–24. Oxford: Oxford University Press.

Wuiame, Nathalie. 1994. "Night Work for Women—*Stoeckel* Revisited." *Industrial Law Journal* 23: 95–100.

"Zwei Pässe—warum nicht?" 1995. *Die Zeit*, January 27.

CONTRIBUTORS

TANJA A. BÖRZEL is Coordinator for Environmental Studies at the European University Institute and Research Fellow at the Max Planck Project Group on Common Goods: Law, Politics and Economics, Bonn, Germany.

JAMES CAPORASO is Professor of Political Science at the University of Washington, U.S.A.

JEFFREY T. CHECKEL is Senior Researcher and Coordinator, Research on European Identity Change, ARENA (Advanced Research on the Europeanization of the Nation State), at the University of Oslo, Norway.

LISA CONANT is Assistant Professor of Political Science at the University of Denver, U.S.A.

MARIA GREEN COWLES is Assistant Professor of International Relations at American University, Washington, D.C., U.S.A.

ADRIENNE HÉRITIER is Professor and Director of the Max Planck Project Group on Common Goods: Law, Politics and Economics, Bonn, Germany.

JOSEPH JUPILLE is Assistant Professor of Political Science at Florida International University, Miami, U.S.A.

CHRISTOPH KNILL is Senior Researcher at the Max Planck Project Group on Common Goods: Law, Politics, and Economics, Bonn, Germany.

ANDREA LENSCHOW is Assistant Professor of Political Science at Salzburg University, Austria.

THOMAS RISSE is Professor of International Relations and Joint Chair of the Robert Schuman Centre and Department of Social and Political Sciences at the European University Institute, Florence, Italy.

263

ALBERTA SBRAGIA is UCIS Research Professor of Political Science and Director of the Center for West European Studies and of the European Union Center at the University of Pittsburgh, U.S.A.

VOLKER SCHNEIDER is Professor of Political Science in the Department of Administrative Sciences at the University of Konstanz, Germany.

INDEX

265

Cornell Studies in Political Economy
A SERIES EDITED BY
PETER J. KATZENSTEIN